PSEUDO-PHILO

About the Author

Associate Professor and Chair of the Department of Religious Studies at the College of the Holy Cross in Worcester, Massachusetts, Frederick J. Murphy received his Ph.D. from Harvard University. He is the author of *The Structure and Meaning of Second Baruch* (1985) and *The Religious World of Jesus: An Introduction to Second Temple Palestinian Judaism* (1991), along with numerous journal articles.

PSEUDO-PHILO

Rewriting the Bible

FREDERICK J. MURPHY

New York   Oxford
OXFORD UNIVERSITY PRESS
1993

Oxford University Press

Oxford   New York   Toronto
Delhi   Bombay   Calcutta   Madras   Karachi
Kuala Lumpur   Singapore   Hong Kong   Tokyo
Nairobi   Dar es Salaam   Cape Town
Melbourne   Auckland   Madrid

and associated companies in
Berlin   Ibadan

Copyright © 1993 by Frederick J. Murphy

Published by Oxford University Press, Inc.
200 Madison Avenue, New York, New York 10016

The English translation of the *Biblical Antiquities* of Pseudo-Philo used here is by
Daniel Harrington, found in *The Old Testament Pseudepigrapha,* edited by James
H. Charlesworth (Vol. 2, Doubleday: 1985) copyright © 1985 by James H. Charlesworth, pp. 297–377. It is used by permission of Daniel J. Harrington, James H.
Charlesworth, and Doubleday, a division of Bantam Doubleday Dell Publishing
Group, Inc. I am most grateful for this permission, especially since the translation
is itself a major contribution to the study of Pseudo-Philo. Harrington's indication
of agreement with known biblical texts throughout the translation was a particularly
helpful feature of his work.

Quotations from the Bible are from the New Revised Standard Version, copyright © 1989 by the Division of Christian Education of the National Council of the
Churches of Christ in the United States of America, and are used by permission.

Library of Congress Cataloging-in-Publication Data
Murphy, Frederick James.
Pseudo-Philo : rewriting the Bible / Frederick J. Murphy.
p. cm.   Includes a concordance to Pseudo-Philo's
Liber antiquitatum biblicarum.
Includes bibliographical references and index.
ISBN 0-19-507622-2
1. Pseudo-Philo. Liber antiquitatum biblicarum.
2. Bible. O.T.—History of Biblical events—Historiography.
I. Title.   BS1197.P523M87   1993
221.9′5—dc20   92-44041

1 3 5 7 9 8 6 4 2

Printed in the United States of America
on acid-free paper

To Leslie,
Wife, Companion, and Friend,
with Love

Preface

Like many Christians, I first came to the study of Judaism because of my interest in the historical and religious origins of Christianity. Early in my studies I came to appreciate the richness and beauty of Judaism for its own sake, not merely as a background for Christian beginnings. Indeed, most scholars now recognize that if we ask only those questions about ancient Judaism that are of direct interest for the early church, we end up with a distorted picture of Judaism of the first century. Paying due attention to ancient Judaism in its own right will be more useful in the end, even to those whose primary interest is in Christianity, because it will make possible a more balanced appreciation of the dynamics of first-century Judaism and earliest Christianity.[1]

I first became fascinated with Judaism through the Hebrew Bible, the major source for Israelite religion and one of the sources for Early Judaism. It seemed clear that to understand the New Testament one needed a deep appreciation of the Hebrew Bible. Further study made obvious the sizable gap, chronological and religious, between the Hebrew Bible and later Jewish literature. My interests turned to the late Second Temple period, for which the primary sources are the collection of texts now usually referred to as the Pseudepigrapha. I did my dissertation on *2 Baruch,* now published in the Society of Biblical Literature dissertation series. I also had the pleasure as a graduate student of directing Susan Berman's Harvard undergraduate dissertation on 4 Ezra, and of conducting a tutorial on the Pseudepigrapha with Harvard undergraduates.

Several years ago, I decided to turn my attention to the *Biblical Antiquities* of Pseudo-Philo, a rewriting of the Bible from Adam to Saul's death composed

1. It is in this spirit that I wrote *Religious World.*

in Palestine in the first century C.E. The work is often associated with *2 Baruch* and *4 Ezra*. The three works come from first-century Jewish Palestine and share many concepts and motifs. The *Biblical Antiquities* is a book that ought to be of great interest to biblical scholars of all stripes. Whether one's interest is in biblical interpretation in the first century, historical studies of Jewish and Christian traditions, worldviews of first-century Jews, or narrative theology, the *Biblical Antiquities* is a fertile source. Most recently, the work's unusually positive attitude toward women has interested several scholars.

Pseudo-Philo has attracted the attention of several fine scholars since it was reintroduced to the scholarly world by Leopold Cohn in 1898. James produced an English translation in 1917 preceded by a long introduction dealing with a number of introductory and critical points. This was reprinted by Ktav in 1971 with a superb "prolegomenon" by Louis Feldman. Feldman's contribution is an impressive commentary that notes parallels to particular points in the *Biblical Antiquities* elsewhere in Jewish tradition. His commentary is preceded by succinct and incisive discussions of a wide range of issues. As Feldman was bringing out Pseudo-Philo again, Daniel Harrington was hard at work determining the biblical text type used by Pseudo-Philo and producing a critical Latin text. In 1976, Source Crétiennes published a two-volume edition of Pseudo-Philo by Daniel Harrington, Charles Perrot, and Pierre-Marie Bogaert. The first volume is Harrington's Latin text with a critical introduction. The second is a literary introduction, commentary, and index. Each of the three scholars contributed to the literary introduction, which gives an overview of Pseudo-Philo and provides a wonderful synthesis of its "theological thought" by Perrot. Perrot wrote the commentary. Numerous other scholarly pieces on Pseudo-Philo have appeared in the last century.

My notes show the substantial debt I owe to previous scholars on Pseudo-Philo, but most especially to Feldman, Perrot, and Harrington. Their work provided me with a firm and broad foundation on which to build my own interpretation. They were particularly helpful in determining how Pseudo-Philo relates to other Jewish documents and how it works with Jewish traditions. Harrington's Latin text, for which I have produced a concordance, and his English translation are models of careful scholarship, and I have depended on them entirely. I have seldom second-guessed him in translation or in the choices he has made among variant readings. My interpretation rests upon his sound judgments at every turn.

As important as all foregoing work on Pseudo-Philo is, I still saw a need for an interpretation of the work as a unified narrative that maintains a consistent ideological point of view throughout and has an overarching concept of Israel's history that goes beyond individual episodes. I have envisioned my task as analogous to both redaction and narrative critics of the Gospels. The form I have chosen has recently been called "narrative commentary," going through the work chapter by chapter to see how each works and is related to the whole.[2] Such a study will I hope be of use to experts on Pseudo-Philo, as

---

2. See Moore, *Literary Criticism*, 17–24.

an encompassing framework within which their work can advance. It should also prove helpful to biblical scholars and those whose specialties are in other areas of the Pseudepigrapha because it offers an interpretation of the whole of the *Biblical Antiquities* in an accessible format.

It is a pleasure to acknowledge the many people who have played important roles as I worked on this project. The members of the Department of Religious Studies at the College of the Holy Cross continue to offer me support both as professional colleagues and as friends. I am grateful to the College of the Holy Cross for a grant for the summer of 1991 to work on this book, awarded through the Committee on Professional Standards. The library staff of the College, led by Dr. James E. Hogan, has given me prompt, professional, and cheerful service in all my projects, and in this one in particular. I thank John Esposito of Holy Cross and Andy Overman of the University of Rochester for their ongoing encouragement for this project. Daniel Harrington of Weston College School of Theology offered me generous and sustained assistance in the early stages of my work on Pseudo-Philo, for which I am grateful. I thank Tom Tobin of Loyola University in Chicago, who read some of my early work on Pseudo-Philo and offered suggestions that continue to influence my work. I am grateful to John Kearns, Patricia Johnson, Christopher Simon, and Blaise Nagy, all of the Classics Department at Holy Cross, for their help on the Latin concordance at the end of this volume. I also thank Suzanne Sylvester, who makes it possible for me to juggle diverse roles by her efficiency and kindness. Roz and Joe Halpern, my mother-in-law and father-in-law, are constant supporters. Their visits to our home have been a pleasure and a help to me as they have pitched in with the children, Rebecca and Jeremy.

Speaking of the children, I must admit that this book probably would have been completed earlier had they not found a multitude of reasons to interrupt me during its writing. The book would have been done sooner, but my life would have been infinitely less full and meaningful. I am gifted with their presence. No one understands one's labors, joys, and sorrows like a spouse. Leslie has shared the ups and downs of this book like no one else. Indeed, I could not imagine carrying on my professional life without her faithful support. I write this as we celebrate our twelfth anniversary of marriage, and I take this opportunity to dedicate this book to her in love and gratitude.

Worcester, Mass.   F.J.M.
July 1992

Contents

Abbreviations

Except for the following, abbreviations are in accordance with the style sheet for the *Journal of Biblical Literature* (*JBL* 107 [1988]: 579–96). It should be noted that this book uses "LAB" for the *Biblical Antiquities* of Pseudo-Philo, whereas the *JBL* uses *"Bib. Ant."*

Apoc. Abr.	*Apocalypse of Abraham*
Apoc. Elij.	*Apocalypse of Elijah*
2 Bar.	*Syriac Apocalypse of Baruch*
3 Bar.	*Greek Apocalypse of Baruch*
4 Bar.	*Fourth Baruch*
1 En.	*1 Enoch (Ethiopic Enoch)*
2 En.	*2 Enoch (Slavonic Enoch)*
EJMI	*Early Judaism and its Modern Interpreters.* Edited by Robert A. Kraft and George W. E. Nickelsburg. Philadelphia: Fortress, 1986.
HBMI	*The Hebrew Bible and Its Modern Interpreters.* Edited by Douglas A. Knight and Gene M. Tucker. Philadelphia: Fortress, 1985.
IFAJ	*Ideal Figures in Ancient Judaism: Profiles and Paradigms.* Edited by George W. E. Nickelsburg and John J. Collins. Chico, Calif.: Scholars, 1980.
LAB	*Liber Antiquitatum Biblicarum,* Latin title of the *Biblical Antiquities*
OTP	*The Old Testament Pseudepigrapha,* vol. 2. Edited by James H. Charlesworth. Garden City, N.Y.: Doubleday, 1985.
SBFLA	*Studii biblici franciscani liber annus*
SC 229:	*Pseudo-Philon: Les Antiquités Bibliques.* Vol. 1, *Introduction et Texte Critiques,* Daniel J. Harrington and Jacques Cazeaux. Paris: Cerf, 1976.

SC 230	*Pseudo-Philon: Les Antiquités Bibliques.* Vol. 2, *Introduction Littéraire, Commentaire et Index.* Charles Perrot and Pierre-Maurice Bogaert, with the collaboration of Daniel J. Harrington. Paris: Cerf, 1976.
T. Adam	*Testament of Adam*
T. Moses	*Testament of Moses* (also called *Assumption of Moses)*

I

Prologue

1

Introduction

The *Biblical Antiquities* of Pseudo-Philo retells the Hebrew Bible from Adam to the death of Saul. Its retelling is quite free and extensive. It does quote the biblical text at times, but more often it paraphrases, condenses, summarizes, omits material, and adds much that has little or no corresponding material in the Bible. Many of the additions take the form of speeches, prayers, and conversations among the characters.

The *Biblical Antiquities* dates from the first century of the Common Era, probably before the war with the Romans began in 66 C.E. It was written in Jewish Palestine. It is a valuable source for understanding how Jews of first-century Palestine used and retold their sacred stories and for Jewish thought of the late Second Temple period. Because it was transmitted with Latin translations of works by Philo of Alexandria, the *Biblical Antiquities* was thought to be his. However, Philo and Pseudo-Philo have little in common in their dealings with the biblical text. Furthermore, it is likely that the *Biblical Antiquities* was originally written in Hebrew, whereas Philo wrote in Greek.[1] The work's title, *Liber Antiquitatum Biblicarum,* first appears in the 1552 edition of Sichardus's text. Its earlier title (from a fourteenth-century manuscript), *Liber Antiquitatum,* may be in imitation of Josephus's *Jewish Antiquities.*[2]

Text, Translation, Biblical Text Type, Language

The *Biblical Antiquities* survives in "eighteen complete and three fragmentary Latin manuscripts" dating from the eleventh to the fifteenth centuries.[3] Daniel Harrington has produced the critical Latin text of the *Biblical Antiquities,* available in *Sources Crétiennes* 229.[4] He has also provided the best English translation, which is used throughout this study and is based on his Latin text.[5] The translation stays close to the Latin text, to the point of preserving its

1. See *OTP,* 299–300.
2. See SC 230, 10.
3. *OTP,* 298.
4. SC 229, 60–386. For a short explanation of the manuscripts and their relationships, see *OTP,* 298. For a more detailed explanation, SC 229, 15–59.
5. *OTP,* 304–77.

3

awkwardness and ambiguity where they occur. Harrington keeps proper names in their familiar biblical form where possible, a practice followed in this book. Harrington says, "Where the text agrees with a recognizable ancient biblical text (the MT, LXX, Samaritan Pentateuch, etc.), we have signaled these agreements by placing the relevant words in italics."[6] The italics have been retained in this book. They furnish a handy if rough way to compare the *Biblical Antiquities* to its biblical source and determine how Pseudo-Philo rewrote it.

Harrington also determined the biblical text type used by Pseudo-Philo.[7] He found it to be a Palestinian text type, as opposed to Babylonian (Masoretic Text) or Alexandrian (Septuagint).[8] In a seminal article published in 1898 that brought the *Biblical Antiquities* to the attention of the scholarly world, Leopold Cohn suggested that the Latin manuscripts were translations from Greek and that a Hebrew original underlay the Greek. Harrington tested his proposal in detail and confirmed it.[9]

Genre

In recent years, there has been a tendency to use the term "midrash" for a wide variety of modes of ancient biblical interpretation. Saldarini notes, "R. Bloch (1955, 1957) understood midrash as a set of attitudes and a process that resulted in various interpretations of scripture with related purposes."[10] If the definition of midrash is as broad as Bloch's, then Pseudo-Philo is indeed midrash.[11] But if the element of focus on explication of text is added to the definition, then Pseudo-Philo falls into a different category.[12] Perrot's distinction between *texte expliqué,* which includes midrash, and *texte continué,* which includes Pseudo-Philo, is useful here.[13] In the first *(texte expliqué),* the written biblical text is the focus, and the point is to explain it. In the second *(texte continué),* the focus is on the sacred history known both through the Bible and other traditions. The latter category would include the *Book of Jubilees,* the

6. *OTP,* 303.

7. See Harrington, "Biblical Text" and *Text and Biblical Text.*

8. SC 230, 77–78. He uses Cross's classifications (see Cross, "History" and "Contribution").

9. "Original Language."

10. "Reconstructions," 445.

11. "Midrash." Porton ("Defining Midrash") claims that Pseudo-Philo is midrash. Saldarini ("Reconstructions," 446) insists that the term "midrash" "would be better restricted to rabbinic midrash or to those works that closely resemble rabbinic midrash." This would not include Pseudo-Philo.

12. Vermes *(Post-Biblical,* 59–91) uses "midrash" more broadly, and prefers to distinguish "pure" exegesis, which has as its object the explication of problematic aspects of the biblical text, such as word meanings, insufficient detail, contradictions with other biblical texts, and unacceptable meanings, and "applied" exegesis, which used as the point of departure not Torah itself but "contemporary customs and beliefs which the interpreter attempted to connect with Scripture and to justify" (80).

13. SC 230, 24–28.

Genesis Apocryphon, Josephus's *Jewish Antiquities,* and the *Testament of Moses.* Pseudo-Philo's genre is far closer to these works than to rabbinic midrashim or even targums.

Vermes categorizes Pseudo-Philo as "rewritten Bible."[14] Harrington takes up this term in a recent review of such literature and defines it as follows: "The expression 'rewritten Bible' is used simply to refer to those products of Palestinian Judaism at the turn of the era that take as their literary framework the flow of the biblical text itself and apparently have as their major purpose the clarification and actualization of the biblical story."[15] This is a good description of Pseudo-Philo's purpose. Harrington is reluctant to call Pseudo-Philo midrash "because the focus is not the explication of the biblical text," or targum, "because the reworking is too free." Pseudo-Philo's purpose is not explication of the text per se. Many details can be explained as the solving of problems in the biblical text itself, but major parts of the narrative are not susceptible to such an explanation.[16] Nor is the *Biblical Antiquities* meant to replace the biblical text. It refers to scriptural books by name several times. Furthermore, it assumes knowledge of biblical stories and details not present in the *Biblical Antiquities.* Actualization of sacred stories is the best way to describe what Pseudo-Philo does.

The *Biblical Antiquities* is not a collection of sermons, neither is it a theological treatise in which the Bible is mined for helpful hints or proof texts. Pseudo-Philo builds a new narrative on the foundation of the biblical stories, using other traditional materials as well. The new narrative has a life of its own and does not just clear up inconsistencies in the biblical account or preserve various traditions. The process of forming a canon, although underway in Pseudo-Philo's time, had not yet resulted in a completely fixed text. However, it had progressed sufficiently far to allow some form of the written Bible to be familiar to readers and hearers. Using traditional stories that he assumes his audience already knows, Pseudo-Philo enables readers to experience them in new ways. Such fluidity in the sacred stories is of course common in the Second Temple period and before. Experiencing those stories in a different form could have been a powerful way to get a message across, to change behaviors, and to reshape society.

Narratives of all sorts are particularly attractive genres because of the nature of storytelling. Humans experience their lives as a narrative with a past, present, and future, and they often interpret their lives as a plot in which events are causally related, persons are meaningful, and settings are significant. Narratives tend to pull people in so that they participate in the imagined world. Nonbiblical literary critics have been investigating this for a long time, but it is only fairly recently that biblical scholars have looked at narrative in terms of plot, character, setting, point of view, and so on. Chapter 2 details how such study can illuminate a work like the *Biblical Antiquities* of Pseudo-Philo.

---

14. *Scripture,* 95.
15. "Palestinian Adaptations," 239.
16. Bauckham ("Liber") has examined biblical elements in Pseudo-Philo in detail.

Place and Date

The *Biblical Antiquities* was composed in Palestine. Harrington lists the reasons for this conclusion. It was written in Hebrew, and the author used a Palestinian biblical text. The work shows many parallels with 4 Ezra and *2 Baruch,* both written in Palestine. "Some of the author's theological interests (the Temple, the rules of sacrifice, the covenant and the Law, eschatology, and angelology) point toward a Palestinian provenance." Finally, the author seems to have known Palestine's geography.[17]

Few doubt that the *Biblical Antiquities* was written in the first century C.E.[18] Pseudo-Philo uses a biblical text type current in Palestine before the destruction of the temple but later overshadowed by a Babylonian text type. The work is sparse in internal indications of its time of composition, but in 39:8–9 the Ammonite king confronted by Jephthah is named "Getal," which may be a Semitic variant of "Kotylas," mentioned by Josephus as the ruler of Philadelphia to whom Ptolemy, son-in-law and murderer of Simon the Hasmonean, fled.[19] That would have been in 135 B.C.E., indicating that the *Biblical Antiquities* could not have been composed prior to that time. The parallels with 4 Ezra and *2 Baruch,* both written around the turn of the second century, suggest a date in the first century.

Conflict on dating the *Biblical Antiquities* has centered on whether it was written before or after the war against the Romans. Cohn took 19:7 as a reference to the destruction of the temple in 70 C.E., but others see that reference as uncertain, possibly indicating the first destruction of the temple in 587 B.C.E. or the desecration of Jerusalem by Antiochus IV or Pompey the Great.[20] Nickelsburg thinks that the message of hope in times of oppression and the emphasis on leadership suggest a setting during the war itself.[21] Bogaert sees the frequent references to sacrifice and the repeated use of the phrase *usque in hodiernum (hunc) diem* (15:6; 22:8; 26:5, 15) as pointing to a prewar date.[22] He adds that the work's genre, *texte continué,* died out after 70 C.E.

No arguments will convince all parties. Works written after the war, specifically 4 Ezra and *2 Baruch,* show a marked preoccupation with this momentous event. It seems unimaginable that Pseudo-Philo could have written such a long work without that disaster leaving a more recognizable mark. This tips the balance of evidence, sparse as it is, to a pre-70 C.E. date.

---

17. *OTP,* 300.
18. For dating, see Murphy, "Retelling," 285; SC 230, 66–74.
19. *Ant.* 13.8.1 § 235; *J.W.* 1.2.4. § 60.
20. See *OTP,* 299; Feldman, "Epilegomenon," 305–6; SC 230, 67–70; but see Wadsworth, "New," 186–91.
21. "Leaders," 63.
22. SC 230, 72.

Author's Social Location

Scholars have no idea who composed the *Biblical Antiquities,* but numerous suggestions have been made concerning his probable social location (i.e., class and group of Second Temple Jewish society). The suggestions rest on interpretations of alleged polemics or peculiar doctrines in the book. Obviously the author could read and write, knew many Jewish traditions, and was an intelligent and creative storyteller, so to some degree he was scribal. But scribes occupied many different positions in society and were found in most if not all Jewish groups.[23] To say that the author was a scribe says little.

Feldman goes through each of the suggestions about the social origin and purposes of the *Biblical Antiquities* and finds most wanting.[24] He investigates the ideas that it is an anti-Samaritan work; an anti-Tobiad polemic; an anti-Mithraic piece; an "Essene pamphlet"; a product of the Dead Sea Scrolls community, Gnosticism, or Jewish mysticism; or a work with connections to the sort of community that produced the Dura Europus artwork. There are features of the text that support each of these positions, but none of them is sufficiently prominent to justify confident assertions about Pseudo-Philo's origins. Neither is there any evidence to tie the work to the Pharisees, Sadducees, or the priestly establishment in Jerusalem.

The reason that such widely divergent interpretations are possible may be that Pseudo-Philo represents fairly mainstream scribal Judaism in first century Palestine. Elements shared with narrower groups are present, but they are not developed in the way they would be in Pharisaism, Essenism, Christianity, Gnosticism, or more apocalyptically oriented settings. But precisely because the book does represent aspects of mainstream Judaism in the first century, it is a valuable text and should be studied in detail.

The Approach of This Book

This book is a literary commentary on the *Biblical Antiquities.* Its methodology is a combination of redaction criticism, using the Bible as the point of comparison, and narrative criticism. The predominant form is that of narrative commentary, examining Pseudo-Philo chapter by chapter. Such commentary does not seek to address in detail all questions of parallels, translation, variant readings, and so on, as do more conventional commentaries. Feldman and Perrot have already provided helpful commentaries of that kind.[25] Rather, it concentrates on how the plot and characterization of each episode works, how it relates to the larger complex in which it is located, and how it contributes to the unified narrative of the work as a whole. Chapters 10 and 11 treat

23. On scribes, see Saldarini, *Pharisees.*
24. "Prolegomenon," xxxiii–xlvii.
25. Feldman, "Prolegomenon;" Perrot, SC 230.

characters and themes, respectively. Chapter 12 investigates some issues of history. The aim of the whole is to arrive at a comprehensive interpretation of the *Biblical Antiquities* that will be of use to a wide range of scholars.

Before any document can increase knowledge about the period in which it was written, its genre, purpose, and ideological point of view must be understood. Although I address historical matters in chapter 12, the other chapters do not deal with such matters directly. Most comments about historical context are confined to the notes and to chapter 12. The Bible, which Pseudo-Philo rewrites, is a fixed point of comparison for the analysis, but most other literary parallels are relegated to the notes.[26]

I have tried to avoid the masculine pronoun in reference to God. Language reflects and influences thought, and our efforts to rectify distorting, gender-based language about God are right and important. However, that effort at times has made for somewhat awkward constructions, such as the repetition of the word "God" in certain passages.

References to secondary sources are made by author and short title only. The bibliography contains all cited works, as well as other works on Pseudo-Philo for the sake of completeness. The concordances at the end of this book should prove useful for future studies of the *Biblical Antiquities.* In the analysis I do not always make full listings of key words and concepts since such lists are available in the concordances.

26. See Nickelsburg, "Leaders," 51.

2

Pseudo-Philo as Narrative

Literary Criticism, the Bible, and Pseudo-Philo

Most students of the Pseudepigrapha have been trained as biblical scholars, so developments in the study of the Pseudepigrapha should be viewed in light of similar developments in biblical studies. Although the Bible has long been the object of "literary criticism," that criticism has been fairly narrow until recently. It has concentrated on such matters as isolation of sources, investigation of smaller units within the text, use of tradition, biblical quotations and allusions, and genre. Concerns of literary critics from other fields were not prominent.[1] Recent years have witnessed growing interest in a wide range of approaches to the Bible, including many varieties of literary criticism. New studies are constantly appearing, even in the most traditional journals and presses, applying to Scripture methods of criticism developed for nonbiblical literature.

Current scholarship on Pseudo-Philo's *Biblical Antiquities* resembles scholarship on the synoptic Gospels during the advent of redaction criticism in the 1950s. At that time the Gospels had been scrutinized in terms of sources, interrelationships, constituent units, dating, and incorporation of traditional material. Under the influence of form criticism, the Gospels were often treated as depositories of small units. The small units were the principal objects of study and interest.[2] There were exceptions to this, but the exceptions tended to prove the rule. With the arrival of redaction criticism, the synoptic evangelists began to receive their due as authors and theologians.[3] No longer were they seen as mere collectors and arrangers of tradition. Scholars started to appreciate the evangelists' originality and the extent to which they produced new creations. But both the strength and the weakness of redaction criticism lay in its attention to the ways in which the Gospels modified their sources. The strength of the method was close analysis of the detailed rewriting of the

1. For literary criticism in New Testament studies, see Moore, *Literary Criticism;* Beardslee, "Recent Literary Criticism"; Peterson, *Literary Criticism.* For the Hebrew Bible, see Knierim, "Criticism of Literary Features"; Culley, "Exploring"; Sternberg, *Poetics.*

2. McKnight, *Form Criticism.*

3. See Perrin, *Redaction Criticism;* Rohde, *Rediscovering.*

evangelists' sources. That analysis revealed patterns that were then used as keys for understanding the viewpoints of the authors, but there was often too little time spent on features of the text not covered by the rewriting of sources. For this reason, several critics began to use the term "composition criticism," which was perceived to be wider than "redaction criticism" since it addressed broader structural issues.[4] However, the new method still tended to operate from the model of a text assembled from preexisting bits of tradition and did not attend sufficiently to many narrative features of the Gospels. Literary criticism of the Gospels is now broader and takes many forms. Prominent among these forms is narrative criticism. In narrative criticism, each Gospel is seen as a unit in which each part contributes to the text's larger story.[5]

Pseudo-Philo's work is comparable to the synoptic Gospels in that he uses traditional material extensively. Studies investigating Pseudo-Philo's views have tended to be analogous to redactional critical studies of the Gospels, in that they often focus on how the work rewrites traditional material, or to tradition historical studies, in that they have tried to determine the place of Pseudo-Philo's version of specific stories within the broader transmission and use of that story. Interest in the traditions in *Biblical Antiquities* has sometimes, as in the case of the synoptic Gospels earlier in this century, eclipsed the study of the work as a whole.[6] But since the *Biblical Antiquities* is a narrative, it too can be analyzed in terms of its narrative features.

The methodology of this study consists in large measure of a combination of redaction and narrative criticism. Pseudo-Philo reworks traditional material freely and with a genuine flair for storytelling. The primary foundation for my narrative analysis is the work of Seymour Chatman in *Story and Discourse*. I have chosen only those elements of his work that apply directly to the *Biblical Antiquities* and have modified them as appropriate. The work of numerous biblical scholars, some of whom have also found Chatman helpful, has provided models for this study.[7]

In redaction criticism, it is important to determine what sources the redac-

---

4. See Beardslee, "Recent Literary Criticism," 163–64.

5. See, for example, Tannehill, *Narrative Unity*, xiii–xiv.

6. The image of eclipse as applied to biblical studies is taken from Frei, *Eclipse*. Vermes (*Scripture*) shows how Pseudo-Philo's treatment of stories and traditions compares with other treatments. He delineates important exegetical traditions to which Pseudo-Philo is heir. Bauckham's work focuses on discovering biblical elements and influences in Pseudo-Philo. See also Jacobson, "Biblical Quotation." The value of such work is clear. Dimant ("Use and Interpretation," 379) offers the following caution about being content with such approaches: "Here lies another pitfall; to set out from unresolved difficulties of a given biblical episode in order to review the solutions offered to them in later writings is to look for common interpretative aims. Such an investigation usually entails playing down or disregarding the specific function of a biblical text in individual compositions." "Comparative midrash" does more justice to the narrative context of individual traditions (see Callaway, *Sing,* and the work of her mentor, J. A. Sanders, in Callaway's bibliography).

7. Literary studies of the Bible are becoming too numerous to list. Especially influential have been Culpepper, *Anatomy;* Kort, *Story;* Rhoads and Michie, *Mark as Story;* Tannehill, "The Disciples in Mark," "The Gospel of Mark," and *Narrative Unity;* Kingsbury, *Matthew as Story;* Alter, *Art.*

tor uses. This study assumes that the author of the *Biblical Antiquities* had a version of the Bible before him and consciously rewrote it. Comparison with the Bible as a "fixed point" characterizes this study.[8] Of course, the Bible was but one element, albeit the prime element, in the traditional material available to the author. Pseudo-Philo demonstrates extensive knowledge of a wide range of Jewish exegesis, as is clear from exegetical material shared with Josephus, *Jubilees,* rabbinic literature, and other works. But emphasis on the text's treatment of the Bible is justified both because of the privileged place of the Bible in first-century Palestinian Judaism and because it is the only continuous source the author uses, as far as can be determined. The Bible furnishes Pseudo-Philo's basic narrative structure and most episodes can be related in one way or another with biblical material.[9]

Historical questions are important in treating ancient texts. While literary critics correctly object to the rather overwhelming interest in history in the sense of "what actually happened," an ahistorical approach is equally one-sided. A certain ahistoricism is perhaps a legacy of the New Criticism, but there is now a renewed interest in the dependence of texts on their social context for meaning. Communication depends on cultural codes. Literature that originates in a culture radically different from that of the critic utilizes codes and assumes worldviews that require study. Biblical studies of the past yield a rich store of crucial information on language, genre, historical and social context, and so on that furnishes a foundation for our present investigation. Lest the abundance of such information detract from the analysis of Pseudo-Philo as a consistent and connected narrative, most of it is relegated to notes except as directly useful for this analysis. In chapter 12, historical concerns are dealt with explicitly. Although one can bracket specifically historical concerns in concentrating on texts, it must not be forgotten that texts are produced by real people in real-life situations. In the case of Pseudo-Philo, the book is a valuable witness to one perception in first-century Judaism of Israel's identity, its relation to God, and its relation to outsiders.

The rest of this chapter discusses narrative features and literary techniques in Pseudo-Philo. References to Pseudo-Philo in the present chapter are illustrative, and are not intended to be exhaustive.

Narrative Features

Story and Discourse

Chatman explains the title of his book *Story and Discourse* as follows.

---

8. The image of the Bible as a "fixed point" is taken from Nickelsburg, "Leaders," 51. We do not have the biblical version used by Pseudo-Philo, but Harrington's English translation notes where the text corresponds to a variety of biblical texts.

9. Nickelsburg ("Leaders," 64, n. 1) says, "It seems more likely that, as a whole, the *Antiquities* are based on the Bible than on earlier traditions transmitted apart from the Bible."

> Structuralist theory argues that each narrative has two parts: a story *(historie),*
> the content or chain of events (actions, happenings), plus what may be called
> the existents (characters, items of setting); and a discourse *(discours),* that is,
> the expression, the means by which the content is communicated. In simple
> terms, the story is the *what* in a narrative that is depicted, discourse the *how*
> (19).

"Discourse" denotes a particular manifestation of a story, but any discourse
is but one possible manifestation. The distinction between story and discourse
is problematic because one can never actually locate the "story." Any rendi-
tion of it is discourse.[10] If a given discourse involves flashbacks and flashforwards, one might construct a version in which each element occurs in its proper
chronological place. But that would also be only one possible rendering of the
"story." One never arrives at the story but is always left with discourse. The
present study adopts much of Chatman's discussion of narrative features, but
the dichotomy between story and discourse is misleading.

The *Biblical Antiquities* retells of some of Israel's sacred stories.[11] It is a
particular expression of a much larger series of stories that have many other
expressions within the Bible and in extracanonical literature. By the time
Pseudo-Philo's book was written, Israel already had a long tradition of retelling its stories to make them useful for its present life. Such a process has been
called "actualization."[12] The stories continue to "live" within communities
that change and adapt them in the context of new situations and problems.
Different renditions of stories can be used simultaneously by different communities or by different segments of a single community.

The process of adapting tradition to new situations occurs within the
boundaries of the canon itself.[13] The Chronicler retells parts of Samuel and
Kings, for example.[14] Long retellings of the Bible found outside the canon
have been called "rewritten Bible." Major examples are the *Jewish Antiquities*
of Josephus, the *Book of Jubilees,* the *Genesis Apocryphon* from Qumran, and
the *Biblical Antiquities* of Pseudo-Philo.[15] Judaism's evolving canon was a privileged version of its sacred stories to be commented upon and against which
to measure adaptations of the sacred stories.[16] As the canon of the Hebrew

10. See Moore's (*Literary Criticism,* 60–61) discussion of this. He rightly claims, "Narrative
is ubiquitously rhetorical," and criticizes Chatman as well as Rhoads and Michie for not realizing
that. Dividing Mark into the "what," the content, and the "how," the rhetoric, is misleading. Form
and content are inseparable (an insight that Moore attributes to the New Criticism), and therefore
all analysis comes under "how."

11. Extensive work on this aspect of Pseudo-Philo has been done by Vermes, *Scripture;* Cohn,
"Apocryphal Work;" Feldman, "Prolegomenon;" Bauckham, "Liber."

12. For a recent discussion of the concept, see Groves, *Actualization.*

13. See Fishbane, *Biblical Interpretation;* Vermes, *Post-biblical.*

14. It has been suggested that the *Biblical Antiquities* is modeled on 1 and 2 Chronicles and
is meant to supplement them. See Spiro, "Samaritans," 304–8; Le Déaut, *Nuit,* 188; Feldman,
"Prolegomenon," xxxii.

15. For a recent discussion of such texts, see Harrington, "Palestinian Adaptations."

16. For a short list of recent works on the process of the canon's development in light of
insights on how sacred stories are interpreted and applied in different contexts, see Callaway,
Sing, 1, n. 1.

Bible moved toward closure, a process whose culmination traditionally has been traced to the council at Yavneh at the end of the first century C.E.,[17] long retellings of the Bible gave way to extended commentaries on the canonized text, as in rabbinic midrash.[18] Pseudo-Philo's work is one of the last examples of the rewritten Bible. He shows awareness of the sacred text of the canon by quoting it, building upon it, and making direct references to it (35:7; 56:7; 63: 5). Pseudo-Philo assumes his readers are familiar with the larger context of the Hebrew Bible and of Jewish tradition in general. He makes frequent references to incidents in Israel's sacred traditions not recounted in the *Biblical Antiquities.* Although Pseudo-Philo demonstrates awareness of and respect for the sacred text, the author writes when that text is but one version of Israel's sacred stories, although a privileged one. The author freely adds, omits, and rewrites to produce a version of the sacred stories of use to his community in its own circumstances.

Author, Narrator, Point of View

Chatman conceives of narrative as the communication of a story. But that communication is not a simple matter of one person talking to another. A real reader may have little idea who the real author of a given work is. The complexity of the communication is expressed in the following scheme, which lays out its logical steps:[19]

Real author → [Implied author → (Narrator) → (Narratee) → Implied reader] → Real reader

Subsequent paragraphs explain these terms. The real author and the real reader are outside the narrative; elements within the square brackets are inside the narrative.

The term "implied author" was coined by Wayne Booth, who defines it as follows: "The 'implied author' chooses, consciously or unconsciously, what we read; we infer him as an ideal, literary, created version of the real man; he is the sum of his own choices."[20] A reader's impression of the "author" based on choices, reliable generalizations, judgments, and attitudes toward the material found in the narrative is the "implied author." Culpepper comments, "This impression may be more or less accurate as a picture of the real author depending on how he or she has crafted the work."[21] Of course, a real author can write so that the author inferred from the text is at some distance from his or her real self in terms of outlook, values, and knowledge, although there is no evidence that this is so in the case of Pseudo-Philo.

Corresponding to an implied author is an implied reader. The implied

17. For a reassessment of Yavneh in the light of rabbinic evidence, see Leiman, *Canonization.* For a bibliography on canonization, see Sanders, *Sacred Story,* 195–200.
18. SC 230, 22–28.
19. Chatman, *Story and Discourse,* 151.
20. *Rhetoric,* 74–75.
21. *Anatomy,* 16.

reader is not the concrete, real person reading the work, whether it be a first-century Jew or a twentieth-century critic. The implied reader is the reader implied by the narrative. It is the reader who follows the leads of the implied author, accepts his or her judgments, and is moved in precisely the ways intended by the implied author. Throughout most of the analysis in this book, the word "reader" refers to the implied reader.

All narratives imply a narrator, one telling the story within the work. Corresponding to the narrator is a narratee, one to whom the narrator speaks. Narratives vary widely in the extent to which the real reader is aware of the narrator. How a narrative is experienced is influenced by the degree of presence of the narrator, by whether that narrator is reliable, and by the narrator's point of view. In the *Biblical Antiquities,* the narrator is omniscient spatially, temporally, and psychologically, and is completely reliable. The narrator brings the reader to the beginning of history or to its end, sees and hears what happens in heaven or on earth, and knows the innermost thoughts not only of humans but even of God. The narrator makes trustworthy judgments and generalizations about characters and events. Although the reader does hear the narrator's voice several times, the narrator prefers to stay backstage and let the readers hear and see the characters. Rather than pronounce a generalization or judgment, he tends to put it in the mouth of a major character such as Moses, Joshua, Kenaz, Deborah, or God. Since the narrator conveys to the readers information not available to the characters, the narration is in the ironic mode.[22]

Most of my analysis is on the level of the narrative itself; it concentrates on what happens within the square brackets of the scheme I am using. For the sake of convenience in the following analysis, "author" means the implied author and "reader" means the implied reader. Following usage common in biblical scholarship, "Pseudo-Philo" is used to refer both to the implied author and to the text itself. Chapter 12 reflects on how the story world of Pseudo-Philo relates to the real world of first-century Palestine.

Plot

Chatman adopts Aristotle's definition of plot as the "arrangement of incidents" but indicates that the arrangement itself falls within the realm of the "story-as-discoursed."[23] He quotes Hardison to develop this notion.[24] The author

> can arrange the incidents in a story in a great many ways. He can treat some in detail and barely mention or even omit others, as Sophocles omits everything that happened to Oedipus before the plague in Thebes. He can observe chronological sequence, he can distort it, he can use messengers or flashbacks, and so forth. Each arrangement produces a different plot, and a great many plots can be made from the same story.

22. The term "ironic mode" comes from Frye, *Anatomy,* 34.
23. *Story and Discourse,* 43.
24. Hardison, "A Commentary," 123; quoted by Chatman, *Story and Discourse,* 43.

Central to plot is causality. A plot does not usually merely juxtapose events but explains their causes and relations and shows the role and character of actors within the story.[25] Pseudo-Philo is especially concerned with God's role in history and the relation between divine and human causality. God's decisions about whether or not to act through particular persons and God's reactions to human acts are major recurring strands in the *Biblical Antiquities*. Pseudo-Philo also makes a strong case for moral causality: The righteous are successful and the evil fail.[26]

The *Biblical Antiquities* is episodic. Much of the analysis of plot must be carried on at the level of individual episodes. Especially significant are narrative patterns that suggest overall purposes and techniques in Pseudo-Philo. But the episodic nature of Pseudo-Philo does not negate its overall plot structure.[27] Pseudo-Philo constructs larger complexes from small subunits. Examples are the complexes developed around the figures of Moses, Joshua, Kenaz, Deborah, and Samuel. Furthermore, there is a structure informing the work as a whole that is essential for appreciating Pseudo-Philo's viewpoint. Subsequent chapters investigate the subunits and complexes making up the *Biblical Antiquities*, but it is necessary here to consider the larger plot of the work within which those smaller units should be read.

Kort offers a helpful way of thinking about the temporal element of plot.[28]

> A formal study of fictional plots will reveal three kinds of temporal patterns. One is rhythmic or cyclical; such plots, because they emphasize return, favor the past and are most easily expanded by natural metaphors. Other plots are patterned by the interaction of contemporary figures and forces. We can term such plots "polyphonic," and we can anticipate that they will most easily be elaborated with social and political metaphors. The actualization of a particular person's or group's potential is a third kind of pattern. It is oriented toward the future and is most easily associated with psychological implications. To continue with the musical terminology, we can call such plots "melodic." While all three patterns may appear in a single narrative, one of them will be more inclusive and important in a narrative than the other two.

The overall plot of the *Biblical Antiquities* involves a complex interweaving of these types of plot.[29] The "melodic" aspect, which could be called teleological, dominates chapters 1–21, from the Creation up to the establishment of Israel in the land. Chapters 1–7 are early history up to the time of Abraham. Except for Abraham and his family, all of humanity is depicted as sinful and unworthy of God. God chooses Abraham and makes a covenant with him and promises to bless his seed and be his Lord forever (7:4). Chapters 8–21 narrate

25. Role is defined by Tannehill (*Narrative Unity*, 1.1) as "character in action and interaction within an unfolding plot."

26. Perrot (SC 230) uses the term *causalité morale* throughout his commentary.

27. This is exactly the point made about the Gospel of Luke by Tannehill (*Narrative Unity*, 1.xiii). But see Moore, *Literary Criticism*, 29–30, 35–38.

28. *Story*, 16.

29. Tannehill's (*Narrative Unity*, 1.4) terminology is different. What Kort calls "rhythmical," Tannehill calls "iterative." What Kort calls "melodic," Tannehill calls "progressive."

fulfillment of the promises. A thanksgiving ceremony in 21:7–10 claims that the promises of God have been completely fulfilled, and the tension implicit in God's making promises is resolved by their fulfillment. It is a climax that could end the narrative. Israel could now live happily ever after.

The remainder of the *Biblical Antiquities* (chaps. 22–65) is a narrative explanation of why Israel has not lived happily ever after. The reason is that Israel has not lived up to its side of the bargain; it has not been faithful to God. This section of the *Biblical Antiquities* is "rhythmical." In a pattern based on the Book of Judges, Israel is unfaithful, suffers for its sin, is rescued by God (usually through a human agent), and is restored to God's favor. But this is always simply a return to a situation that Israel fully enjoyed as early as chapter 21, by its own admission. The "rhythmical" pattern illustrates and proves Pseudo-Philo's assessment of Israel's situation. Israel always has potential access to God's favor and protection; that is a constant. But Israel continually disrupts the equilibrium that divine support could bring. The narrative proves that God is always faithful and fulfillment and security are always available to Israel, but Israel's own actions incur misfortune.

In an interesting twist that provides a distinctive flavor to the narrative, God is repeatedly portrayed as wishing to end this special relationship with Israel. But God is constrained by the divine promises to Israel's fathers. God can punish individual Israelites or even whole generations but cannot destroy Israel. This increases the readers' confidence in the covenant because the covenant is truly secure if not even God can annul it.

Throughout the *Biblical Antiquities,* there are repeated references to Israel's past.[30] This is appropriate to the plot's "rhythmical" nature. Explicit analogies are often drawn between something in the narrative present and something that happened before. Often, the earlier episodes are not even narrated by Pseudo-Philo, since the author assumes knowledge of a larger story by his readers. Recurring analogies foster the conviction that Israel's history is unified by God. Nothing is new under the sun in Israel's life, and a correct understanding of Israel's history will reveal the meaning of the present. That outlook relates to the purpose of the writer of the *Biblical Antiquities,* an interpretation of Israel's past that aims to provide guidance in the present. The analogies contribute to the "rhythmic" quality of Pseudo-Philo's use of time.

Although the "rhythmical" aspect of the plot dominates the *Biblical Antiquities* from chapter 22 on, two possible "melodic" elements still remain, but their precise place in the plot is debatable. The first concerns Davidic kingship; the second involves the eschaton.

The topic of leadership helps drive the plot.[31] The book ends with Saul's death. Interactions between Samuel, Saul, David, and Jonathan are portrayed in chapters 45–65. Given Pseudo-Philo's interest in leadership and the fact that the narrative extends to the time of David, it is puzzling that there is no

30. See Eissfeldt, "Kompositionstechnik."
31. See Nickelsburg, "Leaders."

mention of David's ascent to the throne. It is unlikely that the omission indicates a deemphasis of the Davidic dynasty, because the last chapters of the book point forward to David's kingship. Alternatively, the abrupt halt of the narrative at the death of Saul has prompted scholars to suggest that the original ending of the work has been lost. If that is true, then no conclusions based on the way the work ends are possible.

There is no sure way to decide whether or not chapter 65 is the original ending of the *Biblical Antiquities,* but one can see the present ending as original and yet compatible with an interest in Davidic monarchy. There are indications that suggest a "melodic" line leading to the establishment of a monarchy faithful to God. One such indication is the connection between Kenaz and David. Kenaz is one of Pseudo-Philo's most important leaders; his ancestry is altered so that he belongs to Judah, David's tribe (LAB 25:9). Kenaz is the son of Caleb, who in 15:3 is said to be descended from Judah. Joshua himself quotes Gen. 49:10 ("A ruler will not be lacking from Judah, nor a leader from his loins") in apparent reference to him. The verse from Genesis is often applied to the Davidic king in Jewish and Christian tradition. In LAB 49, when Israel again undergoes a crisis of leadership, the people long for a leader like Kenaz (49:1). God responds to the people's prayer by sending Samuel, but Samuel's major significance is that through him God inaugurates first the monarchy of Saul and then the projected reign of David. In a departure from the biblical account, Samuel objects to the people's request for a king, not because kingship is wrong in itself, but because it is not yet time for a king. But Samuel does expect monarchy as part of God's plan. In chapter 59, Samuel is ordered to anoint David, who is probably the one like Kenaz of 49:1. David is then anointed and sings a psalm of praise to God for protecting and anointing him. The rest of Pseudo-Philo presents a very favorable picture of David. The words of David and Jonathan in chapter 62 elaborate on David's righteousness and, by implication, his right to rule. David is an ideal leader in the *Biblical Antiquities*, but his leadership is more potential than actual, at least as the work now stands. Pseudo-Philo ends with David well poised to be a good leader. His righteousness is admirable, and he is chosen by God and anointed by Samuel. His hymns show him to be aware of his dependence on God (59:4) and demonstrate wide knowledge of the universe and the supernatural world (60:2–3). His military prowess is impressive (59:5; 61:1–9) and he has angelic support (61:8).

If the *Biblical Antiquities* originally ended with Saul's death, its ending could be compared to the equally controversial ending of the Gospel of Mark. Debates still rage over whether Mark actually ended with 16:8. One interpreter has shown how ending with 16:8 serves the theme of discipleship.[32] Christian readers identify with the disciples. As the Gospel progresses and the disciples lack perception and understanding and show themselves more interested in power and security than in following Jesus, the readers become dissatisfied with their behavior. The final failure of the fearful women leaves the narrative

32. Tannehill, "Disciples."

hanging (16:8). The ending shifts the burden of being good disciples to the readers themselves, who ought not repeat the mistakes of the disciples.

Pseudo-Philo's ending also leaves readers hanging. Throughout the *Biblical Antiquities,* good leadership depends upon faithfulness to God's will and trust in divine guidance. The righteous person motivated by devotion to God and the covenant, not by riches and glory, is the good leader. Many biblical stories concerning David's rise to royal power and his exercise of that power do not demonstrate good leadership in Pseudo-Philo's terms. Those stories, as well as the stories about kings of Israel and Judah in 1 and 2 Kings, document misuse of royal authority. Rather than rewrite such stories, the author decided to present David's potential as something to be realized. Ending the narrative before David's enthronement also keeps the exact nature of the leader's office ambiguous. David was a king, but kingship per se is not in the forefront of Pseudo-Philo's narrative. Righteousness and potential for leadership is stressed. Whether or not that potential is expressed through the office of king is secondary.

The second "rhythmical" element that goes beyond chapter 22 concerns the eschaton. There are various temporal patterns at work in the narrative, but there is one overarching temporal framework. Pseudo-Philo pays attention to what could be called protology and eschatology.[33] There are repeated references to the beginning and end of the world. Such references are often put into the mouths of reliable characters or occur through a description of God's revelation to someone, such as Moses. Those references, especially to the eschaton, do not have the urgency found in such works as *2 Baruch,* 4 Ezra, and the *Apocalypse of Abraham,* works close in time and geography to the *Biblical Antiquities,* nor do they play the same role in the narrative as in those other works. Protology and eschatology supply a temporal frame within which all of the action takes place. There is a nesting effect in the plot that comes from its temporal aspects. Individual episodes such as Kenaz's judgment of the Israelite sinners must be seen within larger complexes, such as the entire career of Kenaz (the first judge to rule when the people are established in the land). That career must in turn be seen within the context of Israel's behavior in the land of Israel, which occupies the work from chapter 21 onward; that story is nested within the larger story of nascent Israel and God's relationship with it. The whole is framed by recurring references to the beginning and the end of the world. The nesting could be represented as follows: [Creation ({Israel before entering the land} {⟨Kenaz⟩ Israel after entering the land}) Eschaton].

As becomes clear later in this book, Pseudo-Philo's use of protology and eschatology contributes less to the "melodic" aspect of time than to the "polyphonic." In other words, the use of eschatology does not so much move events forward as shed light on the present and the interaction of characters in individual episodes. Protology and eschatology really explain the present, which is the focus of attention.

33. See SC 230, 53–57.

Characters

Chatman defines character as a "paradigm of traits," taking "trait" in the sense of "a relatively stable or abiding personal quality."[34] Characters are revealed through their thoughts, words, and actions, by the way the other characters look at them and interact with them, and by the narrator's comments about them. A main concern of the *Biblical Antiquities* is to examine key characters from Israel's past. God is also a character. In many cases the characters are "round," that is, they are complex and not unidimensional.[35] "Flat" characters possess a single or a few traits. Round characters "possess a variety of traits, some of them conflicting or even contradictory—they are capable of changing, of surprising us, and so on."[36] The latter description certainly fits God, whose inner conflicts concerning Israel and the human race are graphically depicted, but it is also true of several characters in the text—Kenaz, for example. Chapter 10 investigates character in Pseudo-Philo.

Atmosphere and Setting

"Atmosphere" is a vague term. Chatman comments, "Setting is practically terra incognita; my brief pages hardly do justice to the subject, particularly its relation to that vague notion called 'atmosphere.'"[37] Kort offers the following definition of atmosphere: "Atmosphere is that element that establishes the boundaries enclosing the narrative's world. These limits are secured by the sense of what might be expected to occur, of what is and what is not possible."[38] Temporal and spatial boundaries help determine what is possible within a narrative, and so setting is included in this definition of atmosphere.

Time elements have been examined in the previous section on plot. Perhaps most significant for atmosphere is the observation that all of the action is framed by references to the beginning and the end of the world. This lends a supernatural atmosphere to the entire work. All history can be viewed from its farthest limits, cosmic boundaries that can be encompassed only by God or by someone instructed by God. In terms of space, Israel is limited to its occupation of a small area in Egypt, the desert, and the land of Israel, but the readers are permitted to see God talking to the angels or the stars or even to himself. There are numerous flashbacks and flashforwards that give readers the temporal perspective of the narrator and even of God at times.[39] The readers are able to see much more than the characters. The fact that the readers can see the realm of God also contributes to the supernatural atmosphere of the narrative.

34. *Story and Discourse,* 126. See his discussion of character, 107–38.

35. The terms "round" and "flat" were coined by E. M. Forster (Chatman, *Story and Discourse,* 131–32).

36. *Story and Discourse,* 132.

37. *Story and Discourse,* 264; quoted by Kort, *Story,* 17. It is in reaction to such ambiguity that Kort advances his own definition.

38. *Story,* 17.

39. For time in narrative, see Genette, *Narrative Discourse.*

Throughout the *Biblical Antiquities,* God acts directly in human history. In addition, the divine enters history through human agents and through angels. Miracles are common, as are signs and prophecies. Pseudo-Philo adopts these elements from its sources and enhances them.

Irony

Dramatic irony occurs when "the spectators understand the speech or action more fully than do the dramatic figures."[40] Dramatic irony pervades the *Biblical Antiquities*. In many cases, the readers share the narrator's knowledge and are often treated to God's perspective.

Literary Technique

Extent of Rewriting the Bible

The extent to which passages in Pseudo-Philo depend upon biblical passages varies. A simple categorization is the following.

1. Passages that depend heavily upon quotations of biblical passages and in which Pseudo-Philo's interpretation depends upon small-scale changes in the text. An example of this kind of use of the Bible is found in the story of the Flood in chapter 3. This sort of rewriting is fairly rare in the *Biblical Antiquities*, for the author prefers to rewrite rather freely.
2. Passages that quote the Bible to set up the situation of a passage or to constitute the structure of an incident but in which there is extensive rewriting, often with the addition of lengthy passages that do not appear in the Bible. This kind of rewriting is common in the *Biblical Antiquities*. It occurs in the story of Abraham and the fiery furnace combined with the story of the tower of Babel, for example.
3. Passages built around a biblical figure, but consisting of material not found in the Bible. Examples are the stories of Jair (chap. 38), Zebul (chap. 29), and the judges Abdon and Elon (chap. 41).
4. Passages with no counterparts in Scripture. An example is the story of the Midianite magician Aod (chap. 34).

Direct Address and Dialogue

Pseudo-Philo prefers direct rather than indirect address. This accounts for the numerous speeches by characters as well as the prevalence of dialogue that both advances the plot and expresses judgments, generalizations, and explanations. Direct address allows readers to experience the characters' words and

40. Barnet, Berman, and Burto, *Dictionary,* 63.

actions firsthand, creating the illusion that the readers witness the action directly, not through a narrator. Paradoxically, this makes the narrative more authoritative.

God is really the principal character, and the narrative makes liberal use of God's words. The reader frequently hears God speak and even hears God's thoughts. One also hears God holding conversations with the people of Israel, with particular characters, and with angels and stars. God is the most reliable commentator on everything.

Words of characters other than God also figure largely and can be reliable. Moses, Joshua, Kenaz, and Deborah make speeches, pray, and converse with the people, and it is through seeing and hearing them that the readers understand the meaning of history and gain the proper attitudes toward life. There are also characters whose words are not reliable and whom the narrator holds up for disapproval. The words of evil people usually appear in the context of conflict between them and the good characters or between them and God, so that it is evident how wrong they are. In other cases the narrator allows ambiguity concerning the goodness or badness of certain characters and their thoughts, plans, and actions.

Speeches and prayers abound in Pseudo-Philo. Through them the characters reflect on situations and apply general principles, draw conclusions, and express attitudes the narrator wishes to encourage or discourage. The technique of using speeches and prayers allows the narrator to keep a low profile and creates the impression that the readers are hearing words directly from key characters. A special form of speech in the *Biblical Antiquities* is the testament. Testaments were popular late in the Second Temple period because they enlist the authority of an ancient sage or hero to support certain ideas or actions.[41] Much direct address takes the form of short exchanges between characters. The action in many passages is carried forward by such dialogue. The author often seems less interested in exactly what happens than in what characters have to say about it, what conclusions they draw from it, and what attitudes they have toward it.

Related to direct address is soliloquy. When the narrator wants to inform the reader about the motivations of a character, including God, he usually lets the reader hear the character thinking or speaking in a soliloquy. Although the term "soliloquy" more properly applies to staged drama, Chatman defends its use for narrative.[42] The following is his definition of narrative soliloquy.[43]

> Soliloquy is perhaps best used as a term to refer to nonnaturalistic or "expressionistic" narratives in which the only informational source is that of characters formally presenting, explaining, and commenting upon things. These are formal declamations—not speech or thought in the ordinary sense but a stylized merging of the two.

41. See Kolenkow and Collins in *EJMI*, 259–85.
42. *Story and Discourse*, 178–81.
43. *Story and Discourse*, 181.

By this definition, soliloquy is common in Pseudo-Philo and is a major device by which the author conveys important information, judgments, and generalizations to the readers.

Direct Quotation

The characters share the narrator's penchant for direct address. Like the narrator, the characters find direct address vivid and authoritative, for it proves that they report things exactly as they happened. As might be expected, God is the one most often quoted. God quotes the divine words to prove divine faithfulness to promises, threats, and predictions. The people or specific characters quote God to prove either divine faithfulness or its absence. The people quote Moses to justify their request for a king. The people are often quoted by God or a good leader to show their unfaithfulness or their errors in understanding.

Direct quotation reaches remarkable proportions several times. In 32:3, Deborah quotes Isaac's words to Abraham and within that quote Isaac himself quotes Abraham. Since the narrator is quoting Deborah here, the narrative reads as follows: Deborah said, "Isaac said, 'Abraham said, "(Abraham's words)." ' " Three sets of quotation marks are needed. In chapter 28, the narrator quotes Phinehas, who quotes his father Eleazar, who quotes what Phinehas should say, which involves a further quotation of Eleazar, who quotes God. The narrative reads as follows: Phinehas said, "Eleazar said, 'Phinehas should say, "Eleazar said, 'God said, "(God's words)." ' " ' " Five sets of quotation marks encompass these nested quotations.

Quotation in Pseudo-Philo is not always exact. Even when something from Pseudo-Philo's own narrative is quoted, the quotation is often rephrased. Pseudo-Philo is more interested in essential meaning than precise words.

Stock Words and Phrases

Pseudo-Philo has a predilection for specific words and phrases expressing important themes. Frequently the very occurrence of those words and phrases is enough to evoke a theme, and their insertion into biblical passages amounts to an interpretation of the Bible. A prevalent example is the verb "command." God's direction of the action is often signaled by the observation that something has taken place in accordance with divine command. A related word is the verb "direct," used to show that God controls things. An example of a phrase commonly used in Pseudo-Philo is "inhabitants of the land (or earth)." Its use often evokes Pseudo-Philo's theme of the separation of Israel from other nations.

Condensation and Summary

The distinction between condensation and summary is not absolute, but the following working definitions will help indicate more precisely what sort of technique is being used. Condensation is the enumeration of specific events, but in a markedly shortened form. Most frequently the narrator uses this technique to set up the situation for an episode from the Bible. In this case, the purpose of the technique is to provide essential knowledge for understanding a situation or to advance the plot to a desired point, as in chapter 8, whose main purpose is to get the Israelites to Egypt so that they can be saved through Moses. At other times, such as in the case of the Flood (chap. 3), the biblical passage is shortened to highlight certain aspects of it.

Summary is the characterization of repeated events or situations without isolating particular instances. An example is in 4:5, where the following general pattern is seen as characterizing the activity of humans and God: Humans cultivate the land; they pray to God in times of drought; God answers by sending rain; a rainbow appears in the clouds after the rain; humans offer thanksgiving sacrifices. The pattern summarizes a whole period of history.

Biblical Elements

Pseudo-Philo often transfers details from one biblical context to another. Such details are often hard to isolate, partially because they are embedded in the text and partially because the *Biblical Antiquities* is a translation into Latin of a Greek translation of a Hebrew original. More extensive uses of the Bible to comment on the Bible are clearer. For example, the story of Korah's rebellion is influenced by the trial pattern also found in Daniel 3 and 2 Maccabees 7.[44] Portions of the story of Kenaz, a story not present in the Bible, are modeled on that of Gideon in Judges 6–8 (LAB 27).

Prediction and Fulfillment

A pattern of prediction and fulfillment permeates the *Biblical Antiquities*. One category of prediction and fulfillment is that of God's promises, which see their fulfillment within the narrative. In that case, both the promises (a form of prediction by God) and their fulfillment are clearly marked in the text and the fulfillment is seen as an explanation of events. Israel's unfaithfulness is also regularly predicted. The unfaithfulness comes to pass in the episodes of the story, but the climax of Israel's repeated unfaithfulness is projected to a time beyond that of the narrative. For example, in 19:7 God predicts that Israel's sin will result in the destruction of the temple, which is yet to be built. There are also references to the eschaton, when punishment will descend on all the wicked.

Other instances of prediction and fulfillment abound. God predicts that Agag, the Amalekite king spared by Saul, will have a son who will kill Saul, and it comes to pass. The births of important characters such as Abraham and Moses are foretold and come to pass. God predicts that the divine plans concerning Seila, daughter of Jephthah, will be put into effect, and they are. The

44. See Murphy, "Korah's Rebellion."

all-encompassing pattern of prediction and fulfillment implies that everything is under the direction of God and that God's word is to be trusted absolutely.

Generalizations and Judgments

Generalizations are statements about life that go beyond the boundaries of the narrative.[45] In Pseudo-Philo they are ethical, philosophical, or explicitly religious. Judgments are evaluations of the morality of characters or of the rightness or wrongness of their actions, words, or attitudes.[46] The narrator attributes many generalizations and judgments to the direct address of the characters.

Recognition

Recognition or lack of it occurs several times in Pseudo-Philo.[47] It heightens the ironic nature of the text because it shows that humans are often fooled by appearances. Their sudden recognition of a person or a situation is an effective technique for showing that there is an understanding of things only occasionally available to the characters, but usually available to the readers. The changing of a character's appearance is a subtheme of the recognition motif. For example, Moses' appearance is changed in 12:1, as is David's in 61:9.

Explanations

At times, the narrator explains something, either by intruding into the narrative to furnish information, or through a character. Explanation of characters' motivations is common.

Use of Angels

Although God acts directly in the narrative, God also frequently works through agents, both human and angelic. Not much attention is paid to angels as such. They are taken for granted as being God's messengers and agents on earth. They deliver a particular message or perform a specific task and then disappear. Angels work side by side with humans in several instances, but in those cases it is really the angel who does the work, in keeping with the author's insistence on divine causality.

45. Chatman, *Story and Discourse*, 243–48.
46. *Story and Discourse*, 241–43.
47. See 7:5; 8:10; 9:5; 12:1; 27:7; 28:7; 38:3; 47:4; 53:5; 61:8–9 (twice); 64:4. For recognition as a literary technique in the ancient world (discussed by Aristotle, for example), see Culpepper, *Anatomy*.

Narrative Patterns

Narrative patterns are occasionally shared by several episodes in the *Biblical Antiquities*. For example, there is a pattern of evil plans, countered by plans by apparently good people, which are in turn objected to by a dissenter, and a final resolution by God.[48] That pattern or a variation of it occurs in chapters 6, 9, 10, and 44. A trial pattern is traceable in the story of Abraham in chapter 6 and the story of Korah in chapter 16.[49]

Conclusion

This chapter provides a broad framework within which to view the *Biblical Antiquities*. The set of questions implied by that framework does not replace more traditional questions of tradition criticism, form criticism, source criticism, and redaction criticism, but supplements them.

48. See Murphy, "Divine Plan."
49. See Murphy, "Korah's Rebellion."

II

Narrative Commentary

3

From Adam to Joseph: *Biblical Antiquities* 1–8

These initial chapters, which depend on Genesis, serve three main goals: to locate Abraham and his progeny in a "human geography" through genealogies, to contrast righteous Abraham with sinful humanity, and to set the stage for the Exodus.[1] The two versions of the Creation in Genesis 1–2 are omitted. Pseudo-Philo reverses the order of the genealogies from Genesis 4–5. LAB 1 recapitulates Genesis 5 and LAB 2 does the same for Genesis 4. By this reversal, humanity's positive side is presented before the negative. The genealogy of chapter 1, which names Adam's descendants through Seth, does not contain much editorial comment. It culminates in Noah's birth. The genealogy in chapter 2 offers several editorial comments showing that various evils originated in Cain, the first murderer, and his descendants. By presenting humanity's positive side first, Pseudo-Philo suggests humanity's potential before detailing its failures. This pattern, potential for good followed by failure, is repeated several times in Pseudo-Philo. It is related to the plot's structure noted in the previous chapter: Israel's potential for living at peace with God is portrayed before its failure to realize that potential is recounted. Chapters 3–8 tell the story of humanity from the Flood to Israel's descent to Egypt. The chapters stress humanity's sinfulness, Abraham's refusal to join in their wickedness at the tower of Babel, the subsequent election of Abraham and his seed, and the migration of Abraham's progeny to Egypt.

Chapter 1: Adam's Descendants Through Seth

The genealogies in LAB 1–2 belong to the first category of rewriting listed in the previous chapter. Pseudo-Philo merely adds names to Genesis 4–5 and alters comments about or by individuals in the genealogies. Most of the added names in these and other genealogies are not found elsewhere in Jewish tradition. Multiplication of names gains the readers' confidence. Surely an author

---

1. The *Biblical Antiquities* uses the name "Abram" until God formally changes it in 8:3. The present study uses "Abraham" whenever referring to that figure.

with such intimate knowledge of the specifics of biblical history, specifics that do not appear in the Hebrew Bible or even elsewhere in Jewish tradition, is a trustworthy guide to that history. Since LAB 1–5 locates Abraham's place within the human race, the impression of accuracy is especially important.[2] For example, Gen. 5:4 says that after Adam had Seth, "he had other sons and daughters." LAB 1:2–3 specifies that after Seth Adam had twelve sons and eight daughters, and then gives the names of most of them.[3] Feldman notes that the Talmud sees the filling in of gaps in the biblical text, such as the absence of names, as justifiable in order to combat heretics who use such gaps against believers.[4]

Besides adding names, Pseudo-Philo alters Genesis 5 by rewriting the words of Lamech, Noah's father (1:20). The language and concepts of LAB 1:20 are characteristic of Pseudo-Philo. In Gen. 5:29, Lamech says, "Out of the ground which the LORD has cursed this one shall bring us relief from our work and from the toil of our hands." "Shall bring us relief" translates the Hebrew *ynhmnw* as being from *nhm,* "console," so Gen. 5:29 is based on an etymology of "Noah" deriving it from *nhm.* In LAB 1:20, Lamech says, *"This one will give rest [requiem] to us* and to the earth *from* those who dwell on it—on account of the wickedness of whose evil *deeds [propter iniquitatem operum malorum]* the earth will be visited." Pseudo-Philo derives "Noah" from the Hebrew *nwh,* "rest."[5] "Rest" is a common image in the *Biblical Antiquities.* Pseudo-Philo sees the world as an often-hostile place. Rest is needed and desired. Noah is the first human through whom God works to effect rest. The fact that Noah is the culmination of the first genealogy, before the sinfulness of the world is detailed, strengthens hope for deliverance from this evil world.

"Inhabitants of the earth" is a stock phrase in the *Biblical Antiquities.* It emphasizes that God is in heaven and humans on earth and that God sees all human activity. This image is found in various places in the Bible.[6] Pseudo-Philo uses the phrase "inhabitants of the earth" both to generalize about the human race and to contrast Israel with everyone else.

The noun *opus* and the verb *operari* used in 1:20 are stock words in the *Biblical Antiquities.* They most frequently refer to humanity's and Israel's evil deeds. (Pseudo-Philo's evaluation of humanity is fairly pessimistic.) The word *iniquitas,* a favorite of Pseudo-Philo, is used in much the same way.[7] The ref-

---

2. See Johnson, *Purpose.*

3. Perrot (SC 230, 82) points out the frequent occurrences of the number twelve in Pseudo-Philo: 1:2; 6:3; 8:1, 6; 15:1; 17:2; 25:9–13; 26:10; 51:2.

4. *B. Bat.* 91a ("Prolegomenon," xlvi, lxx).

5. Harrington points out that "the LXX is similar to Ps-Philo here" (*OTP,* 305, n. w). Feldman ("Prolegomenon," lxxxiv) notes that "rest" is the meaning given to Noah's name by the Latin translators before Jerome. "Rest" and "console" are both found in *Gen. Rab.* 25:2 (SC 230, 83).

6. For example, Gen. 23:7, 12, 13; 42:6; Num. 14:9; Ezra 4:4; Isa. 40:22–23.

7. *Opus* (or *operari*) and *iniquitas* (or *iniquus*) are found in the same context ten times (1:20; 2:8, 10; 3:3, 6; 12:4; 22:7; 23:6; 34:5; 44:9).

erence to God's visit is characteristic of Pseudo-Philo's emphasis on eschato-logical judgment.[8]

Noah is to give rest to "us" and to the earth. The "us" in 1:20 comes from Gen. 5:29, but the readers would identify with "us." Although the readers do not live in Noah's time, humanity's sinfulness, to be described in LAB 2, extends to the remaining history of the world, as seen in subsequent chapters. Desire for relief from that sinfulness and for subsequent restoration of God's favor is a dominant motif in Pseudo-Philo. The earth needs rest from human-ity's sins because those sins affect it. As in Gen. 3:17, Adam's sin results not only in his own condemnation but in that of the earth as well (LAB 37:3). Although no mention of rest for the earth occurs in Genesis, Pseudo-Philo's mention of the earth is occasioned by the use of the word "ground" in Gen. 5:29. Gen. 5:29 promises rest from the toil caused by sin, whereas LAB 1:20 offers relief from sinners themselves. Pseudo-Philo keeps the focus on the sinfulness of humans.

The rewriting of Lamech's words demonstrates how the narrator places important ideas on the lips of characters. The readers know that Noah did play the role Lamech predicts for him, a role narrated in chapter 3. This is but the first of numerous instances of prediction and fulfillment in the book.

Chapter 2: Humanity's Sinfulness

LAB 2 modifies the genealogy of Genesis 4.[9] In Gen. 4:12, God commands Cain to wander the earth as punishment for his brother's murder. Then, with-out explanation, Gen. 4:16 says, "[Cain] settled in the land of Nod, east of Eden." LAB 2:1 reads: *"Now Cain dwelt in the land trembling,* as God had appointed for him after he had killed Abel his brother." That Cain lives in the *"land trembling"* results from deriving the place name "Nod" from the Hebrew *nwd,* "tremble." The participle is nominative, so modifies "Cain." LAB 2:1 makes it clear that God orders Cain to dwell fearfully in the land as a punishment. The retention of God's role illustrates divine causality. LAB 2:3 says, "Cain was fifteen years old when he did these things, and from that time he began to *build cities* until he had founded seven cities." In Gen. 4:17, Cain founds just one city, so here his city-building activity is enhanced.[10] The narrator proves his knowledge by supplying the names of all the cities. The mention of Abel's murder thus serves primarily to characterize the first city-

8. The word *visitare* is used of God's coming for the Last Judgment here and in 19:12, 13, and 26:13. In 13:8 it refers to God's punishment of humanity through the great Flood.

9. It has been suggested that Pseudo-Philo names Cain's wife Themech to avoid the conclusion that his marriage was incestuous (LAB 2:1). *Jub.* 4:8 says that Awan was his wife, and *Jub.* 4:1 claims that she was also his sister (see Spiro, *Manners,* 184, n. 126, and SC 230, 84). But there is no indication that Pseudo-Philo knew the traditions contained in *Jubilees* about Awan, and it is unclear that he would be interested in improving the picture of Cain or of Adam's children.

10. For the number seven, see 25:11 and 61:5.

builder, hinting that this key element of human civilization, the city, was tainted from the start.[11]

LAB 2:5–10 rewrites Gen. 4:18–26 with three additions. In Gen. 4:21, Jubal is "the ancestor of all those who play the lyre and the pipe." Pseudo-Philo's addition expands that description to connect the making of music with sexual immorality: "*Jobal . . . was the first to teach all kinds of musical instruments.* In that time, when those inhabiting the earth began to do evil deeds (each one with his neighbor's wife) and they defiled them, God was angry. And he began to play the lyre and the lute and every instrument of sweet song and to corrupt the earth" (2:7–8). Music leads to immorality.[12] Jobal bears special responsibility for adultery because of his playing, but the guilt is truly communal, for the narrator generalizes that all of humanity engages in adultery.[13] This generalization is conveyed by his use of two favorite terms, "those inhabiting the earth" and "evil deeds." God's anger is a common theme in Pseudo-Philo. The narrator is omniscient; he knows God's reaction to Jobal, even though the Bible does not make that explicit.

Pseudo-Philo's second addition to Gen. 4:18–26 concerns Tubal-cain from Gen. 4:22, called Tubal in the *Biblical Antiquities*. Genesis says that Tubal-cain "made all kinds of bronze and iron tools." The narrator of the *Biblical Antiquities* goes further: "This is the Tubal who showed men techniques in using lead and tin and *iron and bronze* and silver and gold. And then those inhabiting the earth began to make statues and to adore them" (LAB 2:9). Idolatry is the fundamental sin in Pseudo-Philo; this passage places its beginnings very early in history and generalizes it through the stock phrase "those inhabiting the earth."[14]

Pseudo-Philo's third addition concerns Lamech (not Noah's father). In Gen. 4:23, Lamech addresses his wives and says, "I have killed a man for wounding me, a young man for striking me." Pseudo-Philo's Lamech says, "*I have destroyed men* on my own account and snatched sucklings from the breasts, in order to show my sons and those inhabiting the earth how to do evil deeds" (LAB 2:10). Lamech's ferocity is increased here, and he does not only act violently as in Genesis but teaches the entire human race to do likewise. The familiar terms "those inhabiting the earth" and "evil deeds" are present. Evil is generalized. Humanity's sinfulness is stressed.

Genesis quotes Lamech's words. Pseudo-Philo builds on this device to let Lamech himself explain his effect on humanity. There may be antithetical parallelism between the two Lamechs. In 1:20, Noah's father predicts that his son will be the agent of God's salvation. In 2:10, the evil that Lamech teaches is part of the evil from which Noah must rescue humanity.

---

11. The notion that human civilization is the result of a fall or of sinful actions is frequent in ancient literature. Such a notion has been called a "negative application of the culture-hero motif" (Hanson, "Rebellion," 229).

12. The rabbis also connect music with sexual immorality (SC 230, 85).

13. The MT has "Jubal."

14. See Murphy, "Retelling."

Chapter 3: The Flood

In LAB 3, most of the material comes from the Bible but is reworked. Pseudo-Philo's alterations are editorial comments and additions to God's words. In the Bible, most of God's original world is wiped away in the Flood. When Noah leaves the ark, there is a new beginning in history. Pseudo-Philo takes this opportunity to comment on the nature of the world and of God's relations with it.

The first words not found in any biblical manuscript appear after God's statement concerning the limitation of the human life span to 120 years. Pseudo-Philo adds, "For them he set the limits of life, but the crimes *[scelera]* done by their hands did not cease" (LAB 3:2). *Scelus* is a *hapax legomenon* in Pseudo-Philo but is a stylistic variation on the frequent *opus* attended by a negative qualifier found in 3:3, 4, 6, and used neutrally in 3:10. The sentence highlights humanity's stubborn sinfulness. God's limitation on human life does not stem the tide of human evil. The pessimistic theme that humanity (or Israel) seldom obeys God no matter what God does is common in the *Biblical Antiquities.*[15]

In LAB 3:4, Noah finds favor in God's eyes, as in the biblical narrative, but Pseudo-Philo adds that he also finds "mercy." Mercy is one of God's major attributes in the *Biblical Antiquities*. Noah finds mercy because he is righteous and blameless. Later in 3:4 God says to Noah, *"I will establish my covenant with you,* to destroy those inhabiting the earth." This motivation for God's establishment of the Noachic covenant occurs nowhere else in Jewish tradition. In the biblical narrative, the covenant with Noah focuses on God's promise never to destroy the earth by flood again (Gen. 9:9–17). In Gen. 6:17, God says that everything on the earth will be destroyed. Pseudo-Philo incorporates the notice of destruction into the covenant itself, making it part of God's promise to Noah; this underlines God's anger at sin. This may be a promise that Noah will no longer have to tolerate the evil of humanity. After all, Noah is the one who is to bring *"rest to us* and to the earth *from* those who dwell on it—on account of the wickedness of whose evil *deeds* the earth will be visited" (1:20). The use of the stock phrase "inhabitants of the earth" in both 1:20 and 3:4 signals one of Pseudo-Philo's generalizations and sets off Noah from all other human beings.

LAB 3:6 is an editorial comment: "Now it was then the sixteen hundred and fifty-second year from the time when God made heaven and earth, in which the earth along with those inhabiting it was destroyed on account of the wickedness of their deeds." This may be a scribal gloss. Precise dating of events does not preoccupy the *Biblical Antiquities* as it does *Jubilees,* for example.

---

15. A similar example is in chapters 6–7 concerning the tower of Babel. Although God foils the builders' plans to murder those who will not cooperate with them, "the people of the land were not turned from their malicious plottings" and carry on their work as if nothing had happened.

Further, the chronology here is incompatible with LAB 1.[16] The sentence is permeated with language typical of Pseudo-Philo, but the originator of the gloss could well have made the comment fit the book. In any case, the repetition of the reason for the destruction of the earth—the sinfulness of its inhabitants—conforms to the rest of the chapter.

The addition of the phrase "as God commanded him" in 3:8 is typical of Pseudo-Philo and emphasizes God's direction of the action. The interpretation of *hnyḥḥ* from Gen. 8:21 to mean "restful" reflects Pseudo-Philo's interest in rest.[17]

LAB 3:9–10 contains general statements about God's retribution. LAB 3:9 deals with punishment in this life, and 3:10 concerns judgment at the eschaton. Both aspects of retribution attract considerable attention in the *Biblical Antiquities*. In this early chapter, the principle for the rest of the book is clearly delineated: Sin will inevitably result in punishment in this life, the life hereafter, or both.

LAB 3:9 quotes Gen. 8:21, God's promise that the earth will never again be cursed because of humanity, since the tendency of the human heart is *"foolish from his youth,"* and Gen. 8:22, God's assurance that the earth's seasonal cycles will not cease *"in all the days of the earth."*[18] Pseudo-Philo's inclusion of the idea of the evil yetzer here reinforces a pessimistic view of humanity. Pseudo-Philo makes two insertions, one after Gen. 8:21 and the other after Gen. 8:22. To God's promise of Gen. 8:21 Pseudo-Philo adds that although the earth will not be cursed again, all human sins will be punished in this life. Famine, sword, fire, death, earthquakes, and exile to uninhabited places are all punishments for "those inhabiting the earth" when they sin. Then Pseudo-Philo uses the opportunity supplied by Gen. 8:22 ("while the earth remains") to refer to the time when the earth will no longer remain. The seasonal cycles will last "until I remember those who inhabit the earth, until the appointed times are fulfilled." This addition is replete with terminology typical of the *Biblical Antiquities*. The word "remember" is used several times to refer to God's eschatological judgment of humanity.[19] The phrase "those who inhabit the earth" has already been noted several times. "Fulfillment" is a frequent term in Pseudo-Philo; its objects are prophecy, God's predictions and plans, and preordained times. Here the concept of "fulfillment" implies that history is planned out in advance and that there is a preordained end. Pseudo-Philo uses features of the biblical text to stress the themes of punishment in this world of all sin, the inevitability of God's visitation of the earth at the end of time, and the correspondingly limited nature of present existence.

LAB 3:10 elaborates on God's visitation of the earth, going into detail

---

16. Perrot, SC 230, 87–88; *OTP,* 306, n. f.

17. *OTP,* 306, n. i. Such an interpretation is different from the MT, LXX, and Vulgate (SC 230, 88).

18. LAB: *figura cordis hominis;* MT: *yṣr lb h'dm.* We follow Harrington's emendation of *desiit* to *desipit.* See Harrington, *OTP,* 306, n. j; and SC 229, 70.

19. *Rememorari:* 3:9; 16:2 (twice); 19:2; *memor:* 16:3; 26:13.

concerning the Last Judgment. It is an important source for Pseudo-Philo's eschatology.[20] A certain number of years have been appointed for the earth; when they are fulfilled, "the light will cease and the darkness will fade away." This reverses God's creation of light and darkness in Genesis 1.[21] Then comes the resurrection of the dead (the raising of "those who are sleeping from the earth"), seen as hell paying its debt and returning what has been deposited in it (see 33:3). That the dead sleep in the earth is also found in 11:6, 19:12, 35:3, and 51:5. This eschatology resembles that of 4 Ezra 4:41–43, 7:32, *2 Bar.* 11:4, 21:23–24, and *1 En.* 51:1, and so probably reflects common thought in first-century Palestinian Judaism.[22] At the end of time, "the world will cease." For Pseudo-Philo, *seculum* means the present world, with emphasis on its human inhabitants and their history. A new earth and heaven are anticipated, a common notion in Judaism and Christianity.[23]

Although all receive their just recompense, emphasis in 3:10 falls upon the fate of those "justified" *(iustificatus)* by God.[24] They inhabit the new earth and there will be no death. The new earth will be fruitful and its inhabitants will not be defiled.

LAB 3:11–12 concludes the story of Noah and the Flood. Pseudo-Philo strengthens the causal connection between the injunction against eating blood and the prohibition of killing humans, who are in the image of God.[25] God's command to increase and multiply and fill the earth (Gen. 9:7) is enhanced by the added metaphor of fish multiplying in water.[26]

Chapter 4: The New Beginning

LAB 4 is a genealogy combining Genesis 10 and 11. As in Genesis, genealogies introduce humanity's new beginning represented by Noah and the other survivors of the Flood. Pseudo-Philo retains the tripartite division of humanity according to the descendants of Japheth, Ham, and Shem. In Genesis the focus of the genealogies is on the names themselves. Pseudo-Philo shows the usual interest in adding names, most of which are unknown to other extant Jewish traditions, but the focus is changed in that each of the three divisions culminates in general statements. Japheth's section ends with a description of humanity praying to God for rain; Ham's ends with city-building activities; and Shem's includes a prediction of the election of Abraham, ending with a

20. See SC 230, 89, for a long list of parallels to LAB 3:10. The clearest parallels are in *4 Ezra* and *2 Baruch.*

21. Compare 4 Ezra 7:39–42; Matt. 24:29; Rev. 21:23.

22. For a parallel to "mouth of hell," see *2 Bar.* 59:10.

23. See Isa 65:17, 66:32; *1 En.* 45:4–5, 91:16; *Jub.* 1:29; *T. Adam* 3:9; *Apoc. Elij.* 3:98; 2 Pet. 3: 13; Rev. 21:1.

24. The same word is used in 32:17, 49:4, and 51:2. For a discussion of election and predestination in the *Biblical Antiquities,* see Philonenko, "Essénism," 406–7.

25. In Latin, the connection is made clear by the use of *enim.* Presumably, this would have been *kî* in Hebrew, whereas the MT has *'ak* at the beginning of Gen. 9:5.

26. For the image, see also *Tg. Neof.* and *Tg. Yer. 1* (SC 230, 89).

statement about the idolatry of all of humanity except Serug and his descendants, among whom is Abraham.

The genealogy's first division, that of Japheth, ends with 4:5:

> And then they began to work the land and to sow upon it. And when the land was dry, its inhabitants cried out to the LORD; and he heard them and gave rain in abundance. And it happened that, when the rain descended upon the earth, the bow appeared in the cloud. And those inhabiting the earth saw this memorial of the covenant and fell upon their faces and made sacrifices and offered burnt offerings to the LORD.

This passage sets the stage for the rest of the *Biblical Antiquities,* showing how things should be. The familiar notion of the inhabitants of the earth (twice here) recalls that all humans act upon the stage of the earth created by God and under divine control. The correct response to drought is to pray, and God answers with abundant rain. Rain symbolizes God's nourishing the earth and its inhabitants and depends on humanity's obedience to God. Rain makes its first appearance in the *Biblical Antiquities* in a negative way, as part of the destruction of the earth by water (3:5). It is later seen as a reward for obedience and proper worship (4:5; 11:9; 13:7, 10; 23:12). It is under God's control (21:2), and the sin of lying before God will result in its being withheld (44:10).

After God's life-giving rain, the rainbow appears. By combining God's answer to humanity's plea for rain with a reminder of the potentially destructive force of rain, Pseudo-Philo touches on one of his themes—creation serves God's purposes; elements of the natural world can be at once good for good people and bad for evil ones.[27] Rain once destroyed sinners and now nourishes the human race. The rainbow fills earth's inhabitants with gratitude and they sacrifice to God. Sacrifice as thanksgiving is common in Pseudo-Philo.

One should ask why Pseudo-Philo includes the insertion about rain here within the section about the sons of Japheth (4:1–4). Pseudo-Philo is making a general statement about the situation of humanity at its new beginning after the Flood. Humanity in a proper relation with God will receive support from nature, and humanity protected from another flood will show God gratitude. It would be inappropriate to include this description while enumerating the sons of Ham, for they are depicted negatively in 4:6–8 and in Jewish tradition generally. There is no place for it in the enumeration of the sons of Shem, for there the prediction of the election of Abraham is in the foreground. The sons of Japheth furnish a more neutral context for the general statement about humankind and its proper relation to God.

In Gen. 10:11–12, the sons of Ham construct cities. Pseudo-Philo repeats this and, as with Cain (2:3), emphasizes their city-building activities by adding to the list of cities, including Sodom and Gomorrah (4:8). In Gen. 10:8–9, it is said that Nimrod was a mighty hunter and was the first on earth to be a "mighty warrior." In LAB 4:7 this becomes a more negative characterization: Nimrod *"began to be arrogant [superbus] before the Lord."* Negative evaluation of

---

27. Wisd. 16:24 states the principle: "For creation, serving you who made it, exerts itself to punish the unrighteous, and in kindness relaxes on behalf of those who trust in you."

Nimrod is rife in Jewish tradition, so Pseudo-Philo is not unique in attributing to him the beginning of arrogance before God.[28] But the inclusion of the judgment here reinforces Pseudo-Philo's pessimistic view of humanity in general and Ham in particular. Further, it puts the city building of the descendants of Ham into a negative context, and so suggests a nostalgia for simpler days when cities were not the focus of life.

There is a significant addition to Shem's descendants in LAB 4:10–11:

They [the sons of Peleg] took wives for themselves from the daughters of Joktan and became fathers of sons and daughters and filled the earth. Now Reu took as his wife Melcha the daughter of Ruth, and she bore to him Serug. And when the day of his delivery came, she said, "From him there will be born in the fourth generation one who will set his dwelling on high and will be called perfect and blameless; and he will be the father of nations, and his covenant will not be broken, and his seed will be multiplied forever."

The Shemites will give birth to Abraham, whose seed is Israel. In Gen. 10:21–31, Shem's descendants are traced down through Joktan. There Peleg is Joktan's brother (both are Eber's sons [Gen. 10:25]), but Peleg's progeny is not enumerated. Rather, Joktan's descendants are listed. In an apparently independent genealogy in Gen. 11:10–32, the line of Shem is traced down through Peleg, and Joktan is not mentioned. Pseudo-Philo combines the two genealogies by the clever device of having the sons of Peleg marry the daughters of Joktan. Subsequent members of the Shemites are descendants of both Peleg and Joktan. This allows Pseudo-Philo to tap into the traditions of Genesis 11, which are important because they trace the Shemite line down to Abraham and Sarah, and also to use the traditions of Genesis 10, which situate Abraham in the context of the tripartite division of humanity. In chapter 6, Joktan plays a major role in a narrative crafted completely by Pseudo-Philo. In that story the Shemites are set in opposition to the other divisions of humanity, and it is integral to the narrative of chapter 6 that Joktan and Abraham belong to the same tribe. Thus, 4:10–11 prepares for chapter 6.

The descendants of Shem "filled the earth" (4:10). It is the Shemites who fulfill the divine command to humanity to multiply and fill the earth (LAB 3: 11), so their special position among humans is already apparent. Abraham's ancestor Reu takes Melcha as wife and she bears Serug. When Serug is born, Melcha utters a prophecy whose reliability is apparent to the readers, who already know the subsequent history of Abraham and his progeny. The prophecy and its fulfillment show that history evolves as God decided in advance. Melcha's prophecy in 4:11 has five parts, each of which is examined in turn below.

The first part of Melcha's prophecy states that Abraham will set his dwelling "on high" *(super excelsa).* The precise meaning of the phrase "on high" is uncertain. The Septuagint translates "Moreh" of Gen. 12:6 and Deut. 11:30 and "Moriah" of Gen. 22:2 as *hypsēlos.* If the Greek behind the Latin of Pseudo-Philo depends on a similar translation, then the original Hebrew of

---

28. See Ginzberg, *Legends,* Vol. 1, 177–78; SC 230, 96.

the book may have said that Abraham would live at Moreh or Moriah. But since Gen. 12:6 and Deut. 11:30 refer to the oak of Moreh near Shechem, and since Pseudo-Philo is not well disposed toward the Samaritans, it is unlikely that the text signifies that Abraham will live there.[29] The LXX of Gen. 22:2 says Abraham took Isaac *eis tēn gēn tēn hypsēlēn* (a translation of the Hebrew: *'l-'rṣ hmryh)* to sacrifice him. This location is elsewhere identified as the mountain on which Solomon builds the temple. However, it is unlikely that Pseudo-Philo has Jerusalem in mind, for Abraham never goes there.

There are two other possibilities for *super excelsa* that ought to be considered. One concerns Abraham's elevation above the firmament so as to see the entire creation in 18:5.[30] In that case, Abraham's setting his dwelling "on high" in 4:11 would be equivalent to his being lifted "above the firmament" in 18:5. The other possibility is that the phrase in 4:11 refers to Abraham's reward after his death. LAB 19:16 furnishes an imperfect parallel when Moses is told that God will bury him "on a high place" *(super excelsam terram)*.[31] Either of the latter two possibilities is more satisfactory than either of the first two. Whatever the exact reference of the phrase in 4:11, its function is to glorify Abraham and to assert that his exalted status was preordained, thus reinforcing the idea that God controls all.

The second part of Melcha's prediction is that Abraham "will be called perfect and blameless." Apart from Abraham, only Noah is called "blameless" in the *Biblical Antiquities* (3:4), and no one but Abraham is called "perfect."[32] Again, Abraham is glorified.

The third part of the prediction is that Abraham will be the father of nations. This is clearly dependent on Gen. 17:4–6. The notion that Abraham is the father of nations is not pursued in the rest of the *Biblical Antiquities*. In fact, it emphasizes the distance between Israel and the nations. The idea that Abraham is father of nations is used here to stress his importance for the whole world.

The fourth section of Melcha's prediction is that Abraham's covenant will not be broken. This reflects the unconditionality of the covenant found in Gen. 17:7 and elsewhere. Throughout Pseudo-Philo, the eternity of God's covenant with Israel is consistently affirmed.[33] This is frequently put in terms of God's unwillingness to renege on promises made to the fathers. LAB 4:11 prepares for the rest of the work by stating in clear terms that God's covenant with Abraham will never fail. Readers can experience the rest of the story with that assurance in mind.

29. Although Spiro's hypothesis that the *Biblical Antiquities* was written as a polemic against the Samaritans is not tenable, the work does share the anti-Samaritan disposition characteristic of first-century Palestinian Judaism (see Feldman, "Prolegomenona," xxxiv–xxxvi).

30. Suggested in SC 230, 91–92. See the *Apocalypse of Abraham* 15–29 and *Testament of Abraham* 10.

31. Note the close verbal parallel between the LXX of Gen. 22:2 *(tēn gēn tēn hypsēlēn)* and LAB 19:16 *(excelsam terram)*.

32. Here Pseudo-Philo is concerned to justify Abraham's election. In LAB 6, Abraham admits that he is not sinless.

33. See Murphy, "Eternal Covenant."

The final element of Melcha's prediction is that Abraham's "seed will be multiplied forever." God's command to multiply and fill the earth, expressed in God's words to Noah and his sons in 3:11 (cf. 3:8), finds true fulfillment in the sons and daughters of Abraham, as foreshadowed in the statement about the Shemites in 4:10. This multiplication of the seed of Abraham will be "forever," a further assurance for readers of the *Biblical Antiquities* to keep in mind throughout the stories of Israel's failings and misfortunes.

The genealogy of the Shemites culminates in this observation of LAB 4:16: "Then those who inhabited the earth began to observe the stars and started to reckon by them and to make predictions and to have their sons and daughters pass through the fire. But Serug and his sons did not act as these did." This statement recalls those in 2:8–10, which trace the beginning of human wrongdoings to particular figures from Genesis 4. This time, astrology and child sacrifice are practiced by all but Serug and his offspring. Such an assertion contradicts Jewish traditions that see Abraham as the originator of the study of the stars and divination, as well as those that see Abraham's father Terah and other relatives as idolators.[34] Pseudo-Philo is preoccupied with idolatry, but this is the only clear instance of an attack on astrology. It may occur here because Terah and Abraham lived in Ur, known for its practice of astrology.[35] It may also be a refutation of the tradition that Abraham invented astrology. The exculpation of Serug and his offspring (Israel's ancestors) may also oppose other traditions that saw Abraham as engaged in idolatry with his family before he began to worship God alone.

Chapter 5: The Census of Noah's Descendants

Chapter 5 begins as each of humanity's three divisions selects its own leader. The sons of Ham choose Nimrod, the sons of Japheth choose Fenech, and the sons of Shem choose Joktan. Pseudo-Philo is very concerned with the issue of leadership. Much of the plot of the *Biblical Antiquities* depends upon the interaction between leaders on the one hand and the people, the non-Israelites, and God on the other. The story of the tower of Babel in chapters 6–7 contrasts the Shemite leader Joktan with Abraham. LAB 5 sets the scene for chapters 6–7. In that connection, it is significant that God does not choose Joktan in 5:1; the people do.

LAB 5:2 observes, "While Noah was still alive, all gathered together in one place and lived in accord, and the earth was at peace." This falls into a pattern traceable throughout the *Biblical Antiquities,* in which the presence of a good leader brings God's blessings. The claim about Noah resembles the one made for Joshua in Judg. 2:7.

That all humanity is present in one place contradicts the view expressed in 4:17 that the nations were divided *(divise sunt)* after the Flood. It is possible

34. For astrology and divination, see Philo, *Abr.* 15:69–70; *Gen. Rab.* 11:28; etc. For idolatry, see Josh. 24:2, *Jub.* 11:6–7, *Apoc. Abr.* 1–8 (SC 230, 92).
35. Harrington, *OTP,* 309, n. s2.

that *divise sunt* should be taken in the sense that the nations became distinguishable after the Flood but still lived together, but the Latin seems close to the Hebrew of Gen. 10:32 *(nprdw hgwym b'rs)*, which probably means that the nations were scattered to their own territories. It would appear that the beginning of Genesis 11, where humanity migrates together from the east to the plain of Shinar, was originally independent of Genesis 10, where the nations are divided on the earth. Another view is that Gen. 10:32 reflects God's plan to divide up the nations so as to fill the earth, but in Gen. 11:1–9 the nations refuse to conform to that plan.[36] Such could not be the view of Pseudo-Philo, because having all humans together is associated with the peace connected with the presence of Noah, and dispersal of the human race is associated with war in LAB 6:1.

The census of LAB 5 is not present in the biblical text. Using material from Genesis 10, Pseudo-Philo fabricates the census episode as another means of preparing for the narrative to follow. Although the text does not record a negative reaction to the census, numbering the people implies authority over them and should be undertaken only with God's approval, as 2 Samuel 24 indicates. The appointment of leaders and the taking of the census, although not explicitly condemned by the narrator, shows the ambiguity of humanity's relationship with God at this point.

The census has a distinctly military tone.[37] The count is given for the three divisions of humanity, each broken down into its clans. Each group of men passes in review under their captains' staffs.[38] The formula is *transeuntes secundum sceptra ducationis sue,* repeated with only slight variation. The total number for each division is summarized in a military context. For the sons of Japheth, it is: *Omnes virtutificati et omnes in procinctu armorum positi in conspectu ductorum suorum.* For the sons of Ham, it is: *Universi virtutis viri et in apparatu armorum positi in conspectu ducationum suarum.* For the sons of Shem, it is: *Omnes erant proficiscentes in virtute et in precepto belli in conspectu ducationum suarum.* In each case it is specified that the numbers given do not include women and children because the census is only concerned with men fit for battle. The sons of Shem receive a stronger statement than the other two, for its members are distinguished in military prowess. They also predominate numerically: Japheth has 142,200, Ham 244,900, and Shem 347,600.[39]

It is appropriate that humanity be pictured as three groups of armed camps, for much of the rest of the *Biblical Antiquities* concerns military activities. The dominant place assigned to the descendants of Shem fits Pseudo-Philo's intent to trace Israel's history and show how all history leads to and centers on God's chosen people. Chapter 5 shows that Abraham belongs to the strongest and most numerous of the divisions and that Israel descends from this group.

36. See Clifford, 17.

37. The census of Numbers 1 also has a military tone, since Moses is told to count "everyone in Israel able to go to war."

38. Perrot suggest that these are commanders' staffs (SC 230, 93).

39. The totals for each division do not match the sum of their parts (Feldman, "Prolegomenon," lxxxviii), but Pseudo-Philo is problematic with respect to numbers.

Chapters 6–7: Abraham and the Tower of Babel

Chapters 6 and 7 display two distinct methods of dealing with the biblical narrative of the tower of Babel (Genesis 11). Chapter 6 exemplifies the second kind of rewriting discussed in the previous chapter (this volume) by using the first verses of Genesis 11 to provide a setting for a narrative almost entirely independent of Genesis. The biblical material occupies only parts of 6:1–2. The narrative of Abraham and the furnace takes up 6:3–18 and does not directly incorporate any biblical material. Chapter 7 rewrites Gen. 11:4–9 and belongs to the first category of rewriting because it sticks closer to the biblical plot.

Chapters 6–7 incorporate a number of themes important to Pseudo-Philo. The first is the contrast of Abraham and a few others with the rest of the human race on the issue of worship of God. The narrative also contrasts Abraham's trust in God with Joktan's more "practical" leadership, and so concerns the theme of leadership. Third, the chapters deal with reward and punishment. Finally, as a specific example of the third theme, the election of Abraham and his seed is presented as a result of Abraham's faithfulness, seen against the backdrop of humanity's sinfulness. All of these themes have a cosmic dimension, since the narrative concerns the whole of humanity and the setting consists of the entire earth.

Chapter 6: Abraham and Joktan

Chapter 6 opens with words that harmonize Genesis 10 and 11.[40] Genesis 10 implies that God scattered humanity to different parts of the earth. Genesis 11 claims that the entire human race migrated together from the east to the land of Shinar. LAB 6:1 begins, "Then all those who had been separated and were inhabiting the earth gathered and dwelt together." The sentence explains how the nations could be scattered but end up migrating together.

The rest of LAB 6:1–2 interprets Gen. 11:3–4. "Behold it will happen that we will be scattered every man from his brother and in the last days we will be fighting one another. Now *come, let us build for ourselves a tower whose top will reach the heavens, and we will make a name for ourselves* and a glory *upon the earth*" (LAB 6:1). The biblical text has the builders propose the tower before they say why. Pseudo-Philo puts their motivation up front.[41] This corresponds to his interest in humanity's motivations and the assignation of clear guilt to sinners. What Genesis puts last, Pseudo-Philo puts first.

Associating the scattering of humanity with warfare in 6:1 is the opposite side of the coin from connecting living together with peace in 5:2. It is ironic that the building of the tower, the step humans take to avoid dispersal, leads

---

40. SC 230, 94.

41. The phrase "in the last days" is not eschatological here. On the motif of bricks in Jewish tradition, see SC 230, 94–95.

directly to dispersal. This irony is present in the biblical story, but Pseudo-Philo heightens it by the placement of the motivation at the beginning. The irony is sharpened by the introduction of brotherhood, since the builders' plans violate true human unity based on the worship of God. Abraham and eleven others oppose the building, so the builders' plans result in a rupture in the human race. A final irony is that this episode is immediately preceded by the depiction of humanity as a series of armed camps (LAB 5), so that the predisposition for division is inherent in humanity even before the building of the tower.

Pseudo-Philo's addition of "and a glory" to the biblical phrase "make a name for ourselves" interprets the latter. Desire for earthly glory propels the builders, a common motivation in Pseudo-Philo (see LAB 44; 64:1).

The builders decide to write their names *(nomina nostra)* on bricks and burn them in fire to make them suitable for building. Vermes states, "LAB vi. 2–4 is incomprehensible unless 'nomina nostra' be taken to mean 'our gods.' "[42] His point is that the building of the tower is clearly taken as idolatry in LAB 6:4, but unless *nomina nostra* is taken as a reference to false gods there is no mention of idolatry in the narrative. He supports his interpretation by referring to *Gen. Rab.* 38:8, where "name" in Gen. 11:4 is interpreted: *"Shem* means nothing but an idol."[43]

Making a name for oneself is explicitly connected with idolatry in 44:2. But contrary to Vermes's interpretation, it can be observed that the interpretation of "name" as "idol" is unnecessary for the narrative in LAB 6 since the building of a tower whose "top will reach the heavens" is itself an act of rebellion against God in Genesis 11. Pseudo-Philo has merely taken over that interpretation of the builders' action and motivations. In addition, in LAB 44:2 "name" is singular and "gods" is plural, so the parallel between the two terms is imperfect. Further, the parallel to the phrase "make a name for ourselves" in LAB 64:1, as well as Pseudo-Philo's interpretive phrase "and a glory" in 6:1, suggest that in this text *nomen* denotes the builders themselves.

There is irony in the idolaters' burning bricks with their own names on them. Fire is frequently mentioned in Pseudo-Philo in connection with the punishment of sinners.[44] In 6:17, the idolaters try to burn Abraham in the furnace meant for the bricks, but Abraham is saved while 83,500 of the idolaters are burned up instead. Burning the bricks in 6:2 ironically foreshadows the resolution in 6:17.

The rest of chapter 6 follows a four-step pattern, a "plan form," that can also be discerned in chapters 9, 10, and 44.[45] The form is as follows: (1) Humans plan something contrary to God's will; (2) an individual or group opposes the first plan and proposes a counterplan; (3) a dissenter arises who objects to the counterplan on the grounds that it does not conform to God's will; (4) God intervenes, bypassing the counterplan and proving the dissenter right. In LAB

---

42. *Scripture,* 77.
43. Vermes also refers to *b. Sanh.* 190a in the same context.
44. See SC 230, 55–58; LAB 6:11; 20:7; 26:1; 32:11; 37:4; 38:3.

6, part 1 consists of the plan to build the tower and to destroy dissenters. Part 2 is Joktan's counterplan, designed to rescue the twelve resisters. Part 3 is Abraham's refusal to cooperate with Joktan's plan. Part 4 is God's intervention, which bypasses Joktan's scheme and saves Abraham and the other eleven by God's own means. This pattern is especially suitable for Pseudo-Philo since it incorporates direct address. It also expresses central themes. The story of the tower is transformed into one concerning leadership. Joktan, who proposes the plan that counters that of the builders, is leader of the Shemites. Abraham, a Shemite who opposes Joktan's plan, contrasts with Joktan.

The story in chapter 6 also illustrates the opposition between divine and human plans that permeates Pseudo-Philo. Humans left on their own inevitably make wrong choices and anger God. On one level, the decision to build the tower seems reasonable. Human unity and the evasion of war are laudable goals. But the means of effecting those goals contravenes God's plans, so the builders' action is doomed to failure. Even Joktan's plan, which seems good insofar as it is meant to rescue those faithful to God, does not receive God's approval.

In 6:3 the people take bricks to build the tower. Twelve persons refuse to participate. True to his interest in names, Pseudo-Philo lists their names.[46] That there are twelve resisters foreshadows the creation of the twelve tribes of Israel, whose identity rests on their resisting idolatry. The first is Abraham. In the Bible no direct connection is drawn between Abraham and the tower, although Abraham is introduced immediately after the tower narrative in Genesis 11. Pseudo-Philo makes the connection between Abraham and the tower explicit. That move conforms to the tendency of Jewish interpretation to analyze contiguous elements or episodes in terms of each other. But only Pseudo-Philo inserts Abraham so fully into the tower scene.[47]

"The people of the land" take the resisters to their leaders, which sets another narrative pattern, a "trial form," in motion.[48] In LAB 6, the trial form (also found in LAB 16, 38, Daniel 3, and 2 Maccabees 6 and 7) is interwoven with the plan form.[49] The following are narrative elements shared by both Daniel and LAB 6: (*a*) Someone reports to a leader(s) about those who disobey the leader's commands; (*b*) the leader interrogates the offenders; (*c*) the offenders stand firm, refusing to recant and demonstrating full awareness of the punishment awaiting them; (*d*) the leader angrily passes sentence; (*e*) the sentence is carried out; (*f*) some of those who carry out the sentence are killed by the very punishment meant to consume their victims; (*g*) the victims are miraculously saved. This pattern is particularly suited to Pseudo-Philo's predilection toward direct address because of the dialogue between the leader and those on trial.

45. See Murphy, "Divine Plan."
46. The names are based on Genesis 10. See *OTP,* 310, n. c; Feldman, "Prolegomenon," lxxxviii.
47. In *Pirqe R. El.* 24, Abraham tells God to confuse the language of the builders.
48. See Murphy, "Korah's Rebellion."
49. Feldman ("Prolegomenon," lxxxix) notes the influence of Daniel 3 on LAB 6–7.

The accompanying chart represents the interweaving of the plan and trial forms.

Plan Form	**Trial Form**
1. people plan to build a tower and kill resisters	
	a. Abraham and the other resisters brought before leaders
	b. Leaders interrogate resisters
	c. Resisters stand firm
	d. Leaders pass sentence
2. Joktan's plan to free resisters	
3. Abraham's dissent from Joktan's plan	
	e. Leaders try to carry out sentence
4. God intervenes	f. God saves Abraham
	g. God punishes those who wished to kill resisters

LAB 6:4–5 embodies parts *a* through *d* of the trial form. First, the people take the resisters to their leaders (part *a*). The people report, "These are the men who have gone against our plans and would not walk in our ways." When questioned by the leaders (part *b*), Abraham and the others respond (part *c*), "We are not casting in bricks, nor are we joining in your scheme. We know the one LORD, and him we worship. Even if you throw us into the fire with your bricks, we will not join you" (6:4). As in Genesis 11, the building of the tower is construed as rebellion against God. The resisters' courage is confirmed by their acknowledgment of the punishment awaiting them. The leaders proclaim that they will indeed die by fire if they persist in their resistance (6:5; part *d*). The connection of Abraham with fire and a furnace is common in Jewish tradition.[50] Genesis 11:31 says that Abraham and his family went forth from the Chaldean city of *'wr*. Since the Hebrew *'wr* can mean "flame," the association of Abraham with fire is understandable. Nonetheless, the narrative in LAB 6 is unique to Pseudo-Philo.

At this point, the trial form is temporarily interrupted to introduce the counterplan comprising part 2 of the plan form (6:6–14). Joktan, leader of the Shemites and already known from chapter 5, takes steps to rescue the resisters from the clutches of the other leaders. Readers who expect the trial form to play itself out would be surprised at Joktan's intervention, but the narrator portrays Joktan in a positive way. Readers are seduced into placing their trust in Joktan's plan until it is brought up short by Abraham's negative response.

LAB 6:6 says Joktan was the "chief of the leaders," a title that is new but

---

50. For references, see SC 230, 96–97; Feldman, "Prolegomenon," lxxxix. For analysis, see Vermes, *Scripture*, 85–90.

that accords with the prominence of the Shemites, of whom he is leader (LAB 5). Although Joktan is chief of the leaders, he does not simply order them to release the resisters but resorts to subterfuge. He deceives the other leaders by calling the decision of the resisters "evil plans" and by not opposing the death sentence directly. Instead, he proposes that the resisters be given seven days to "repent," at the end of which time the sentence can be carried out if they do not give in. Joktan's deception fools the other leaders, but the readers know his secret intentions since the narrator comments, "He, however, sought how he might save them from the hands of the people, because he was of their tribe and served God" (6:6). The observation that Joktan serves God implies that all Shemites serve God, whereas in other Jewish traditions Abraham differs from his own family in that they are idolaters and he is not.

In LAB 6:7, Joktan orders fifty "men of might" (the traditional biblical term for warriors) to take the twelve prisoners to the mountains and hide there. Joktan makes a considerable material contribution to the project, so his stature is enhanced for the readers. In LAB 6:8, the soldiers do as they are told. Their obedience is emphasized by using the biblical technique of repeating the details of the commands in the description of their performance. Clearly Joktan is a man of authority. The mission's secrecy is reinforced by Joktan's warning at the end of 6:7: "If anyone learns what I have said to you, I will burn you in the fire." The severity of the warning highlights the mission's danger, and suggests the risk Joktan runs. The warning increases the readers' trust of Joktan. But God does not initiate Joktan's plans. This is a purely human endeavor, undertaken without God's authorization. It is a venture dependent on secrecy and deception.

In 6:9, Joktan addresses the prisoners. He begins with the assurance, "Be confident and do not fear, for you will not die. For the God in whom you trust is powerful, and therefore be steadfast in him because he will free you and save you." Joktan then describes the steps he has taken to ensure the safety of the resisters in the mountains and says that their hiding will last "until the hatred of the people of this land *[populi terre]* subsides and until God sends his wrath upon them and destroys them. For I know that the evil plan *[consilium iniquitatis]* that they have agreed *[consiliati sunt]* to carry out will not stand, because their plot is foolish *[vana est cogitatio eorum]*."The Latin terms are characteristic of the *Biblical Antiquities.* Joktan says he will tell the people that the prisoners escaped by night and that he has sent men to look for them.

In 6:9 Joktan continues to appear in a favorable light. His trust in God seems exemplary. Ironically, although it is the resisters whose lives are endangered by their courageous stand, Joktan lectures them on the nature of their God and assures them of God's help. He says that God is "powerful" *(fortis),* a trait that typifies God throughout the *Biblical Antiquities,* where *Fortissimus* is frequent as a divine title.[51] The narrative creates the impression that Joktan is even more conscious of God's sovereignty and faithfulness than the twelve. He explains God's ways to them. Focus has shifted from the resisters' courage

51. 16:5 (twice); 18:10, 11 (three times); 20:4; 31:5; 32:4, 8, 10, 13; 61:5, 6; 62:4.

to Joktan's plans. His conviction that God will act appears to be real trust in God. Joktan's plan does not so much save the resisters as allow God to save them within a specified time frame. His mention of drinking water from the rocks (6:9) shows that God will support the escapees in their hiding.

Joktan's apparent confidence is really presumption. He "knows" that God will save the resisters, not because God said so, but because of his own convictions. Joktan's speech appears to place full trust in God, but the hope for God's action is vague. What is concrete and specific is Joktan's catalog of what *he* has done and will do.

The reaction of all the resisters except Abraham to Joktan's speech is, "Your servants have found favor in your eyes, because we are rescued from the hands of these arrogant men *[superborum horum]*" (6:10).[52] Their response intensifies the focus on Joktan. Joktan has been characterized as one who serves God (6:6), but now the resisters call themselves the servants of Joktan.[53] They attribute their salvation to having obtained Joktan's favor. They make no mention of hope of being delivered by God. Up to this point, readers might be caught up in the drama and sympathize with Joktan. When the flow of the narrative is compared to the direction indicated by the trial form, one can see that attention usually directed toward miraculous rescue by God has shifted to a human leader acting without God's direct authorization. Nonetheless, since that leader is on God's side, the readers might accept the new direction of the story, thinking God would act through such a person.[54]

The narrative's movement stops with the simple sentence "But Abram alone was silent" (6:11). Abraham's silence contrasts with what suddenly seems the wordiness of Joktan. Another contrast is between Abraham's uncooperative attitude and the respectful gratitude of the eleven. The story continues, "And the leader said to him, 'Why do you not answer me, Abram servant of God?'" (6:11). Joktan is called "the leader," thus accenting his position. Abraham's silence turns the readers' attention to him and Joktan's question intensifies the spotlight. Joktan voices the question raised for the readers by Abraham's silence. Joktan calls Abraham "servant of God," a title applied to Abraham, Kenaz (27:7), Moses (20:2), the resisters to Jair's idolatry (38:4), Phinehas (47:1), and the "fathers" (15:5; 22:7).[55] There is irony in the fact that the eleven call themselves servants of Joktan, whereas Joktan calls Abraham God's servant. Joktan is unaware that Abraham deserves the title servant of God precisely because of his ultimate trust in God, a trust that leads Abraham to reject Joktan's plan. The title is bestowed on Abraham at the very point when full attention suddenly turns to him.

52. *Superbus* occurs only in 4:7 (applied to Nimrod) and here in the *Biblical Antiquities*. Nimrod is also connected with the tower of Babel elsewhere in Jewish tradition (Feldman, "Prolegomenon," lxxxix).

53. That the eleven call themselves Joktan's servants here contrasts with God's characterization of the resisters to Jair's idolatry as God's servants in 38:4.

54. The story of Joktan occurs nowhere else in Jewish tradition, so even first-century Jewish readers would not know how the story turns out.

55. See Delling, "Morija," 1–2. In 18:4, Balaam applies it to himself, and in 25:6 Kenaz calls Israel God's servants.

Abraham replies that escaping from the builders will not ensure safety. The resisters could be killed by wild beasts or famine. Then they will have escaped the idolaters but perished for their sins. He says, "And now as he in whom I trust lives, I will not be moved from my place where they have put me. If there be any sin of mine so flagrant that I should be burned up, let the will of God be done" (6:11). Abraham's trust in God is absolute. He points to his trust as the reason he decides not to accept Joktan's aid. Abraham asserts that misfortune is not random but is punishment from God. Suffering and death are always God's judgment, so it is futile to try to escape them. The good are rewarded and sinners are punished both in this life and in the life to come. Abraham is a spokesman for the view already encounted in LAB 3:9 and prominent throughout the *Biblical Antiquities.*

The narrative continues, "And the leader said to him, 'May your blood be upon your own head if you are not willing to go forth with these men. Now if you are willing to do so, you will be freed; but if you wish to stay, stay as you wish'" (6:11). There is a tone of panic in Joktan's voice. His words stress Abraham's responsibility for his own fate: *si nolueris, . . . si autem volueris, . . . si volueris, . . . secundum quod vis.* Joktan insists that the only escape for Abraham lies in leaving with the others to await God's action. To go forth will result in freedom *(liberaberis);* to remain is to reject it. Ironically, by putting such faith in his own plan by which he means to give God room for action, Joktan shows his trust in God to be inadequate. Until the narrator notes Abraham's silence, Joktan's trust seems admirable. In comparison with Abraham's trust, Joktan's appears superficial.

Despite Joktan's impassioned speech, Abraham is adamant: "I will not go forth, but I will stay here" (6:11). Joktan implements his plan. Again, the choice of words draws attention to Joktan's leadership: "And the leader took those eleven men and sent another fifty with them and commanded them . . ." (6:12). The risk of the venture and the possibility that Joktan's own men will not be loyal to him is recalled with his words to the second fifty: "And know that if anyone disregards any of these words that I have spoken to you, he will be burned in the fire" (6:12).

The narrative continues:

> And after seven days had passed, the people gathered together and said to their leader, "Give us back the men who were unwilling to join in our plan, and we will burn them in the fire." And they sent the leaders to bring them out, and they found no one but Abram. And they gathered together with their leaders and said, "The men whom you locked up have fled; they have evaded our scheme" (6:13).

Pseudo-Philo's interest in leadership is evident in the occurrence of the word for "leader" *(dux)* three times in this short passage. Fire, Pseudo-Philo's favorite instrument of punishment, appears again.[56] The language of the passage recalls the aim to highlight the evil plans of humans.

Joktan lies to the other leaders, saying that the prisoners escaped by night

56. SC 230, 53–55.

and that he sent a hundred men to look for them, with orders to burn them when caught (6:14). Abraham is brought out to be burned. When interrogated about the eleven, he says, "I was sleeping during the night; when I awoke, I did not find them" (6:15). His terse answer says nothing false, but his questioners are misled, taking it to mean that he slept during the escape.

Now the narrative resumes the trial form. Part *e* occurs in LAB 6:16, where Abraham is cast into the furnace. Pseudo-Philo focuses on Joktan: "And then the leader Joktan with great emotion took Abram and threw him along with the bricks into the fiery furnace" (6:16). The narrator draws attention to the intense emotional conflict inside Joktan. On the one hand, Joktan is convinced that his "practical" approach to dealing with the other leaders and the people is the only one that can succeed. On the other hand, Joktan does not want to carry his charade so far as to execute Abraham. Joktan represents the classic person in the middle, caught between those whose evil plans he must pretend to endorse and those whose loyalty to God he supports but cannot emulate publicly. He must choose between throwing Abraham into the fire or dropping his mask. He chooses the former.

LAB 6:17 contains parts *f* and *g* of the trial pattern: "But God caused a great earthquake, and the fire gushing out of the furnace leaped forth in flames and sparks of flame. And it burned all those standing around in sight of the furnace. And all those who were burned in that day were 83,500. But there was not the least injury to Abram from the burning of the fire." God finally takes action, but sooner and in a different manner than Joktan expected. God's action could not have taken place as it does if Abraham had acceded to Joktan's scheme. God vindicates Abraham and reveals Joktan's activity as irrelevant to the outcome of events.

In 6:18, Abraham leaves the furnace, which promptly collapses. He then goes to the eleven, tells them what has happened, and returns with them, "rejoicing in the name of the LORD." Abraham's behavior leads to his rescue by God and results in the liberation of the eleven as well. Joktan fades from the picture and is not heard from again. Abraham's trip to the mountains to lead the eleven out of hiding shows that his choice had implications for the others who were loyal to God but stopped short of embracing martyrdom.

Chapter 7: The Tower Halted and Abraham Chosen

LAB 7:1 states that Abraham's rescue did not stop the plans of the people to build a tower. Quoting words from the beginning of Genesis 11, the narrator has the people make a second start at carrying out their "malicious plottings." The evil plans of the builders become still more evil because they attempt to follow them through despite God's action at the furnace. The people urge their leaders to go forward with the project (7:1). In 7:2, God notes the building with disapproval in much the same terms as in Gen. 11:5–6. Pseudo-Philo adds God's observation: "Neither the earth will put up with it nor will the heavens bear to behold it." In several places in the *Biblical Antiquities,* heaven and earth are witnesses to human action, an idea that has its origin in Moses' words in Deut. 4:26, 30:19, and 31:28.[57] This contrasts with the words of the tower planners in 6:1: "Now *come, let us build for ourselves a tower whose top will reach the heavens, and we will make a name for ourselves* and a glory *upon the earth.*" Rather than receiving glory on earth, the sinners will have the earth witness against them.

LAB 7:3–4 contrasts God's judgments concerning humanity and Abraham. God scatters humanity, confuses its languages, and says that humans will live in caves and straw huts like animals. God says, "And thus they will remain before me all the time so that they will never make such plots again, and I will consider them like a drop of water and liken them to spittle" (7:3).[58] This sentence displays the pessimistic view of humanity found in Pseudo-Philo and shows that view to be reliable by placing it in God's mouth. God's words in Genesis do not make such sweeping judgments about the human race, but merely indicate God's steps to stop the tower.

In LAB 7:4, God chooses Abraham and his seed:

> And before all these I will choose my servant Abram, and I will bring him out from their land and will bring him into the land upon which my eye has looked from of old, when all those inhabiting the earth sinned in my sight and I brought the water of the flood and I did not destroy it but preserved that land. For neither did the springs of my wrath burst forth in it, nor did my water of destruction descend on it. For there I will have my servant Abram dwell and will establish my covenant with him and will bless his seed and be lord for him as God forever (7:4).

God contrasts Abraham and the rest of humanity. It is "before all these [humans]" about whom God has just spoken that Abraham is chosen. Further, God separates Abraham geographically from the rest of the human race by bringing him to a new land, a land that figured in God's plans "from of old" *(ab initio)* since God preserved it from the Flood.[59] There is a correspondence between land and people here that is essentially biblical and that permeates Pseudo-Philo. God recalls the human sinfulness that caused the Flood. Conversely, Abraham's righteousness makes it appropriate for him and his seed to inhabit a land untouched by the Flood. Indeed, God always *(ab initio)* planned to preserve the chosen land. God plans to make a covenant with Abraham that will extend to his seed and last forever, a clear statement of the eternal nature of the covenant.

Pseudo-Philo's additions to the end of the tower story serve primarily to illustrate the effectiveness of God's action in stopping the builders (7:5). Noteworthy is the phrase that once again draws attention to human plans: "And so their plan was frustrated" (7:5). God changes the appearances of humans

---

57. See LAB 19:4; 24:1; 32:9, 13; 62:10.

58. Harrington emends the Latin from *scuto*, "shield," to *sputo*, "spittle," because of the LXX of Isa. 40:15 and LAB 12:4; see *OTP*, 313, n. a. For a similar use of the same Isaian passage, see 4 Ezra 6:56 and *2 Bar.* 82:5.

59. For other examples of the tradition that the chosen land escaped the Flood, see SC 230, 99.

so that they do not even recognize their own brothers. This is an instance of
the theme of recognition (or lack of it). It is ironic because it attributes
humans' inability to know how things are, even to the extent of knowing their
own siblings, to their sinfulness and even to their desire to band together and
make a name for themselves (6:1).

Chapter 8: Getting to Egypt

Chapter 8 is largely transitional. Pseudo-Philo uses enough of Genesis 12–50
to form a bridge between the story of Abraham and the tower of Babel on
the one hand and the birth of Moses and the Exodus on the other. LAB 8 is
built almost entirely of biblical verses and so falls into the first category of
rewriting. LAB 8:1–3 assembles a smattering of information from Genesis 12,
13, 16, 17, 21, and 25 to convey some facts of interest to Pseudo-Philo. The
three elements stressed are God's overcoming the sterility of Sarah, Abraham's separateness from the nations, and the covenant between God and
Abraham. Pseudo-Philo retains mention of Sarah's sterility since it reinforces
his emphasis on God's role in human affairs. The narrative recalls that because
of Sarah's sterility Abraham took her maid Hagar for a concubine and that
Hagar's son Ishmael had twelve sons. Pseudo-Philo makes clear that the covenant does not apply to Abraham's offspring though that union (8:3). LAB
8:2 quotes Gen. 13:12–13 to contrast Lot and Sodom's evil inhabitants with
Abraham dwelling in Canaan. Lot dwells apart from Abraham in an evil land,
and Abraham is geographically separated from Lot and the evil that surrounds
him because he dwells in the land whose special status was already mentioned
in 7:4.

LAB 8:3 combines elements of Genesis 13 and 17 to compose a speech by
God establishing a covenant with Abraham. This fulfills 7:4, where God said
that he would establish such a covenant. *"And* God *appeared to Abram, saying, 'To your seed I will give this land, and your name will be called Abraham,
and Sarai, your wife, will be called Sarah. And I will give* to you from her *an
everlasting* seed, *and I will establish my covenant with you.'* And Abraham
knew Sarah, his wife, *and she conceived and bore* Isaac" (8:3). In the MT of
Gen. 17:7–8, "everlasting" applies to the covenant and to possession of the
land. In LAB 8:3, it modifies Israel itself, Abraham's seed. Pseudo-Philo uses
Genesis 17, where the covenant is unconditional, as opposed to other passages
in the Hebrew Bible where it is contingent on Israel's obedience. The last
sentence of the passage reemphasizes God's overcoming of Sarah's sterility.

The rest of chapter 8 uses little of Genesis 25–50. Isaac's marriage to the
daughter of Bethuel is mentioned, as is the fact that she bore Jacob and Esau.
It remarkable that Rebekah's name is never mentioned. In fact, the name
Rebekah never appears anywhere in the *Biblical Antiquities*. Rebekah is
prominent in Genesis because she is Isaac's wife, and because she single-hand-
edly changed the course of salvation history through deception. Pseudo-Philo
omits this incident and even goes so far as not to mention Rebekah. It is God's

role in events that is important, and it may be that Pseudo-Philo sees the story of Rebekah as problematic in terms of human and divine causality.

The sons and daughters of Esau and Jacob are enumerated in 8:5–6. LAB 8:7 summarizes in a short space the story of the rape of Dinah. Pseudo-Philo may include this because of its interest in military matters, particularly ones that involve Israel fighting its enemies in Palestine. LAB 8:8 contains the tradition that Dinah married Job.[60]

LAB 8:9–10 briefly summarizes the story of Joseph with little commentary. Significant for Pseudo-Philo's purposes is the statement *"And Joseph recognized his brothers, but was not known by them.* And he did not deal vengefully with them" (8:10). This moral judgment by the narrator fits the high evaluation of Joseph found in Jewish tradition generally. Joseph's brothers' hatred contrasts with Joseph's lack of desire for vengeance. Joseph epitomizes the way a good Israelite should relate to his or her fellows. Pseudo-Philo finds recognition and nonrecognition in the biblical text, but it is also one of his own devices. It heightens the irony of the narrative by showing the inability of most humans to know the meaning behind events. Here the righteous person, Joseph, knows what is happening, but his sinful brothers do not. The brothers' sinfulness is shown by the words, *"And these hated* their brother Joseph, whom *they delivered into Egypt to Potiphar"* (8:9). Later Joseph, model of proper behavior, is contrasted with Samson (43:5).

LAB 8:11–14 rounds out the chapter with a list of the Israelites who went down to Egypt, another example of Pseudo-Philo's interest in names. The chapter ends with "And they went down to Egypt and dwelt there 210 years" (8:14).[61]

---

60. See SC 230, 100 for other references to the same tradition.
61. See the discussion of this figure in SC 230, 100; Heinemann, "210 Years."

4

Moses: *Biblical Antiquities* 9–19

Moses is the most dominant figure in the *Biblical Antiquities,* as is evident in the sheer number of chapters devoted to him. The narratives about Moses in chapters 9–19 also concern the Exodus, the giving of the Law, and the first approaches to the land of Israel. These chapters lay the foundation for Israel itself, and so describe the presuppositions of the rest of the book. In Moses' story, the tension between God's mercy and God's justice is particularly evident, and as the ideal mediator between God and humanity, Moses addresses it specifically.

LAB 9:1–8: Amram, Father of Moses

Most of LAB 9 is not from the Bible. The chapter is important as an introduction to the birth and career of Moses, as well as for its incorporation of several themes crucial to Pseudo-Philo's worldview. It exhibits the four-part "plan form" discerned in LAB 6: plan, counterplan, dissent, and divine intervention. Pharaoh proposes a plan that is accepted and added to by the Egyptians (9:1); the Israelite elders propose a counterplan (9:2); Amram objects to the counterplan (9:3–6); God intervenes, rewarding Amram and saving Israel from the Egyptians' plan through Amram's son Moses (9:7–10).[1] The message is that human plans tend to be ineffective or even evil, and God's plans always prevail.

Pseudo-Philo condenses the story of Pharaoh's oppression of Israel, going directly to the killing of all male Hebrew babies (Exod. 1:22). The element of human planning is highlighted when Pharaoh says, *"Let us make a plan against them"* (9:1). As in the biblical text, LAB 9:1 says that female babies are to be spared. Then there is a significant addition to the story: "And the Egyptians answered their king, saying, 'Let us kill their males, and we will keep their females so that we may give them to our slaves as wives. And whoever is born from them will be a slave and will serve us.' And this *[hoc]* is what seemed wicked before the LORD" (LAB 9:1). The referent of *hoc* is not clear in the last sentence. It may indicate all of the Egyptians' plans or it may denote the

---

1. See Murphy, "Divine Plan," 10–12.

enslavement of the Hebrew women and their future children. God may find this enslavement particularly heinous because one can enslave the Israelites only when they sin, which is not the case here.

In part 2 of the plan form, the Israelite elders lament and devise a counterplan: "And now we are lost, and let us set up rules *[terminos]* for ourselves that a man should not approach his wife lest the fruit of their wombs be defiled and our offspring serve idols. For it is better to die without sons until we know what God may do" (9:2). The elders' plan resembles Joktan's in that it is a temporary measure intended to leave room for God's action. Like Joktan's plan, that of the elders is their own and is not initiated by God. There is irony in the use of the word *terminos* here, since elsewhere in Pseudo-Philo it refers to God's commands.[2] As in Joktan's case, the elder's motivation is good; they wish to avoid idolatry's defilement. Given Pseudo-Philo's polemic against idolatry, readers might expect God to heed the elders' words.

Amram objects to the elders' plan in a long speech (9:3–6). with the following structure:

a. General claim about Israel's indestructibility (9:3);
b. Assertion that God's covenant as expressed in Gen. 15:13–14 will be fulfilled (9:3);
c. Interpretation of Gen. 15:13, showing that the Egyptian slavery is part of the 400 years God mentions (9:3);
d. Statement of Amram's plans (9:4);
e. Support of Amram's plans through reference to the covenant (9:4);
f. Restatement of Amram's plans (9:5);
g. Exhortation to the elders (9:5);
h. Support of Amram's plans through the observation that Hebrew pregnancies will not be noticed for three months, an observation leading to the example of Tamar (9:5);
i. Tamar's story as a precedent for Amram's present plans (9:5);
j. Restatement of the exhortation to the elders to adopt Amram's plan (9:6); and
k. Suggestion that God's approval of Amram's actions will issue in divine liberation (9:6).

The structure of Amram's speech reveals it to be firmly based on the covenant between God and Abraham. Statements of Amram's plans or exhortations to follow his plans (parts *d, f, g, j*) are supported by reference to God's commitments to Israel (parts *a–c, e*), by reference to Tamar, who wished to stay in the covenant (parts *h, i*), and by hope of God's action on the basis of the covenant (part *k*). The following paragraphs analyze Amram's speech section by section.

(*a*) Amram says, "It will sooner happen that this age will be ended forever or the world will sink into the immeasurable deep or the heart of the abyss

---

2. LAB 15:6 and 51:3, perhaps reflecting the Hebrew *hwqym*, which can be translated "commands" or "limits." See also LAB 3:2. See *OTP*, 323, n. d.

will touch the stars than that the race of the sons of Israel will be ended"
(9:3).[3] The association of Israel's existence with the existence of the entire
universe is common in Jewish literature, but such a clear claim for Israel's
indestructibility is rare.

(*b*) Amram continues, "And there will be fulfilled the covenant that God
established with Abraham when he said, 'Indeed your sons will dwell *in a land
not their own and will be brought into bondage and afflicted 400 years*' " (9:3).
The theme of the fulfillment of God's words is prominent in the *Biblical Antiquities*. But here, early in the book, there is a special case of fulfillment to which
all other cases are subordinate. It is special because it concerns the foundation
of Israel. The central divine promise is the promise to Israel's fathers that
Israel will never pass away, that it will always enjoy a special relationship with
God, and that it will possess the land of Israel except during times of chas-
tisement. The notion that God will always be faithful to that promise is basic
to Pseudo-Philo's worldview.[4]

Amram quotes Gen. 15:13, where God predicts the bondage in Egypt. This
quotation authoritatively explains the suffering Israel undergoes under Pharaoh. This is especially important since the Egyptian bondage was atypical
because it was not a punishment from God. The elders view the Egyptian
oppression as undeserved, and their plan is a temporary measure until God
acts to correct the injustice. Amram's quotation of Gen. 15:13 uses God's
words to argue against the elders' plan. If Israel's suffering was predicted by
God and is part of the divine plan, then the elders should not take steps to
confront the crisis.

(*c*) Amram interprets the 400 years of Gen. 15:13 by pointing out that 350
years have passed since God spoke to Abraham, 130 of which have been
passed in Egypt.[5] This implies that Israel's deliverance is only fifty years away.
Alternatively, 8:14 says that Israel's sojourn in Egypt lasted 210 years. If 130
of those years are already passed, as Amram says in 9:3, then eighty years are
left before liberation. It is true that Pseudo-Philo is notoriously unreliable with
numbers. In any case, Amram's point is that salvation is near.

(*d*) Amram rejects the elders' plans: "Now therefore *[Nunc ergo]* I will not
abide by what you decree, but I will go in and take my wife and produce sons
so that we may be made many on the earth" (9:4). The *nunc ergo* bases part
d on Amram's argument prior to this point, so his decision is based on Israel's
indestructibility and the reliability of God's covenant (parts *a–c*). Amram

---

3. Note the similarity to Jesus' words about the Torah in Matt. 5:18. *In victoria* is translated
"forever" because it probably translates the Greek *eis nikos* which mistranslates the Hebrew
lnṣḥ, a mistranslation that would not be possible were the original text in Aramaic instead of
Hebrew (*OTP*, 315, n. c; SC 230, 103).

4. For such statements before chapter 9, see 4:11 and 7:4.

5. Jewish tradition resolved the contradiction between the 430 years of Exod. 12:40 and the
400 years of Gen. 15:13 by saying that 400 years counts from Isaac's birth, whereas 430 years
begins the count from thirty years prior to Isaac's birth. For references for this solution, see SC
230, 103. See also Feldman, "Prolegomenon," xci. Pseudo-Philo does not explicitly state this
solution, but he agrees with the figure of 430.

acknowledges that the elders have authority, for they can "decree." But Amram promises disobedience if they do so. The purpose of Amram's decision is "that we may be made many on the earth." This recalls God's intentions for the human race and for Israel in particular (3:8, 11; 4:10, 11).

The opposition between Amram and the elders is unique to Pseudo-Philo. In rabbinic texts, Amram and the elders agree to stop having intercourse with their wives. There Amram's daughter persuades him to take back his wife.[6] Josephus lacks these opposing plans.

(*e*) Amram continues, "For God will not abide in his anger, nor will he forget his people forever, nor will he cast forth the race of Israel in vain upon the earth; nor did he establish a covenant with our fathers in vain; and even when we did not yet exist, God spoke about these matters" (9:4). This sentence reasserts the indestructibility of Israel and of the covenant, as do parts *a* and *b*, but here the connection between the covenant and God's present protection of Israel is explicit. The first four of the five clauses in part *e* are mutually implicative. God's abiding in anger amounts to forgetting Israel, which would be equivalent to casting forth Israel, which would be the same as having the covenant in vain. Pseudo-Philo frequently uses the phrase "in vain" of human plans made without God's approval that are bound to fail. The final clause emphasizes the firm basis of the covenant by asserting that God's plan to establish a covenant with Israel was formed before Israel came to be.

(*f*) Part *f* begins as did *d*, with the words *nunc ergo* (9:5). Just as Amram's plans are based on his statements in *a–c*, so here his restatement of those plans is connected to his assertions about the covenant in *e*. He reasserts his intention to have intercourse with his wife and reminds his hearers that he is aware this means disobedience to the king.[7]

(*g*) Amram now says, "If it is right in your eyes, let us all act in this way" (9:5). His argument has made disagreement with him tantamount to rejection of the covenant. The narrator never informs the readers of the elders' decision, so attention remains firmly fixed on Amram.

(*h*) Amram says that adoption of his plan still leaves the Israelites three months before their action becomes evident to the Egyptians, implying that God may act within that time (9:5).[8] "Three months" comes from Exod. 2:2. There it refers to Moses' mother hiding him for three months after his birth. The figure of three months allows Amram to connect his plan to the example of Tamar, who deceived Judah into sleeping with her and hid the pregnancy for three months (Gen. 38:24–25), and simultaneously it transfers the hiding done by Moses' mother from the three months after birth to the first three

6. *B. Sota* 12a, *Exod. Rab.* 1:13; *Pesiq. R.* 43, *Num. Rab.* 13:20; *Eccl. Rab.* 9:17, etc. See Feldman, "Prolegomenon," xci.

7. Although this seems to imply that Amram is already married, 9:9 seems to mean that he gets married later. Other works have him already married (SC 230, 103). Pseudo-Philo reflects the confusion of Exod. 2:1–2, where Moses seems to be born shortly after Amram's marriage, even though Aaron and Miriam are already born.

8. On the three months, see Feldman, "Prolegomenon," xcii.

months of pregnancy.[9] The comparison of Tamar's situation to Israel's is related to a technique frequent in the book—the narrator or a character says that something happening in the narrative's present is "like" something that happened earlier in Israel's history.[10] Frequently, the analogous situation from the past is not even narrated in the *Biblical Antiquities,* showing the narrator's assumption that the readers know a larger story. The technique implies that as God has acted in the past, so God acts in the present and will act in the future.

The connection of Tamar with Israel's present situation is made even closer by Amram's calling Tamar "our mother." This is part of Pseudo-Philo's remarkable enhancement of Tamar's status, which in turn is an example of his high estimation of women. Van der Horst notes that the phrase "our mother" is analogous to the phrase "our father Abraham." He also points to the lack of interest in Judah in this passage, and says, "It is not that Judah is 'our father', but that Tamar is 'our mother', and this can only be meant as the highest praise of this woman, elevating her to matriarchal status."[11]

(*i*) Amram's treatment of Tamar involves her intention:

> For her intent *[consilium]* was not fornication, but being unwilling to separate from the sons of Israel she reflected *[recogitans]* and said, "It is better for me to die for having intercourse with my father-in-law than to have intercourse with gentiles." And she hid the fruit of her womb until the third month. For then she was recognized. And on her way to be put to death, she made a declaration saying, *"He who owns this staff and this signet ring and the sheep-skin, from him I have conceived."* And her intent saved her from all danger *[salvavit eam consilium]* (9:5).

Tamar's plan saves her. The language of human thought used in this passage (*consilium* twice and *recogitans*) is atypical for Pseudo-Philo since human planning is shown in a positive light.[12] The biblical story ends with Tamar's vindication and rescue from death, so God's approval of her plans is manifest. She is a worthy model for the Israelites as they plan to respond to the crisis initiated by Pharaoh.

Tamar's intention is relevant to the situation depicted in LAB 9. Were she to leave Israel, she would have to go to the Gentiles.[13] Tamar wishes to avoid intercourse with Gentiles, so she settles on a desperate plan that apparently transgresses Torah. Amram asserts that because her intention was in accord with the spirit of Torah, it resulted in her salvation. The biblical account says nothing of Tamar's desire to avoid contact with Gentiles. The issue of intercourse with Gentiles is read into Genesis 38 and occurs nowhere else in Jewish

9. Bauckham, "Liber," 55.

10. See Eissfeldt, "Kompositionstechnik;" and "Plot" in chapter 2, this volume.

11. "Portraits," 31–32.

12. See Chapter 11, this volume, under "Plans and Plots, Human and Divine."

13. Van der Horst ("Portraits," 32) notes that whether or not Tamar was an Israelite was much debated in Jewish sources. He says that Pseudo-Philo clearly sees her as an Israelite because Amram refers to her as "our mother."

interpretation of the Tamar story. Amram transforms the Tamar incident into a suitable precedent for his own problem. The narrative is remarkable because Amram reads the thoughts and intentions of a figure from the past. By this technique Amram is shown to be reliable in his comments. The negative attitude of the elders, Tamar, and Amram toward marriage with Gentiles characterizes the *Biblical Antiquities* as a whole.[14]

(*j*) For the third time in the speech, Amram exhorts the elders to abandon their plan (9:6). Earlier he based his exhortation on theoretical arguments involving the covenant. He has now cited the example of Tamar and has proven that God endorses such action.

(*k*) Amram concludes, "Who knows if God will be provoked on account of this so as to free us from our humiliation?" His humble statement of hope for God's liberating action contrasts with the elders' presumption, a presumption that recalls Joktan in chapter 6. Amram does not assume that God will act, any more than Abraham assumed that God would act (LAB 6). Like Abraham, Amram leaves things in God's hands and hopes in God's promises. The narrator discloses God's reaction to Amram's plan: "And the strategy that Amram thought out *[cogitavit]* was pleasing before God" (9:7). Amram is right, the elders are wrong. Like Tamar, Amram "thinks" correctly. He is one of the few humans who reasons on the basis of his knowledge of the covenant and God's ways and gets it right.

Because Amram's plan pleases God, God proclaims that Amram's son will free Israel. God makes this important pronouncement directly. God addresses no one in particular, so this passage allows the reader to witness God's own thoughts.

> Because Amram's plan is pleasing to me, and he has not put aside the covenant established between me and his fathers, so behold now he who will be born from him will serve me forever *[in eternum]*, and I will do marvellous things in the house of Jacob through him and I will work through him signs and wonders for my people that I have not done for anyone else; and I will act gloriously among them and proclaim to them my ways. And I, God, will kindle for him my lamp that will abide in him, and I will show him my covenant that no one else has seen. And I will reveal to him my Law and statutes and judgments, and I will burn an eternal light for him, because I thought of him in the days of old, saying, *"My spirit will not be a mediator among these men forever, because they are flesh and their days will be 120 years"* (9:7–8).

God says that Amram's plan is pleasing because it is faithful to the covenant with Israel's fathers. To be true to the covenant is to be true to one's ancestors and heritage. Because Amram is faithful to the covenant, God works through him to bring forth the most important figure in Israelite history, Moses. Moses is the servant of God par excellence (see 20:2). His service to God is eternal, something said of no other character in the *Biblical Antiquities*. Reference to

---

14. See 18:13–14; 21:1; 30:1; 44:7; 45:3. For the attitudes of other works toward mixed marriages, see SC 230, 104.

God's signs and wonders is common in the *Biblical Antiquities,* but God insists that Moses was unique. Perrot notes that *in eternum* only occurs one other time; in 7:4 it applies to the covenant with Abraham.

The rest of God's words refer to Moses' role in bringing the Torah into the world.[15] Through Moses, God reveals the divine ways, to make it possible to please God. The statement that God will make known the divine ways occurs at the end of 9:7 and leads to a series of clauses associating Moses and the Law. These statements are introduced solemnly with God's self-identification: "I, God *[Ego Deus]"* (9:8). God will kindle his lamp for Moses. "Lamp" is an image commonly used for the Torah.[16] It stresses the instructional and revelatory aspects of Torah. To know Torah is to know God's ways and so to know the basis and meaning of everything. God shows Moses his covenant that "no one else has seen." Pseudo-Philo does not distinguish between the covenants with the patriarchs and the Mosaic covenant. Here God implies that the covenant with the fathers had aspects revealed only to Moses, so that through Moses Israel has access to the entire covenant and all of its provisions. God stresses statutes (*iusticias*) and judgments of Torah. In 11:15 and 12:2, 10 *iusticias* means the Decalogue.[17] The "eternal light" that God burns for Moses probably also refers to the Torah.

God claims to have thought of Moses when setting the limit of human life at 120 years (Gen. 6:3). Here God quotes Genesis as saying that the divine spirit would not be a mediator among men forever, whereas LAB 3:2 quotes Gen. 6:3 as saying that God's spirit will not judge people forever.[18] The point of the text is that Moses is God's ultimate mediator and judge. Before the Flood, God's spirit was available to all humanity, but now one can approach God only through Moses and the Torah. Pseudo-Philo may have associated Gen. 6:3 with Moses because in Deut. 34:7 Moses is said to have been 120 years old when he died.[19] For Pseudo-Philo, Gen. 6:3 assumed added meaning when applied to Moses, so the version of Gen. 6:3 that appears in LAB 9:8 reflects that additional significance.

15. Harrington's note (*OTP,* 316, n. j) on his translation of *superexcellentiam* as "Law" must be quoted: "Lit. 'superexcellence.' This expression (or one like it) must mean 'law' or 'statute' as in 11:1; 12:2; 19:4; 30:2; and 44:6, but its origin is not now recognizable." See the discussion of this term in SC 230, 104–5.

16. See LAB 11:1; 15:6; 19:4. See also the following (SC 230, 104): Prov. 6:23; *2 Bar.* 17:4; 18:1–2; *T. Levi* 14:4; 19:1; *M. 'Avot* 6:7; *Sipre* on Deut. 32:2; *Deut. Rab.* 4:4; 25:7; *b. Meg.* 16b. See also SC 230, 30; Vermes, "The Torah Is a Light."

17. SC 230, 105.

18. The LXX, Philo (*Gig.* 3:19), and *Jub.* 5:8 have "my spirit will not remain," whereas Symmachus has "my spirit will not judge," as in LAB 3:2 (SC 230, 86). Perrot says that the Hebrew also has "will not judge," but the MT's meaning is not clear.

19. See Feldman, "Prolegomenon," xcii, for the same connection in rabbinic literature and Philo.

LAB 9:9–16: The Birth of Moses

The full text of Harrington's note about the birth of Moses is as follows.[20]

> There are striking parallels between Moses' birth as narrated here and that of Jesus in Mt 1f.: communication by dreams, the spirit of God, interest in name and mission, concealment, and the slaughter of the male children. Literary dependence is doubtful; the points in common show a lively interest in the birth of heroes in the NT period. The "new Moses" motif in Mt 2 is well known. See also Ps-Philo 42.

Perrot draws attention to the similarity of the births of Moses, Samson, and Samuel in the *Biblical Antiquities.* Common elements are the situation of the nation's distress, the impossibility of having children, and the announcement of liberation through an angel.[21] These elements stress the theme that God liberates the people.

After God's words of 9:7–8, the narrator says that Amram takes his wife and that others follow his example. Amram's speech must have had some success, although he does not seem to have convinced the people as a whole, and no mention is made of the elders. Then the narrator says that Amram had children, Aaron and Miriam.

In 9:10 the spirit of God comes upon Miriam and God communicates with her in a dream.[22] Revelation through dreams draws attention to God's direction of events.[23] The readers hear the dream from Miriam's own lips through the device of her telling it to her parents the next morning: "I have seen this night, and behold a man in a linen garment stood and said to me, 'Go and say to your parents, "Behold he who will be born from you will be cast forth into the water; likewise through him the water will be dried up. And I will work signs through him and save my people, and he will exercise leadership always" ' " (9:10). The man in the linen garment is an angel, as comparison with Ezek. 9:11, Mark 16:5, and Luke 24:4 shows.[24] The analogy between Moses being cast into the water and his drying up the Red Sea is unique to Pseudo-Philo. It underlines the structure and interconnectedness of history, which in turn illustrates God's control of events. The word "signs" is frequent in the *Biblical Antiquities,* for it is often through signs that God communicates with humans. God will work through Moses to save his people. "Saving" and "liberating" are two of God's most characteristic activities in Pseudo-Philo. As elsewhere in the *Biblical Antiquities,* salvation means freeing the people from the domination of non-Israelites. Leadership is a constant concern of

---

20. *OTP,* 316, n. k. See Harrington, "Birth Narratives," "Pseudo-Philo, *Liber Antiquitatum Biblicarum*"; and Le Déaut, "Miryam."

21. See SC 230, 102; Perrot, "Récits."

22. For rabbinic parallels, see Feldman, "Prolegomenon," xcii. Winter ("Jewish Folklore," 38–39) looks at parallels with the Gospels' infancy narratives.

23. 8:10 9:15; 18:2; 23:6; 28:4;

24. Jewish tradition identifies the angel who appeared to Miriam as Gabriel. See Ginzberg, *Legends,* Vol. 5, 396, n. 40; SC 230, 59–63.

Pseudo-Philo, and here it is stated that Moses will "exercise leadership always." Since the Torah comes through Moses, his influence lasts forever in Israel. When Miriam relates her dream to her parents, they do not believe her.

In LAB 9:11, the narrator says that Pharaoh's plan against the Israelites succeeds, for they are "humiliated *[humiliabantur]* and worn down in making bricks." This is the first mention of bricks in the story. The narrator assumes that readers know a fuller story than the one in the *Biblical Antiquities.* The humiliation of the Israelites is the setting into which Moses is born. The use of *humiliare* creates a verbal link with Amram's hope in 9:6: "Who knows if God will be provoked on account of this so as to free us from our humiliation *[humiliatione]."* In 9:12, Amram's wife Jochebed conceives and conceals her pregnancy for three months, as Amram had said in 9:5. The narrative then suddenly shifts to the placing of Moses in the river, so that some commentators believe material describing the birth of Moses has been lost.[25] LAB 9:12 infers from Exod. 1:22 that Israelite children were killed by being thrown into the water.[26] There follows a summary of the story of Moses being placed in a container in the river. In 9:13 is the Jewish tradition that Moses was born "in the covenant of God and the covenant of the flesh," which means that he was born circumcised.[27]

LAB 9:14 brings the narrative back to the elders, last mentioned in 9:2. Although the readers know that God approves of Amram's plan and that Israel will be saved through Moses, the elders do not know. All they see is that Israel's woes continue: "All the elders gathered and quarreled with Amram, saying, 'Are not these our words that we spoke, "It is better for us to die without having sons than that the fruit of our womb be cast into the waters"?' " And Amram did not listen to those who were saying these words" (9:14). The elders' doubt contrasts with Amram's faith.

As in Exodus 2, Pharaoh's daughter discovers Moses in the basket in the Nile (9:15). Pseudo-Philo adds that she came to the river to bathe because she had been instructed in a dream, a detail that stresses God's direction of the action. Her recognition of Moses as a Hebrew child (Exod. 2:6) is explained by her observing his circumcision (9:15). As in the Bible, Pharaoh's daughter takes Moses and raises him as her own, and gives him the name Moses. The narrator adds that Moses' true mother names him Melchiel (9:16).[28] The name comes from the Hebrew, *malkî 'el,* which means "God is my king." Moses' name hints that he never owed real allegiance to Pharaoh, particularly important in view of Pseudo-Philo's concern with foreign oppression.

The story of Moses' birth ends with a statement by the narrator that shows

---

25. Harrington, *OTP,* 316, n. m; Feldman, "Prolegomenon," xciii; SC 230, 106.

26. The killing of the children recalls Matt. 2:16.

27. *Exod. Rab.* 1:24; *b. Soṭa* 12a. Feldman notes that this is the only allusion to circumcision in the *Biblical Antiquities.* The word "circumcision" is not used, but Harrington (*OTP,* 316, n. o) notes, "In post-biblical Heb., 'covenant' had become a technical term for circumcision."

28. In Clement of Alexandria (*Strom.* 1.23.1), Moses is called "Melchi." For a discussion of the name, see Feldman, "Prolegomenon," xciii.

knowledge of Moses' entire career: "And the child was nursed and became glorious above all other men, and through him God freed the sons of Israel as he had said" (9:16). This sentence contains several points typical of Pseudo-Philo. Moses is glorified and seen to be the greatest of humans. God's action is stressed, since Moses is only God's instrument. God's characteristic action on behalf of Israel is freeing them. "As he had said" indicates that God is true to the divine word.

Chapter 10: The Exodus

Chapter 10 relates Israel's escape from Egypt and brings the story up to Sinai.[29] LAB 10:1 condenses Exodus 1–13 to several sentences, using only those elements important for setting up the following story. LAB 10:1 is typical of the *Biblical Antiquities* in depicting the people as crying to God in their distress, in focusing on God's action, and in characterizing God's action as bringing freedom. The divine action is summarized in "And he sent Moses and freed them from the land of the Egyptians" (10:1). This sentence restates the comment of 9:16 that God liberated the people through Moses.

With the Bible story, first-time readers would be unsure whether the people would escape Pharaoh. The narrator of the *Biblical Antiquities* states twice, once at the birth of Moses and again at the beginning of the Exodus story, that God "freed" *(liberavit)* Israel through Moses. The verb "freed" is in the past tense in both cases. There is no suspense in Pseudo-Philo on this point. The narrator's statements emphasize God's action, God's use of Moses, and the role of the people. Although the plagues are enumerated, no interest is shown in their details.[30] They are mentioned only to remind the readers of God's action on behalf of Israel.

Chapter 10 does not narrate the burning bush incident.[31] Instead, it focuses on how Moses' leadership works in the context of the people undergoing a crisis, a focus common in Pseudo-Philo. The meeting between God and Moses at the burning bush would detract from the clear connection between God's intentions as stated in 9:7–8, 16, and the Exodus in chapter 10. God decides in LAB 9 to save Israel because of Amram's faithfulness, while Exodus 3 reads as if God has just decided to save Israel.

LAB 10:2–6 follows the pattern of the plan form: (1) The Egyptians plan to pursue the Israelites (10:2); (2) three groups of four tribes each propose

29. For another treatment of this chapter that covers some of the same ground, see Murphy, "Exodus." In that piece I examine the work of Olyan, "Israelites," in detail. Olyan's work is particularly valuable for its comparison of Pseudo-Philo's version of the tribes' division at the Red Sea with the Samaritan and rabbinic versions.

30. Feldman ("Prolegomenon," xciii) points out that only nine plagues are listed. He compares Pseudo-Philo's list with that of Josephus and Philo.

31. LAB 37:3 does alludes to the burning bush. As usual, Pseudo-Philo assumes knowledge of a larger story than its expression in the *Biblical Antiquities*. LAB 10:4 does allude to Moses' call on Sinai.

plans to deal with the crisis (10:3); (3) Moses turns to God, implicitly rejecting the people's plans (10:4); (4) God saves the people, making their plans unnecessary (10:5–6).[32] As in chapters 6 and 9, the plan form contrasts human and divine plans.

The people's words when they find themselves pursued by the Egyptians are very different in the *Biblical Antiquities* than in the Bible. In Exod. 14:11–12, the people accuse Moses of having brought them out of Egypt to die; it would have been better to serve the Egyptians. In LAB 10:2, the people say to Moses,

> Behold now the time of our destruction *[perditionis]* has come. For the sea is ahead of us, and the throng of enemies is behind us, and we are in the middle. Is it for this that God has brought us forth, or are these the covenants that he established with our fathers, saying, *"To your seed I will give the land in which you dwell"* that now he might do with us whatever is pleasing in his sight?

In Exodus the people challenge Moses; here they challenge God. Their looming destruction leads them to accuse God of deserting the covenants with the fathers. The people quote God's words to Moses, another example of Pseudo-Philo's predilection for direct quotation. The direct quote makes the attack on God even stronger because it "proves" God's unfaithfulness through God's own words.

The readers know that God will rescue the people through Moses (9:16; 10:1). The narrative is ironic, since the readers know what the characters do not. It is also ironic that the people, who mistrust God's covenants with the fathers and so prove themselves unfaithful, accuse God of being unfaithful. Especially ironic is the use of the word *perditio. Perditio, perdere,* and *disperdere* are associated with the theme of moral causality. The Latin words are common in the text and are almost always used in the context of the destruction of the wicked and the salvation of the righteous. In light of the view of moral causality that pervades the *Biblical Antiquities,* if *perditio* has overtaken the people, they deserve it.

A final irony is that the people accuse God of failing to live up to the promise of their own land and of instead bringing them into the desert to do "whatever is pleasing in his sight." They imply that what is pleasing to God is their destruction. But God's liberating them from Egypt is part of fulfilling the promise of land and that fulfillment pleases God. The kernel of chapter 10 is the contrast between people's lack of understanding and trust and God's constancy and faithfulness.

32. See Murphy, "Divine Plan," 12. Some have suggested that the division of opinion among the tribes is related to Judg. 5:15–16 (*OTP,* 317, n. b; SC 230, 109; Feldman, "Prolegomenon," xciv; James, *Biblical Antiquities,* 104.) The Samaritan version has a threefold division of the tribes at the Red Sea, but later rabbinic and talmudic texts have a fourfold division, in which the first three positions are supported by biblical verses and the fourth is close to Moses' position as seen in the *Biblical Antiquities.* See Olyan, "Israelites," for comparison of the versions of the story. Perrot sees the threefold division of Pseudo-Philo as earlier than the fourfold division.

"Then in considering the fearful situation of the moment, the sons of Israel were split in their opinions according to three strategies" (10:3). The Israelites attend only to the present crisis. They cannot see things as do God and the readers. Pseudo-Philo, who is interested in human motivation, attributes their "strategies," their plans, to their fear mentioned in Exod. 14:10. The plans are not based on trust.

The first group of tribes plans suicide, since suicide is better than death at enemy hands. The irony is that such death is not in question since God intends to save the people through Moses, although they do not know that. If the people commit suicide, they will obliterate the covenant. Ironically, their proposed measure would accomplish the very thing they seek to escape.

The second group plans to return to Egypt and serve the Egyptians. This has its origin in the biblical text (Exod. 14:12). The readers know that service of the Egyptians implies idolatry (9:2).[33] Their plan would return them to the very situation that initiated God's action.

The third group suggests fighting, hoping for God's assistance. This plan may seem heroic to the readers, but anyone who remembers the narrative of Joktan in chapter 6 should think twice. Joktan also counseled specific action based on hope of God's help. He was sorely mistaken and his apparent trust turned out to be presumption. His action contrasted with Abraham's complete trust in God.[34]

Moses' portrayal in 10:4 is revealing for the author's view of leadership. In Exod. 14:13, Moses confidently reassures the people of God's help. That does not happen in the *Biblical Antiquities*. Rather, Moses cries out to God. This represents part 3 of the plan form because in ignoring the tribes' plans and crying to God, Moses rejects their plans. In Exod. 14:15, God asks Moses, "Why do you cry to me?" but Moses has not done so. Pseudo-Philo makes sense of this by quoting words of Moses to God. Instead of leaving out God's reference to Moses' cry, he creates a prayer for Moses. This plays into Pseudo-Philo's predilection for adding direct words of characters. *"Moses* cried out *to the Lord* and *said, 'Lord God of our fathers,* did you not say to me, "Go and *tell the sons of Israel,* 'God has sent me to you' " ' ?" And now behold you have brought your people to the edge of the sea, and the enemy *has pursued them;* but you, LORD, remember your name'" (10:4). Moses' prayer alludes to parts of Exod. 3:13–14, 14:9, 15–16. Pseudo-Philo again uses direct quotation. Moses quotes God and God quotes previous divine words. In 10:2, the people's quotation of God is an accusation, but Moses' prayer is based on trust. When the people observe the sea and the enemies, they picture their own destruction. Moses observes the same things and hopes for divine action. Moses bases his plea on God's previous acts of liberation. He remembers his own calling and being sent to Israel, an allusion to Exodus 3. He addresses God as "Lord God

---

33. *Servire* often occurs in a context that contrasts service to God and service to foreign gods. See concordance.

34. I disagree with Olyan's view ("Israelites") that the author favors this third, "martial," option.

of our fathers," a title that also occurs in 22:3, 5, 7; 25:6; 43:7; and 47:1, 2, and recalls the covenant. The people use the reference to the fathers to accuse God; Moses refers to the fathers to show the ground of his trust. Moses' prayer ends, "LORD, remember your name." If Israel perishes, that denigrates God's name since God is known as Israel's protector (see LAB 12:8–9).

The readers already know about Israel's impending liberation (9:16; 10:1). God seems to think that Moses should know about it, too. It is perhaps with some annoyance that God urges, *"Why have you cried out to me? Lift up your rod and strike* the sea, and it will be dried up" is (10:5). "It will be dried up" is not in Exodus 14. It connects 9:10 and 10:5 (where it occurs twice), emphasizing the fulfillment of the angel's words in 9:10. The narrative continues, "And when Moses did all this, God rebuked the sea and the sea was dried up" (10:5). This divine intervention constitutes part 4 of the plan form. The cosmic dimensions of God's saving action are enhanced in 10:5, when the *"depths* of the earth" and the "foundations of the world" are disclosed.

In Exod. 14:17, God plans to harden the Egyptians' hearts so that they will pursue Israel into the Red Sea, but the text leaves the precise meaning of "hardening" ambiguous. Pseudo-Philo explains that the Egyptians' "perception" was hardened so that they went into the sea unwittingly (10:6). In LAB 10:7, the narrator remembers the manna, the well of water, and the pillar that leads the people as three things God did to support Israel in the wilderness.[35] LAB 10:7 forms an inclusion with 20:8, which names the same things. LAB 20:8 mentions that the manna ended when Moses died and then recalls the well, the pillar, and the manna. The three gifts are associated with Miriam, Aaron, and Moses, respectively.[36] The section 10:7–20:8 is framed by manna, since it is mentioned first and last, but the order manna, well, and pillar is the same in both 10:7 and 20:8. The section describes the establishment of Israel at Sinai, its guidance and protection by God in the desert, and Joshua's succession of Moses as its leader. This is a foundational period in Israel's history on which its subsequent fate rests.

Chapter 10 emphasizes divine action. A brief listing of the verbs of which God is the object makes the point graphically. God hears the people, sends Moses, frees the people, sends the plagues, strikes down the Egyptians, brings the people forth from Egypt, establishes the covenants, will give the land to the people, speaks to Moses, rebukes the sea, lays bare the foundations of the world, hardens the Egyptians' perception, commands the sea, leads the people into the wilderness, rains down bread from heaven, brings forth quail and water, and leads them with pillars of cloud and fire.

---

35. On traditions about the well, see Feldman, "Prolegomenon," xciv, xcvi; SC 230, 110.
36. For other texts that make the same connections, see SC 230, 137.

Chapter 11: Sinai

The giving of the Torah on Sinai is as central to the *Biblical Antiquities* as to the Bible. Chapter 11 exemplifies the first category of rewriting since it proceeds through the biblical text (Exodus 19–20) in order and interprets it. After borrowing a short chronological notice from Exod. 19:1, Pseudo-Philo introduces the giving of the Law with God's words. God speaks to no one in particular, so the divine words are a soliloquy disclosing God's intentions and motivations. Ironically, the readers know more than Moses does. "God remembered his words and said, 'I will give a light to the world and illumine their dwelling places and establish my covenant with the sons of men and glorify my people above all nations. For them I will bring out the eternal statutes that are for those in the light but for the ungodly a punishment'" (11:1). God quotes divine words so that the giving of the Torah is interpreted as a fulfillment of an earlier divine promise. The note in Exod. 19:5 that Israel will be God's "treasured possession out of all the peoples" is interpreted by LAB 11:1 to mean that Israel will be "glorified" above all nations. LAB 11:1–3 is framed by the mention of God's intention to "establish his covenant" with Israel in 11:1 and 3. The association of the giving of the covenant with bestowing light on the world echoes God's words concerning Moses in 9:8 and signals their fulfillment.[37] Torah's statutes are the only source of light for those on earth.[38] Those who have it are in the light; those who do not follow it are ungodly and will be punished by it.[39] This is an instance of the idea that the same thing benefits the righteous and punishes the wicked.[40]

After telling Moses to command the people to prepare for the giving of the Law (11:2, following Exod. 19:15), God says,

> I will put my words in your mouth, and you will enlighten my people, for I have given an everlasting Law into your hands and by this I will judge the whole world. For this will be a testimony. For even if men say, "We have not known you, and so we have not served you," therefore I will make a claim upon them because they have not learned my Law (11:2).

Pseudo-Philo substitutes his own version of what God tells Moses at the beginning of the covenant on Sinai. God's statement in 11:1 that the Law is light to the world and the further statement in 11:2 that the whole world will be judged by Torah support the conclusion that all the world is accountable to the Law. That the whole world had the opportunity to receive the Law is absent from

37. See our comments on 9:8.

38. The Latin has "heights" *(excelsa)*, but, as Harrington rightly claims *(OTP*, 318, n. a), the context demands "statutes."

39. God speaks of the Torah here as the Gospel of John speaks of Jesus. Note also the similarity in formulation to 1 Cor. 1:18, where Christ's cross is folly to those who are perishing but the power of God to those who are being saved (cf. 2 Cor. 4:3).

40. See 4:5 and our comments there.

Exodus but is known from other Jewish documents.[41] The failure of the ungodly to "serve" God is language characteristic of Pseudo-Philo. The depiction of the Law as "everlasting" corresponds to the insistence that the covenant is eternal and may be occasioned here by God's statement in Exod. 19:9 that the people will believe Moses forever.

LAB 11:4–5 describes the cosmic signs accompanying the giving of the Torah. It quotes Exod. 19:16–17. Pseudo-Philo embellishes the cosmic disturbances associated with the theophany. Cosmic imagery expressing the significance of the giving of the Torah is also seen in LAB 15:5–6; 23:10; and 37:7–8. Whereas in Exodus the theophany shakes Mount Sinai, Pseudo-Philo says that the abysses are shaken.[42] In Exodus there are thunders and lightnings, but in Pseudo-Philo the stars and the angels participate and the heavens are folded up.[43] In Exodus, the theophany focuses on the glory of God and the danger God's presence poses for human witnesses. In Pseudo-Philo, the focus is on the Law itself. The cosmic disturbances serve less to highlight God's majesty than to dramatize the significance of the giving of the Law by God to human beings. The section ends with a reemphasis of the reason for the theophany. These things happen "until God should establish the Law of his eternal covenant with the sons of Israel and give his eternal commandments that will not pass away" (11:5).[44]

LAB 11:6–13 limits itself to altering the Ten Commandments (Exod. 20:1–17) without fully rewriting them.[45] This passage demonstrates Pseudo-Philo's concern for proper behavior and its consequences. Obedience brings success; disobedience brings misfortune. In 44:6–7, God demonstrates in detail how the people violate the Ten Commandments so that they deserve punishment.

In 11:6, Pseudo-Philo combines the injunction against other gods (Exod. 20:3) with the prohibition of graven images (Exod. 20:4). The result is: *"You shall not make for yourselves graven* gods." In this combination, "other gods" disappears from the Decalogue entirely because of Pseudo-Philo's strong opposition to idolatry. Although the people may make graven gods, other gods do not exist. The idea that God will punish people for the sins of their ancestors (Exod. 20:5) is altered to say that God will do so only "if they will walk in the

41. *2 Bar.* 41–42 says that all people will be judged according to their degree of adherence to Torah. For rabbinic reflections of the same idea, see SC 230, 110. Sirach claims that Wisdom sought a dwelling place throughout the world and was finally told by God to dwell in Zion (24:7–8). In Sir. 24:23, Wisdom is equated with the book of the Law.

42. Pseudo-Philo several times uses "abysses" to illustrate the cosmic dimensions of some event: foundation of Israel (12:8); Red Sea (15:5); giving of the Torah on Sinai (11:5; 23:10; 32:8); a combination of the Red Sea and Deborah's victory (32:17).

43. See *2 Bar.* 59:3 on the heavens being disturbed at Sinai. On Christian views of the role of angels at Sinai, see Gal. 2:19; Heb. 2:2; Acts 7:37, 53. Where the Christian sources claim that the angels gave the Law, Pseudo-Philo says only that they were present. See also the Jewish references in SC 230, 111.

44. The phraseology used here to express the eternity of the covenant recalls Jesus' statement about the Law in Matt. 5:18.

45. The Ten Commandments exercised a fascination for Jews and midrashic texts frequently reflect on them (see SC 230, 112).

ways of their parents." This accords with Pseudo-Philo's strict sense of moral causality.[46] LAB 11:7 supplies a reason for the command not to take God's name in vain: "Lest my ways be made empty." This may refer simply to not obeying God's commands (ways) or may mean that taking God's name in vain will cause desolation of the land, where "my ways" would mean the roads of Israel.[47] LAB 11:8 embellishes the statement in Exod. 20:11 that God created "heaven and earth, the sea, and all that is in them" with the words "and all the world and the uninhabitable wilderness and all things that labor and all the order of heaven." The addition underlines God's power and sovereignty over the cosmos. The section repeats the reason for God's hallowing of the seventh day ("Because he rested on it"), thus emphasizing the connection of observance of the Sabbath with God's action, already found in Exod. 20:11.

The command to honor father and mother in Exod. 20:12 is supported by the assertion that obedience will result in living long upon the land (11:9). Pseudo-Philo adds that "your light will rise" and makes it specific with the promise of rain, fertility of the land, and numerous progeny.[48] The alterations of Exodus fit well into Pseudo-Philo's usual emphases on God's control of nature (God "commands" heaven to bring forth rain), the correspondence between the righteousness of the people and nature's cooperation with them, and the permanence of Israel.

The remaining four commandments are each supplied with a reason. For two, the reason is something in the past, and for two it is so that a certain result will follow. Adultery is to be avoided because the people did not have adultery committed against them (11:10). Killing is prohibited because the people were not killed by their enemies (11:11). Both of these reasons allude to God's protection. False witness is forbidden lest the people's "guardians," probably guardian angels, bear them false witness, presumably in heaven before God (11:12).[49] Finally, coveting of one's property is to be avoided lest others covet the people's land. Coveting another's property leads to loss of the land of Israel. The introduction of the "golden rule" into the Decalogue is unique to Pseudo-Philo.

LAB 11:14 paraphrases several biblical passages with little change in meaning. Pseudo-Philo's main contribution is the reference to the earth quaking, corresponding to the highlighting of cosmic disturbances in 11:5. LAB 11:15 condenses into a very small space the rest of God's revelations to Moses on Sinai. First, it summarizes most of the other commands as "statutes and judgments" and says that God "commanded him many things." Second, it speaks of the tree of life and the water of Marah. Finally, it summarizes the commandments dealing with the sanctuary. The first part requires little comment except to point out that it assumes the readers have access to far wider sources

---

46. Pseudo-Philo was not alone in making this change to this problematic text (see Feldman, "Prolegomenon," xcv).

47. This may be what *b. Šab.* 33a has in mind. See SC 230, 112.

48. For rain as a sign of God's blessing, see 4:5; 13:7; 21:2; 60:2.

49. See 15:5 and 59:4.

of information than the *Biblical Antiquities*, and that it emphasizes statutes and so behavior.

The second part of 11:15 deserves attention. The tree of life is seen as the wood that sweetened the water of Marah (Exod. 15:22–25) here, as elsewhere in Jewish tradition.[50] Further, Pseudo-Philo says that the sweetened well followed the Israelites in the desert. Jewish legend, building on Exod. 17:6 and Num. 20:7–11, holds that a well followed the Israelites in the wilderness and associates that well with Miriam.[51] That tradition appears in LAB 10:7, but only Pseudo-Philo identifies Miriam's well with that of Marah (20:8). Ginzberg considers this a confusion of "Marah" with "Miriam," but the identification may be part of the ongoing attempt to present Israel's history as a web held together by divine plans.[52]

Chapter 11 ends by noting God's cultic commands. The cult is one of the few things singled out by Pseudo-Philo in his condensation of the Sinai commandments. That the cult is structured according to the divine will is emphasized by including the tradition that Moses was shown the pattern of the sanctuary when he was on Sinai.[53]

Chapter 12: The Golden Calf

Since idolatry is a major theme for Pseudo-Philo, it is no surprise that the author chose to include the episode of the golden calf from Exodus 32.[54] Pseudo-Philo's version highlights Moses' leadership and God's faithfulness to the divine promises.

Pseudo-Philo prefaces the golden calf narrative with the story of Moses' face shining from later in Exodus (34:29–35). In Exodus 34, the people are frightened when Moses descends from Mount Sinai with his face shining because of his exposure to God's glory. The biblical story emphasizes the reality of Moses' contact with God and so underscores his ability to act as a divine spokesman. In Exodus, fear of direct contact with the divine characterizes Israel's stay at Sinai. Pseudo-Philo changes fright to lack of recognition—when Moses descends from the mountain with his face shining, the people do not recognize him, a point unique to Pseudo-Philo (12:1). The element of recognition accords with the ironic mode in which the *Biblical Antiquities* is written. Humans' inability to understand God's ways is symbolized by the radical difference between the world above visited by Moses, where he is

50. Ginzberg, *Legends,* Vol. 6, 14, n. 82; see Feldman, "Prolegomenon," xcvi.

51. See 1 Cor. 10:4 for Paul's thoughts on the spiritual rock that gave the Israelites water in the desert and followed them. See also LAB 10:7; 20:8.

52. See Ginzberg, Vol. 6, 15, n. 82; SC 230, 113.

53. Exod. 25:8–9; Heb. 8:5; *2 Bar.* 4:5. This belies the notion that the author opposed or was indifferent to the Jerusalem cult.

54. Feldman ("Prolegomenon," xcvi) notes that Josephus omits the incident, but Pseudo-Philo "chooses to narrate the incident of the Golden Calf at some length."

bathed in invisible light, and the world below, where the light of Moses' face surpasses that of the sun and moon.[55] Only one who has access to the light of the world above, as do Moses and (vicariously) the readers of the *Biblical Antiquities,* can fully understand earthly events. LAB 12:1 likens the Israelites' lack of understanding to the failure of the eleven sons of Jacob to recognize their brother Joseph in Egypt (8:10). The analogy is another example of the tendency to see similarities between different times in Israel's history. The same verb *(cognoscere)* is used in both LAB 8:10 and 12:1. The word carries the same ironic tone elsewhere in Pseudo-Philo, particularly in the narratives about Kenaz, Samuel, and David. In 12:1, *cognoscere* occurs four times. The people recognize Moses when he speaks, since his speaking best characterizes him.[56]

The use of 12:1 as a preface to the golden calf incident stresses the immense difference between God and people. The verse also shows Moses' authority and ability to bridge the distance between God and Israel. Conversely, it highlights the people's failure to understand God's ways, a failure that becomes graphically evident in the making of the calf.

LAB 12:2–3 describes the sin of the golden calf. Most remarkable is the diminishing of Aaron's culpability. In Exodus, the people ask Aaron to make gods for them and he does so without resistance. In Pseudo-Philo, Aaron tries to dissuade the people and then cooperates only because of his fear of their strength (12:3). This indicates the author's concern for the cult. The first head priest is to some degree exculpated for Israel's first cultic sin following its reception of the Torah. In the process, one of Israel's ancient and honored citizens is portrayed in a more favorable light than in the Bible. Chapter 12 provides two instances of a realistic streak in Pseudo-Philo that tempers the strict rule of moral causality. Aaron gives in to the people because of fear, and there is no punishment of Aaron here. Later, those who worship the calf because they are forced to do so are excused (12:7).[57]

In 12:2 the narrator says that the people's heart was corrupted when Moses ascended the mountain.[58] This recalls the statement in 3:9 that the human heart is foolish from youth. Pseudo-Philo has a fairly pessimistic view of humanity in general, and Israel is not much different except for God's relationship with its ancestors. The connection of the corruption of the people's heart with Moses' absence serves the theme of leadership.

Pseudo-Philo generalizes the people's request for gods in Exod. 32:1 by changing the specific references to the Exodus and the desert to a more general

---

55. In *Sipre* 140 on Num. 27:20, the light of Moses' face is like the light of the sun, but here it surpasses it. For other references to this, see SC 230, 114.

56. A parallel to this recognition scene is in Luke 24, where two disciples recognize Jesus in the breaking of bread.

57. An interesting parallel to this attitude is that of the Gospel of Matthew which makes stringent demands on Christians but is realistic about the fact that the church is actually composed of good, bad, and everything in between.

58. The author takes this detail from Exod. 32:7, where God tells Moses that the people have "corrupted themselves."

context. In Exod. 32:1, the people say to Aaron, "Come, make gods for us, who shall go before us; as for this Moses, the man who brought us up out of the land of Egypt, we do not know what has become of him." LAB 12:2 changes this to: *"Make gods for us* whom we may serve, as the other nations have, *because that Moses* through whom wonders were done before our eyes has been taken away from us." Pseudo-Philo generalizes what the people seek. It is not just gods who can lead them through the desert, but gods to "serve." This generalization concerns the opposition between service to God and service to idols so prominent in the *Biblical Antiquities.* Similarly, Pseudo-Philo generalizes the description of Moses from the one who led them out of Egypt to the one who did wonders before their eyes. The connection between seeing wonders and obedience recalls Judg. 2:7: "The people worshipped the LORD all the days of Joshua, and all the days of the elders who outlived Joshua, who had seen all the great work that the LORD had done for Israel." The book of Joshua then tells of Israel's sins after Joshua's death. In LAB 12:2 the people go astray even before Moses' death just because he is absent for a time.

The people's motivation in asking for new gods in LAB 12:2 is the same as that attributed to them by 1 Sam. 8:5 when they ask for a king. They want to be like the other nations.[59] The association of idolatry with being like the nations is important to Pseudo-Philo.

Aaron tries to argue the people out of idolatry in LAB 12:3. He tells them to be patient because Moses will return with the Law, which he will explain to them and which will constitute "rules for our race." The distinctiveness of Israel lies in its possession of the Law and its service of God. The narrator editorializes in 12:3: "They did not heed him, so that the word spoken in the time when the people sinned by building the tower might be fulfilled, when God said, 'And now unless I stop them, *everything that they propose to do they will dare,* and even worse.'" This is another example of the pattern of prediction and fulfillment. The iniquity of fashioning the golden calf surpasses that of the tower.

LAB 12:4 contains a short speech by God to Moses. It begins as in Exod. 32:7–10, where God informs Moses that the people have gone astray, but in Exodus God gives a more extended description of the people's sin and then says that they will be destroyed and Moses set up as a great nation in their place. Instead of this, Pseudo-Philo has God reflect on the status of the divine promises to Israel in light of the people's idolatry, and then God predicts the future behavior of the people and its consequences. LAB 12:4 is one of the many passages in which the covenant's existence is questioned. This time, God poses the question of whether the fabrication of the golden calf annuls the promise of land. God points out that the people violated the covenant even before entering the land and asserts that if they had entered the land, their transgressions would be even worse. This view of the Israelites is characteristically pessimistic. Fulfillment of God's promises paradoxically makes their allegiance to the covenant less likely.

---

59. The influence of Samuel's story on Pseudo-Philo's Moses cycle reemerges in chapter 19.

God says that God will indeed forsake the people but will then make peace with them again (12:4). It is noteworthy that God passes from forsaking to peace without an intervening stage where the people repent. Although repentance is present in the *Biblical Antiquities* and although the author advocates the connection between sin and punishment, the full pattern of sin–punishment–repentance–forgiveness is not always present.[60] At times, repentance is not mentioned. This makes the eternity of the covenant more prominent. God punishes the people for their sins but always turns back to them, even when repentance is not present.

God will forsake the people but then turn back to them so that a house (temple) will be built among them, but when they sin again the house will be destroyed (12:4). Then, "The race of men will be to me like a drop from a pitcher and will be reckoned like spittle." This expression derives from Isa. 40:15 and was already used in LAB 7:3, where the human race attempted to erect the tower of Babel and so is likened to spittle. In 7:4 Abraham and his seed are separated from the rest of humanity, who are likened to spittle. That makes the expression in 12:4 even more striking. In view of Israel's failure and the resultant destruction of the temple, all humanity, including Israel, is now alienated from God. Israel should be humanity's connection with God, but that connection appears broken by Israel's disobedience.[61] This looks like a grim prediction of God's abandonment of the human race. Since it does not mention the second temple, it may reflect a negative view of it.[62]

LAB 12:4–10 embodies "intercessory bargaining."[63] The form has three parts: (1) God appears to a representative of the people and threatens their destruction because of their sins but exempts the representative from the punishment; (2) The representative intercedes, advancing arguments to dissuade God; (3) God relents. Exod. 32:7–14, which Pseudo-Philo rewrites here, contains the form. LAB 12:4–10 eliminates certain problems in the flow of Exodus 32. In Exodus the sequence is as follows: God tells Moses of the people's sin and of the divine intention to destroy them; Moses intercedes; God relents; Moses descends from the mountain and apparently discovers the sin of the people for the first time; he smashes the tablets; he makes the people drink water containing dust from the destroyed calf; he confronts Aaron, who blames the people; Moses wreaks vengeance on the people through the Levites; he reascends the mountain to intercede again; God claims that the sinners will be punished; a plague afflicts the people. Everything in Exodus 32 that comes after Moses' first intercession and God's change of heart is redundant. The sequence in Pseudo-Philo is less complicated. God threatens destruction; Moses goes down and punishes the guilty; Moses reascends the

60. See Steck *(Israel)* for this theme in Jewish literature.

61. For a similar train of thought, see *2 Bar.* 3:8. See Murphy, "Temple," 674–75.

62. Knibb ("Exile") shows that many Jewish works of the Second Temple period hold that the exile did not come to an end with the building of the second temple, and that therefore the Second Temple period was but a continuation of God's punishment of Israel.

63. See Murphy, *Structure,* 72–77. The form is also found in *2 Bar.* 1–9; Gen. 18:1–28; Num. 14:10b–25; 16:19b–24. See Murphy, "Temple," 672–80.

mountain and intercedes for Israel; God relents. LAB 12:4–10 stands out from other instances of the intercessory bargaining form in that Moses is not explicitly exempted from God's punishment. This may be because all of humanity is doomed because of Israel's sin (12:4). It may also be because Pseudo-Philo is so intent on the indestructibility of the covenant with Israel that no other option could be contemplated.

LAB 12:5–7 advances the themes of leadership, the eternity of the covenant, and moral causality. LAB 12:5 attests to the tradition, also found in rabbinic sources, that God's writing fled from the tablets before Moses broke them.[64] The tradition avoids the idea that Moses committed sacrilege in breaking the tablets. In LAB 12:5, Moses breaks them only after looking at them and seeing that the writing is gone. Moses' anguish is represented through the striking image of a woman in childbirth who is unable to bring forth her child by her own strength.[65] Moses' pain is caused by the disruption of a process through which he was to bring Israel to birth through the giving of Torah. This situation lasts only one hour. In a display of true leadership, Moses takes the situation in hand and says, "Will bitterness win the day always, or will evil prevail forever? And now I will rise up and gird my loins because even if they have sinned, what was declared to me above will not be in vain" (12:6). Moses' leadership flows from his conviction that God's words will be fulfilled in spite of all obstacles. Even the golden calf cannot interfere with God's plans. Moses comes to this conclusion on his own, not because God informs him of it.

In Exod. 32:20, Moses burns the calf, grinds it to dust, mixes it with water, and makes the people drink it. The biblical text gives no explanation for this action, although it may be connected to the plague that overtakes the people in 32:35. In. Num 5:16–28, a similar ritual constitutes a trial by ordeal. The *Biblical Antiquities* interprets the drinking of the water as a trial by ordeal: "If anyone had it in his will and mind that the calf be made, his tongue was cut off; but if he had been forced by fear to consent, his face shone" (12:7). This sentence supports Pseudo-Philo's idea of moral causality, since the guilty parties suffer for their crime. It also shows Pseudo-Philo's lenience toward those forced to commit the act. Finally, it indicates sensitivity toward the issue of intention. What matters is not just the act itself, but the intention in performing the act.

In LAB 12:8–9, Moses reascends the mountain to intercede with God. As in Exodus 32, Moses' argument connects God's well-being to Israel's survival. Destruction of God's people would mean no one will glorify God, because only Israel can properly praise God. Even if God were to choose another nation, that nation would never trust God because of the destruction of the first chosen people. Further, if God forsakes the entire world, no one will be left to do the divine will. The idea that God's well-being depends on humans is present elsewhere in Jewish tradition.[66] Israel's close relationship with God

64. SC 230, 115, refers to *Tg Yer. I* Exod. 32:19 and *Pirqe R. El.* 45.

65. For references to the image of childbirth, see SC 230, 115; Vermes, *Scripture,* 56–57.

66. It is used in the intercessory bargaining form (see Murphy, *Structure,* 72–85).

is expressed through the image of the vine planted by God and rooted in the abyss and stretching to God's throne.[67] Moses prays, "You are he who is all light" (12:9). Light is most often applied to the Torah in this work, but God is the source of Torah and so the source of all light.[68]

Typical of Pseudo-Philo is the interplay between God's anger and mercy that Moses makes explicit (12:8–9).[69] Moses asks God not to act out of anger even if that anger is justified, for it would result in the destruction of God's labor in the Creation being "in vain." Such an argument is persuasive, since a major theme of the book is that God's plans or work are never "in vain." Any human plans or actions that challenge God's plans are futile. Moses' intercession ends with a plea that God's inheritance, Israel, not be allowed to be pulled apart "in humiliation." In 9:6 Amram expresses the hope that Israel will be rescued from its humiliation in Egypt. God does this through Moses, so Moses' intervention here concerning Israel's humiliation is poignant.

Chapter 12 ends with God's statement to Moses, "Behold I have been made merciful according to your words," and with God's command to Moses to cut two new tablets from the original source and to write the commandments on them.[70.] Whereas in Exod. 32:14 it is merely said that God repents of the evil that was to have come upon the people, the *Biblical Antiquities* characteristically stresses God's mercy.

Chapter 13: Cultic Commands

Chapter 13 contains five sections: (1) commands concerning the sanctuary, priests, and sacrifices (13:1–2); (2) commands concerning leprosy (13:3); (3) commands concerning festivals (13:4–7); (4) reference to the time of Noah and to paradise (13:8–9); and (5) God's prediction of the future (13:10). The chapter is an authoritative condensation of parts of Torah, since most of it is in God's words. Concerning sections 1 and 2, a few short comments will suffice. First, of all aspects of the Law given on Sinai, the author chooses to highlight cultic commands. This is significant with respect to the question of Pseudo-Philo's attitude toward the cult—he supports it. Second, Moses' obedience to God and God's command of the situation are stressed. God is the sovereign Lord who controls nature and history and in whose hands lies Israel's fate. Finally, the attention to the problem of leprosy is due to a general interest in skin diseases apparent in Israelite and Jewish laws and in the New Testament.

In section 3, the author assigns a rationale for each of the feasts.[71] Unleavened Bread memorializes Israel's liberation from Egypt. Weeks has only agri-

---

67. See 1 QH 6:15. God's care for Israel and the temple is described using traditional Jewish terms. See SC 230, 115, for references.

68. For references to God as light, see SC 230, 115.

69. See Murphy, "God;" and chapter 10, this volume, under "God."

70. Jewish tradition is divided on whether God or Moses wrote on the second set of tablets (SC 230, 115; Feldman, "Prolegomenon," xcvii).

71. The list of feasts is essentially the same as that found in *m. Roš Haš.* 1:2.

cultural content and is not connected with a historical event. Trumpets (later called New Year) is the time for offerings for "your watchers." "Watchers" are the guardian angels encountered in *1 En.* 1:5; 10:7; etc., as well as Dan. 4:13, 23. The negative view of angel worship in LAB 34 does not contradict this, since in that chapter it is worship of the angels in charge of magicians for the purpose of gaining illicit powers that is condemned. The New Year is the anniversary of Creation in *b. Roš Haš.* 11a. Here it is the time to remember that God foresaw all that was to happen on the earth and to remember the earth, probably because it is God's work.[72] God's control over history is illustrated by the fact that at the New Year God decides on all births and deaths for the following year.

The Day of Atonement is called a "fast of mercy." Mercy is an attribute of God emphasized in the *Biblical Antiquities*, so this name is appropriate. The fast is for the souls of the people, and "so that the promises made to your fathers may be fulfilled" (13:6). Attention to the promises made to the fathers characterizes Pseudo-Philo as a whole. Pseudo-Philo's list ends with Tabernacles.[73] The text connects Tabernacles with rain, as is common in Jewish tradition since Tabernacles occurs at the beginning of the rainy season.[74] Pseudo-Philo goes beyond the simple mention of rain to highlight God's control of all elements of the universe—seasons, stars, clouds, wind, lightning, and thunder. The next words are, *"Et hoc erit in signum sempiternum."* It is unclear whether the *hoc* refers to the preceding list or to what follows, the dew that the nights produce seen as a fulfillment of something God predicted after the Flood (13:7). Neither the Bible nor Pseudo-Philo records a prediction of dew. However, LAB 3:9 does follow Gen. 8:22 in seeing the succession of the seasons as part of God's postdiluvian promise that the earth will never again be destroyed by water. It is possible, then, that *hoc* should be taken to refer not just to dew but to the seasons as well, and probably to the whole range of things Pseudo-Philo mentions in this context. The orderly working of the universe is predicted by God and ensured by Israel's cultic prayers.

In LAB 13:8, the "command regarding the year of the lifetime of Noah" refers to the limitation of human life to 120 years (LAB 3:2; Gen. 6:3).[75] God tells Moses that at the divine visitation, probably at the time of the Flood, God limited human life and showed humans the "place of creation and the serpent."[76] Thus, Noah was granted a vision of the Garden of Eden. God makes that explicit by identifying the place as the one where Adam was told that all things would be subject to him if he obeyed God. God recalls that

---

72. This interpretation depends upon the translation of *prespexi* as "I foresaw" rather than "I watched over," and thus is a departure from Harrington's translation (*OTP*, 321). Our interpretation follows that of SC 230, 117.

73. The word for the feast here is *scenophegia*, as found in the LXX of Deut. 16:16.

74. SC 230, 118, mentions *m. Ta'an.* 1:1 and *b. Roš Haš.* 16a.

75. For Pseudo-Philo's treatment of Noah, see Lewis, "Study," 74–77.

76. Instead of "serpent" *(colubrum)*, the manuscripts have "color" *(colorem)*. I follow Perrot and Harrington here.

Adam *(protoplastum)* transgressed since he was persuaded by his wife, who was deceived by the serpent, with the result that death was decreed for all.[77]

LAB 13:9 reads, "And the LORD continued to show him the ways of paradise and said to him, 'These are the ways that men have lost by not walking in them, because they have sinned against me.' " The most probable recipient of the vision here is Moses.[78] That God shows Moses paradise and everything humankind had lost through Adam's sin recalls *2 Bar.* 4:3–6, where paradise is shown to Adam but removed from him when he sinned. In that same passage paradise is shown also to Abraham (Gen. 15:9–21; see also 4 Ezra 3:14–15) and Moses on Sinai (as in Pseudo-Philo).

LAB 13:8–9 is an example of the protology of Pseudo-Philo. Everything within the work is framed by the Creation and the eschaton. Creation and eschaton are portrayed so as to highlight their judgmental aspects. Moses' vision provides a context for the giving of the Law. The negative aspects of the human condition are a result of disobedience, implying that what was lost can be regained only by obedience.

The lesson of moral causality is explicit in 13:10. Obedience brings God's merciful blessing. Rain and fertility embody that mercy. This recalls the paradigmatic statement in 4:5 of how the world ought to work—prayer and obedience bring rain, which brings fertility. But God knows in advance that Israel will not be faithful. They will forget the covenants with the fathers and so will be abandoned by God for a time. Then God says, "But nevertheless I will not forget them forever." It is remarkable that Israel's repentance is not mentioned. God's words mean that the covenant is indestructible. God knows Israel will not live up to its side but has decided beforehand to turn back to Israel and not to abandon it permanently. Chapter 13 ends with God's reminder that divine abandonment of Israel will be due to its own sins, as the people will indeed know "in the last days," because God is faithful.[79]

Chapter 14: A Census

In Num. 1:2–3, God tells Moses to number the males that are at least twenty years old and ready for war. The census of chapter 14 is based on that of Numbers 1, but Pseudo-Philo deletes its military aspects. This is especially striking given the military tone of the census in LAB 5, where the divisions of humanity are depicted as armed camps. Instead, the census in LAB 14 holds

77. The "feminism" of Pseudo-Philo, striking as it is, has its limitations. Although this passage does not go nearly as far as several Jewish and Christian texts in using Genesis 3 to denigrate women, it does show some influence of the tendency to blame Eve for the Fall. Pseudo-Philo does not lay all of the blame at Eve's doorstep but makes no alteration to the story of Genesis on this point.

78. It is possible that it is Noah. See Harrington, *OTP*, 322, n. j, who opts for Moses. Perrot (SC 230, 118) notes that even Adam is possible.

79. This may be a reference to the eschaton, though Perrot (SC 230, 118) thinks that it is not necessarily such.

in tension the ideas that God's promises are indestructible and all sin is punished. The text does this by using the notion of the remnant. One-fiftieth of the people survive punishment so that the promises can still be fulfilled. Moses is to count the people,

> that I may show your tribes what I declared to your fathers in a foreign land, because from the fiftieth part I raised them up from the land of Egypt, but forty-nine parts died in the land of Egypt. When you make them stand and pass in review, write down their number until I fulfill all that I have spoken to their fathers and until I set them firmly in their own land; for not a single word from what I have spoken to their fathers will I renege on, from those that I said to them: *"Your seed will be like the stars of heaven in multitude."* By number they will enter the land, and in a short time they will become without number (14:1–2).

The number of people turns out to be 1,620,900 (14:3). Moses reports this number to God, who tells him that in Egypt Israel numbered 9,295,000. The smallness of Moses' number is stressed when the narrator says it includes all Israel, whereas God's tally excludes women. In LAB 14 nothing is said about counting only warriors, as in Exodus, and the age restriction of Num. 1:3 is removed in LAB 14:3. Moses' number does not amount to one-fiftieth of God's number, but Pseudo-Philo is not trustworthy on specific numbers.[80] The point of the figure of one-fiftieth is the same as that of the specific numbers: The people have become few. God explains Israel's decrease by saying, "I put to death the whole crowd of them because they did not believe in me" (14:4). God consecrated the remnant and assigned tithes as a reminder of the hardships from which they were saved.

In Deut. 28:62, Moses says, "Although you were once as numerous as the stars in heaven, you shall be left few in number, because you did not obey the LORD your God." He goes on to predict the exile. In both Deuteronomy and the *Biblical Antiquities,* Israel's faithfulness determines its size. Deuteronomy compares Israel's past greatness to its future smallness. Pseudo-Philo sees Israel about to enter the land as small and compares this to its great number in Egypt and its future size in the land. For Pseudo-Philo, Israel's smallness is both a warning based on past punishments and a hope for future blessings. Especially important is that Israel's future multitude will be proof of fulfillment of the divine promises contained in Gen. 22:17. The text's insistence on the complete fulfillment of all that God has spoken is typical. God requires the census as proof of divine faithfulness.

In the last sentence of the chapter, Moses conveys all of this information to the people. Their reaction is one of sadness and mourning. This expresses the tragic element in Israel's history that Pseudo-Philo highlights. The people always and everywhere have at their disposal the means to ensure God's mer-

---

80. Harrington notes that "fiftieth" is "based on a midrashic explanation of the Heb. *ḥmšym* in Ex 13:8, which can mean 'equipped for battle' or 'fifties' " (*OTP*, 322, n. a). Ginzberg (*Legends,* Vol. 6, 138, n. 806) notes that the figure of one-fiftieth appears also in *Mek. Beshallah* 1, 24a, and *Mek. d'R. Shimon. 38* on Exod. 13:18.

ciful blessing and to bring themselves prosperity and success. If the people find themselves in any other situation, it is of their own making.

Chapter 15: The Twelve Spies

Chapter 15 condenses Numbers 13–14. The condensation is as remarkable for what it leaves out as for what it includes. In Numbers 14, the full intercessory bargaining form is present. God threatens to abandon Israel, Moses intervenes, and God forgives. Given Pseudo-Philo's use of that form in LAB 12 and his interest in Moses as a mediator, one might expect the full form to reappear in LAB 15. That is not the case. The first two parts of the form do appear—God threatens to destroy Israel and Moses intercedes, but there is no explicit report of God's relenting. Pseudo-Philo skips to Numbers 16. In so doing, the author also intensifies the pace of rebellion in the wilderness. Before God can forgive the people for the first rebellion, they engage in another.

LAB 15:1 follows the biblical text in that the sending of the spies is due to God's initiative. In Deut. 1:22–23, the people generate the idea, which is then approved by Moses. In Josephus *(Ant.* 3.14.1 § 302) as well as in Philo *(Vit. Mos.* 1:40 § 221), Moses takes the initiative. Pseudo-Philo follows the biblical version as consonant with the emphasis on the action of God. Pseudo-Philo's leaders are good not when they devise their own plans, but when they follow God's will.

LAB 15:1 interprets the effect of the spies' report on the people by borrowing phrases from Joshua 14, where Caleb recalls the incident of Numbers 13–14. The spies' words *"troubled the heart of the people"* (LAB 15:1), or "made the heart of the people melt" (Josh. 14:8). In Josh. 14:9, Caleb recalls Moses' reassurance that the land would be their inheritance. It may be due to the influence of the passage from Joshua 14 that Pseudo-Philo's spies tell the people, "You cannot inherit the land" because of the strength of the inhabitants (15:1). The rephrasing clarifies what is at stake in the people's fear. To allow the strength of the Canaanites to deter them from following God's instructions would be to lose their inheritance, which means that God's promises would be in vain.

In the next few sentences Pseudo-Philo streamlines the story from Numbers. In the biblical version, it appears at first as though all of the spies are discouraging the people. Then Caleb speaks up and tells the people to trust in God. The people are not persuaded, and then Joshua and Caleb speak up together. In the *Biblical Antiquities,* the spies' initial report is followed immediately by the editorial comment, "Yet two men of the twelve did not speak in this way" (15:2). Their names and genealogies are given in 15:3. They express their confidence in God's power to overcome human opponents: "Just as iron can overcome the stars, or as weapons conquer lightning, or thunder is shut off by the arrows of men, so can these men fight against the LORD"

(15:2). These words stress God's cosmic might. Joshua and Caleb are so confident because as they go into Canaan they see a vision of lightning from the stars and thunder coming with them into the land.[81]

Israel's protest in LAB 15:4 is sharper than in Num. 14:2–3. In the biblical text, the people regret having left Egypt and ask why God brought them out. The *Biblical Antiquities* has them quote God's words found in Exod. 3:8: "Are these the words God spoke to us, saying, 'I will bring you *into a land flowing with milk and honey.' " This is another example of Pseudo-Philo's penchant for direct quotation, and in this case it falls into that subcategory of quotation that proves or disproves God's faithfulness to the divine promises. The people virtually taunt God by contrasting their situation with the divine pledges.

God's angry speech in 15:5–6 is rife with elements typical of Pseudo-Philo. As usual, the readers get firsthand access to God's thoughts and plans. God says that despite the people's failure to listen, "behold now the plan of action that has issued from me will not be in vain." This states a major theme: God's ways will prevail. God says that the people will be sent into dark chambers and word will be sent to the fathers, saying, "Behold this is the seed to which I have spoken, saying, *'Your seed will stay a while in a land not its own, and I will judge the nation whom it will serve' "* (15:5). Often God would prefer to abandon Israel, as its conduct merits, but the covenant with the fathers always prevents that. Here the fathers are made witnesses to Israel's transgression. God quotes the divine words (Gen. 15:13–14), as did the people in 15:4. The people try to prove God false; God uses the same device to prove the divine words true—the divine words recorded in Genesis found their fulfillment in the sojourn in Egypt and in the liberation of the people. The judgment of Israel's enemies (Gen. 15:14) occurred when God "killed their enemies" (15:6). God's liberation of the people through the division of the Red Sea is shown to have cosmic proportions and was an event greater than any between the parting of the waters at the Creation and the present day (15:6). Again, God quotes the divine words when referring to the creative act of separating the waters (Genesis 1).

The second great act of God on behalf of the people, besides the liberation from Egypt, is the giving of the Torah. Borrowing language from Isa. 64:1, God describes the theophany at Sinai as bending the heavens to descend (15:6). The application of this image to Sinai is known elsewhere in Jewish tradition.[82] Significant here is Pseudo-Philo's characteristic reference to the Law as something that enlightens (see 9:8; 11:2) and the claim that the Law is "for creation."

God's speech goes on to sanctuaries given to the people for proper worship so that God might dwell with them (15:6). If God cannot remain among the people, it is their fault, not God's. The people did not believe God's words

---

81. The vision recalls the song of Deborah where the stars fight from heaven on the side of the Israelites (Judg. 5:20). In *Mek. Shirah* 9:43a, the spies are miraculously protected.

82. SC 230, 121, 148. See LAB 11:5; 32:7–8.

and abandoned God, "and their mind grew weak."[83] God's words are always true. The people's failure to believe them results in the weakening of their minds—they cannot reason properly. God sees banishment to the wilderness as giving the people what they want: *"Faciam eis sicut voluerunt"* (15:6). As usual the people's fate is in their own hands.

Moses' intercession employs an argument not found in Numbers 14: "Before you took the seed from which you would make man upon the earth, was it I who did establish their ways? Therefore let your mercy sustain us until the end, and your fidelity for length of days; for unless you had mercy, who would ever be born?" (15:7). Moses' logic is subtle. He first reminds God that God created humanity, and then says that he (Moses) did not establish humans' ways. He does not directly blame God for the way humans are, but he borders on doing so. The argument recalls 4 Ezra 3:20–36, where Ezra tells God that God did not remove humanity's "evil heart," that no human group can be considered to be without sin, and that therefore God is unjustified in removing favor from Israel. Israel is actually no worse than anyone else and is more mindful of the commandments than any other nation. Ezra is careful not to blame God for the evil heart, only for not removing it.[84] Although Pseudo-Philo does not explicitly mention the evil heart here, he alludes to it in 3:9 and 33:3. It should also be noted that 4 Ezra 4:30 uses the image of an evil seed sown in the human heart, an image that expresses the same reality as that of the evil heart. That the word "seed" is used in both LAB 15:7 and 4 Ezra 4:30 in the context of the inveterate evil of humanity makes at least a linguistic connection between passages for which we have already recognized a conceptual connection.

Moses appeals to two qualities of God stressed throughout the *Biblical Antiquities:* mercy and fidelity. He sees God's mercy as necessary for the very existence of humankind and looks forward to it being there "until the end."

Chapter 16: Korah's Rebellion

In Num. 15:37–41, God tells Moses to have the people put tassels on their clothing as a reminder of all the commandments.[85] LAB 16:1 reduces those verses to the short notice "In that time he commanded that man about the tassels." Once again, Pseudo-Philo assumes that the readers know more than he tells them about the biblical story. Pseudo-Philo goes on to say that Korah and two hundred companions revolt against the order, protesting, "Why is an

---

83. Perrot suggests that the meaning here is that to abandon the Law is to lose oneself (SC 230, 121). He refers to the study of K. Berger *(Gesetzesauslegung,* 216), who stresses the importance of the two ways of Deut. 30:15–20 for the *Biblical Antiquities.*

84. See Stone, *4 Ezra,* 63.

85. The analysis of this chapter is based on my earlier study, "Korah's Rebellion."

unbearable law imposed upon us?"[86] Numbers makes no connection between the law of the tassels and Korah's rebellion, but the connection is attested to in rabbinic literature.[87] Jewish interpretation often reads adjacent passages in terms of each other.[88] Although at first glance it appears that Korah is upset merely at the rule of the tassels, it is clear from the rest of the chapter that the issue is the larger one of obedience to God in general.[89] The author assumes that the readers know of the connection established by Numbers between the tassels and the Torah as a whole.

Korah's rebellion exercised considerable fascination for later Jewish tradition. Korah became a paradigm for those who would not accept Torah or who engaged in illegitimate argument over Torah, as contrasted with the lawful controversy of the rabbinic schools.[90] In rabbinic tradition, Korah's lies contrast with the truth of Moses and the Torah.[91] Korah is sometimes pictured as trying to make the Law appear absurd so as to discredit it or prove that it is from Moses and not from God.[92] This last point has a parallel in LAB 25:13, where some Israelites claim that it was Moses who wrote the Law, not God.

In Numbers 16, there is a pronounced power struggle between Moses and Korah. Korah directly attacks the legitimacy of the Aaronic priesthood (Num. 16:3), and Moses responds with an attack on the presumption of the Levites (Num. 16:8–11). Josephus and the rabbis embellish the power struggle.[93] Josephus sees Korah's jealousy of Moses as the cause of the trouble and his Korah presents his birth and wealth as factors that entitle him to the role of high priest.[94] In his version, Korah attacks not Torah but Moses. Korah even insists that Moses acts in violation of Torah when he appoints his brother, Aaron, as high priest. Given such interest in the power struggle between Korah and Moses, it is remarkable that Pseudo-Philo has omitted this aspect of the story from his narrative. In Pseudo-Philo no explicit confrontation between Korah and Moses exists; chapter 16 plays down the direct opposition between Moses and Korah in favor of an emphasis on conflict between Korah and God.

In the *Biblical Antiquities,* when Korah protests against God's Law, it is God, not Moses, who responds immediately with an angry speech (16:2–3). God's speech in LAB 16:2–3 has no direct analogue in Numbers 16. In having God react directly to Korah's action, Pseudo-Philo follows his usual procedure of increasing God's role. God's speech begins with another device character-

86. Only Pseudo-Philo has the number two hundred, but the work is unreliable with respect to numbers. The MT, LXX, and Josephus have two hundred fifty.

87. For example, *Num. Rab.* 16:3; *b. Sanh.* 110a. See *Tg. Yer. I* Num. 16:2.

88. See Bauckham, "Liber," 38, 69, n. 17. Bauckham refers to Wadsworth ("Making," 10–16) for a discussion of this interpretive principle.

89. Sanders *(Jesus,* 247) considers it a principle accepted by all Jews of the first century that "the law is unitary—it was all given by God to Israel, and all parts are thus equally binding."

90. *M. 'Abot* 5:17; *'Abot R. Nat.* 46; *b. Sanh.* 110a.

91. See *b. Sahh.* 110b; *b. B. Bat.* 74a; *Num. Rab.* 16:20.

92. *Num. Rab.* 16:3; *b. Sanh.* 110a.

93. *Ant.* 4.2.1–3.4 §§ 11–58; *b. Sanh.* 110a; *Num. Rab.* 16:20.

94. See *b. Sanh.* 110a; *Tg. Yer. I* Num. 16:19; *Num. Rab.* 16:15.

istic of Pseudo-Philo—reference to the past. God recalls the creation of humanity and the subsequent murder of Abel. God says that the earth swallowed up the blood of Abel and that God then said to the earth, "You will swallow up blood no more."[95]

Pseudo-Philo draws together the stories of Cain and Abel and of Korah through the idea of swallowing.[96] The word occurs in Num. 16:30, 32, 34 *(bl')*, but not in Gen. 4:1–16. But in later Jewish tradition, the idea that Abel's blood cried out to God from the ground (Gen. 4:10) is embellished with the ground having swallowed the blood.[97] After recalling Abel's murder, God continues, "And now the thoughts of men are very corrupt; behold I command the earth, and it will swallow up body and soul together" (16:3). This comment about human thoughts recalls that in chapter 15 when the Israelites forgot the Law, their minds were weakened. To depart from God's way of reasoning is to lose the power to reason properly and leads to disaster. Pseudo-Philo makes a sweeping generalization on the basis of Korah's sin. God does not see the problem as confined to Korah and his followers—it extends to the whole human race. This pessimistic view of humanity is characteristic of the work.

Korah and his people are condemned to dwell in darkness and destruction. Their punishment is unusual; they do not die but "melt away" until the Judgment. At that time, when the rest of humankind is raised, they will die unremembered.[98] Hell will not "spit them back." They share this fate only with the Egyptians and those who perished in the Flood. Meanwhile, the earth will swallow them up. Pseudo-Philo sees this event as vitally important because as an early revolt against Mosaic authority it is the paradigm for all subsequent rejections of Torah.[99]

Pseudo-Philo uses Korah to elucidate true leadership by portraying its opposite. A true leader in Israel is completely devoted to God's will, acts only at God's behest, and is willing to die for Torah. Korah opposes God's will, follows his own impulses, and is willing to die to resist Torah's claim on him.

Numbers 16 is rewritten as a trial scene by using four elements from trial scenes in 2 Maccabees 6, 7. The following is the structure of LAB 16:4–6.[100]

a. Moses tells the people (and Korah) of the punishment that awaits Korah and his men if they persist.

b. Korah and his men remain defiant.

c. Korah summons his seven sons.

95. The Latin actually says that God spoke to Zion, but that reading is probably based on a misreading of the original Hebrew *ṣywn* "parched earth" (*OTP*, 324, n. d).

96. Jude 11 brings together Cain's sin, Balaam's error, and Korah's rebellion. LAB 16 connects Korah's rebellion to Cain's sin, and LAB 18 deals with Balaam.

97. *Tg. Yer. I* Gen. 4:10. In *b. Sanh.* 37b, R. Judah says that after the death of Abel the earth did not open its mouth again (SC 230, 122).

98. The rabbis preserved the tradition that Korah and his fellows would not rise *(m. Sanh.* 10:3; *'Abot R. Nat.* 36:2; *b. Sanh.* 109b; *y. Sanh.* 10:4).

99. The revolt of Miriam and Aaron had already occurred in Numbers 12, but the author did not want to make them prototypes of those who oppose Torah.

100. Murphy, "Korah's Rebellion," 116.

   d. The sons refuse to join Korah. They answer that Korah has not begotten
     them, but God has formed them. If they walk in God's ways, they will
     be God's sons.
   e. The earth is opened before Korah and his men.
   f. The sons accuse him of madness in his day of destruction.
   g. Korah refuses to listen to his sons' appeal.
   h. The earth opens its mouth, swallows the rebels and their households,
     and Korah and the others cry out until the earth closes again.

Pseudo-Philo enhances the trial elements of Numbers 16.[101] Those on trial
stand before a person of authority, the punishment that will come upon them
if they refuse to recant is announced, they remain steadfast despite the efforts
of some to persuade them, and the sentence is carried out. The idea that the
punishment is announced to Korah and that he persists in spite of awareness
of it is absent from Numbers 16. It is precisely this idea that leads to 2 Maccabees 6 and 7 for parallels to LAB 16, since it is present in all three chapters.
Eleazar's martyrdom in 2 Maccabees 6 and that of the mother and her seven
sons in chapter 7 of the same book are examples of those who prefer to
undergo martyrdom rather than violate Torah.[102] In contrast, Korah refuses
to obey Torah and dies for his steadfastness in this resolve.

    LAB 16 and 2 Maccabees 6, 7, all contain the following elements: standing
before a figure of authority; announcement of punishment; refusal to recant;
and punishment. This abbreviates the full trial scene as found in Daniel 3 and
LAB 6. In addition to this basic fourfold pattern, LAB 16 shares the following
elements with 2 Maccabees 6: Eleazar's friends and Korah's sons try to dissuade them from standing fast; both Eleazar and Korah are accused of madness; each refuses to listen to those trying to persuade them; each utters a cry
before death.

    There are numerous parallels between LAB 16 and 2 Maccabees 7. Both
the mother and Korah have seven sons. Furthermore, the mother's words find
echoes in the words of Korah's sons. The mother encourages her sons as follows: "It was not I who gave you life and breath, nor I who set in order the
elements within each one of you. Therefore the Creator of the world, who
shaped the beginning of humankind and devised the origin of all things, will
in his mercy give life and breath back to you again, since you now forget
yourselves for the sake of his laws" (2 Macc. 7:22b–23).

    Antiochus promises the youngest son "with oaths that he would make him
rich and enviable if he would turn from the ways of his ancestors *[patriōn]*"
(7:24b). In LAB 16:5, Korah's sons say, "Our father has not begotten us, but
the Most Powerful has formed us. And now if we walk in his ways, we will be
his sons. But if you are unbelieving, go your own way."[103] In 2 Maccabees the

    101. In later Jewish tradition, the scene of Numbers 16 is considered a formal trial scene
(*Mo'ed. Qat.* 16a; *Tg. Yer. I* Num. 16:12).

    102. See Doran, "Martyr." The story of Taxo and his seven sons in *Testament of Moses* 9
combines the two stories in 2 Maccabees.

    103. Perrot (SC 230, 44, 123) suggests that Pseudo-Philo can be seen as an extended medi-
tation on the two ways of Deut. 30:15–20.

mother says that it was not she who gave her sons life, but God. In Pseudo-Philo, the sons say Korah is not their father; God is. In 2 Maccabees, following the ways of the fathers means following Torah. In Pseudo-Philo, the sons see following their father's ways as abandonment of Torah. One last echo of 1 Maccabees 7 in LAB 16 is the interest in resurrection. The mother's sons go to their deaths in the hope of receiving resurrection as a reward. They warn Antiochus that he will not see resurrection (7:14). According to LAB 16:3, Korah is one of the few who will not participate in the Resurrection. Pseudo-Philo has subtly and creatively used the trial scenes of 2 Maccabees 6 and 7 to strengthen Korah's function as foil.

In both Numbers 16 and LAB 16, Korah and his followers are separated from Israel. In the biblical account they are separated so that the people will not be destroyed when Korah perishes. In LAB 16:7, after Korah and company are swallowed up, the people say they cannot stay in that place. Moses responds, *"Take up your tents from round about them; do not be joined [nec coniungamini] in their sins."* The words are reminiscent of those of Abraham and the other resisters concerning the tower of Babel: "Nor are we joining *[nec coniungimur]* in your scheme" (6:4). Separation means refusal to participate in Korah's ways.

Like the good leaders, Korah is portrayed in relation to other individuals and groups.[104] Like them, he plays his role before a public assembly. As with the other leaders, Korah's importance lies in his attitude toward God's covenant. Whereas the good leaders "enact their leadership in actions that implement God's purposes and set good public examples,"[105] Korah opposes God's purposes and sets a bad example, a lead followed by the two hundred. Finally, the good leaders put themselves in mortal danger on behalf of Torah. Korah puts himself in mortal danger by rebelling against God over a specific rule of Torah.

The role of Korah's sons in LAB 16 solves a specific biblical puzzle. Whereas in Num. 16:32–33 it appears that Korah and his entire family perish, in the books of Chronicles and in the Psalms they appear as a group of singers.[106] A biblical solution to the problem is the claim in Num. 26:11 that the sons of Korah did not die, and later Jewish tradition asserts that they repented of their sin. The *Biblical Antiquities* solves the problem by having the sons oppose their father's sin from the beginning.

Chapter 17: Aaron's Rod

A few brief comments will suffice for this short chapter. One effect of Pseudo-Philo's rewriting of Numbers 16 was the exclusion of the direct power struggle

---

104. This paragraph analyzes Korah according to the profile of a good leader developed by Nickelsburg ("Leaders," 60–61). He does not analyze Korah as a leader.

105. Nickelsburg, "Leaders," 61.

106. See 2 Chron. 20:19; Pss. 42; 44–49; 84–85; 87–88. In 1 Chron. 9:19; 26:1, 19, they are gatekeepers, and they appear as bakers of sacrificial cakes in 1 Chron 9:31.

between Moses and Korah. LAB 17 rewrites Numbers 17, where Aaron is appointed high priest in the context of a power struggle in Israel. The power struggle is omitted from Pseudo-Philo's version. The choice of the high priestly family happens calmly and without opposition. Emphasis is on God's initiative. The high priestly family is "revealed," implying that it was a decision made by God long before. Finally, this passage provides another example of Pseudo-Philo's comparing an event in the narrative's present to one in the past. In this case, the choice of Aaron through almond rods is like Jacob's use of almond rods to produce certain kinds of sheep (Gen. 30:37–39).[107] The analogy reinforces the idea that at this solemn moment in Israel's history God exercises complete control. Pseudo-Philo includes Aaron's election because he sees it as a key event in Israel's history.[108]

Chapter 18: Balaam

This chapter is a showpiece for Pseudo-Philo's ideological point of view expressed through the characters' words. Most of the chapter consists of direct address, either in dialogue or soliloquy. Numbers 21, the conquest of Sihon and Og, is summarized in LAB 18:1. In Num. 22:5–6, Balak, king of Moab, tries to get Balaam to come and curse Israel. He stresses Israel's power and Balaam's ability to utter effective curses. In the biblical version Balaam tells Balak's emissaries to stay the night and let him consult God (Num. 22:8). Later in the chapter, he tells them he can do nothing of which God disapproves (22:18).

Pseudo-Philo improves the biblical picture of Balaam.[109] He enhances Balaam's strength by adding that Balak's father Zippor had previously availed himself of Balaam's services, which were effective against the Amorites. Then Balaam speaks to the messengers: "Behold this has given pleasure to Balak, but he does not know that the plan of God is not like the plan of man. Now he does not realize that the spirit that is given to us is given for a time. But our ways are not straight unless God wishes it. And now *wait here,* and I will see *what the Lord may say to me this night*" (18:3). This short speech goes beyond Num. 22:18: "I could not go beyond the command of the LORD my God, to do less or more." It enunciates a basic principle of Pseudo-Philo, that divine plans are not like human plans. Only after uttering this didactic speech

---

107. The connection is also made in *Midr. Tanḥuma* 3.66–67 (Ginzberg, *Legends,* Vol. 6, 106, n. 600).

108. This argues against the view that the author opposed the cult.

109. Vermes (*Scripture,* 174) points out that Pseudo-Philo's story of Balaam is much more favorable than the biblical version or any other segment of Jewish tradition. Feldman ("Prolegomenon," c) qualifies that judgment, finding the biblical passages upon which Pseudo-Philo depends less negative than Vermes and pointing out other positive aspects of Balaam present in Jewish tradition. Perrot (SC 230, 124–25) is correct in claiming that Balaam's picture is favorable at the beginning of chapter 18 and deteriorates as the chapter proceeds.

does Balaam tell the messengers to stay and that he will consult God, as he does in Num. 22:8.

The next section deals with a problem created by Num. 22:9. There God asks Balaam who the men are who have come to him, implying that God does not know. In the *Biblical Antiquities,* Balaam's response solves the problem: "Why, LORD, do you try the human race? They cannot endure it, because you know well what is to happen in the world, even before you founded it. And now enlighten your servant if it be right to go forth with them" (18:4). Balaam proclaims God's omniscience and creation of the world. He takes God's question as a test and uses it to confess God's attributes. Balaam's characterization of the human race here as incapable of withstanding God's testing is borne out by the entire book. Balaam refers to himself as God's servant here. If the readers were to accept that as a reliable judgment, Balaam would fall among a very select group in the *Biblical Antiquities*—Abraham (6:11), Moses (20:2), the resisters to Jair's idolatry (38:4), and the "fathers" (15:5). As the narrative progresses, the readers learn that Balaam does not really deserve the title, but his answer to God in 18:4 is a marked improvement over the one depicted in the Bible.[110]

Balaam asks God whether he should go with Balak's men, presumably to curse Israel. God responds with a strong statement of commitment to Israel, ending with the warning that if Balaam curses Israel then no one will bless Balaam (18:5–6). The statement begins and ends with rhetorical questions that underline the absurdity of Balaam's own question. If what God says about Israel is true, how could Balaam even ask whether he should curse it?

God first recalls the promise of numerous progeny to Abraham. The promise occurs several times in Genesis; Pseudo-Philo quotes it from Gen. 22:17.[111] This is yet another example of God quoting the divine words, this time to remind Balaam of God's special relationship with Israel. God goes on to join the promise of a numerous progeny to the tradition that God lifted Abraham above the firmament and showed him the universe.[112]

God reminds Balaam of the sacrifice of Isaac, the Aqedah.[113] God says that God demanded Isaac "as a holocaust." Because Abraham did not refuse, God found his sacrifice acceptable.[114] Although Pseudo-Philo is aware that Isaac was not actually sacrificed, God declares that Israel was chosen because of Isaac's blood.[115] The *Biblical Antiquities* refers to the Aqedah three times, all

110. Feldman ("Prolegomenon," ci) notes, "LAB has Balaam give the reply which, according to Bamidbar Rabbah, 20.6, he *ought* to have given."

111. Gen. 12:2; 13:16; 15:5; 16:10; 17:2, 4–6, 16, 20; 18:18; 21:12; 22:17; etc.

112. That tradition was developed into a complete literary piece in the *Apocalypse of Abraham.* It also appears in the *Testament of Abraham* 10 and *2 Bar.* 4:4, all dated to the first or early second century C.E., so all are roughly contemporary with the *Biblical Antiquities.* See SC 230, 125.

113. For treatments of the Aqedah, see Daly, "Soteriological;" Davies and Chilton, "Aqedah;" and Feldman, "Josephus;" Vermes, *Scripture,* 193–227; SC 230, 125–26.

114. Harrington *(OTP,* 325, n. f) points to the similarity between this treatment of the Aqedah to that of Josephus *(Ant.* 1.13.2–4 §§ 225–36) and *Tg. Jon.* of Gen 22:1.

115. The same idea is present in rabbinic literature *(b. Yoma* 5a and *Mek. d'R. Shimon.* 4; *OTP,* 325, n. g).

at key points in the narrative (18:5; 32:2–4; 40:2). In chapter 18, Israel experiences the first external threat to its existence since the Sinai covenant. Now
Balak tries to enlist Balaam's power against Israel, but the Aqedah caused
God to choose Israel, thus establishing a bond with Israel that means ruin for
anyone who opposes it. As usual, Pseudo-Philo locates the basis for God's
present protection of Israel in the past: It is due to God's relationship with
the fathers.

God reveals to Balaam that God spoke to the "angels who work secretly."
This is one of the many times in the book that readers get "inside information." This case is unusual in that Balaam, not one of the good leaders, gets
the same information. God discloses words spoken privately to the angels.
This sentence is an instance of nested quotations in Pseudo-Philo, a phenom-
enon that attests to the author's interest in direct quotation. In this case, the
passage works in the following way. God says to Balaam, "Then I said to the
angels who work secretly, 'Did I not say concerning this, "*I will reveal everything I am doing to Abraham* and to Jacob his son, the third one whom I called
firstborn, who, when *he was wrestling in the dust* with the angel who was in
charge of hymns, *would not let him go* until *he blessed him*" ' " (18:5–6). The
sentence unites elements from Gen. 18:17, where God decides to reveal to
Abraham the actions to be taken with respect to Sodom, with Gen. 32:24–27,
where Jacob wrestles with the angel. Words from Genesis 18 that originally
referred to Sodom are now applied to Israel's election. Here it is his election
that God discloses to Abraham. Furthermore, God's decision to reveal the
election is extended to Jacob through an interpretation of the blessing contained in Gen. 32:29 as being the same blessing (election) revealed to Abraham.[116]

God's final words to Balaam are a rhetorical question concerning Balaam's
proposal to curse Israel, and an implicit warning that Balaam will not be
blessed if he does so. This is an application of God's words (not quoted here)
spoken to Abraham the very first time the promise to Abraham appeared in
the Bible: "I will bless those who bless you, and the one who curses you I will
curse" (Gen. 12:3).

As in the Bible, Balaam refuses to go with Balak's men after he talks with
God. When Balak's messengers return to him with this news, Balak engages
in typically erroneous human reasoning. He supposes God will not help him
because of his sins, and he thinks that holocausts gain reconciliation with God's
favor. He tells Balaam to offer as many holocausts as necessary to win God
over. Balak says that if the sacrifices are successful, then both God and Balaam
will profit. God will get sacrifices, and Balaam will get a reward from Balak.
The biblical version of the story contains only Balak's offer of reward to
Balaam. Pseudo-Philo adds the element of bribing God, which illustrates the
truth enunciated by Balaam in 18:3: "The plan of God is not like the plan of
man."

---

116. The specification of the angel with whom Jacob wrestled as the angel in charge of hymns
is an example of the author's angelology. Such identifications are not pursued.

Balaam first responds to the second group of messengers with the puzzling words "Behold the son of Zippor is looking around and does not recognize that he dwells among the dead" (18:8). Harrington interprets this to mean that Balak's idols are dead, though he does not realize it.[117] Perrot suggests that Balak is like a soothsayer unable to predict his own fate, which does not bring him success but assigns him to the realm of the dead.[118] Whatever the precise meaning of the sentence, Balak lacks knowledge of God's ways. He is trapped in human, "practical" ways of reasoning.

In Num. 22:20, God tells Balaam to go with Balak's men. Pseudo-Philo adds God's prediction that Balak will go to ruin and Balaam's way will be a "stumbling block." This added prediction emphasizes God's control of events and foreknowledge. It is not clear to whom Balaam's way is a stumbling block, but the rest of the chapter concentrates not on Balak's fate but on Balaam's. The rest of LAB 18:8–9 condenses into a very small space the narrative of Num. 22:21–35. Balaam's anger at his donkey is omitted. Only the elements of the donkey's recognition of the angel, Balaam's subsequent recognition of the angel, and the angel's opening Balaam's eyes are kept. The section ends with the angel's words, "Hurry and be gone, because whatever you say will come to pass for him." Recognition scenes are important in the *Biblical Antiquities,* so it is natural that this one would be preserved. The thrust of the passage is again God's control of the action. All of Balaam's words—words that come from God—will come to fulfillment.

In the next sentences, Pseudo-Philo alters the order of the biblical account. In Numbers, God tells Balaam to go to Balak but then is angry that he does so (Num. 22:20–21). In the *Biblical Antiquities,* God is not angry that Balaam goes to Balak, for God had told him to do so. In the Bible when Balaam comes to Balak, they converse about Balaam's reluctance. Then Balak performs sacrifices and sends them to Balaam and those with him. On the next day, they go to where they can see Israel and Balaam performs sacrifices, saying that perhaps God will give him a message. Pseudo-Philo lessens the impression that Balaam is already cooperating fully with Balak and instead focuses on Balaam's understanding that the mission to destroy Israel is doomed from the start. Balaam arrives in Moab and immediately performs his own sacrifice before having any contact with Balak. Then he sees Israel, again without Balak's company.[119] In the Bible, Balaam does not deliver his first discourse until he has a conversation with God, after having observed Israel. In the *Biblical Antiquities,* Balaam utters his words spontaneously upon seeing Israel's encampment. Balaam says,

> "Behold *Balak brought me* to *the mountain, saying, 'Come,* run into the fire of those men.' What fire the waters will not extinguish, I cannot resist; but the fire that consumes water, who will resist that?" And he said to him, "It is easier to take away the foundations and the topmost part of the earth and

117. *OTP*, 325, n. k.
118. SC 230, 126.
119. See Feldman ("Prolegomenon," cii) for variations on who performed sacrifices.

to extinguish the light of the sun and to darken the light of the moon than for anyone to uproot the planting of the Most Powerful or to destroy his vine" (18:10).

Harrington suggests that "run into the fire" is the result of a pun depending on the Hebrew words *'wr*, "fire," and *'rh*, "curse."[120] The pun would imply that Balaam's cursing of Israel results in his own destruction. The pun leads into a metaphorical expression of God's invincible power. A fire more potent than any known on earth cannot be opposed by Balaam. He goes on to say that the very existence of the universe is less secure than the existence of Israel. This is another example of Pseudo-Philo's belief in Israel's indestructibility. The belief is all the more compelling in that Balaam spoke his words spontaneously at the very sight of Israel. God's title here is *Fortissimus*. For those with eyes to see what is happening (and Balaam's eyes have just been opened by the angel), the contrast between God's power and that of Balaam or Balak is striking. Balaam's words are interrupted by an editorial comment, "And he did not know that his consciousness was expanded so as to hasten his own destruction" (18:10). This is another instance of the ironic mode at work. God puts words into Balaam's mouth of which Balaam is not conscious. The readers know more than Balaam.

"And when *he saw part of the people, the spirit of God* did not abide *in him*" (18:10). Perrot draws attention to 18:11, where Balaam says, "There is little left of the holy spirit that abides in me." This implies that as he proceeds with his task, the Holy Spirit slowly leaves him. That the Holy Spirit leaves Balaam when he views the people means that the Spirit cannot dwell in anyone who looks at Israel with evil intent. Nonetheless, Balaam's words following the editorial comment are indeed inspired by the Spirit, as is implied by the narrator's aside that Balaam uttered them with an "expanded consciousness" of which he was unaware.[121]

LAB 18:11 resumes the speech of Balaam that was interrupted by the editorial comment at the end of 18:10. The section is replete with features typical of Pseudo-Philo. Its theme is God's commitment to Israel. Israel is the "heritage" of God, whose title *Fortissimus* is used here for the second time in the chapter. Then a dire fate is predicted for Balak because of his attempt to bribe God, and his fate is compared to that of Pharaoh, who dared try enslaving Israel. Next, Israel is called a "desirable" vine, an appellation used in 18:10 in connection with Israel's indestructibility; it also recalls Moses' successful intercession on behalf of Israel, God's vine, in 12:8–9. Opposition to Israel is due to "jealousy" of its desirability. The next sentence encapsulates a major theme of the *Biblical Antiquities:* "But if anyone says to himself that the Most Powerful has labored in vain or has chosen them to no purpose, behold now I see the salvation and liberation that will come upon them." The very thought that God is not entirely committed to Israel is blameworthy and

---

120. *OTP*, 326, n. p.
121. Balaam's prophecies lack any messianic overtones (SC 230, 127).

false. Again God's strength is highlighted by the title *Fortissimus.* That God's work is never "in vain" is a refrain of the *Biblical Antiquities.* Finally, one of God's most characteristic activities in the book is effecting Israel's liberation.

Balaam says that his eyes, opened by the angel earlier, are dimming because the Holy Spirit is leaving him. He then says, "For I know that, because I have been persuaded by Balak, I have lessened the time of my life" (18:11). This is somewhat enigmatic, since until now Balaam has seemed careful not to transgress God's wishes. However, the idea that God gave Balaam permission to go to Balak but that somehow Balaam was still blamed for it is present in the biblical text as well. Perhaps because of Pseudo-Philo's interest in moral causality he must find something of which Balaam is clearly guilty, and so at the end of this chapter Balaam is said to have advised Balak to arrange for the temptation that resulted in Israel's seduction by Moabite women. The attribution of the sin described in Num. 25:1–3 to the counsel of Balaam is found elsewhere in Jewish tradition.[122]

LAB 18:12 continues Balaam's prophecy and repeats the pattern of 18:11: Israel's exalted station is noted, the evil fate awaiting Israel's opponents is referred to, and Balaam's own dismal future is predicted. Israel's light is said to be brighter than lightning, and its course swifter than an arrow. Moab's "plots" against Israel will be punished. Finally, Balaam correctly predicts that his prophecy will be public, long-lived, and "remembered" by the "wise and understanding," who will comprehend Balaam's words that end this prophecy, "When I cursed, I perished, but though I blessed, I was not blessed." This alludes to Gen. 12:3, where God tells Abraham that those who bless him will be blessed and those who curse him will be cursed. The same biblical verse was alluded to in LAB 18:6, discussed above. Although Balaam had wonderful and true things to say about Israel, so that he in effect blessed it, his negative activity toward Israel wiped out the blessing. As a result, Balaam ends up with a curse. Balak comments that God "has cheated" Balaam of the reward that Balak was prepared to give him (Num. 24:11).

As mentioned above, LAB 18:13–14 claims that Balaam and Balak plotted the seduction of Israel by the Moabite women. Balaam states a truth consistently applied in the *Biblical Antiquities*—Israel cannot be conquered unless it sins. It is remarkable that there is no mention of the punishment of Israel in this passage, as there is in Numbers 25. This is one of the few instances in the *Biblical Antiquities* where there is no clear punishment for a sin.

Chapter 19: Moses' Farewell, Prayer, and Death

This chapter concludes the Moses cycle. Although it uses biblical materials, it is mostly an original creation filled with elements characteristic of Pseudo-Philo. It has six parts:

122. See Josephus *(Ant.* 4.6.6 § 126–30); see SC 230, 128, for Targumic references.

    a. Moses' testamentary speech to the people (19:1–5)
    b. God's prediction of the future to Moses (19:6–7)
    c. Moses' prayer on Mount Abarim (19:8–9)
    d. God's revelations to Moses (19:10–13)
    e. A further divine revelation to Moses (19:14–15)
    f. Moses' death and burial (19:16)

In Numbers 31:2, God tells Moses, "Avenge the Israelites on the Midianites; afterward you shall be gathered to your people." LAB 19:1 generalizes the enemies whom Moses attacks, making them "the nations." Moses gives half of the spoils to the people, as in Num. 31:27. LAB 19:1 thus attributes to Moses military victories that benefit Israel.

The Book of Deuteronomy is summarized with the brief sentence, "He began declaring to them the words of the Law that God had spoken to them on Horeb" (19:1). In LAB 19:2, the text shifts to direct address, quoting the words of Moses to the people. Moses' first words, "Behold I am to sleep with my fathers and will go to my people," establish a testamentary framework.[123] In Deut. 29:19–30:5, Moses predicts the exile of those who do not enter the covenant with a pure heart. Then he says, "When all these things have happened to you, the blessings and the curses that I have set before you, if you call them to mind among all the nations where the LORD your God has driven you, and return to the LORD your God, . . . then the LORD your God will restore your fortunes . . ." (Deut. 30:1–3). The restoration of Israel will depend upon their repentance. In LAB 19:2 the case is different. Moses foretells the punishment of unfaithful Israel, but it is not by exile: "God will be angry at you and abandon you and depart from your land. And he will bring upon you those who hate you, and they will rule over you." It is God, not the people, who departs from the land.[124] Restoration depends upon repentance in Deut. 30:1–2, but not in LAB 19. Moses says that foreign domination will not last forever, "because he will remember the covenant that he established with your fathers" (LAB 19:2). God's commitment to Israel depends not upon Israel's repentance but upon God's original compact with Israel's ancestors.

The next section of Moses' speech connects Israel's oppression under foreigners in its own land and its longing for a leader like Moses. When the people find themselves punished in their land, they will mourn Moses' death and say, "Who will give us another shepherd like Moses or such a judge for the sons of Israel to pray always for our sins and to be heard for our iniquities?" (19:3).[125] It is noteworthy that the leader desired is neither royal nor military but is called a "judge" and an intercessor. To be sure, the judges frequently performed a military role and the word "shepherd" can be used to refer to

---

123. Harrington points out other testaments of Moses in Deuteronomy 31–34, *Jubilees* 1, *Testament of Moses* (also called *Assumption of Moses*), and Josephus's *Ant.* 4.7.44–48 §§ 302–26 (*OTP,* 326, n. a.).

124. In Ezekiel 9–11, God is depicted as departing from the temple, and in Ezekiel 43 and Isaiah 40 God returns to Jerusalem after having been absent from it.

125. Harrington (*OTP,* 327, n. c) refers to a similar depiction of Moses in *T. Moses* 11:11, 17, and 12:3, and of Jeremiah in 2 Macc. 15:14 and *2 Bar.* 2:2.

kingly figures, but Pseudo-Philo chooses intercessory prayer for sinful Israel as the most important characteristic in a leader.

LAB 19:4 alludes to Deut. 4:26 (32:1), where Moses calls heaven and earth to witness the covenant. The role of heaven and earth as witnesses is emphasized with the following: "For heaven will hear this, and earth will know it with its ears." In LAB 24:1, Joshua recalls Moses' words about heaven and earth, and in 32:9 Deborah alludes to them. Pseudo-Philo goes beyond Deuteronomy in its sweeping protology and eschatology. The entire universe, past, present, and future, is attuned to the relationship between Israel and God. Moses invokes eschatology with his next words: "God has revealed the end of the world so that he might establish his statutes with you and kindle among you an eternal light" (19:4). Knowledge of the eschaton makes possible the establishment of the statutes. When humans know the Judgment to take place at the end of the world, they might follow God's will. The reference to Torah as light is familiar in the *Biblical Antiquities.*

Moses says that when the people sin and are being punished, they will recollect their own words to Moses: "*All that God has said to us, we will do and hear.* But if we transgress or grow corrupt in our ways, you will recall this as a witness against us, and he will cut us off." The words in italics quote Deut. 5:27. Pseudo-Philo considerably elaborates the people's statement from Deuteronomy. The elaboration underlines the people's responsibility for their own misfortunes—they are condemned by their own words. Pseudo-Philo uses the usual technique of having Moses quote the people to prove his case.

Moses' testament ends in LAB 19:5 with his reference to manna, Moses' blessing of the people, and an insistence that the people acknowledge his work on their behalf during his life. Blessing is a typical feature of testaments and occurs in Deuteronomy 33. The demand for a testimony to good service by Moses recalls the same demand made by Samuel before his death (1 Sam. 12:1–5) and draws attention to another parallel between LAB 19:1–5 and 1 Samuel 12. Both passages stress the role of the intercessor. As Samuel says, "Far be it from me that I should sin against the LORD by ceasing to pray for you" (1 Sam. 12:23).

In LAB 19:6–7, God tells Moses that he is about to die. Moses has already told the people this in 19:2. LAB 19:6 follows Deut. 31:16, where God informs Moses of his impending death before predicting the people's sin. The people will forget God's Law, which is again characterized as enlightening. God says that they will be abandoned "for a time," thus setting a limit on the divine anger in advance.[126] God's next words are based on Deut. 32:49–52; 34:1–4. God says that Moses will see the land but not enter it. The reason for Moses not entering the land is unique to the work: "Lest you see the graven images with which this people will start to be deceived and led off the path" (19:7). Deut. 31:16 specifies idolatry as the sin that will be committed when they enter the land but does not say that the people's future sin prevents Moses from entering. Pseudo-Philo is particularly interested in idolatry.

126. See *2 Bar.* 4:1, 5:3, for a similar limitation.

In 19:7 God predicts that the temple is to be turned over to Israel's enemies and destroyed. God draws a parallel between that disaster and the breaking of the tablets on Sinai, another instance of connecting two events in salvation history.[127]

LAB 19:8–9 is Moses' last intercessory prayer, delivered on Mount Abarim. He invokes God's mercy (twice), pity, and long-suffering, and twice refers to Israel as God's "heritage." Moses looks to the past, recalling God's calling him, Moses' bringing the people to God on Horeb, the liberation from Egypt and the slaying of the Egyptians in the water, and the giving of the Torah. The formulation of the giving of the Law is intriguing: "You gave them the Law and statutes in which they might live and enter as sons of men" (19:9). The next sentence says, "*For who is the man who has not sinned against you?*" This leads Moses to a plea to God not to hold Israel's failings against it. Perrot offers the following interpretation: "*Il s'agit apparemment ici de l'entrée dans le pays de la promesse, signe de l'entrée dans la vie, alors que les hommes sont faibles et pécheurs.*"[128] This interpretation does justice to the flow of thought in the passage. Israel lives under the Law as human beings, but human beings are always sinful. The next step in the syllogism would be that therefore Israel will also be sinful.

Moses' characterization of the human race as universally sinful grounds his final intercession with God on behalf of Israel: "*For who is the man who has not sinned against you?* And unless your patience abides, how would your heritage be established, if you were not merciful to them? Or who will yet be born without sin? Now you will correct them for a time, but not in anger" (19:29). The argument recalls 4 Ezra 3, where Ezra says God did not remove the evil heart from the humans and so all are sinful (see also *2 Bar.* 84:11). Pseudo-Philo shares this pessimistic view of humans. Israel's very existence depends upon God's mercy, since Israel, being human, will inevitably transgress. Moses acknowledges that God must "correct" Israel but prays that God do so without anger. God's direct answer to that prayer appears a bit later in the passage: "When they sin, I will be angry with them but I will recall your staff and spare them in accord with my mercy" (19:11). Anger is God's legitimate response to Israel's sin, but it will be followed inevitably by divine mercy. God's mercy depends on remembrance of Moses' staff, symbol of the covenant. Once again the maintenance of God's relationship with Israel depends not upon Israel's repentance but on God's past commitments.

Next comes a section in which God shows Moses certain things and then speaks to him at length (see Deut. 34:1–3).[129] God's revelation is made cosmic by the addition of "the place from which the clouds draw up water to water the whole earth, and the place from which the river takes its water," as well

127. See SC 230, 131, for the complex traditions surrounding these events and for a discussion of the figure of 740 years.

128. SC 230, 131. Perrot also advances an argument for seeing "sons of men" as a reference to humanity before the Fall, but his argument, though fascinating, is not compelling.

129. Stone (*Fourth Ezra*, 25) says this is an example of a list of revealed things. See *2 Bar.* 59:5–11; 4 Ezra 4:5–8; 5:36–37; etc. See Stone, "Lists."

as "the place in the firmament from which only the holy land drinks. And he showed him the place from which the manna rained upon the people, even unto the paths of paradise" (19:10). Pseudo-Philo puts the story of Israel into a cosmic framework both spatially and temporally.

In 19:10, the holy land is central. There is progression in the revelation of sources of water, from the place from which the whole world is watered to the place from which "the river" (the Euphrates or perhaps the Jordan) originates. Finally, Moses sees the place "in the firmament," a superterrestrial source, from which the holy land itself is watered.[130] Throughout the *Biblical Antiquities,* water and rain are important symbols of God's favor. The uniqueness of the land of Israel in God's plans is proven by the special cosmic source for its watering. The connection between provision of water and the presence of God in Jerusalem was seen in 12:8–9. Here it should be noted that as the holy land gets special treatment from God, so the chosen people should be in that land to get the full benefit from their election. Ironically, it is precisely when they enter the land that their sinfulness is fully exposed, as foretold by God in 19:7 and illustrated by subsequent chapters.

Moses also sees paradise and the source of manna. Adam, and so the entire human race, lost paradise through sin. Now Moses sees paradise, which is apparently also the source of the manna. After an intervening sentence about the cult, God tells Moses, "These are what are prohibited from the human race because they have sinned against me" (19:10). This recalls the earlier revelation to Moses on Sinai: "And the LORD continued to show him the ways of paradise and said to him, 'These are the ways that men have lost by not walking in them, because they have sinned against me'" (13:9). The human condition results from human sinfulness. Israel is a special instance of that general rule. Israel is the nation to which God has offered some of the blessings denied humanity in general, such as the manna from paradise. If God removes these blessings from Israel, it is Israel's own doing and testifies to the near hopelessness of humanity.

Between the revelation of paradise and God's statement that humanity has been deprived of these "ways" because of sin, Moses is shown "the measurements of the sanctuary and the number of sacrifices and the signs by which they are to interpret the heaven" (19:10). The inclusion of the sanctuary, here associated with the ability to "interpret the heaven," in this short list of things revealed to Moses indicates the importance of the cult to Pseudo-Philo.

Chapters 13 and 19 share a complex of elements: sanctuary; cult; a cosmic context; special revelation to Moses including paradise; humanity's loss of the original blessings; reference to God's mercy; prediction of the sinfulness of the people, their punishment, and the restoration of God's favor; association of rains and water with God's favor; and reference to the previous establishment of the covenant. The replication points to the centrality of these elements to the establishment of Israel, its foundation in Sinai, and its cosmic significance.

---

130. Perrot (SC 230, 132) sees this as built on the four rivers of Gen. 2:10–13.

LAB 19:11 reiterates God's dedication to the covenant, here symbolized by Moses' staff. It is an appropriate symbol for the covenant, for Israel's liberation at the Red Sea was accomplished through it (LAB 10:5–6). This passage contains another instance of one event of salvation history being compared to another. Moses' staff is compared to the rainbow, symbol of the covenant between God and Noah (Gen. 9:13, 15; LAB 3:12). Water is a motif that holds together the Noachic covenant, the liberation at the Red Sea, and the Mosaic covenant with its promise of rain and fertility.

In LAB 19:12–13, God again tells Moses of his impending death and foretells his resurrection. The rest of God's words refer to the end of time, when God will "visit the world." Moses and the fathers buried in Egypt will be raised and brought to "the immortal dwelling place that is not subject to time" (19:12). Traditional cosmic images, including the passing away of the present heaven, describe God's visitation. As God approaches, the time is shortened, a feature known from other works.[131] The eschatological scenario ends with Moses and "all who can live" inhabiting the "place of sanctification" that God showed Moses. The precise referent here is uncertain but may be paradise.

LAB 19:14–15 contains one last request by Moses: He desires to know how much time is left before the end. It is frequent in the Bible for characters to request things of their superiors or God with great trepidation, real or conventional. Moses follows this pattern here, but does so in a way typical of Pseudo-Philo. He appeals to God's mercy and says he wishes to avoid God's anger. The tension between divine mercy and anger was seen in Moses' previous prayer and prevails throughout the book. God's answer is cryptic, and the text appears to be corrupt (19:15). Harrington's suggestion, emending *istic mel, apex magnus* to *stigma et apex manus,* is very helpful.[132] The first part of the answer would then read, "An instant, the topmost part of a hand, the fullness of a moment, and the drop of a cup; and time has fulfilled all things." The time is left vague, but is not too far away. The second part of the answer is "For four and a half have passed, and two and a half remain." This appears to leave a fair amount of time before the end, but the unit of measurement is unspecified. Harrington connects this passage with LAB 28:8, where human history is said to last for seven thousand years. If such a connection is to be drawn, then there are twenty-five hundred years from the death of Moses to the eschaton.

LAB 19:16 describes the death and burial of Moses. God's revelation fills him with understanding and his appearance changes, another instance of the importance of human appearance to Pseudo-Philo. In this case it signifies Moses' passage from earthly existence to a higher plane, just as earlier Moses' appearance changed because he was in God's presence (12:1). Moses' glorification is stressed and the magnitude of his passing is expressed through God's burial of him and the angels' mourning. Even the heavenly liturgy is halted,

---

131. Harrington refers to 2 *Bar.* 20:1; 54:1; 83:1, and Mark 13:20 (Matt. 24:22) (*OTP,* 328, n. r). Perrot adds 4 Ezra 4:26, 34; *1 En.* 80:2; and *3 Bar.* 9:7 (SC 230, 133).

132. (*OTP,* 328, n. s). For other suggestions about this difficult passage, see SC 230, 134–35.

an event that never happened before and will never be repeated, according to the narrator.[133] Lightning, torches, and arrows precede Moses in procession. The simple statement "He [God] loved *[amavit]* him[Moses] very much" is striking given the scarcity of the word *amare* in the *Biblical Antiquities.* God buries Moses "with his own hands on a high place and in the light of all the world" (19:16).[134] The phrase "with his own hands" emphasizes Moses' exalted status.[135]

133. Other Jewish traditions claim that the angels' hymn did stop at other times (Ginzberg, *Legends,* Vol. 6, 397, n. 32).

134. "That Moses' death took place in public and that God buried him is also found in Josephus' *Ant.* 4.8.48 § 326 and AsMos 1:15. There may be conscious opposition to the view that Moses did not really die" (*OTP,* 328, n. u). Pseudo-Philo retains the biblical notion that Moses' grave is unknown. See SC 230, 136.

135. See SC 230, 135, for other traditions about who buried Moses.

5

Joshua: *Biblical Antiquities* 20–24

Joshua connects the formative period under Moses with the period of settlement in the land. As in the Bible, the new era of the people's presence in the land is inaugurated with a covenant ceremony. Pseudo-Philo rewrites this to stress the complete fulfillment of all God's promises that possession of the land involves, thus setting the stage for the rest of the book, where Israel repeatedly fails to live up to its side of the covenant.

Chapter 20: Division of the Land

LAB 20:1 introduces the Joshua cycle. Pseudo-Philo says God established a covenant with Joshua, a statement not found in the Bible. He bases his statement on passages such as Deut. 31:23, 34:9, and Josh. 1:1–9, which imply that God established a special relationship with Moses' successor, but Pseudo-Philo makes the idea of covenant explicit.

LAB 20:1 identifies Joshua as one of the spies sent into Canaan who survived. The rest of the verse summarizes the incident in LAB 15, where the people refused to enter the land because of the intimidating report brought back by all the spies except Caleb and Joshua (LAB 15:2–3). Pseudo-Philo says, "The lot went forth upon them that they should not see the land because they had spoken badly about it, and on account of this that generation died" (20:1). Here it is the people's lack of appreciation for the land itself that prevents their entering it rather than their disobedience, as in 15:5–6. There is no mention of lots in connection with this event either in the Bible or in LAB 15, but in LAB 20:1 the "lot went forth" upon the people. Lots emphasize that the people fail to enter the land because of God's decree.

LAB 20:2 begins the career of Joshua with God's direct address to him, as in Joshua 1, but the words are quite different. In the Book of Joshua, God encourages Joshua to be strong and obedient. In the *Biblical Antiquities*, God's words are meant to overcome Joshua's reluctance to succeed Moses that is based on his hope that Moses has not really died. God assures Joshua that Moses is indeed dead. The text may be arguing against a position that Moses

96

never died.[1] God tells Joshua to put on Moses' garments of wisdom and knowledge (based on Deut. 34:9, where Joshua inherits Moses' spirit of wisdom) so that he might become "another man." Finally, in a touch characteristic of the *Biblical Antiquities,* God quotes divine words spoken previously to Moses that prove God always intended to appoint Joshua as Moses' successor. Moses is called God's "servant," an appellation reserved for a very few in the *Biblical Antiquities.* God says that Joshua's leadership will result in the conquest of the Amorites.

In LAB 20:3–4, Joshua puts on Moses' garments of wisdom and understanding and they inflame his mind and move his spirit. He delivers a short speech that is at first directed to the people, but most of which is addressed to their leaders, showing that keeping Israel obedient is primarily a responsibility of its leaders. Joshua tells the people that the previous generation died in the wilderness because of their rebellion against God. His words to the leaders contain the deuteronomistic theology basic to Pseudo-Philo. The covenantal status of the people is alluded to in the use of the possessive pronoun: "*their* God" and "*your* God." Punishment for disobedience is that one's name will perish from the earth. The desire to be remembered is an important motivation for various characters in the *Biblical Antiquities.*[2] Particularly important is Joshua's question about what will happen to the promises to the fathers if the people disobey. At stake is a tension that drives the *Biblical Antiquities* as a whole, the tension between God's promises to the ancestors and the strict deuteronomistic theology that demands punishment for disobedience. Joshua raises the question of the continued existence of Israel if it follows the example of the desert generation and refuses to obey. He asks the question in the context of his affirmation of the reward/punishment scenario found throughout the book.

The rest of Joshua's speech deals with the tension between Israel's disobedience and God's faithfulness to the promises to the ancestors.

> For even if the gentiles say, "Perhaps God has failed, because he has not freed his people"—nevertheless they will recognize that he has not chosen for himself other peoples and done great wonders with them, then they will understand that the Most Powerful does not respect persons; but because you sin through pride, so he took away his power from you and subdued you. And now rise up and set your heart to walk in the ways of your Lord, and he will guide you (20:4).

The Gentiles are right in seeing Israel's liberation as a consequence of the covenant. Throughout the *Biblical Antiquities,* God liberates the people. Israel's servitude raises questions in Gentile minds, but they realize that God has done such wonders for no other nation. Combining these two incontrovertible facts—Israel's slavery and its glorious history—leads the Gentiles to

---

1. See the comment on LAB 19:16 in the previous chapter, this volume, as well as SC 230, 136. Joshua also hesitates to take Moses' place in *T. Moses* 11:9–19; 12:3. For Joshua's mourning, see Ginzberg, *Legends,* vol. 6, 165, n. 957.

2. Micah in LAB 44:3–4 and Saul in 64:1.

the following conclusions: Israel is indeed the chosen people; God is still the Most Powerful; being the chosen people does not exempt Israel from God's punishment when it pridefully disobeys; for Israel, punishment means removal of God's power from them, a power that works on their behalf when they are faithful; the result is Israel's subjection. These conclusions are the more powerful in that even Gentiles can reach them merely by observing certain obvious facts: Israel's history and its present state. Joshua's speech ends with the command to "walk in the ways of your LORD." The reference to the divine ways and the possessive with God's name are typical of Pseudo-Philo. They stress Israel's election and its being distinguished from the nations by the possession of the Torah and consequent knowledge of God's ways. Joshua promises that God will "guide" *(diriget vos)* Israel if it obeys. The word *dirigere* is common in the *Biblical Antiquities* and indicates God's guidance of all history. If Israel submits to divine guidance, it can only be successful and prosperous.

LAB 20:5 is the people's response to Joshua. It reflects the author's concern for leadership and displays Pseudo-Philo's technique of extensive direct address. In Numbers 11, Israel goes out of its camp to meet God at the Tent of Meeting. Two prophets, Eldad and Medad, remain in the camp and prophesy; what they prophesy is not disclosed. Pseudo-Philo supplies the content of the prophecy: "After Moses goes to rest, the leadership of Moses will be given over to Joshua the son of Nun."[3] This is an instance of nested quotations; the narrator quotes the people, who quote the prophets. The point is to prove that Joshua's succession is foreordained by God, as the people knew beforehand. When Moses heard the prophecy, he "was not jealous" (20:5). Leadership is important, not the individual who holds it.

The people continue, "And from then on all the people believed that you would exercise leadership over them *and divide up the land* among them in peace. And now even if there is conflict, *be strong and act manfully,* because you alone are ruler in Israel" (20:5). In 20:2, God reveals that Joshua's leadership will result in the conquest of a foreign enemy. The people focus more on conflicts within Israel. They expect him to divide up the land in peace. Even if there is conflict, presumably in the process of dividing up the land, Joshua is to "be strong and act manfully." That injunction is found on God's lips in Josh. 1:6, 9, in connection with God's command to conquer the land. The people finish by asserting that Joshua alone is ruler in Israel. The concentration on the division of the land, the mention of internal conflict, and the declaration that Joshua alone is ruler all point to a concern with the effects of good leadership on Israel's internal harmony.

Upon receiving the people's acclamation, Joshua decides to send spies into Jericho, as in Joshua 2. To Joshua's commission of the spies, Caleb's sons Kenaz and Seeniamias, Pseudo-Philo adds words based on a speech of Caleb in his old age from Josh. 14:6–12, in which Caleb recalls the earlier failure of Israel to follow God's directions and invade the holy land. Joshua reminds

3. For other references for the content of their prophecy, see Feldman, "Prolegomenon," cvi. The MT has "Medad," but the LXX has "Modad."

them that he, Caleb, and ten other spies went into the land, and that ten of the spies "came back and spoke badly about the land *and discouraged the heart of the people*" (20:6). Only Caleb and Joshua did not join in the disparagement of the land, so they alone are alive in chapter 20. The contrast between obeying the Lord and discouraging the heart of the people comes from Josh. 14:8. Pseudo-Philo transfers Caleb's words to Joshua to keep the focus on him. The transfer also allows Joshua to draw a lesson from the fact that he and Caleb obeyed God and so are alive. He ends with the exhortation, "Imitate your father, and you also will live." Joshua expresses here a principle that inspires the narrative as a whole, since the *Biblical Antiquities* furnishes Israel with models from the past to imitate. In 20:7 the spies carry out their mission. They apparently bring back a positive report, for the people conquer Jericho. Thus Kenaz and Seeniamias do imitate their father Caleb. Focus in the narrative is not on the conquest and its mechanism, as in the Book of Joshua, but on the spies' role and on Joshua's first act of leadership in commissioning them.

An interesting feature of Pseudo-Philo's retelling of Joshua's sending of spies is the degree to which the earlier failure (LAB 15) is attributed to the action of the spies, and the success of the Jericho operation depends on the attitude of the spies. It is up to the spies, who are really public figures in this case and therefore exercise a limited leadership role, to encourage or discourage the people, and on that rests the fate of the operation. Pseudo-Philo sees the people as directionless without leaders. Success or failure depends more on the leaders than on the people themselves.

Pseudo-Philo ties Joshua's leadership and the subsequent history of Israel more securely into the career of Moses in several ways. LAB 20:8 develops Josh. 5:12. In Joshua, it is said that when the people began to eat of the produce of the land of Canaan, the manna ceased. The *Biblical Antiquities* associates the cessation of the manna with Moses' death and says that from that time on, the people began to eat the fruit of the land. In LAB 20 the failed mission of Numbers 14–15 (LAB 15) is recalled twice (20:1, 6). The spies' mission to Jericho undoes the earlier disaster. Pseudo-Philo thus establishes a connection between an event under the leadership of Moses and Joshua's first act as leader. Finally, Moses learned through the prophets Eldad and Modad that Joshua would succeed him, and he approved. The close ties between the careers of Moses and Joshua reinforce the author's presentation of the ideal leadership exercised by both figures.

LAB 20:8 and 10:7 form an inclusion that frames the desert wanderings and Moses' leadership. In 10:7, the narrator summarizes the desert period as that time when God showered manna from heaven on the Israelites, brought them quail from the sea, had a well of water follow them, and led them with the pillars of cloud and fire. In 20:8, the narrator says that God gave the Israelites the well of Marah for Miriam, the pillar of cloud for Aaron, and the manna for Moses.[4] The removal of each gift is associated with the death of

4. See our comments on 10:7.

each figure. The effect is to idealize the past, when under the leadership of Israel's heroes God gave the people gifts.

In LAB 20:9, Joshua divides the land by lot: "Joshua gave the land to the people by lot, to each tribe according to the lots, as it had been commanded him." The repetition of "lot" and the reference to command imply that God really divides the land.

Chapter 20 ends with Caleb's request that his son Kenaz be given land. The scene is from Josh. 14:12–13, where Caleb's speech to Joshua about his exploits as a spy lead up to it. Pseudo-Philo transfers elements of Caleb's speech to Joshua as noted above, but he retains the idea that Caleb requested and got a distribution of land. In the Bible the land is given to Caleb himself, but here Caleb seeks it for his son, Kenaz. Kenaz's introduction as one of the spies sent to Jericho and as Caleb's son to whom land is given foreshadows his important role in the *Biblical Antiquities* and ties the next step of Israel's history to this stage.

Chapter 21: Joshua's Prayer; Ceremony at Gilgal

Chapter 21 is the climax of the first section of the *Biblical Antiquities* because it solemnly declares the fulfillment of all God's promises to Israel. LAB 21:1, based on Josh. 13:1, situates the scene at the end of Joshua's career. It consists of God's words to Joshua. It preserves unexplained the biblical contradiction that Joshua conquered and divided up the entire land and that he neither conquered the whole land nor apportioned it all. The rest of the chapter consists of Joshua's prayer in response to God's words (21:2–6) and a climactic ceremony at Gilgal (21:7–10).

After God tells Joshua that he is old and that there is much land with no one to divide it up by lot, God predicts Israel's unfaithfulness and God's consequent abandonment of them (21:1). God does not quote the divine words but does say that Moses also received a divine prediction of Israel's iniquity and punishment. Seduction by foreign gods is found in God's words to Moses in Deut. 31:16. Pseudo-Philo has God tell Joshua, "After your departure this people will be intermingled with those inhabiting the land, and *they will be seduced after strange gods.*"Intermarriage is frowned upon by Pseudo-Philo and is frequently related to idolatry. "Inhabitants of the land" is biblical usage for non-Israelite nations living in Canaan who pose a threat to Israel's identity as Yahweh worshipers.

God ends by telling Joshua to bear witness to the Israelites before he dies. The notion of witness against the people given in anticipation of their unfaithfulness is common in Deuteronomy. It is less so in Joshua. In Joshua it occurs in connection with the building of the altar across the Jordan (chap. 22) and the setting up of the stone by Joshua (chap. 24). In Deuteronomy, heaven and the earth are witnesses against the people (4:26; 30:19; 31:28), as are the words of Moses' song recited by both Moses and Joshua (31:19; 32:44–46) and the book of the Law (31:26). Pseudo-Philo's retelling of Joshua's story is influ-

enced here by the recital of Moses' song as a witness against Israel in Deuteronomy 31–32, especially since that song warns against idolatry, as do Joshua's words in LAB 21.

Joshua's prayer in response to God can be divided as follows:

1. Praise of God's omniscience (21:2)
2. Request that God give the people a wise heart (21:2)
3. Reason for request in the form of anticipated result (21:2)
4. Recollection of the Achan incident and Joshua's words at that time (21:3)
5. Assertion that the promises do not rest on the fate of any one generation (21:4)
6. Request for a leader (21:4)
7. Quotation of Jacob's prediction of a leader (21:5)
8. Request that God fulfill Jacob's words (21:5)
9. Reason for request in the form of anticipated result (21:5)
10. Addendum concerning Israel's repentance (21:6)

Part 1 stresses God's knowledge of the universe, particularly the sea, the con-
stellations, and the number of stars. God also regulates the rain. Throughout
the *Biblical Antiquities* rain symbolizes God's blessing; divine regulation of
rain implies ability to bestow or withhold blessing.[5] Connected with God's
knowledge of the universe and control of rain is knowledge of "the number
of all generations before they are born." It is common in Judaism of the Second Temple period to associate knowledge of the universe with knowledge of
history. The mention of a number of generations prepares the way for part 5
of Joshua's speech.

Parts 2 and 3 can be taken together, since part 3 is a direct result of part
2. Joshua asks God to give the people a "wise heart and a prudent mind."
The result will be that they will obey God's orders and so avoid divine anger.
The equivalence of wisdom and obedience is routine in Jewish thought, as is
the idea that disobedience angers God. Of note here is that Israel appears
passive. God must give the people a new heart if they are to obey. It is implied
that they now have a foolish heart (LAB 3:9; Gen. 8:21), which characterizes
both Israel and humans in general. Left to themselves, they go wrong.

In part 4, Joshua recalls his own prayer uttered during the Achan incident,
not narrated in the *Biblical Antiquities* (Joshua 7; LAB 21:3). In Josh. 7:7,
Joshua says that Israel would have been better off settling in Transjordan
rather than perishing at Amorite hands in Canaan. In the *Biblical Antiquities,*
Joshua says that Israel would have been better off dying in the wilderness like
their fathers (another reminder of the desert generation) or drowning in the
Red Sea than being destroyed by the Amorites. Since God saved the people
from drowning in the Red Sea and brought them safely out of the desert,
Joshua suggests that God's work would be in vain were Israel to perish now.
The basis of his prayer is like that of Moses' in LAB 12.

5. See 4:5; 13:7; 60:2; and other concordance listings.

Part 5 contains the most intriguing part of Joshua's prayer. It quotes words whose origins are unknown: "And the word concerns us: 'No evil will befall us'" (21:4). What follows shows that those words are true in spite of appearances. Although they seem to be words of the people ("us"), they are taken as authoritative and are proven through the reasoning that follows them. Joshua claims that the death and failure of a single Israelite generation does not prove that God does not live up to the promises, for God's purposes are for Israel as it exists over time. An individual human being who experiences only one generation might say, "God has destroyed the people whom he has chosen for himself," but Joshua claims that such words are spoken by "man, who cannot place one generation before another" (21:4). God is the one who "before all ages and after all ages" lives; Joshua has already said in part 1 that God is the one who numbers all generations. Only God can truly judge matters that go beyond the purview of a person's lifetime. Joshua realizes that even the destruction of an entire generation does not mean God has permanently abandoned Israel: "And behold we will be in Sheol but you will make your word alive." Making God's word alive means that all God's predictions and promises will be fulfilled. God's plans are never in vain.

Joshua now prays for a leader (part 6). Leadership in Israel is an expression of God's mercy. Joshua reminds God of the divine relationship with Israel ("your people" and "your heritage"). In part 7 Joshua strengthens his argument in a fashion familiar to the *Biblical Antiquities* by quoting Jacob's words, recorded in Gen. 49:10, predicting a leader from Judah. The quotation leads to another direct request in part 8: "And now confirm those words spoken beforehand so that the nations of the earth and the tribes of the world may learn that you are eternal" (21:5). The readers know that anything spoken by God or under inspiration comes to pass. The fulfillment of Jacob's words will prove again that God is eternal (part 9). Such motivation for God's actions is common in Jewish literature, and is often used in Jewish prayer of petition.[6]

LAB 21:6 is part 10 of Joshua's prayer: "LORD, behold the days will come when the house of Israel will be like a brooding dove who on placing her young in a nest does not leave or forget her place. So also these, having repented of their deeds, will hope for the salvation that is to be born from them." This passage is odd in a number of respects. First, it is separated from the rest of the prayer with the phrase "And he added, saying." Second, Joshua himself makes a prediction to God. Finally, the metaphor is obscure and so its function in the prayer is not clear. These considerations suggest the section is a later addition. It has even been proposed that the salvation to be born of the people is Jesus, making this a Christian interpolation. However, this is hardly a very explicit reference to Jesus and the absence of any clear Christian interpolations in the *Biblical Antiquities* argues strongly against this being the case here.[7] It is best to interpret the passage as original. The image of the dove

6. See Murphy, *Structure*, 72–96.

7. Perrot (SC 230, 139–40) rightly rejects Klausner's suggestion (*Messianic Idea*, 367) that the Christian Messiah is in mind, or that this passage concerns an eschatological savior.

is also found in 23:7 and 39:5. The center of Joshua's prayer is the request for
a leader, and in part 7 Joshua quotes Jacob to the effect that a leader will be
forthcoming from Judah. In the present passage Joshua predicts that when
Israel brings forth that leader, it will not abandon him. The dove to which
Israel is compared does not leave her young, and Joshua says that the people,
also, "having repented of their deeds, will hope for the salvation that is to be
born from them." In this case, salvation is liberation from the Amorites.

The rest of chapter 21 is taken up with the ceremony at Gilgal.[8] LAB
21:7–9 describes a ceremony based on Joshua 8, including setting up the white-
washed stone with the Law written on it, reading the Law, sacrifices, songs,
and a procession with the ark of the covenant. The account of the ceremony
in Josh. 8:30–35 contains no words attributed to the people. As usual in the
Biblical Antiquities, direct quotes of the people are added, revealing the
event's significance.

> Behold our LORD has fulfilled what he said to our fathers: "*To your seed I
> will give the land* in which you may dwell, *a land flowing with milk and honey.*"
> And behold he led us into the land of our enemies and delivered them broken
> in spirit before us, and he is the God who sent word to our fathers in the
> secret dwelling places of souls, saying, "Behold the LORD has done everything
> that he has said to us." And truly now we know that God has established
> every word of his law that he spoke to us on Horeb. And if our heart keeps
> to his ways, it will be good for us and for our sons after us (21:9).

Were it not for Israel's unfaithfulness, this could be the climax not just of the
first part of the *Biblical Antiquities* but the end of the entire book. God made
promises, went to great lengths to fulfill them, and achieved that goal in full.
As usual, Pseudo-Philo has Joshua quote the divine words to demonstrate that
they have come to pass. Since the covenant is described as having been made
with the fathers, the fathers receive word that it is now completely realized.
The fulfillment finds expression three times in this short passage. "Every
word" spoken on Horeb has now been actualized. The phrase "every word"
depends on Josh. 8:35, where Joshua reads the Torah to the people, and leaves
out not a word, and Josh. 23:14, where Joshua tells the people that every word
promised by God has been fulfilled for them. The witness to the fulfillment of
God's promises is even more powerful in Pseudo-Philo in that it occurs on the
lips of the people, who recall Horeb explicitly, the scene of the giving of the
Law and of their first transgression of it. It would only require obedience on
Israel's part to preserve the idyllic situation created by the fulfillment of God's
promises.

Israel does not remain faithful. The rest of the *Biblical Antiquities* shows
how the perfect situation celebrated by the tribes at Gilgal is continuously
jeopardized by Israel's behavior, and how God, though faithful and merciful,
is frequently tempted to revoke the covenant. The ceremony of LAB 21 sets

---

8. Since part of the ceremony involves Mount Ebal, Pseudo-Philo locates Gilgal there, in
accord with Deut. 11:30 and Samaritan tradition. Josh. 4:19–20 and Josephus (*Ant.* 5.1.4 § 20)
locate it near Jericho. (See SC 230, 140.)

the stage for the rest of the book by showing what is ideally possible, given Israel's obedience. The remainder of the *Biblical Antiquities* describes the real-life world of Israel.

Joshua's blessing ends the ceremony and the chapter (21:10). He prays that Israel will be faithful, the covenant unbroken, and a dwelling built for God in the midst of the people. This would consummate what God planned when God sent Israel into the land and would result in joy for Israel.

Chapter 22: The Altar in Transjordan

This story comes from Joshua 22. There are several major differences between the biblical version and Pseudo-Philo's. First, in Josh. 22:23–29 it is said emphatically that the tribes to the east of the Jordan did not build their altar for the purpose of sacrifice. LAB 22:1 flatly contradicts this by saying that the Transjordanian tribes established a priesthood and offered sacrifices. Second, the two-and-a-half tribes are not commanded to destroy their altar in Joshua 22, but in the *Biblical Antiquities* they are so ordered. Third, although both versions recall an incident in Israel's past by which to interpret the present circumstances, Joshua 22 chooses the story of Achan, whereas the *Biblical Antiquities* speaks of the golden calf. Fourth, in the Bible the narrator presents the tribes' explanation of their motivation as accurate and it is accepted without question by the other Israelites. In Pseudo-Philo, the tribes' explanation is questioned. Fifth, in the Bible the matter is dropped after the tribes explain themselves. In the *Biblical Antiquities* they are still considered to have sinned. Not only must their altar be destroyed, Joshua and all the people of Israel must offer a thousand rams on their behalf and pray for their forgiveness. Sixth, there is commentary on the role of Torah in Pseudo-Philo's version.

LAB 22:1 begins the story of the Transjordanian altar. It differs from the biblical introduction in that priesthood and sacrifice is part of the establishment of the altar. Also different is that in Joshua the other tribes prepare to make war on the offenders, but in Pseudo-Philo they merely go to talk to them. The confrontation takes place in Shiloh in the *Biblical Antiquities,* but in the Bible it occurs in Gilead. In LAB 22:2, Joshua and the elders ask the Transjordanian tribes why they have sinned before the other tribes have even settled in their land. Joshua goes on to quote a prediction of Moses, resulting in yet another of Pseudo-Philo's quotes-within-quotes. Joshua says that Moses said, "Beware that on entering your land you grow corrupt in your own deeds and destroy this people." In LAB 21 (Josh. 8:30–35), the entrance into the land was celebrated as a complete fulfillment of all that God promised Israel, but now in LAB 22 the author skips to Joshua 22 to relate the first transgression of the people. This results in a closer connection between presence in the land and sinfulness. Whatever the people's motivation, building the altar transgresses God's Law. Pseudo-Philo chooses cultic violation here as the first example of sinning as Israel enters the land. The choice argues against those who think Pseudo-Philo plays down the cult. As Moses sees destruction of the people as a result of corrupt deeds, so Joshua attributes Israel's difficulty with its enemies to the illegitimate altar.

In Josh. 22:22, the offending tribes begin their self-defense with the assertion that God knows their intentions. LAB 22:3 does the same but embellishes the notion of God's knowledge by extolling divine control of humanity (God "counts out the fruit of the womb of men") and the divine gift of light to the world. Since in the *Biblical Antiquities* the Torah is associated with light and Torah is at issue later in this passage, it is undoubtedly the giving of the Torah that is envisaged here. The Torah is an expression of God's own knowledge: "Because *he himself knows what are in the hidden places* of the abyss *and the light abides with him*" (22:3).

The motivation for the altar is similar in Joshua and the *Biblical Antiquities,* but there is an intriguing difference. In Joshua, the Transjordanian tribes build the altar as a witness between them and the other Israelites. It is not for sacrifice, but only proves to the rest of Israel that the tribes east of the Jordan truly belong to Israel. In the *Biblical Antiquities,* the altar is for sacrifice. The builders say that they were afraid their posterity would say, "Behold our brothers who are across the Jordan have an altar and offer sacrifices on it, but we in this place do not have an altar and are far from the LORD our God; for our God is so far from our ways that we may not serve him" (LAB 22:3). They reason that God will be present only where there is altar and sacrifices. Service to God motivates building the altar, a service that must include cultic activity. In LAB 22:4, the defenders again quote themselves to the effect that their intention was to make "zeal. . . for seeking the LORD" possible and claim that they are therefore "guiltless."

Joshua's answer to the offending tribes is in LAB 22:5–6. It begins, "Is not the LORD the King more powerful than a thousand sacrifices? And why have you not taught your sons the words of the LORD that you heard from us? For if your sons had been meditating upon the Law of the LORD, their mind would not have been led astray after an altar made by hand." That the temple and altar were made "by hand" was used in Christian circles to relativize or even denigrate the cult.[9] But it need not carry that connotation. In 1 Kings 8:27–30, Solomon acknowledges that the temple he had built could not contain God, but nevertheless could serve as a center for Israelite piety and a place of communication between Israel and God. In LAB 22:7, Joshua sacrifices a thousand rams for the erring tribes, so he hardly attacks the cult as such. Rather, he challenges those who see God as needing or being coerced by sacrifice. Joshua opposes a view like that of Balak, who thought Balaam could change God's mind by holocausts (LAB 18). More important is the idea that one need not resort to guesswork in discerning the will of God. God's will is expressed clearly and definitively in Torah. The basic sin of the eastern tribes was their failure to read and understand the Law. It is only through the study and teaching of the Law that Israel can follow God's will and abide in the divine favor.

9. Acts 7:48–50; Mark 14:58 and parallels. See SC 230, 142–43.

In accord with his emphasis on Torah's centrality, Pseudo-Philo bypasses the reference to the Achan episode found in Joshua 22 and substitutes a recollection of the people's sin at Sinai. The Israelites' idolatry in Moses' absence parallels the building of the illegitimate altar by the tribes who were far from Joshua. Only by God's mercy did the sin at Sinai not lead to the destruction of the people, and the same applies to the Transjordanian altar. The two events are run together in the last sentence of 22:5, where "your foolishness" is not clearly distinguished from the sins at Sinai.

In LAB 22:6, Joshua tells the violators they must destroy their altar (unlike in Joshua 22) and "meditate" on the Law "day and night" (see Josh. 1:8). In Joshua 22, the altar itself is a witness between the eastern and western tribes. In Pseudo-Philo, God, accessible through Torah, is both witness and judge of the erring tribes' posterity. God is also to be witness between Joshua and the offending tribes. Joshua cannot see into the offenders' hearts. He cannot know whether or not they acted from a good motive, but he warns them that they gain nothing by deceiving him. Appealing to a strict deuteronomistic pattern, Joshua certifies that if they are guilty in their hearts they will suffer for it, but if they truly acted for the reason that they claim, then God will be merciful. What the tribes did was a violation of Torah that must be undone, but their motivation makes all the difference in terms of what God will do about it. The tribes agree with this resolution by saying, "Amen, Amen."

LAB 22:7 resolves the problem of the Transjordanian altar. Joshua and the people pray and sacrifice on behalf of the erring tribes and send them away "in peace," thus reestablishing order within Israel. The tribes destroy the altar as commanded and pray, lament, and fast. Their prayer is unique to Pseudo-Philo. It echoes the tribes' words in 22:3, dwelling on God's knowledge of the human heart and therefore divine knowledge that the tribes acted out of praiseworthy motives. Straying from God's ways contrasts with serving God, formulations familiar from the rest of the *Biblical Antiquities*. The prayer ends with a plea for God's mercy "on your covenant with the sons of your servants." This phrase connects the survival of the covenant itself with God's mercy, and it frames the covenant with contemporary Israelites in terms of their descent from the "servants" of God. As noted before, the term "servants" is one that Pseudo-Philo uses sparsely. God is faithful to the covenant because of the promises made to the fathers, who were truly faithful to God.

LAB 22:8–9 reveals a concern for cultic matters. LAB 22:8 recounts Joshua's transfer of the cult from Gilgal to Shiloh, and 22:9 explains why a cult outside of Jerusalem was allowed.[10] The mention of the Urim and Thummim in 22:8–9 is unusual in the pseudepigraphical corpus. They appear several times in the *Biblical Antiquities* to indicate that God determines the action.[11] In 22:8 the Urim and Thummim reveal what "holocausts" are to be offered throughout the year. Pseudo-Philo asserts continuity between the cult

10. LAB 22:8 seems to have been confused at some point in its transmission. See SC 230, 143–44.
11. See LAB 22:8, 9; 25:5; 46:1.

at first Gilgal, then Shiloh, then Jerusalem. He also claims cultic unity for Israel even before the building of Solomon's temple.[12] Gilgal and Shiloh are associated with Joshua and Eleazar the priest, and both the order of sacrifices and the use of Urim and Thummim to reveal God's will are related to both of these shrines and then to Jerusalem in 22:9. This belies any attempt on Pseudo-Philo's part to play down the cult. The sacrifices are offered "to this day," indicating that the cult is still in operation in the author's day.[13]

LAB 22:9 explains that the cult was permitted in Shiloh because the temple had not yet been built in Jerusalem.[14] The Urim and Thummim reveal "all things" at Shiloh, stressing that the people have full access to God's will there, thus removing any excuse the people might have for error in following God's ways. The chapter ends by saying that Eleazar, who the readers are reminded is the son of Aaron, serves at Shiloh. This passage portrays Israel at peace in its own land, in God's favor, and with the God-given capability to maintain its favored position, since it can know and follow God's will.

Chapter 23: Joshua's Covenant

LAB 23 rewrites Joshua 24. LAB 23:1 gathers together various elements from the Book of Joshua to furnish a clear introduction to Joshua's last words. Joshua's status as a "mighty man" is stressed. Because of his might, he can divide up the land. Joshua prepares to die while there are still enemies in the land. Knowing that he is nearing the end of his life, Joshua gathers all Israel, as in Josh. 23:2. Pseudo-Philo elaborates, saying that Joshua "*summoned all Israel* in all their land, along with women and children." This emphasizes Israel's presence in its own land, as does the climactic ceremony of LAB 21. Whereas Josh. 23:2 and 24:1 mention elders, heads, judges, and officers, Pseudo-Philo substitutes women and children. The inclusion of women is perhaps influenced by Neh. 8:2, which is in the context of a covenant ceremony.

Joshua's tells the people, "Gather before the ark of the covenant of the LORD in Shiloh, and I will establish a covenant with you before I die" (23:1).[15] That Joshua is about to die makes his last words a testament. Testamentary speeches are a common device in the *Biblical Antiquities* because of Pseudo-Philo's concern for leadership and his didactic interests. In Josh. 23:2, Joshua informs the people that he is old, and in 23:14 he says he is about to die, but the word "covenant" does not appear until 23:16 (see 24:25). Pseudo-Philo specifies the covenant-making function of the speech from the outset, a natural development given the book's emphasis on covenant.

The narrative continues:

12. SC 230, 141.

13. This is Harrington's interpretation (*OTP,* 332, n. h). *Usque in hodiernum diem* reflects the Hebrew *'d hywm hzh,* a phrase common in Joshua and Judges.

14. This is the only time that Pseudo-Philo mentions Jerusalem by name.

15. Perrot (SC 230, 144) suggests that Pseudo-Philo situates this in Shiloh so as to stress Israel's cultic unity.

> And on the sixteenth day of the third month *all the people* along with women
> and children *gathered together before the Lord in Shiloh,* and *Joshua said* to
> them, *"Hear, O Israel.* Behold, I am establishing with you a covenant of this
> Law that the LORD established for your fathers on Horeb. *And so wait here
> this night* and see *what God will say to me* on your behalf." And while the
> people were waiting that night, the LORD appeared to Joshua in a dream
> vision and said to him, "According to these words I will speak to this people"
> (23:2–3).

Harrington notes that the fifteenth day of the third month is the date set by
Jubilees (1:1; 15:1; 44:1–4) for the celebration of Pentecost, later associated
with the giving of the Torah.[16] Pseudo-Philo again insists that all of Israel
includes women and children and omits mention of the various types of leaders
enumerated in Joshua 23 and 24. Joshua addresses the people with the initial
words of the "Shema," found on Moses' lips in Deut. 6:4 but absent from
Joshua 24. This confirms the weight the author gives the scene as a covenant-
making ceremony. Joshua explicitly identifies the covenant he establishes with
the one at Sinai. Joshua 23–24 says nothing of Sinai explicitly, although 23:16
may imply it. The absence is especially striking in chapter 24, where Joshua's
rehearsal of Israelite history passes from the rescue at the Red Sea to the
victories over the Amorites without mentioning Sinai, a fact long noted by
biblical scholars. The *Biblical Antiquities* ties Sinai firmly to Joshua's covenant
in the land, since an aim of the book is to portray Israel's history as interconnected and determined by its relationship with God. As noted in our analysis
of LAB 20, Pseudo-Philo emphasizes Joshua's ties to Moses.

Joshua's speeches in LAB 23 and in Joshua 24 are both presented as God's
speech mediated by Joshua. In the *Biblical Antiquities,* Joshua begins, "The
LORD says this," and in Joshua he begins, "Thus says the LORD." But Pseudo-
Philo adds the idea that Joshua had to retire for the night to receive a revelation from God before making his covenant (LAB 23:2–3). Joshua's words
about needing to consult God at night resemble those of Balaam in LAB
18:3. Night is a important time for communications from God.[17] Their narrative function is to show that everything that follows in LAB 23 is directly from
God. Pseudo-Philo typically emphasizes or increases God's role in the narrative. LAB 23:3 says summarily that God told Joshua everything he was to say
to the people, so Joshua's speech is not really his own.

In LAB 23:4, Joshua rises in the morning and begins his speech with the
words "The LORD says this," as in Josh. 24:2. This picks up on the dream and
its significance for the divine origin of his words (23:3). His speech is in the
form of a long interpretive review of Israel's history, a common form in Jewish
literature, spanning various genres.[18] The speech has the following content:

16. See SC 230, 144–145, which discusses the dates and comments on the importance of covenant in Pseudo-Philo. See Feldman, "Prolegomenon," cviii–cvix.

17. For example, it is at night that God communicates with Samuel, Miriam, Balaam, and
Joshua.

18. For example, see Pss. 78; 105; 106; 1 Macc. 2:51–61; Wisdom 10–12; Deuteronomy 1–4;
4 Ezra 14:28–36; etc.

1. Creation of Abraham, Nahor, Sarah, and Melcha and their marriages (23:4)
2. Recollection of Abraham's belief in God (23:5)
3. God's rescue of Abraham and promise of land (23:5)
4. Vision of the future given to Abraham (23:6–7)
5. Gift of Isaac (23:8)
6. Jacob and Esau, and Jacob's descent into Egypt (23:9)
7. Liberation from Egypt (23:9)
8. Sinai (23:10)
9. Gift of the land (23:11)
10. Rewards in this world (23:12)
11. Rewards in the world to come (23:13)

Characteristic of Pseudo-Philo are the emphasis on the Torah as enlightenment and on its cosmic significance, insistence that all of God's promises have already been fulfilled, focus on God's activity, earthly and nonearthly rewards, and reference to the fathers. Joshua's speech is clearly modeled on the one in Joshua 24. The shared elements are as follows: starting with Abraham and Nahor and their life across the Euphrates; God's taking Abraham out of that land; Isaac's birth; the births of Jacob and Esau, and the mention that Esau gets Seir, whereas Jacob descends to Egypt; the Red Sea events; entrance into the promised land and God's giving Israel that land and dispossessing its inhabitants for them.

The differences between the two speeches are striking. The most noteworthy difference is the absence from Joshua 24 of the giving of the Torah on Sinai. Pseudo-Philo devotes considerable attention to Sinai, giving it pride of place in the speech through the very volume of words devoted to it, as well as by its specific treatment (23:10). The mention of the matriarchs Sarah and Melcha reflects Pseudo-Philo's interest in women (23:4). LAB 23:5 sees the gift of the land as a reward to Abraham for his belief in God, a notion missing in Joshua 24. LAB 23:6–7 contains an extensive vision of Abraham associated with the sacrifice in Genesis 15, absent from Joshua 24. The brief notice of the birth of Isaac found in Josh. 24:3 is expanded. Finally, where Joshua demands that the people serve the Lord and then tells them of the punishment for disobedience (Joshua 24), the *Biblical Antiquities* has Joshua lay before the people the blessings that will result if they serve God. The blessings are in both this world and the next.

The mention of the afterlife points up a parallel between Joshua's speech in LAB 23 and Ezra's in 4 Ezra 14:28–36. Both passages are testamentary speeches of a major figure in Israel's history. In both cases "all Israel" gathers to hear the speech. Both speeches begin with an echo of Deut. 6:4. Both end with a prediction that the people will enjoy God's favor if they obey, and in both cases that favor involves joyful participation in the afterlife.

Pseudo-Philo begins Joshua's review of Israel's history with Abraham and Nahor (23:4), as does Joshua 24. Pseudo-Philo combines this with Isaiah's words in Isa. 51:1–2. There Israel is exhorted by the prophet, "Look to the rock from which you were hewn, and to the quarry from which you were dug. Look to Abraham your father and to Sarah who bore you." Pseudo-Philo takes the combination of Abraham and Nahor from Joshua 24 and the mention of Abraham and Sarah from Isaiah 51, and supplies the missing member of the two couples, Melcha. The complete foursome is found in Gen. 11:29 as well. LAB 23:4 fits with Pseudo-Philo's interest in the patriarchs.

In LAB 23:5 it is said that Abraham was rescued from the flame and promised the land because he was not "led astray" as were "those inhabiting the land" who "were being led astray after their own devices." This refers back to LAB 6–7 and depends on a knowledge of those chapters to make sense. The idea that the land was given to Abraham as a reward for his faithfulness accords with the strict moral causality that permeates the *Biblical Antiquities.* Pseudo-Philo alludes to Gen. 12:7 and 15:2–5 as he narrates God's bringing Abraham throughout Canaan and promising the land to his posterity. In Pseudo-Philo, Abraham points out to God that Sarah is sterile and asks God how he can have descendants.[19] This bypasses the whole incident of Abraham laughing at God in Genesis 17 or his suggestion that the posterity be reckoned through Ishmael (Gen. 17:18). It also supplies an opportunity to insert a lengthy account of Abraham's vision based on Genesis 15.

Abraham's vision includes the places of reward and punishment. In Genesis 15, Abraham, having halved the victims and gone to sleep, observes a flaming torch pass between the halves. Fire is a favorite image of Pseudo-Philo. He sees the place of fire where the wicked are to be punished, and then sees "*the torches of fire* by which the just who have believed in me will be enlightened." To preserve strict parallelism with the fire of punishment, these "torches of fire" would be a postmortem revelation made to the just. But throughout the *Biblical Antiquities,* the Law is that which illumines, as is the case later in this chapter (23:10). In the end such a distinction may not be possible, since it is the same God who enlightens—through the Torah before death and through the divine presence after death. The dynamic is the same as that found, for example, in the *Similitudes of Enoch,* where the wisdom that enlightens the faithful in this life becomes an unending fountain when they reach God's presence (*1 Enoch* 48). The idea of special revelation to Abraham is also included in other Jewish texts.[20] The idea that fire is punishment to the wicked and benefits the righteous is a specific example of the more general pattern that the same element can be good for the good and bad for the bad.[21]

Pseudo-Philo is part of a much wider tradition in which Abraham receives esoteric revelation. What is significant for our purposes is that the author inserts the story of Abraham's vision in Joshua's covenant speech. The whole of Israelite history is thereby woven more tightly. Earlier, Joshua's covenant was identified with the Sinai covenant (23:2). Now the whole of human history between Abraham and the final Judgment is tied together by Abraham's

19. Abraham's question recalls those of Zechariah and Mary in Luke 1:18 and 34.
20. See SC 230, 146, for references.
21. See comments on 4:5.

vision, in which he sees his posterity's history spread before him and knows God's commitment to him and his seed is irrevocable.

Abraham's vision passes from consideration of the Last Judgment to Israel's history (23:7). The section begins and ends with the idea of "witness," a notion important throughout the *Biblical Antiquities.* At the beginning of the section, God says, "These *[hec]* will be a witness between me and you, that I will give you offspring from one who is closed up." It is not obvious whether the *hec* refers to the preceding vision, which then becomes a witness that Sarah will bear a son, or whether *hec* means the future miraculous conception of Isaac, which then becomes a witness for the rest of Israel's history. Given the meaning of the witness that ends the section, the first reference for *hec* is probably correct. Abraham's vision of the end will assure him that the promise of a child from the barren Sarah, as well as the entire history of Israel to follow, will indeed happen as foretold by God. After speaking of Abraham's posterity, God closes the vision by saying, "And these prophecies and this night will be a witness between us, that I will not go against my words." That God is unfailingly faithful to the divine words is an integral theme of the *Biblical Antiquities.* Here Abraham receives proof of that through God's predictions as well as through his visionary experience. This fits with the interpretation of *hec* as referring to Abraham's vision of the torches.

Having established that Abraham's vision is guaranteed to be accurate by God, the content of that vision must be examined. First, Abraham is pledged a posterity through Sarah. Then each of the sacrificed animals of Gen. 15:9–10 is taken to symbolize some category of person within Israel or in relation to it.[22] Abraham himself is the dove, elsewhere a symbol for Israel (21:6;39:5). The city that he takes for God and his descendants build is Jerusalem. The turtledove represents the prophets.[23] The ram symbolizes the "wise men who will be born from you, who will enlighten your sons."[24] Since enlightenment comes from the Law for Pseudo-Philo, these wise men must be teachers of Torah. It is uncertain why the calf stands for the "multitude of the peoples, which are made many through you." If this means the Gentiles, the rest of the book does not seem to relate Abraham to the nations in this way. If this is but a confusing reference to Israel, then it is more understandable. Finally, the she-goat stands for the barren women whose wombs God opens throughout Israel's history. Pseudo-Philo's is concerned to give women their due in salvation history.

God now passes from Abraham's vision to Isaac's birth. God (through Joshua) remarks that Isaac was in the womb only seven months and that thereafter any child born after only seven months' gestation will live, "because upon him have I brought my glory and revealed the new age" (23:8) Perrot briefly

22. For other interpretations of the animals of Genesis 15, see SC 230, 147.

23. Perrot (SC 230, 147) refers to *Tg. Cant.* 2:12 as identifying the turtledove and the Holy Spirit. He sees this as key to understanding the identification of the Holy Spirit with a dove in the Gospels. Jesus' vision signifies the beginning of his prophetic ministry.

24. Aside from the rams sacrificed by Joshua in chapter 22, the only other place a ram appears is in 31:5, where Jael compares Israel to a ram that leads a flock representing the rest of humanity.

considers related Jewish traditions and suggests that all children born after seven months in the womb were considered prophets.[25] That might explain why they would manifest the glory of God and be a sign of the "new age." Pseudo-Philo's tendency to frame Israel's history in grand terms—Creation at one end and the eschaton at the other—could account for the presence of this element.[26]

LAB 23:9 concerns Esau and Jacob and depends on Josh. 24:4–5. As in the Book of Joshua, Esau is given Seir and Jacob goes to Egypt. Pseudo-Philo summarizes the first section of Exodus with "*And the Egyptians humbled* your fathers, as you know; but I remembered your fathers and *sent Moses* my friend and freed them from there, but their enemies I struck down." Characteristic of Pseudo-Philo are the double reference to the fathers, the exaltation of Moses (God's friend), and the statement that God freed Israel. In 23:9 the crossing of the Red Sea and the giving of the Law are summarized. Cosmic signs accompanying the giving of the Law are evident in LAB 11:5; 15:5–6; and 32:7–8.[27] Sinai is a cosmic event for Pseudo-Philo. Each mention of the cosmic disturbances is slightly different. The differentiating factor in 23:10 is the idea that God stopped cosmic processes so the covenant would not be harmed. The covenant is reified here and could be damaged. God explains that the theophany of Sinai caused havoc in nature and the natural elements became dangerous. They had to be restrained. As usual, the Law is a light to Israel so that they might obey it and therefore live and not die.

In LAB 23:11, Joshua finishes the section of his speech recalling God's work for Israel. Joshua reminds the people that God gave them the land with its cities and vineyards even though they had not built them. God's activity on behalf of Israel is summarized with "And I fulfilled my covenant that I promised your fathers." These words, similar to those of the people in 21:9, epitomize the entire first section of the *Biblical Antiquities*.

LAB 23:12–13 enumerates the blessings in store for Israel if it listens to its fathers (equivalent to obeying the Law). LAB 23:12 itemizes the earthly advantages Israel will receive if it listens, and 23:13 tells of the blessings it will inherit after death. LAB 23:12 is particularly warm in its depiction of the relationship between God and Israel. God's heart is set among the people forever and God will "overshadow" it, protecting it from its enemies. Israel will be famous throughout the world. All nations will say that because Israel believed in the Lord, the Lord freed them and planted them. Belief in God, meaning trust in God's words and promises, is the central virtue in the *Biblical Antiquities*. Freeing the people is God's primary activity. Israel as a plant is a common image in Pseudo-Philo. A second image for Israel is added, that of God's flock. Finally, rain and dew are concrete signs of God's blessing, as throughout Pseudo-Philo. These blessings endure "during your lifetime."

LAB 23:13 brings in the afterlife. In this, Pseudo-Philo departs from the model of Joshua 24 but is like documents more contemporary with it, such as

---

25. SC 230, 147–48. See also van der Horst, "Seven Months."
26. Prophecy could be seen as a sign of the end time, as in Acts 2.
27. See SC 230, 148.

4 Ezra 14:34–35. If the people are faithful to God, their souls will be stored in peace until the allotted time of the world expires.[28] The last words of the speech are typical of Pseudo-Philo: "And I will restore you to your fathers and your fathers to you, and they will know through you that I have not chosen you in vain." Relationship with the fathers is assumed throughout the *Biblical Antiquities* and reunion with the fathers after death is integral to Israel's reward.[29] It is important in Pseudo-Philo that the fathers know the promises have been fulfilled. In chapter 21, at the climactic ceremony affirming that all God's promises have been fulfilled, God is said to have sent word to the fathers "in the secret dwelling places of souls" that God had done everything promised. Therefore, God's election of Israel is not "in vain," a phrase that recurs frequently in the *Biblical Antiquities*. "In vain" is a phrase that could often apply to human plans or undertakings, but never to God's words or actions. Although God's words can never be in vain, Israel's behavior usually makes it difficult for the promises to reach their ultimate conclusion.

Joshua ends the speech with the reminder that the words he has just spoken were not his own, but were conveyed to him by God the previous night (23:13). This reminder is not present in Joshua 24. Chapter 23 ends with the people's pledge to serve God alone, a condensation of Josh. 24:16–18, 21, 24. They then have a twenty-eight-day feast and renewal ceremony, lacking in the book of Joshua. Perrot points out that other texts associate a feast with Pentecost.[30]

Chapter 24: Joshua's Last Words and Death

In LAB 24, Joshua delivers his own last words. First he addresses the people as a whole, and then he speaks to Eleazar the priest, although a few other notables seem to be present. LAB 24:1 opens with the narrator saying that Joshua gathered the people again. This is necessary because a twenty-eight-day feast separates Joshua's earlier speech (LAB 23) from the one to follow (LAB 24). The rest of 24:1 uses Josh. 24:15 as a model, forcing the people to choose between service to God and idolatry. Choosing God will result in Israel being a "special people" to the Lord. This is language characteristic of Deuteronomy.[31] Here Joshua mentions only the positive possibility. He does not specify a punishment if they do not choose God, though the punishment implied is that they will not be a special people if they make that choice. Pseudo-Philo reinforces the solemnity of that choice through the language of witness, common throughout the book. He calls heaven and earth to witness against Israel, as does Moses in Deut. 4:26 (cf. Deut. 30:19; 31:28). As an introduction, he says, "Behold now the LORD has testified among you." Thus,

---

28. See *1 Enoch* 22; 4 Ezra 7:88–99 (especially verse 95).

29. Although *2 Bar.* 50:4 speaks of people recognizing each other after the Resurrection, nothing is said of reunion with the fathers.

30. SC 230, 149: Tob. 2:1–2; *Jub.* 22:1–2; Philo, *Contempl.* 65, 75–76; *Ant.* 3.5.2 § 79.

31. SC 230, 149.

the words of God delivered through Joshua in LAB 23 are God's witness to Israel.

In 24:2 the people reason, "Perhaps *[forsitan]* God has accounted us worthy; it is better for us to die in fear of him than to be blotted out from the earth." In Josh. 24:16–18, the people's answer to Joshua's exhortation is confident. In LAB 24:2 their words are more tentative. *Forsitan* suggests that they are still unsure of God's attitude toward them. This is ironic given what God has done for them, so recently celebrated in the ceremony in chapter 21, as well as in Joshua's lengthy speech in LAB 23. The people's thought that it is better to serve God than to be blotted out from the earth implies that they serve God just to avoid destruction.

Joshua blesses the people, kisses them, and prays their words might provoke God's mercy so that God's angel will guard them. He exhorts them to remember Moses and himself and to abide by the covenant. Moses is called "friend of the LORD" once again.[32] The idea of remembering is important in the *Biblical Antiquities* and is built into the very structure of the book. The people are to remember Moses and Joshua. Leaders are central to Pseudo-Philo; the people cannot maintain the covenant unless their leaders make it possible.

Joshua dismisses the people and calls the priest Eleazar to him (24:4). Joshua predicts Israel's future to Eleazar, such prediction being common in testaments. Despite the pledges of the people and Joshua's words of encouragement to them, he knows full well that they will fail. He tells the priest to "strengthen yourself while you are still with them." The priests must be strong even if the people err. This passage shows that Joshua and the priests (and the readers, who hear their conversation) view the people from a superior perspective. This is the ironic mode at work. The people go off to their inheritances apparently thinking all is well, but their leaders know the situation is temporary. Joshua then kisses Eleazar and his father and sons and says, "May the LORD God of your fathers guide *[dirigat]* your ways and those of this people." The word *dirigere* often has God as its subject. The proper situation is for the people's "ways," their behavior, to conform to God's "ways," God's will. Joshua then draws up his feet into the bed (in imitation of Jacob in Gen. 49:33) and dies.

The Joshua cycle ends with the people's lamentation at his death. He is compared to an eagle who has flown away and a lion's cub who has been hidden.[33] After the lament, the people ask, "Who will go and tell the just Moses that we have had a leader like him for forty years?" This reinforces the idea that God provides for continuity of leadership. The people have not had to pine for such a leader as Moses predicts in 19:3, for the period of Joshua is presented as idyllic. The one negative event, the building of the Transjor-

---

32. Perrot notes instances in other Jewish literature where Moses and Abraham are called friends of God (SC 230, 149–150).

33. Note the similar phrasing of 2 Sam. 1:23, David's lament at Saul's death (SC 230, 150).

danian altar, is a mistake and does not result in punishment. Joshua's leadership continues that of Moses. The people want Moses to be apprised of their situation. Israel's status is always of great interest to the dead fathers in Pseudo-Philo, because it depends both on the original promises to the fathers and on the ongoing actions of successive generations.[34]

34. See 31:7; 32:13; *2 Bar.* 11:6.

6

Kenaz: *Biblical Antiquities 25–29*

LAB 25–28 contains the Kenaz cycle. Chapter 29 concerns the judgeship of Zebul, a minor figure who arranges the inheritance of Kenaz's daughters. The attention devoted to Kenaz in the *Biblical Antiquities* has attracted much comment. Kenaz is little more than a name in the Bible. He is the father of the first judge, Othniel (Judg. 3:9, 11), the younger brother of Caleb. Josephus gives him a bit more space (*Ant.* 5.3.3 §§ 182–84). In the *Biblical Antiquities,* Othniel disappears and Kenaz becomes Caleb's son and the first judge. He attains a prominence comparable only to Moses (LAB 9–19), Joshua (20–24), and Deborah (30–33). In Nickelsburg's estimation, "It is evident that Pseudo-Philo has created a character to serve his purpose."[1]

Kenaz's story occurs at a crucial point in the plot. Joshua is a transitional figure who brings the people from the desert to settle the land. Kenaz marks the beginning of a new existence for Israel in which the tribes live together in the land under judges. In these chapters Pseudo-Philo shows patterns of behavior, of leadership, and of relation between God, Israel, and leaders that will inform the narrative in successive chapters. A crucial tension that drives the narrative in the *Biblical Antiquities* is between God's promises and Israel's unfaithfulness. Having demonstrated fulfillment of God's promises, climaxing in Joshua's narrative, Pseudo-Philo now begins to show how that tension works itself out in Israel's life.

Chapter 25: Election of Kenaz and Sinners' Confession

In Judg. 1:1, the people ask who will fight the Canaanites for them after the death of Joshua. LAB 25:1 rewrites this in two ways. First, Pseudo-Philo adds the notion that the land was peaceful after Joshua's death. The picture of Israel established in the land according to God's promise is reinforced. All was perfect when Joshua left the scene. Second, whereas fighting the Philistines is

---

1. "Leaders," 54.

Israel's idea in Judges, in the *Biblical Antiquities* Israel is victimized by belligerent foreigners.[2]

Israel's request to God in LAB 25:1 differs from the biblical text. In the Bible, it is assumed that Israel should fight and the only question is which tribe should go up first. God answers the question simply—Judah should go. The question in the *Biblical Antiquities* is *whether* Israel should fight. This affords Pseudo-Philo an opportunity to explore the conditions for Israel's victory over its enemies. God's answer is not simple: "If you go up with a pure heart *[corde puro]*, fight; but if your heart is defiled, you should not go up." This is the only occurrence of the word *purus,* so it is difficult to ascertain its precise nuance, but the word "heart" occurs often. Here "pure" is opposed to "defiled." When lots are cast later in the chapter to determine whose heart is pure, it is clear that defilement means sin in the form of concrete acts contrary to God's will. Israel cannot advance against its enemies with sinners in its midst. The people ask how they can know whether everyone's heart is the same; things are not always as they appear, and faithfulness to God is not necessarily something that can be read easily from one's demeanor. This rather sophisticated notion of morality appears several times in the book. Joshua's admitted inability to judge the Transjordanian tribes is another example (chap. 22).

Pseudo-Philo shares the concern of the Book of Deuteronomy that Israel obey God's Law from the heart. God's instruction in LAB 25:1 that Israel fight the Philistines only if its heart is pure recalls numerous passages in Deuteronomy that connect obedience from the heart to conquest and possession of the land. The injunction to love God with the whole heart found in Deut. 6:5 underlies all of Deuteronomy, and Deuteronomy centers on possession of the land. Obedience results in living in the land in prosperity, but disobedience brings exile. The word "heart" occurs forty-six times in Deuteronomy, with two main uses. In many instances, it is used to express the completeness of one's dedication to God. In other cases, it refers to having "heart" in the sense of having courage and trust in God in the face of enemies. In Deut. 1:28, Moses, speaking of the spies' report from Num. 13:27–29, says, "Our kindred have made our hearts melt," words that do not appear in Numbers 13–14. This verse from Deuteronomy may have influenced LAB 25:1. Since a melting heart prevented victory over the people of the land once before, Israel can only carry on a campaign if its heart is solid. Examples of other pertinent passages in Deuteronomy are 7:17, where Moses tells Israel it will not dispossess the Canaanites if it questions in its heart, and 20:3, 8, where battle with the enemies requires "heart." In these examples from Deuteronomy 1, 7, and 20, a fearful heart is one that does not trust God and so does not believe God. Thus the two uses of heart observed above merge. Obedience to God from the heart is not possible if one does not have "heart" in the sense of courage born of trust.

In LAB 25:1, God's answer centers more on obedience than courage, as

2. The Latin translated "Philistines" is *Allophili.* The LXX usually translates the Hebrew *plšt* as *allophylos* (SC 230, 150).

the rest of the chapter indicates. When in LAB 25:2 the people ask God to appoint a leader before they use the lots, it brings together three important aspects of Pseudo-Philo's narrative: God's control of the action, God's working through leaders, and Israel's character. The people cannot proceed against the enemy unless they discover who is a sinner, and they are powerless to do that without God's direct revelation through lots. They realize that they should not take any significant action without a leader, so they request one. The subsequent narrative presents Kenaz as an exemplary leader and shows how he depends on God for his every move. He is chosen by lot as decreed by God, so the readers know he serves at God's pleasure. Being son of Caleb means that he comes from a family distinguished by trust in God.

In LAB 25:3, Kenaz begins his rule by calling Israel together so that they may hear "the word of the LORD." He reminds them of the commands of Moses (again called "friend of the LORD") and Joshua not to transgress Torah. These first words of Kenaz establish his continuity with Moses and Joshua and present him as God's spokesman. Kenaz attests to his dependence on God by telling the people that the Lord revealed that some of them have defiled hearts and by commanding the use of lots to discover who is defiled. Kenaz reminds the people of the wrath of God that falls upon sinners, and says that the sinners will be punished by fire. The people reply, "You have proposed a good plan to carry out." Kenaz's plan is good because it conforms to God's will. In fact, he is simply carrying out God's instructions.

In LAB 25:4, 6, 110 sinners are discovered. While the number is substantial, it is but a small percentage of Israel.[3] The sinners are not concentrated in any one tribe, but span Israel.[4] Kenaz imprisons the sinners until it is known what to do with them. In 25:5 Kenaz summons the priest Eleazar and orders the Urim and Thummim to be brought to determine God's will. Inquiry of God is to be made through the priest.[5] Kenaz makes a short speech while summoning the priest. He claims that Moses predicted the existence of the sinners, again proving that history is interconnected and under God's control. Characteristically, he quotes Moses directly (Deut. 29:17), resulting in a quotation within a quotation. He then blesses God, "who has revealed all the schemes of these men and did not let them corrupt the people with their wicked deeds." The language is typical. Revelation of things important to Israel's well-being is one of God's main activities. The plans and intents of people are of great interest in the narrative. "Corruption" is used regularly to describe the situation of the people alienated from God. "Wicked deeds" is used similarly. Kenaz credits God with rescuing the people from themselves, in a sense. Without God's disclosure, the people would not even have known that they had sinners in their midst.

3. The desert census showed that Israel totaled 1,620,900 (14:3). The figure of 6,110 would be a substantial number, but small in comparison to the people as a whole.

4. The tribes of Dan and Naphtali are omitted from this list (*OTP*, 335, n. d). This is either inadvertent on the part of the author or a scribal error, since both Dan and Naphtali are present when the sinners confess later in the chapter (25:9).

5. This is another indication that the author does not reject the priestly establishment.

LAB 25:6 is a prayer of Kenaz, Eleazar, the elders, and "all the assembly" asking God to reveal "the truth," which in this case means the facts about the sinners.[6] The sinners are described as "those who do not believe the wonders that you did for our fathers from the time that you brought them out of the land of Egypt to this day." This description recalls Judg. 2:10, which speaks of the generation after Joshua, which "did not know the LORD or the work that he had done for Israel." As does Judges, LAB 25:6 sees the root of rebellion against God as a lack of belief in God's mighty acts of the past. God tells the community to listen to the confessions of the sinners before consigning them to the fire. God says the sinners have done their deeds "with cunning *[astute]*." Sin can be subtle and God must help to uncover it.

In LAB 25:7 Kenaz reminds the sinners of Achan's confession. This refers to Joshua 7, where Israel incurs God's displeasure because Achan violated *ḥerem.* Achan confesses his sin before being destroyed. The Talmud says that Achan won forgiveness through his confession although he still had to suffer death.[7] Kenaz does not presume to know what God's judgment will be but extends to the sinners the hope that their confession will evoke God's mercy at the Resurrection. One of the sinners, Elas, tells Kenaz that if he wishes to learn all of the facts about what has transpired, including the difference between the sins of each tribe, he should question the tribes individually. Their confessions reveal both differences and similarities. The sins present a picture of the sinners as those who doubt the God of Israel and so turn elsewhere for wisdom and for worship. Many of the confessions involve not the commission of acts but the desire to do something sinful. This continues Pseudo-Philo's interest not just in what is done but also in intention and motivation.[8] Idolatry underlies all the sins.[9] Observing that this list comes after the prayer of the community in 25:6, which sees the sinners as those who do not believe in God's mighty works, Perrot draws a parallel between the idea that disbelief leads to idolatry here and in Judg. 2:10–13.[10] Kenaz has each tribe confess its own sins, in accord with Pseudo-Philo's general tendency to resort to direct address whenever practical. The readers hear of the transgressions from the sinners themselves.

Judah is of Kenaz's own tribe, a fact that makes it more likely that Joshua's prayer for a leader from Judah (21:5) refers to Kenaz and not to a messianic figure. Judah's sin is its wish to make a copy of the golden calf. Not only does Judah want to commit idolatry, it wants to repeat the sin that is paradigmatic

---

6. The word *veritas* is not frequent in the *Biblical Antiquities* except in the denotation of the Urim and Thummim, which are called *demonstratio* and *veritas*. The word has no metaphysical overtones here, but merely designates the facts of the situation.

7. *B. Sanh.* 44b and *b. Semaḥot* 44a–b (SC 230, 152). See also Feldman, "Prolegomenon," cxi.

8. Perrot says that in holding sinners accountable for intention as well as for action, the *Biblical Antiquities* is close to rabbinic thought. He cites Jackson, "Liability," for evidence.

9. See Murphy, "Retelling," especially 280.

10. SC 230, 152.

for all subsequent idolatry. This shocking statement sets the tone for the sins of the other tribes. Reuben is next, and that tribe wants to follow Judah's lead by sacrificing to the gods of the land's inhabitants.[11] The members of the tribe of Levi directly attack the cultic center. They desire to test the tent of meeting to see whether it is holy. To question the holiness of the tent is to doubt that God is really there, undermining the entire cultic institution of Israel. This sin is particularly appropriate for Levi since that tribe is the keeper of the tent. The guardians of the cult are the very ones who undermine it. This reveals a pessimistic view of Israel.

Issachar wishes to go to foreign gods for revelation. Since revelation is a major function of God throughout the *Biblical Antiquities,* Issachar's desire insults the Lord. Zebulun wants to commit the grisly offense of eating its own children. What ties its sin to the rest is not so much the act itself as its motivation—they want to know whether or not God cares for the Israelite children. This is a particularly poignant way of questioning whether God cares for Israel itself, so it is really an attack on the covenant.

The transgression of Dan is not just a desire, but an act. Dan learns forbidden arts from the Amorites.[12] Their motivation is to teach these arts to their children. Their intention to pass the evil knowledge to the next generation betrays a desire to change the nature of Israel for all time. They say that they have hidden the information under "Abraham's mountain."[13] Kenaz has the Amorite secrets retrieved and brought to him. This last narrative element—the sending, finding, and bringing back of the offending articles—is also found in Josh. 7:22–23. Achan's statement that the *herem* is hidden "in the ground" (Josh. 7:21) means it was buried, as are the Amorite secrets in LAB 25:9.[14] The next tribe, Naphtali, commits a crime similar to that of the Danites, except that instead of learning what the Amorites do, they desired to make what the Amorites make. That their violation went beyond desire to commission is proven by the fact that their evil objects can be found beneath the tent of the same Elas who told Kenaz to examine each of the tribes individually. Kenaz sends to the tent and finds the objects. Again, there is an allusion to Josh. 7:22–23.

Gad confesses to adultery. Although adultery is not identical to idolatry, it is frequently a metaphor for serving other gods. With Asher, idolatry is again explicit. They steal the Amorites' idolatrous golden nymphs and some precious stones and hide them under Mount Shechem. This recalls the hiding of cult images under an oak at Shechem in Gen. 35:4.[15] But the hiding of the forbid-

---

11. Harrington (*OTP,* 335, n. g) notes that the tribe of Simeon is omitted. It is present in 25:4, so it must have been omitted here through scribal error.

12. *2 Bar.* 60:1 also attributes arcane magical knowledge to the Amorites.

13. Harrington (*OTP,* 336, n. h) explains that this mountain would be Mount Moriah in Jerusalem, but he suggests emending the Latin to *monte Abarim.*

14. The parallel with Joshua 7 is more complete than the others adduced by Harrington (*OTP,* 336, n. k) and accords well with the mention of Achan in LAB 25:7.

15. *OTP,* 336, n. k.

den goods, the confession of where they are, and Kenaz's act of sending and finding them all echo Joshua 7. The context of the chapter makes it likely that Gad takes the images to use them and so commits idolatry. The idols told the Amorites what to do "every hour" (25:11). Despite the marked emphasis in the *Biblical Antiquities* on God's guidance of Israel, the Gadite sinners look for guidance elsewhere. The Amorite idols and precious stones now come in for a great deal of attention by the narrator, who explains their origin and nature in detail. The evil of the idols is primordial, for they were made by the "seven sinful men" after the Flood. Although only six names are given in the text, they include two to be expected of a list of ancient sinners—Canaan and Nimrod. Kenaz does not know what to do with the idols. He sets them aside until he should receive further instructions from God. The stones are described in terms that underline their mysteriousness and idolatrous nature. Their power is taken seriously; there is no attempt to deny it. Idolatry's attraction is strong, for the idols' power is real and ancient. The stones emit their own supernatural light and can heal blindness. Kenaz does not explain away the idols and their power but removes them from where they can harm Israel.

Manasseh confesses, "We merely profaned the sabbaths of the LORD" (25:13). The word "merely" betrays a cavalier attitude to the Sabbath that undermines Israel's covenantal foundations. Ephraim says that it desires to put its own children in the fire "to know if what had been said would be proved by direct evidence" (25:13). This evil desire is like Zebulun's, the wish to eat its children to see whether God cared for them. It is an attack on the future of Israel and an act of mistrust of God. Ephraim displays skepticism about the covenant and the sacred traditions that support it. It demands concrete proof for all these assertions, implying that they may be only words.

The final tribe, Benjamin, sins in a way that is paradigmatic for all the other sins. The foregoing analysis has revealed a thread of idolatry and distrust of God lying at the base of the tribes' misbehavior. Benjamin says, "We desired at this time to investigate the book of the Law, whether God had really written what was in it or Moses had taught these things by himself" (25:13). This direct assault on Torah itself, charging that it may be merely a human production, is the ultimate sacrilege. This sort of radical skepticism could only lead to apostasy and the destruction of Israel's very reason for existence. Such corrosive uncertainty about Israel's election is the root of the nation's misfortunes, according to Pseudo-Philo. This doubt must be eradicated from Israel if God is to bring it success once more.

Chapter 26: Sinners' Punishment; Twelve Stones

Kenaz writes the confessions in a book and reads them before God (26:1), who then tells Kenaz what to do. Kenaz is God's agent. He does not judge or sentence the sinners himself. The reading of the books recalls similar judgment scenes, as in Daniel 7, for example. Kenaz is told to burn the sinners and all their possessions in the river Fison so that God might turn from the divine anger against them.[16] The reference to God's turning from anger echoes Josh. 7:26. Kenaz then brings up the matter of the stones, a topic that occupies the rest of this long chapter.

Kenaz asks God whether he should burn the precious stones, too, or keep them, "because we do not have any like those" (26:2). Kenaz, too, is intrigued by the stones. The tribe of Asher sinned because of its fascination with the stones and their powers, and now Kenaz admits their uniqueness and wonders whether it might not be desirable to keep and use them. Even Israel's ideal leader can be attracted by the forbidden secrets of the Gentiles. God reminds Kenaz that the stones are under the ban. God commands him to separate the stones and "everything that has been found in the book," and, having arranged for the sinners to be burned, to put the stones and "the books" aside until he receives further instructions about them. "Book(s)" appears both in the singular and plural here. The only book mentioned so far is the one containing the sinners' sins written by Kenaz (26:1), which does not seem to be in question. The most likely referent is mystical books containing the Amorites' esoteric lore. God rejects Kenaz's suggestion that Israel might find the stones beneficial and says Kenaz will be taught how to destroy them. Meanwhile, God tells him once again to proceed with the execution of the Israelite sinners.

God tells Kenaz to gather all Israel after the execution. He is to say to them, "So it will be done to every man whose heart has turned from his God" (26:2). The lesson of this episode is generalized to apply to all Israel and all humanity. This is done in the form of God's direct words being delivered to the leader to convey to the people. The readers have full assurance that God intends to destroy everyone who apostasizes. It is clear that fascination with Gentile secrets is dangerous to Israel. When Israel's leaders say so, they are simply repeating the words of the Lord.

In 26:3, God instructs Kenaz to put the stones and books "on the top of the mountain beside the new altar."[17] God says that the stones and books cannot be destroyed by the natural elements of water, fire, or iron—they are from another realm. God says a cloud will be sent to blot out the books, since no water that has ever "served men" can do the job. Then lightning will be sent to burn them up. This elaborate process reinforces the otherworldliness of the books.

The stones are another matter. They are to be cast into the depths of the sea, which will be ordered to keep them. They cannot be used, not because they would not be helpful to Israel but because of their defilement through the Amorites' practices. God informs Kenaz that Israel will be given twelve stones taken from the same place as the Amorite stones. The new stones will

---

16. Perrot dismisses the thought that this might be the river Pishon (Gen. 2:11) since it is not in Palestine. He suggests instead that it may be the river Qishon, Kison in the LXX (SC 230, 156).

17. The exact referent is uncertain. Harrington (*OTP*, 337, n. b) notes that in 25:10 the stones were hidden on Mount Shechem, but 22:8 speaks of the new altar at Shiloh.

be set on the priestly ephod across from the twelve stones of Exod. 28:17. As each of the twelve stones of Exodus is associated with one of the tribes, so each of the new stones will be associated with one of the tribes, an association to be determined by God alone. The ideal Israel, composed of twelve tribes, will have in its possession and in its cult miraculous stones every bit as powerful and mysterious as the Amorite stones, but unpolluted by the Gentile cult. Israel need not look beyond itself for otherworldly power and potent secrets.

Before executing the sinners, Kenaz makes a short didactic speech to the people, which fulfills God's command in 26:2. He gathers all the people and says,

> Behold you have seen all the wonders that God has revealed to us until this day *[usque in hodiernum diem]*. And behold, when we were seeking out all those who planned evil deeds craftily against the LORD and against Israel, God revealed them to us according to their works. And now cursed be the man who would plot to do such things among you, brothers (26:5).

The people respond, "Amen, Amen," signifying their agreement. Kenaz's speech forms an inclusion with the prayer in 25:6. There the sinners are described as those who "do not believe the wonders that you did for our fathers from the time you brought them out of the land of Egypt until this day *[usque in hodiernum diem]*." The sinners do not remember God's mighty works of the past. Kenaz interprets God's revelation of the sinners as another in the continuous line of God's marvellous deeds for Israel and reminds the people that they have seen this one. God's action on behalf of Israel continues "until this day." The emphasis on the deeds of the sinners as being evil and done "craftily" is typical of Pseudo-Philo, as is the recurrence of the idea of planning such evil deeds. Deeds against God are deeds against Israel, too. Had the sinners been able to operate undetected, they would have destroyed Israel by their iniquity. Kenaz ends his speech with a generalization. Not only must the sinners be punished, but anyone who would follow in their footsteps by plotting similar evil is cursed. Immediately after Kenaz's speech and the people's expression of agreement, the sinners are burned (26:5). The stones are not burned. The books are not mentioned here.

In LAB 26:6, Kenaz indulges his curiosity about the Amorite stones and books. He tries to destroy the stones but fails. Then he tries to blot out the books with water. That also fails. Kenaz does not test God or distrust the divine word, but rather confirms it. Kenaz exclaims, "Blessed be God, who has done so many mighty deeds for the sons of men, and he made Adam as the first created one and showed him everything so that when Adam sinned thereby, then he might refuse him all these things (for if he showed them to the whole human race, they might have mastery over them)" (26:6). Again the focus is on the reality of God's mighty deeds. Those deeds are for the benefit of humankind. The misuse of the mysterious stones both by Amorites and wayward Israelites shows that such power cannot be entrusted to humans. Foreseeing this, God showed the supernatural secrets only to Adam. Adam promptly sinned and these things were removed from him and from all humanity. Otherwise, foolish humans would have had access to powerful heavenly secrets, which would have led to disaster. The idea that human access to forbidden secrets leads to disaster is known elsewhere in Jewish literature.[18] In LAB 13:8, Moses is told that Adam had access to paradise but lost it when he sinned. In *2 Bar.* 4:3, Adam sees the heavenly temple before the vision is taken away when he sins. LAB 26:6 combines a special revelation to Adam that was removed from him with forbidden esoteric secrets becoming available to unauthorized humans. Kenaz's experiment with the stones and books makes him appreciate God's foresight in averting a potentially disastrous situation in which humans would have more knowledge and power than they could handle.

Having satisfied himself about the nature of the stones and books, Kenaz follows God's instructions and places them beside the altar (26:7). He then performs a large number of sacrifices and the people hold a feast. Again, sacrifice is seen as a proper way to relate to God. In 26:8 God takes care of the stones and books, as Kenaz had been told would happen. God uses angels as agents. In 26:9 Kenaz gets up in the morning and finds the twelve new stones associated with the twelve tribes, as God promised. LAB 26:10–11 lists the stones and associates each of them with a tribe.[19]

In 26:12 God tells Kenaz to put the new stones in the ark of the covenant. They are to be placed in the sanctuary when Jahel builds the temple.[20] The stones will be a memorial for God before Israel in the sanctuary. Such a memorial is necessary, for Israel tends to forget God's mighty acts. God says that when the temple is destroyed due to the people's sins, the stones will be removed from the sanctuary and returned to their place of origin, along with the twelve Amorite stones and the tablets of the Law.[21] There they will stay until the eschaton. This implies that the second temple is not as great as the first, a common view in the Second Temple period. God says that at the eschaton God will bring these stones, along with many others like them, and they will be the light for the righteous. The place of origin of the stones is one "where *eye has not seen nor has ear heard.*" These words from Isa. 64:4 again stress the otherworldly origin of the stones. Contemporary humanity has been deprived of the stones because of sin. After the eschaton, the just will enjoy the stones again. In this passage the stones symbolize preternatural blessings lost by humanity. The narrator again brings before the readers the protology and eschatology that frame everything that happens in the *Biblical Antiquities*. The stones recall the idyllic situation that humans lost through sin and the

18. For example, *1 Enoch* 7–8.

19. For similar lists and their relation to this one, see SC 230, 157; Feldman, "Prolegomenon," cxiv.

20. This is an obvious reference to the building of the temple by Solomon, but the name "Jahel" is a puzzle. Harrington (*OTP*, 338, n. e) makes this comment: "Jahel should be Solomon. Ithiel is one of Solomon's ten names in rabbinic literature. But Jahel may be the angel Jaoel as in ApAb 10:4, 9." See Feldman, "Prolegomenon," cxiv, on Ginzberg's solution (*Legends*, vol. 6, 183, n. 13).

21. For parallels with the hiding of the precious stones, Harrington (*OTP*, 338, n. h) cites *2 Bar.* 6:4–10; *4 Bar.* 3:7–14; *As. Mos.* 1:17; *Ant.* 18.4.1 § 85; 2 Macc. 2:4–8.

restoration of that situation for those found righteous in the end. The human condition is a result of God's blessings having been withdrawn because of sin. Kenaz responds by voicing Pseudo-Philo's pessimism about humanity: "And now today I know that the race of men is weak and their life should be accounted as nothing" (26:14).

LAB 26:15 ends the chapter. Kenaz does as God commands and puts the stones in the ark. Their splendor is again stressed: Their light is as potent as that of the sun. A puzzling element is that after Kenaz puts them in the ark, the text says, "And they are there to this day." Perrot avoids the difficulty by assuming that the author is writing from the temporal framework of the time of Kenaz, so there is no contradiction with the idea earlier in the chapter that the stones were not present in the second temple.[22]

Chapter 27: The Victory of Kenaz

Pseudo-Philo uses a large number of elements drawn from the Bible to weave a narrative about Kenaz's victory over the Amorites. Gideon's story in Judges 6–7 is especially influential. Perrot points out that although in 25:1 it is the Philistines who want war with Israel, in 27:1 it is the Amorites against whom Kenaz fights.[23] Since the Amorites' idolatry leads Israel astray in chapter 25, it is appropriate that Kenaz defeat the idolaters. A key dynamic in the narrative of chapter 27 is the interaction between Kenaz and the people. In 27:1, Kenaz's campaign meets with great success. It is a conventional campaign in which Kenaz has mobilized a large number of Israelites. The success of the battles is clear in the numbers—the Israelites kill a number of Amorites, more than four times their own.

Despite the Israelite triumph, some grumble against Kenaz, accusing him of relaxing at home while others do the fighting and risk destruction. Kenaz's servants report this to him and he arrests thirty-seven of his detractors, whose names are supplied.[24] The phrasing implies that the thirty-seven were not the only ones in Israel speaking against Kenaz, for the text says Kenaz "brought thirty-seven men from them who had been his detractors" (27:3). Kenaz voices his confidence in God's support of the Israelite cause when he says that he will punish the grumblers "when God will have worked salvation for his people by my hands" (27:4).

In the story that follows, the author uses that of Gideon as a model. Gideon's story stresses God's ability to conquer a powerful enemy with paltry forces, so that it is transparently obvious that the victory comes not through force of arms but through divine assistance. In the Bible it is God who insists Gideon pare down his army to three hundred men. Here the idea is Kenaz's. This expresses his tremendous trust in God. Unlike Gideon, Kenaz knows in

22. SC 230, 158–59.
23. SC 230, 159 (read "25:1" for "26:1").
24. Only thirty-five names actually appear.

advance that God does not need large numbers of troops. It is the people who must be taught that lesson. Kenaz tells his captain to choose three hundred men and to keep them ready day and night, keeping these plans secret (27:5). The plans must be kept secret so the people cannot interfere and will see only the result of the actions. The three hundred are to be kept ready because Kenaz has not yet consulted God, so he does not know the divine plans. Thus Kenaz shows complete confidence in God without falling into the trap of presumption, as did Joktan in LAB 6.

What follows transpires at night, a significant time for God's action in Pseudo-Philo.[25] Kenaz sends spies to determine the Amorites' location. The spies return with that information, along with news that the Amorites are "planning to come and fight against Israel" (27:6). Once again, the Israelites are portrayed as victims of aggression (see 25:1). Kenaz takes the three hundred men, now termed "horsemen," along with some trumpets (an element from Judges 7), and approaches the Amorite camp. He tells his men to wait while he approaches the Amorites alone. He will summon them with the trumpet if he wants them. In Gideon's story, the three hundred are not "horsemen," each of them has a trumpet and torches hidden in jars, and Gideon brings his servant Purah with him to investigate the camp. The expedition of Gideon and Purah is not preceded by other spies. As will appear later in LAB 27, the three hundred men have no role in Kenaz's victory, so Gideon's ruse of having the three hundred seem to be a much larger number by cuing them all to blow trumpets and bring the torches out of hiding simultaneously is unnecessary. Since Kenaz's men are horsemen, they are a substantial force, but even they are not used in the battle. Thus God's lack of dependence on force finds expression in three ways in LAB 27: The full army is kept out of the battle, even the three hundred are not used (a departure from the model in Judges 7), and no tricks are used. The trumpet becomes simply a means of signaling between Kenaz and his men, and the torches and jars disappear altogether. Pseudo-Philo has no servant with Kenaz when he goes to the Amorite camp. This makes Kenaz's answer to the grumblers in Israel's ranks clearer. They said, "Kenaz alone *[solus Cenez]* is busy at his home while others fight" (27:2). In 27:7, Kenaz alone *[Cenez solus]* goes to the Amorite camp.

Kenaz prays before descending to the enemy camp (27:7). As is usual in the *Biblical Antiquities,* a prayer is the vehicle for expressing important motifs. Kenaz addresses God as "LORD God of our fathers." Pseudo-Philo typically refers to the fathers when God is doing something that fulfills the covenant. Kenaz divulges the reason for his confidence in God when he prays, "You have shown to your servant the wonders that you are ready to do by reason of your covenant in the last days." Kenaz is one of the few characters called servants of God. He claims to have been shown God's eschatological wonders. God's motivation for those wonders is the covenant. Kenaz knows that God is about to save Israel, and he asks that God show one of the divine "wonders." Thus God's action in saving the people is a prolepsis of God's eschatological

---

25. See SC 230, 159, which refers to Le Déaut, *Nuit,* 289.

action. Although Kenaz knows God intends to save Israel, he still does not presume upon that and so prays for the victory. Kenaz says that he wants God to show his wonder through victory "in order that they [the enemies] and all the nations and your people may know that the LORD saves not by means of a huge army or by the power of horsemen." This is the language of holy war. The idea that God can vanquish powerful forces with small ones finds expression in such texts as 1 Macc. 3:16–22; 4:6–11; and *Pss. Sol.* 17:32–38. Kenaz believes in God's power, but everyone else must learn the lesson. It is significant that Israel is put into the same category as the enemy and the Gentiles because of its ignorance of God's power. Kenaz says, "If they but knew the sign of deliverance that you will work with me today!" He puts his own belief into practice by willingly leaving his huge army behind and going to the Amorite camp without his horsemen.

Kenaz will not go into battle presuming upon God's support. He asks for a sign. This request may have been inspired by Gideon's request for a sign in Judg. 6:36–40. Gideon's request was an expression of skepticism and fear, but Kenaz asks so that he can be certain he does God's will. The enemies' recognition of Gideon's sword in Judg. 7:14 comes as a surprise to Gideon and is meant to convince the fearful man. In LAB 27:7, the recognition of Kenaz's sword is suggested by Kenaz himself as a way for him to know God's will. Kenaz says that if the enemies fail to recognize his sword, this will mean God has handed him over to his enemies. But the following is Kenaz's advance interpretation: "For even if I be handed over to death, I know that the LORD has not heard me because of my faults and has handed me over to my enemies. But he will not destroy his inheritance by my death." Kenaz accepts a moral causality that says failure is due to transgression. His words recall Abraham's in LAB 6:11, where he says that any misfortune that befalls him is due to his sins. Kenaz further embodies Pseudo-Philo's views when he denies that the fate of one Israelite, no matter how illustrious, means the downfall of Israel. His words also resemble Joshua's in LAB 21:4, where he proclaims that the deaths of individual Israelites do not mean that God neglects to live up to the promises.

After praying, Kenaz approaches the Amorite camp and hears their boasting. They expect victory, for Israel has stolen their idolatrous nymphs and they think the idols will retaliate (27:8). In 27:9, Kenaz is clothed in the spirit of the Lord, as befits the first of the judges, and holds his sword aloft in the enemy camp. The Amorites immediately identify it as his and know it signals their defeat. Desiring to go down fighting, they seize their weapons. Once again Kenaz is inspired, this time being clothed with the spirit of power, and is "changed into another man" (27:10). This underscores the fact that it is God who wins the victory, not Kenaz. Kenaz invades the camp and begins to slay the enemy, but the narrator reveals that two invisible angels work with him.[26] One angel blinds the Amorites so that they kill one another and the other

---

26. For a discussion of the angels and their names, see SC 230, 159–60; Feldman, "Prolegomenon," cxiv–cxv.

holds up Kenaz's arms as he fights. The holding up of Kenaz's arms recalls Exod. 17:8–13, where Aaron and Hur support Moses' upheld arms to ensure Israel's victory against the Amalekites. There are ninety thousand enemy deaths, half brought about by Kenaz and the other half by the Amorites themselves.

After the battle, Kenaz's hand sticks to his sword. This strange detail has a parallel in 2 Sam. 23:10, where the hand of Eleazar ben Dodo sticks to his sword.[27] Eleazar's hand sticks to the sword because his arm was tired. The story ends there. Here the narrator explains that the power of the miraculous sword has flowed into Kenaz, forming a bond he cannot break. Kenaz seizes a fleeing Amorite and demands that he tell him how to release his hand. The Amorite instructs him to kill a Hebrew and to let the blood run over his hand. Sensing treachery, Kenaz tells the man that if he had said to kill an Amorite, he would have gone free. Since he has shown his hatred for Israel by telling Kenaz to kill a Hebrew, Kenaz kills him, runs the blood over his hand, and is released from the sword. This serves several purposes. It reinforces the idea of Amorite knowledge of arcane matters. At the same time, it portrays Kenaz in a posture superior to that of the Amorite: Kenaz outwits him. Finally, it confirms that Israel is the victim of foreigners. Although the Amorites have been soundly defeated and are on the run, the fugitive's hatred for the Hebrews is found blameworthy.

The battle is now over for Kenaz, the lone Israelite combatant. He undergoes a ritual purification in the river, puts on new clothes, and returns to his servants (27:12). Kenaz may purify himself because of the impurity contracted through contact with corpses.[28] God puts the servants into a deep sleep so that they do not see the battle. This proves they had nothing to do with the victory. They awake to find the field full of dead Amorites. The reality of their experience is emphasized by the phrasing: "They looked at him and saw with their own eyes, and behold the field was full of bodies." Their reaction is one of astonishment. Kenaz says, "Why are you amazed? Is the way of men like the ways of God? For among men a great number prevails, but with God whatever he has decided. And so if God wished to save this people by my hands, why are you amazed?" (27:12). His words repeat the holy war theme of the conquest of many by a few. He combines this with a theme dominant in the *Biblical Antiquities,* that the ways of God are not like the ways of humans. It is the most explicit statement of that theme since Balaam proclaimed it in 18:3, but the theme informs much of the narrative of Pseudo-Philo. Kenaz's questions express frustration with the Israelites' ironic ignorance. They should not be amazed, but they are. Kenaz tells the men to gird on their swords and return with him to the people, their "brothers."

LAB 27:13–14 contains the interaction between Kenaz and the people

27. Perrot points out that Ginzberg (*Legends,* vol. 6, 258, n. 77) found another parallel in a tradition about Joab whose hand stuck to his lance.

28. See Leviticus 21. Perrot (SC 230, 160) rightly refutes Philonenko's hypothesis ("Essénisme," 406–7) that Kenaz performs an Essene ritual.

occasioned by the victory over the Amorites. The people praise God for having appointed Kenaz leader and for showing that the words God spoke to
Kenaz were "worthy of belief." This vindicates Kenaz and his leadership, an
administration questioned in 27:1. The people continue, "And what we have
heard by word, now we have seen, and the work of God's word is manifest"
(27:13). This recalls Ephraim's and Benjamin's confessions. Ephraim's sin was
to desire to make their children pass through the fire, "to know if what had
been said would be proved by direct evidence" (25:13). Ephraim is skeptical
about God's willingness or ability to make good on the divine words. Benjamin
asks whether the Torah is divine rather than being Moses' invention. Such
skepticism shows the people's tendency to drift away from God in the absence
of continuous mighty signs. In 27:13 the people believe and praise God, but
only because they have now seen deeds that support the divine words.

Kenaz knows that the people do not appreciate the significance of his victory, for they probably think the three hundred horsemen fought with him.
They return armed as if coming from battle. Kenaz orders the people to ask
their "brothers" whether they fought with him. The men testify that they did
not even see the battle, just the result. Having heard this testimony, the people
exclaim, "Now we know that the LORD has decided to save his people; he
does not need a great number but only holiness *[sanctificatione]*" (27:14).
There is irony in these words. Not long before, thirty-seven men were arrested
for grumbling against Kenaz's leadership even though chapter 25 made it clear
that he was chosen by God (27:2). The negative attitude toward Kenaz went
beyond even the thirty-seven whom he incarcerated. Now that the people see
the result of God's saving action, they believe the words. This implies that
before seeing the most recent proof of God's word, they did not believe.

It is not clear what "holiness" means in this context. It is also uncertain to
whom or what the word applies. *Sanctificatio* occurs only two other times in
the *Biblical Antiquities,* 11:15 and 19:13. In 11:15, God says, *"Make me a sanctuary [sanctificationem], and the tent* of my glory will be *among you."* This
quotes Exod. 25:8. In 19:13, Moses is told that at the end the just will live in
the "place of sanctification" God had showed Moses (cf. 19:10). *Sanctus* is
used sixteen times. It refers to cultic objects in 13:1; 25:9; 25:10, 12; 27:8, 9;
52:1; and 63:1. It occurs in the phrase "holy spirit" in 18:11; 28:6; and 32:14.[29]
It is used in "holy land" in 19:10. There are four occasions in which it is applied
to humans. Deborah is called holy in 33:6, a hymn in her praise. In 53:9 the
priests are called holy in distinction from the people as a whole. LAB 53:13 is
ambiguous but appears to refer to Samuel or perhaps to God. Finally, Samuel
calls the anointed of the Lord holy in 59:2. The outcome of this survey is that
holiness is an attribute never assigned to the people of Israel as a whole anywhere in the *Biblical Antiquities.* It is applied to Deborah, the anointed, the
priests, and perhaps Samuel. The best interpretation of holiness in 27:14 may

---

29. Perrot (SC 230, 162) notes that the phrase "holy spirit" or "spirit of holiness" is common
at Qumran (twenty-five times), in the *Targum Neofiti* (fifteen times), but is found only three times
in the Old Testament and is rare in the Apocrypha.

be that it refers to Kenaz, the ideal leader. His complete obedience to God allows God to work salvation in Israel (27:12).

Now that Kenaz has proven his leadership to all Israel, he can again confront those who grumbled against him. He commands them to be brought to him so they can speak for themselves. When they come, Kenaz asks them why they grumbled. They respond, "We will die not for this sin that we are talking about now but for that previous one in which we were implicated" (27:15). (They refer to the sins confessed in chapter 25.) They continue, "For then we had joined in their sins, saying, 'Perhaps the people will not find us out,' and then we escaped the people." The sinners tell him that fire is an appropriate punishment because it was received by the sinners of chapter 25. There is no hint in chapter 25 that only a portion of the sinners had been discovered. Indeed, it is God who exposes them there. Now the unexpected news is that these thirty-seven grumblers also joined in the sins confessed by the earlier groups. This is yet another example of sin as subtle and hard to discern. Sinners do not always appear to be such. Kenaz burns them and puts their ashes in the river Fison. LAB 27:16 ends the chapter with the kind of chronological notice common in the Book of Judges. It says that Kenaz ruled Israel for fifty-seven years and that his enemies were fearful all his days. Kenaz's rule is unusually long, not surprising for this ideal leader.

Chapter 28: Kenaz's Covenant, Vision, and Death

As did Moses and Joshua, Kenaz delivers a testamentary speech. He summons "all of them," presumably all of Israel. Two prophets, Jabis and Phinehas, and the priest Phinehas, the son of Eleazar the priest, are singled out as being called. An unusual feature of the testament is that it is interrupted by Phinehas, who reveals a prophetic vision experienced by his father, entrusted to Phinehas when Eleazar was dying.

In 28:1–2, Kenaz introduces his testament. He begins, "Behold now the LORD has shown to me all his wonders that he is ready to do for his people in the last days." This echoes 27:7, where Kenaz acknowledges that he was shown such wonders. These are eschatological wonders whose benefit can be experienced proleptically in the present. God's work for the people is ongoing and leads toward divine blessing on earth, a goal repeatedly thwarted by Israel, and ultimate reward at the eschaton. Kenaz goes on to say that he will establish his covenant with Israel so they may not abandon the Lord. He reminds them of the fate of the sinners who confessed. Their punishment is termed a "wonder." For Pseudo-Philo, that term denotes all God's work, be it to reward the righteous or punish the wicked. He then exhorts the people to "stay in the paths of the LORD your God lest the LORD destroy his own inheritance" (28:2). Kenaz is one of Pseudo-Philo's heroes, and his words are fairly reliable. It is surprising to hear him contemplate God's destruction of Israel. Two things must be remembered. First, no one except God is guaranteed to be fully reliable. Even such figures as Samuel and Moses find themselves in positions that do not completely correspond with what God wants.[30] Second, whether or not God's commitment to Israel is unconditional is a point of tension throughout the *Biblical Antiquities.* In the course of the work, humans both presume on the indestructibility of the covenant and assume that it is destructible. God is often on the brink of annulling the covenant because of Israel's unfaithfulness, but the narrative shows that God cannot annul it. Kenaz is right in that Israel's sin will tempt God to invalidate the covenant, so Israel is indeed playing with fire when it sins, but he is wrong insofar as the narrative demonstrates that God will never succumb to that temptation.

In 28:3 Phinehas interrupts Kenaz's speech. He says that "if Kenaz the leader and the prophets and the elders command it," he will share with them something he heard from his father Eleazar as he lay dying; he says, "And I will not be silent about the command that he commanded me while his soul was being taken away." His tone manifests respect for Israel's leaders. Kenaz and the leaders reply, "Speak, Phinehas. Should anyone speak before the priest who guards the commandments of the LORD our God, especially since the truth goes forth from his mouth and a shining light from his heart?" (28:3). This answer evinces the highest possible regard for the priesthood. It is the priests' privilege and duty to preserve and expound the Torah, here spoken of as truth and light, as is typical of the *Biblical Antiquities.* The repetition of the words for "command" *(precipere, mandare)* is significant. Phinehas recognizes and respects the prerogative of the leaders to command, but they in turn acknowledge that there is a higher authority, God's commands in Torah, and that the guardian of those commands is the priest. "Command" in its various forms is a common term, since Pseudo-Philo is concerned that Israel and its leaders subject themselves to God's direction. The leaders allow Phinehas to proceed, so the text contains a testament within a testament. Eleazar's testament reported by his son is nested within Kenaz's testament. This is similar to Pseudo-Philo's device of nested quotations, and the purpose is the same—to use direct quotation to state something effectively. The readers hear not one vision but two. They receive the testimony of not one illustrious figure but two, Kenaz and Eleazar. One of those testimonies is mediated by yet a third eminent figure, Phinehas.

LAB 28:4 contains the largest complex of nested quotations in the *Biblical Antiquities.* It is structured as follows: Phineas says that Eleazar said Phinehas should say to Israel that Eleazar said that the Lord said. What the Lord says refers to previous divine words, so there could even have been yet another layer of quotation. Such extensive quotation both makes the narrative more vivid and stresses its reliability. The characters speak for themselves.

Eleazar's vision predicts Israel's unfaithfulness and God's faithfulness. In the vision, God reminds Eleazar that he and his father Aaron witnessed the divine toil for Israel. God predicts that after Eleazar's death, Israel will become corrupt and abandon God's commands, provoking the divine anger. God will

---

30. Moses' request in 19:9 that God not be angry is rejected in 19:11. In 55:1–2, Samuel misunderstands God's plans, and in 59:2 God is annoyed at his lack of vision.

then remember the time before the Creation when there were no humans and so no wickedness. This places full responsibility for evil in the world on the human race. God says that humans are created to praise God. The Creation is portrayed through the metaphor of a vineyard, wherein God chooses one vine to belong to God forever. God's intention is to have a permanent relationship with Israel, but Israel does not recognize God as its planter and refuses to yield its fruit.[31] The element of recognition, though it could simply mean to obey God, could tie into Pseudo-Philo's wider motif of recognition. Ironically, the people do not even recognize God as God. They do not see things as they are.

Kenaz, the elders, and all the people lament, "Will the Shepherd destroy his flock for any reason except that it has sinned against him? And now he is the one who will spare us according to the abundance of his mercy, because he has toiled so much among us" (28:5). As in the words of Kenaz in 28:2, the prospect of Israel's destruction is contemplated. They do not assert that God will destroy the people, just that the only thing that could lead to God's destruction of the people is their sin. Nonetheless, the leaders and the people fasten on the first element of Eleazar's vision, that God has toiled much for Israel, as a source of hope. Surely the God who has labored so over Israel will have mercy on it. Yet again God's mercy is balanced against the divine wrath, a dynamic familiar to the readers.

Kenaz receives a prophetic vision in 28:6–9 and conveys it in ecstatic speech as he receives it. The vision can be compared to that of Moses' in LAB 19:10, which he also sees after his testamentary speech. A holy spirit comes upon him and he prophesies. He proclaims that what he experiences is unlike anything he ever conceived of or expected. This fits the general outlook of the *Biblical Antiquities,* in which the characters do not perceive the full scope of the universe, God's action, or history. It is another instance of the ironic mode. Kenaz looks at his own past and realizes that to some degree even he has been operating in the dark. He continues, "Hear now, you who dwell on the earth, just as those staying a while on it prophesied before me and saw this hour even before the earth was corrupted, so all of you who dwell in it may know the prophecies that have been fixed in advance." It is unclear who these former prophets could be. The earth was corrupted rather early on and even Pseudo-Philo records no prophets at that ancient stage. But the corruption of the earth, although it appears to speak of the human condition in general, may refer only to the present situation. Kenaz may mean that previous prophets could foresee it. He may even be referring to Eleazar, already dead. Read this way, Eleazar's vision validates that of Kenaz. Just as the vision of Eleazar proved true, so the vision of Kenaz will also be proven true. The prophecies and the events that they describe are all "fixed in advance" (28:6).

Kenaz' vision begins with the Creation. He sees flames that do not consume, an apparent allusion to the burning bush in Exod. 3:2. It is from that flame that the Creation comes in the subsequent verse. He also sees springs

---

31. This is similar to the parable of the wicked husbandmen (Mark 12:1–9; pars.).

rising up for which there is no foundation. At this point God has yet to engage in creative activity, so 28:7 describes the situation before the Creation—no foundation or firmament, no mountains, a place in which "everything has no appearance and is invisible and has no place whatsoever." Kenaz says that what he sees makes no sense to him, but his heart "will find what to say."[32] The vision is incomprehensible on one level, and yet can be understood as saying something specific about the human condition.

The beginning of 28:8 describes the formation of the upper and lower firmaments. One is a platform formed from a spark from the fire that does not burn, and the other comes from the spring of 27:7.[33] Then comes the creation of humanity: "Now between the upper foundation and the lower there came forth from the light of that invisible place, as it were, the images of men; and they were walking around. And behold a voice was saying, 'These will be a foundation for men, and they will dwell in between them for 7,000 years'" (28:8).[34] Humans receive the name *homo* in 28:9.[35] This sets the stage for human history, which is to last seven thousand years (see 19:15). What is important for human history is covered with a brief sentence: "And when he will sin against me and the time will be fulfilled, the spark will be put out and the spring will stop, and so they will be transformed." This is a pessimistic view of humans since humanity as a whole is seen as sinful. When humans sin and the time is fulfilled, the upper and lower firmaments will pass away and humanity will be transformed. The latter transformation at the eschaton is well known in Jewish thought.[36] Although this short sentence says nothing explicitly about the righteous, the transformation in question must be of the good as well as the bad. For an example of the transformation of a righteous person at death, see 19:16, concerning Moses.

In 28:10, Kenaz emerges from his ecstatic state. The narrator says that he "did not know what he had said or what he had seen," a comment emphasizing the vision's heavenly origin. Kenaz says, "If the repose of the just after they have died is like this, we must die to the corruptible world so as not to see sins." The vision becomes an incentive for avoiding sin. Kenaz has seen the sweep of creation and the beginning and end of humanity. He shares the fruit of that experience with the people. He is their eyes, and from his vision they should learn his lesson. Through Kenaz the people have access to the meaning of creation. Since they know such things, their behavior should reflect that. Subsequent chapters show that the essence of Kenaz's vision is lost on them.

32. This recalls the way apocalyptic texts describe otherworldly realities.

33. Feldman ("Prolegomenon," cxv) finds a passage in the Talmud that seems related to Kenaz's vision here.

34. For a discussion of this number, see SC 230, 163–64. Perrot prefers the reading "four thousand years."

35. For a discussion of this reading, see SC 230, 164.

36. See *2 Bar.* 49:3; 51:1–10; 4 Ezra 6:16; 1 Cor. 15:51, cited by Perrot (SC 230, 164), who refers to Dietzfelbinger, *Pseudo-Philo,* 279, n. 261. See also Heb. 1:12, cited in SC 230, 131. Perrot (SC 230, 131–32) discusses the notion of humanity recovering the lost glory of Adam at the eschaton.

Chapter 29: The Judgeship of Zebul

Zebul is a minor judge in the *Biblical Antiquities.* There is no judge named Zebul in the Book of Judges.[37] One of the major functions of his story is to provide closure to the Kenaz cycle. Chapter 29 is in three parts. In the first, Zebul provides for the daughters of Kenaz. In the second, he establishes a treasury for the temple at Shiloh. In the third, he delivers a brief testamentary exhortation to the people.

Zebul's first act is to summon the people to discuss the situation of Kenaz's daughters. He begins, "Behold now we know all the toil that Kenaz toiled for us in the days of his life" (29:1). Throughout the narrative of Kenaz's judgeship, his role as God's agent was stressed. Zebul makes Kenaz the subject of the same verb, *laborare,* that God applied to the divine action in 28:4. As God "toiled" for Israel, so did Kenaz, devoting his whole life to that effort. Zebul claims that if Kenaz had sons, they would rule the people. Pseudo-Philo does not oppose dynastic rule as such. It is evidence of Kenaz's virtuous leadership that he gave his daughters nothing, "lest he be called avaricious and greedy." Zebul proposes that the daughters be given a "greater inheritance among the people."[38] The people agree. Zebul also gives husbands to Kenaz's daughters, a necessary step if they are really to be taken care of in ancient Jewish society. But the formulation of this matchmaking is unusual. Van der Horst says, "Still more striking, it is stated *not* that they are given to men as spouses but that men are given to them, which seems to be an intentional reversal to indicate their superior status."[39] The entire scene is an example of Pseudo-Philo's high estimate of women. True to Pseudo-Philo's interest in names, the names of the three daughters and their husbands are supplied.

Zebul next establishes a treasury for the temple at Shiloh. This act, not undertaken by any of the biblical judges, indicates strong support for the official cult. Zebul forbids anyone to contribute items contaminated by idols to the treasury, an order reflecting Pseudo-Philo's abiding concern with idolatry. This command is said to help avoid disturbance in the "assembly of the LORD *[synagogam Domini]*."[40] Zebul warns that idolatry incurs God's wrath. The people cooperate with Zebul's proposal, bringing to him all of their precious metal. The universality of the cooperation is emphasized with "All the people, from men to women," and the voluntary nature of the cooperation is disclosed

37. Zebul is the officer of Abimelech in Judges 9. See SC 230, 165; Feldman, "Prolegomenon," cxv.

38. Harrington (*OTP,* 342) indicates a parallel to daughters inheriting land in Numbers 36. There Moses gives land to the daughters of Zelophehad. Other clans of the tribe of Joseph object that the land might pass into the possession of other tribes, contrary to the Lord's commands. Moses stipulates that the land must always remain in the possession of Joseph. No such restriction applies to the inheritance of Kenaz's daughters, but that may be because division of land by tribe was no longer an issue in the real author's own time.

39. "Portraits," 34.

40. Feldman ("Prolegomenon," cxvi) points to parallels to this term in Rom. 16:16 and Acts 20:28.

with the words "whatever gold and silver their heart prompted" (29:3). The amount of gold and silver thus procured apparently pleased both Zebul and God. Kenaz left behind a prosperous and obedient Israel.

Zebul delivers a short testamentary speech (29:4), which accords with Pseudo-Philo's interest in providing guidance to Israel through the words of its good leaders. Zebul exhorts the people to concentrate exclusively on the Law and refers them to the "testimonies that our predecessors have left us as witnesses." Once again, the language of witness is to the fore. It is the past that witnesses to Israel, the only key to understanding its own identity and its special relationship with God.

7

Deborah: *Biblical Antiquities* 30–33

Deborah is one of the most remarkable figures in the *Biblical Antiquities*. Her importance is proven by the number of chapters devoted to her, as well as by the fact that some of Pseudo-Philo's most important ideas are put on her lips. Pseudo-Philo's treatment of her is a testimony to his high regard for women and to his determination to give them their rightful place in Israel's history.

Chapter 30: Deborah

The introduction to Deborah's story is considerably more detailed than in the Bible (LAB 30:1–4; Judg. 4:1–3). Judges says simply that the Israelites "again did what was evil in the sight of the LORD, after Ehud died" (4:1). Pseudo-Philo attributes the people's sin to the lack of a leader: "Then the sons of Israel did not have anyone to appoint for themselves as judge" (30:1). As a result they "forgot the promise and transgressed the ways that Moses and Joshua the servants of the LORD had commanded them, and *they were led astray after the daughters* of the Amorites *and served their gods*" (30:1). The reference to the ways commanded by Moses and Joshua typifies Pseudo-Philo's recollection of Israel's past as guidance for the present.

The people are said to have been seduced by the Amorite women and to be serving their gods. Consorting with foreign women and falling into idolatry are not mentioned in Judges 4, but it is part of Pseudo-Philo's condemnation of intermarriage and of its association of with idolatry.[1] True to Pseudo-Philo's interest in Amorites, the women here are of that nation. In 30:2 the Lord becomes angry and delivers a speech through an angel. There is no indication that the speech is actually delivered to any of the other characters, so this is one of the numerous instances where the readers hear God's reasoning first-hand while the characters in the story do not.

God's speech is in three sections: (1) recollection of Israel's election; (2) proclamation of Israel's sin; and (3) prediction of punishment. Part 1 is in two subsections. The first recalls Israel's election, and the second remembers the

---

1. The language resembles Num. 25:1–2; see *OTP*, 343, margin and n. a; see LAB 18:13–14. In Numbers the women are Moabites.

sending of Moses to implement that election. God chose Israel "from every tribe of the earth." It is appropriate that this notion emerges in this context, for the narrator has just connected idolatry with mingling with foreign women. Israel's identity and its service to its one Lord demands separation from the nations. God says that God's glory dwells within Israel. The term *gloria* has four main uses in Pseudo-Philo, all of which are found in the Bible. The first two uses speak of God's glory, and the second two speak of human glory. First, glory can be cultic. God dwells in the sanctuary and is accessible there (11:15; 15:5; 17:1; 54:6).[2] Second, it indicates God's mighty action on behalf of Israel. In 9:7 and 51:7, God *does* glory (see 32:1).[3] Third, it is used to denigrate human glory (6:1; 35:5; 64:4).[4] Finally, humans are glorified because of their relationship with God (19:16; 23:8).

In 30:2 God remembers that Israel's election meant the divine glory would "reside *[permaneret]* in this world with it." The word *permanere* is used in various contexts in the *Biblical Antiquities.* Here it connotes God's constancy in living with Israel through the cult and in God's reliable activity on Israel's behalf. Israel's election is consummated in the sending of Moses. Moses' role in Israel's history is defined in terms of Torah. Through him, Torah is given. The intimacy of Moses' relationship with God is indicated through the use of the term *famulus,* applied only to Moses (30:2; 47:1; 53:2, 8, 10; 57:2; 58:1).

Part 2 of the speech begins when God says, "And they transgressed my ways." The recollection of God's action for Israel followed by an accusation of Israel is a common pattern in Jewish literature. It can be found, for example, in the *rîb* form.[5] The recollection is the basis of the accusation. In 30:2, it is the giving of the Law that is remembered and Israel's sin is transgression of the divine ways elaborated in Torah.

In part 3, God says that God will raise up Israel's enemies against it. God then quotes what the people will say in the future about their punishment: They will admit they suffer "because we have transgressed the ways of God and of our fathers." The technique of direct quotation to make a stronger case is by now familiar to the readers. The people condemn themselves. This recalls Kenaz's statement in 27:15 that the sinners condemn themselves. The fact that the people parallel the ways of God and the ways of their fathers is another case of remembrance of the fathers.

---

2. This usage pervades the Psalms. Aside from the Psalms, it is found in Exodus with reference to the cloud and Sinai epiphany (16:10; 24:7, 16; 28:40). See also Lev. 9:6, 23; Num. 14:10; 16:19, 42; 20:6; Deut. 5:24; 1 Kings 8:11.

3. The idea of doing glory may ultimately derive from the Hebrew verb *kbd,* as used, for example, when God's glory is manifest in the divine victories over Pharaoh (see Exod. 14:4: *w'kbdh bpr'h;* see also Exod. 14:17, 18). The appearance of God's glory is often active in the Hebrew Bible—to see God's glory means to experience powerful divine activity (for example, Exod. 16:7; Num. 14:22).

4. This use is especially common in Proverbs dealing with personal glory (for example, Prov. 14:28), in Isaiah with reference to national glory (Isa. 8:7; 13:19; 14:18; 16:14; 17:3, 4; 21:16; 23:9; etc.), and in the Psalms with respect to both (Pss. 49:16, 17; 37:20; etc.).

5. See Stone, *Fourth Ezra,* 61. He refers to Ezekiel 20, Joshua 24, and Nehemiah 9.

God goes on to say, "And a woman will rule over them and enlighten them for forty years." This can hardly be part of Israel's punishment, even though in Judg. 4:9 Sisera's deliverance into the hand of a woman is a rebuke to Barak. Pseudo-Philo holds Deborah in high regard. Indeed, she is one of the book's most important characters and is a perfect leader. Pseudo-Philo's interest in Deborah is the more intriguing given Josephus's bias against her.[6] Van der Horst's statement about Pseudo-Philo's treatment of Deborah is as follows.[7]

> Right at the start the importance of Deborah is highlighted in *LAB* by the prediction of her rule—hers alone of all the judges—by God himself: "A woman will rule over them and enlighten *(illuminabit)* them for forty years" (30.2). The verb *illuminare* is used elsewhere in *LAB* (11.1–2; 12.2; 18.4; 19.6; 23.6, 7, 10; 33.1; 37.3; 51.3; 53.8), mostly with God or Moses as grammatical or logical subject. . . . It is as if the author wants to say that like God himself and Moses, Deborah will be a light for her people; it is God who says so at the beginning (30.2) and it is Deborah who echoes God's words at the end (33.1).

LAB 30:3 briefly summarizes Israel's oppression by Jabin the king of Hazor and his general Sisera (Judg. 4:2–3). In Judg. 4:3 the Israelites appeal to God for help. As usual, Pseudo-Philo adds direct address, this time in the form of a reflection by the people on their own predicament (30:4). It is not a prayer; the people talk to themselves. This is common in the *Biblical Antiquities*. The reasoning processes of all the participants are frequently revealed by the narrator, often in the form of allowing the readers to overhear conversations, soliloquies, or even inner thoughts. The people consider the punishment at the hands of Sisera a humiliation. The word *humiliare* is used elsewhere of Israel's oppression by the Egyptians (9:11; 23:9; see *humiliatio* in 9:6), Dinah's defilement by the men of Shechem (8:7), and Samson's defeat of the Philistines (43:1).[8] The people say Israel's shame is increased by the fact that it is supposed to be the most blessed of all the nations, but "now we have been humiliated more than all peoples so that we cannot dwell in our own land and our enemies have power over us."[9] They unambiguously assert their own responsibility for their misfortune. They echo Jer. 2:8 when they claim that they *"have walked in these ways that have not profited us."* They suggest a plan that all Israel—men, women, and children—fast for seven days in the hope that God will not "destroy the plant of his vineyard." The use of "vineyard" for Israel is used to express God's close relationship with it. The people's plan is not presumptuous, since they do not assume that their action will save them. God's salvation is only a "perhaps," hopefully evoked by the people's penitence.

In LAB 30:5, the narrator says that after the people fasted for seven days,

6. Van der Horst ("Portraits," 34; referring to Feldman, "Josephus") attributes this to Josephus's misogyny.

7. "Portraits," 34–35.

8. A use that stands apart from the others is when it is said that the angels' hymn ceased temporarily when Moses died. The word Harrington translates "stopped" in 19:16 is *humilietur*.

9. This plaint recalls 4 Ezra 3:2, 12–36, and *2 Bar.* 11:1–2. Stone (*Fourth Ezra*, 53) adduces rabbinic parallels.

God sent them Deborah. There is an implied connection between the fast and Deborah's appearance. Deborah is the answer to the people's prayer. She begins her judgeship with a speech not present in the biblical text. It underlines the importance of leadership and the hopelessness of the people without it, presents a pessimistic view of Israel, but declares that God continues to be faithful to them because of their fathers. The speech falls into three major sections. The first recalls God's deeds for the people, the second accuses the people of disobedience, and the third predicts what will happen to the people.[10]

The speech begins with the metaphor of the sheep silent before its slaughterer, from Isaiah 53. Pseudo-Philo adapts the image so that both sheep (Israel) and slaughterer (God) are silent. Both are silent because both recognize that the sheep's misfortune follows from its own action, even though the slaughterer "is sorrowful over it." God is not insensitive or vindictive. Punishment saddens God. Israel's image as a sheep leads to the idea that it is a flock whom God leads. Using that metaphor, Deborah describes God's leading Israel into the height of the clouds, putting the angels beneath its feet, and giving it the Law. In 15:5, another place where the giving of the Torah is remembered, God says that Israel received the cloud as a covering for its head and the angels were set beneath its feet. The Torah should have set Israel above the angels. Because of Israel's favored status, God sends them prophets and "leaders" (30:5). Even the "luminaries" stood still for Israel, an allusion to Josh. 10:12–13 when the sun stood still so Joshua could win the battle. In another reference to the same passage, Deborah reminds the people that God threw huge boulders down from heaven on Israel's enemies (Josh. 10:11). It is fitting that Deborah mention specific instances when God fought Israel's enemies since their present crisis is oppression by enemies.

The accusation against Israel in part 2 of Deborah's speech is elaborated in terms of leadership. Despite all God did for Israel, it did not obey when commanded by Moses, Joshua, Kenaz, and Zebul (30:5). In 30:6 Deborah refines that statement by saying Israel did indeed serve God when those four leaders were alive, but when they died Israel's "heart also died." Israel obeys in the presence of good leaders but strays in their absence. This states a principle illustrated throughout the work.

In part 3 Deborah predicts the Lord's favor toward Israel in spite of its sin (30:7). She says, "Behold now the LORD will take pity on you today, not because of you but because of his covenant that he established with your fathers and the oath that he has sworn not to abandon you forever." God is often tempted to abandon the covenant and could do so with justification since Israel often violates it. Nonetheless, God remains faithful to Israel's fathers, despite the failings of their seed. Deborah admits that regardless of God's faithfulness, Israel will continue to sin for the rest of its days. Then she predicts that God will do mighty deeds for Israel and will bring it victory over its

10. Van der Horst ("Portraits," 35) notes that Pseudo-Philo puts many of his main ideas into this speech.

enemies.[11] This fits well with the general viewpoint that sees God's favor based not on Israel's merit but on God's relationship with the fathers.

Deborah ends with "For our fathers are dead, but the God who established the covenant with them is life." The idea that God is life sounds rather metaphysical, but Pseudo-Philo is more interested in God's action and relationship with Israel than in ontological speculations. Deborah's statement affirms that although God's establishment of a covenant with Israel is in the distant past, it informs the present for God, who always lives. God's promises to the fathers determine Israel's present.

Chapter 31: Jael Defeats Sisera

Pseudo-Philo's rewriting of Judges enhances Deborah's status. In 31:1 she foresees everything that is about to happen, including the assistance to be given to the Israelites by the stars and lightning (see Judg. 5:20). Sisera's intentions are revealed by Deborah, who quotes his words directly. She says that Sisera boasts, "I am going down to attack Israel with my mighty arm, and *I will divide* their *spoils* among my servants, and I will take for myself beautiful women as concubines" (31:1). The quotation within a quotation is typical of the *Biblical Antiquities.* Pseudo-Philo bypasses the biblical interchange between Deborah and Barak in which Barak is reluctant to carry the battle to Sisera. In Judges, Barak's reluctance to fight Sisera without Deborah results in glory being taken from Barak because Sisera is defeated by a woman, Jael (Judg. 4:8–9). Pseudo-Philo shifts the focus so that Sisera's defeat by a woman becomes a punishment for his planning to steal Israelite women (LAB 31:1). The fit between punishment and crime serves Pseudo-Philo's interest in moral causality. The narrator says, "And on account of this [the intentions of Sisera] the LORD said about him that the arm of a weak woman would attack him and maidens would take his spoils and even he would fall *into the hands of a woman*" (31:1).

In 31:2 the readers again get a privileged look at God's thoughts and actions. In Judg. 5:20, one hears of the assistance of the stars only in passing, but in LAB 31:2 the narrator discloses that as soon as Deborah and Barak went to face the enemy, "immediately the LORD disturbed the movement of his stars." The readers are then privy to God's words to the stars: "Hurry and go, for your enemies fall upon you; and confound their arms and crush the power of their heart, because I have come that my people may prevail. For even if my people have sinned, nevertheless I will have mercy on them" (31:2). God says to the stars that the attackers are "your enemies." An attack on Israel is an attack on the stars. God stresses Israel's status as the chosen people twice here ("my people") and declares that even their sin will not

11. Harrington treats this as parenthetical. The statement seems to interrupt the flow of thought in the passage since the next sentence begins, "On account of this." The "this" must refer to God's faithfulness to the covenant with the fathers and not to Israel's sin. One manuscript omits most of the statement (see SC 229, 236–37).

prevent God from mercifully coming to their aid. The rest of 31:2 attests to the stars' obedience. They burn up the enemy according to God's command and spare Sisera for his special punishment, as God commanded.

LAB 31:3–9 is the story of Jael, wife of Heber the Kenite, a story from Judg. 4:17–22. Several elements from Judith's story are imported to show how Jael employs her beauty to vanquish Sisera, as Judith did Holofernes.[12] This amplifies the theme that Sisera's punishment fits his crime. He intends to use force to capture beautiful women, but his weakness for their beauty proves to be his downfall. Nickelsburg says, "Like Judith, Jael is a woman of immense courage begotten of her trust in God."[13] Pseudo-Philo also introduces another element that is entirely lacking in the Bible—God's control of Jael's actions.

In Judges, the morality of Jael's tricking of Sisera is questionable since there is peace between her husband's clan and that of Sisera's lord, King Jabin (Judg. 4:17). This troubling element is omitted in the *Biblical Antiquities.* Sisera flees the battle and comes to Jael's tent. Jael goes out to meet him, having beautified herself. The narrator explains, "Now the woman was very beautiful in appearance." The MT says nothing of Jael's beauty or of any attraction of Sisera to her. These elements come from the story of Judith.

In Judges 4, Jael's killing of Sisera comes as a surprise. Nothing in the narrative before 4:21 prepares the readers for her action. In LAB 31, Jael knows from the beginning what she is about to do. She deliberately lays a trap for Sisera. She not only tells him to turn aside, as in the Bible, she also tells him to eat, and it is she who suggests explicitly that he sleep. She has her servants attend him. Sisera enters the tent and finds rose petals scattered on the bed. Jael has prepared well. The seductive relationship between Jael and Sisera is explicit in Pseudo-Philo. Jael coyly suggests that Sisera can pay her back later. The narrator then discloses Sisera's inner thoughts: "If I am saved, I will go to my mother, and Jael will be my wife" (31:3). Sexual attraction is not in Judges, but is a driving force in the story of Judith and Holofernes. It is appropriate that Pseudo-Philo use it here, for he wishes to show that Sisera's desire brings about his defeat. Sisera's mention of his mother is ironic, for at the end of the chapter she waits with ill-founded confidence for his return with Hebrew concubines. The chapter ends with Barak sending her the head of her son with a taunting message.

In LAB 31:4 Sisera requests water, as in Judg. 4:19. In Judges, Sisera simply explains that he is thirsty, but here he connects his thirst to the flame he saw in the stars, against which he had been battling. God's participation in the battle through the stars is thus recalled. In Judges Jael immediately gives Sisera a drink of milk; here she tells him to rest first. She then goes out to get milk from the flock. Pseudo-Philo thus creates an opportunity for Jael to pray, a prayer the readers hear (31:5). Jael's prayer reminds God of Israel's election from all the tribes of the earth and draws attention to its predicament. The

---

12. Feldman ("Prolegomenon," cxvii) points out that rabbinic literature also stressed the effect of Jael's beauty on Sisera.

13. "Leaders," 55.

prayer is especially persuasive coming from a woman who does not belong to the chosen people. She says that God compared Israel to a ram who leads the flock of the nations.[14] This view of Israel is surprising for Pseudo-Philo. The usual picture of Israel is more dismal, as a nation that cannot even guide itself. It always depends on the right leaders to keep it in line.[15] This high estimation of Israel comes from a pious outsider, Jael, who is more capable of recognizing Israel's true destiny than is Israel itself.

Jael's reminder to God of Israel's election sets in relief the full significance of Sisera's attack; it is an assault on God's plans for Israel. Jael quotes Sisera: "And so look and see that Sisera has made a plan and said, 'I will go and punish the flock of the Most Powerful One'" (31:5). Sisera's audacity is all the more shocking given his admission of Israel's special status and his acknowledgment of God's power.

Jael's prayer next proposes steps she will take,thus proving herself innocent of presumption. She knows that she cannot act alone, nor can she follow plans of her own devising unless God approves them in advance. She proposes to take the milk of the flock (the flock to which God has compared Israel) and give it to Sisera so that he will be relaxed and she can move against him. This is another instance of the punishment ironically fitting the crime. Jael shows that she understands God's justice, but still she will not act without God's permission. She says, "This will be the sign that you act along with me, LORD, that, when I enter while Sisera is asleep, he will rise up and ask me again and again, saying, *'Give me water to drink,'* then I know that my prayer has been heard" (31:5). Jael's request for a sign betrays no lack of trust but indicates she is not presumptuous. In 31:6, Jael receives her sign. Sisera asks for a drink, claiming he is burning up so that even his soul is inflamed. This again points to the origin of the thirst, for God told the stars to burn up the enemies. The purposefulness of Jael's behavior is underlined here. She mixes wine with the milk to make Sisera sleep, something not present in the biblical version.[16] Having obtained the sign, she proceeds with resolve and cunning.

In 31:7 Jael finally does the deed, but it takes much longer than in Judg. 4:21. In Judges Jael simply picks up the stake, approaches Sisera, and drives it into his temple. The *Biblical Antiquities* adds to this by revealing Jael's thoughts as she approaches him. Although she has already received a sign, she asks for another. This allows Pseudo-Philo to introduce another narrative element from Judith. In Jdt. 13:9, Judith rolls Holofernes off the bed after killing him. Pseudo-Philo transforms this into a sign. Jael figures she can be sure that God acts with her if she rolls Sisera off the bed and he does not awaken. She does so and he remains asleep. Then Jael utters a brief prayer: "*Strengthen in*

14. Perrot (SC 230, 168) points out that elsewhere Israel is the flock (23:12; 32:5). In 23:7, the ram stands for Israel's wise men.

15. Perrot's (SC 230, 168) parallel of 51:3–4 does not contradict this, for there it is not Israel that guides the nations but Samuel.

16. Perrot (SC 230, 168) notes that *Midr. ha-Gadol* 1, 336 also claims that Jael got Sisera drunk. He remarks on the the similarity of the Hebrew words for "cream" (*ḥm'h;* see Judg. 5:25) and "wine" *(ḥmr').*

me today, Lord, my arm on account of you and your people and those who hope in you" (31:7). Jael does not pray in Judges 4, but in Jdt. 13:7, just before killing Holofernes, Judith says, "Give me strength today, O Lord God of Israel!"

Jael drives the stake into Sisera's temple. "And while he was dying, Sisera said to Jael, 'Behold pain has taken hold of me, Jael, and I die like a woman.' And Jael said to him, 'Go, boast before your father in hell and tell him that you have fallen *into the hands of a woman*' " (31:7). The conversation restates the appropriateness of Sisera's end—having illicitly desired Israelite women, he dies like a woman at the hand of one. Jael's taunt about Sisera's report to his dead father is the mirror image of the message brought to Israel's ancestors that the promises to them have been fulfilled (21:9). All people will know, either in this world or in the hereafter, that God is in control of all, and that moral causality rules the day. Jael leaves Sisera's corpse for Barak to see.

LAB 31:8 provides a brief ironic interlude before Barak arrives at Jael's tent. In Judg. 5:28–30, Sisera's mother waits for him to return and worries at his delay. Her ladies calm her fears with the assurance that Sisera is dividing the spoils, among which are "a girl or two for every man." Pseudo-Philo amplifies the irony of Judges by transferring the confidence of the ladies to the mother. Sisera's mother says, "Come and let us go out together to meet my son, and you will see the daughters of the Hebrews whom my son will bring here for himself as concubines" (31:8). Her complacent words form an inclusion with Deborah's quotation of Sisera in 31:1, where he says he will bring back Israelite women as concubines. His mother is certain that he has accomplished his purpose, but the readers know the truth.

When Barak arrives at Jael's tent, she calls him "blessed of God." Barak is less inadequate than in Judges 4. Jael does not merely show Sisera to Barak, as in Judg. 4:22, she actually hands him over to Barak. When Barak observes Sisera's body, he exclaims, "Blessed be the LORD, who sent his spirit and said, 'Into the hand of a woman Sisera will be handed over' " (31:9). Sisera's fate was decreed by God. The final irony of chapter 31 is that Barak sends Sisera's severed head to his mother with the words "Receive your son, whom you hoped to see coming back with spoils" (31:9). Those who think that they can "punish the flock of the Most Powerful One" (31:5) will taste the wrath of God, and in a way that befits their crime.

Chapter 32: Deborah's Hymn

Chapter 32 consists almost entirely of a hymn sung by Deborah, Barak, and all the people. At the end of the chapter, Deborah sings alone, and 32:18 refers to Deborah ending her words. Although the chapter shows no strict hymnic structure, basic elements of a hymn of praise are present: listing God's benefits, proclamation of determination to sing God's praise, and invitation to others to join in the praise.[17] The composition in LAB 32 has only a few points in common with the hymn in Judges. The hymn can be broken up as follows:

a. Statement that God's glory has been revealed in the victory over Sisera, and claim that this is like God's confusion of languages at Babel (32:1)
b. Abraham's election (32:1)
c. Isaac's birth (32:1)
d. The angels' jealousy (32:1)
e. Sacrifice of Isaac (32:2–4)
f. Jacob and Esau (32:5–6)
g. Exodus and giving of the Law at Sinai (32:7–8)
h. Moses' vision (32:9)
i. The sun and moon aid Joshua in battle (32:10)
j. The stars aid Deborah and the Israelites against Sisera (32:11)
k. Praise of God for present deliverance (32:12)
l. Various persons and elements praise God for fulfillment of promises (32:13–17)

The hymn ties the events of LAB 30–31 firmly to Israel's past and sees God's deliverance of the people from Sisera as of a piece with God's election of Israel, the rescue of Israel from Egypt, the establishment of the covenant, and God's assistance to Joshua in the conquest.[18]

Part *a* links the present to the past: "Behold the LORD has shown us his glory from on high, as he did in the height of the heavenly places when he sent forth his voice to confuse the languages of men" (32:1). This brings the attention of the readers back to the situation that led to Abraham's election. Deborah's hymn makes several connections between Sisera and Babel. God's intervention at Babel results in the "confusion of languages" and humanity's division into nations opposed to one another (LAB 6–7). In 32:1, the unity of God's "voice" is implicitly contrasted with the confusion of the "languages of men." Both at Babel and in the case of Sisera, God showed his glory "from on high," "in the height of the heavenly places." In Genesis 11, God descends from heaven to see the city and tower being built on the plain of Babel; in LAB 7 the narrator brings the readers into God's presence to hear the divine deliberations concerning stopping the tower, and in 31:2 the Lord tells the stars to go down to fight Israel's enemies. The phrase "on high" also connects Babel and Sisera to the sacrifice of Isaac, for in Gen. 22:11, 15, God's angel calls to Abraham from heaven (LAB 32:4).

Part *b* (32:1) equates God's rescue of Abraham from the fire with the nation's election. Abraham was chosen from among "all his brothers," making Abraham's offspring unique on earth. Part *c* (32:1) recalls Isaac's miraculous birth, saying that Abraham was old and Sarah was sterile. Sarah's sterility was mentioned in 8:1, but nothing was said of Abraham's age. The narrator always assumes the readers know a fuller version of events. Part *d* (32:1) says that the angels were jealous of Abraham, presumably because of his special relationship with God.[19]

Part *e* (32:2–4) is longer and more developed than the previous parts of the hymn. It deals with the sacrifice of Isaac, a topic already touched on in 18:5, where God tells Balaam that when Abraham was asked for Isaac in sacrifice, he did not refuse (see also 40:5). For that reason, Abraham's sacrifice was acceptable to God and because of Isaac's blood Israel was chosen. Nothing is said in chapter 18 about Isaac's attitude. In chapter 32, it is still Abraham's willingness to offer his son that is in focus, although Isaac's attitude is also considered. God gives Abraham a chance to prove his worthiness for his special status. Abraham proves worthy: "And Abraham did not argue, but set out immediately" (32:2). At the end of this section (32:4), Abraham's success at passing the test silences anyone who would speak against him, not just the jealous angels.

In 32:2, Abraham tells his son that he is to be offered as a holocaust. This provides an opportunity for Isaac's speech in 32:3.[20] Isaac's speech defends the idea that Genesis 22 describes a sacrifice, and it shows that Isaac, like his father, willingly accedes to God's demand.[21] Israel was chosen because of Abraham, but Abraham's son proved himself worthy of inheriting Abraham's special status.

In 32:3, Isaac questions the appropriateness of his sacrifice. He points out that God accepts animal sacrifices for sin but that humans are destined to inherit the world. He then asks Abraham how he can invite him into the next world.[22] Without waiting for Abraham's answer, Isaac goes on, "Yet have I not been born into the world to be offered as a sacrifice to him who made me?"[23] Isaac's answer to his own query is that the same God who accepts animal sacrifices predestined Isaac's sacrificial death. The rhetorical question signals Isaac's acceptance of God's will. Isaac proclaims that he is blessed to have been chosen to fulfill this role and asserts that no one will be able to question the appropriateness of speaking of his death as sacrifice, since God

19. See *Gen. Rab.* 55:4.

20. See SC 230, 171–72, for a discussion of issues in the interpretation of the speech and of its contacts with other Jewish traditions. See also Vermes, *Scripture,* 193–227; Feldman, "Prolegomenon," cxvii–viii.

21. For the Aqedah as a true sacrifice here, see SC 230, 171–72.

22. Isaac quotes Abraham's words back at him: "Come and inherit life without limit *[securam vitam]* and time without measure." Harrington (*OTP,* 345, n. f) explains, "Lit. 'life secure.' There may be confusion between the Gk. *apeiratos,* 'untroubled,' and *aperantos,* 'limitless.'" I take Abraham's words to be a reference to death and the afterlife. Perrot (SC 230, 171) notes that the idea of time without measure characterizes the world to come in 34:3, as well as in *Pss. Sol.* 14:10; *1 En.* 40:9; Mark 10:17; 4 Ezra 7:96; *2 Bar.* 44:13.

23. Feldman ("Prolegomenon," cxvii) points to *Ant.* 1.13.4 § 232 as a parallel: "He exclaimed that he deserved never to have been born at all, were he to reject the decision of God and of his father."

willed it. But he also insists he is unique. His death does not justify human sacrifice in general.[24]

LAB 32:4 shifts attention from Isaac back to Abraham. In 32:1, the victory over Sisera was compared to God sending his voice "from on high" to confuse human languages. Here God sends the divine voice *"from on high"* to stop him from slaying his son: "For now I have appeared so as to reveal you to those who do not know you and have shut the mouths of those who are always speaking evil against you. Now your memory will be before me always, and your name and his will remain from one generation to another." Abraham need not kill his son because his willingness to do so and Isaac's willingness to be sacrificed are enough to silence the tongues of his detractors. Abraham receives God's solemn promise that God will never forget him. All of the *Biblical Antiquities* proves God's faithfulness to those words.

Part *f* (32:5–6) briefly covers the birth of Jacob and Esau and the descent of Jacob into Egypt. Noteworthy is the emphasis on God's action, for Pseudo-Philo says that God gave Isaac his two sons. Further, the sons were born to Isaac's sterile wife, another indication of divine intervention. The uniqueness of this happening is strongly maintained: "It will not happen in this way to any woman, nor will any female so boast" (32:5).[25] It is remarkable that the name "Rebekah" is not mentioned here, nor does it occur anywhere in the *Biblical Antiquities*. Given the author's special interest in women, one might expect this strong woman to receive some attention. However, the biblical Rebekah dared to change the course of salvation history on her own initiative. Such a figure may have been problematic for an author who placed so much weight on God's initiative and action and defined good leadership not in terms of personal initiative but in terms of following divine instructions. The omission of Rebekah's name may well be due to Pseudo-Philo's mistrust of one who operated independently of divine direction. This suggestion receives support from the brief contrast between Jacob and Esau found at the end of 32:5: "And God *loved Jacob, but he hated Esau* because of his deeds." Pseudo-Philo resorts once again to his theory of moral causality: People get what they deserve. Esau was hated "because of his deeds." Pseudo-Philo even moves Isaac's blessing of Jacob to a position after Jacob's election by God (32:6). The text implies that Isaac's blessing flowed from God's choice of Jacob, not the reverse. This section of the hymn ends with a summary in which Jacob is blessed, sent to Mesopotamia, has twelve sons, and descends into Egypt. The stage is set for the Exodus and Sinai.

The Exodus and Sinai (part *g*; 32:7–8) are introduced in a manner typical of the Book of Judges. The people are oppressed by enemies, they cry out to God, and God hears them. Judges would then go on to narrate the choice of a judge to save the people, but in LAB 32:7 God's direct action in liberating

24. Perrot (SC 230, 172) rightly argues that Pseudo-Philo is not to be interpreted as saying that Isaac's death replaces temple sacrifice. That idea postdates the destruction of the temple by the Romans.

25. The text, which claims that Rebekah gave birth three years into her marriage, is probably corrupt. Originally, it may have read twenty-three years. See SC 230, 172–73.

them from Egypt is noted. God "brought them out of there and brought them to Mount Sinai and brought forth for them the foundation of understanding [*fundamentum intellectus*] that he had prepared from the creation of the world" (32:7). Whether the "foundation of understanding" refers to the Law or to divine wisdom in general is moot, since for the *Biblical Antiquities* God's wisdom is available primarily in the Law. Jewish tradition speculated on what preexisted or was planned before the Creation, and the Torah is often one of those things. Pseudo-Philo's characterization of the Law stresses its cosmic and historical significance. Styled the "foundation of understanding," the Torah is the key to the meaning of history and to the universe itself. God gives this key to Israel. The hymn demonstrates all that God has done for Israel. The rescue from Sisera's threat is but the last in a series of awesome deeds done by God for the chosen people.

The establishment of the covenant is now described. As in other descriptions of the bestowal of the Law, the entire cosmos is shaken to the very abyss.[26] It begins by saying that the "foundation was shaken [*commoto fundamento*]." Harrington rightly adds "of the world" to "foundation," for the text does not mean that the "foundation of understanding" is shaken, though the word *fundamentum* is employed in both cases. The coming forth of the foundation of understanding shakes the very basis of creation. This idea derives from the common idea that when God approaches creation, it quakes in the divine presence.[27] The cosmic effects of the divine presence are well represented in the biblical account of the events at Mount Sinai (Exodus 19). The foundation of understanding coming forth from God creates the same result, for the universe is in the presence of the ultimate divine wisdom. In 32:7–8, the description of the tumult in the universe is richly embellished. As in the other treatments of the Law, Pseudo-Philo presents it as the most important thing in the universe next to the Deity itself. But this portrayal of the events at Sinai centers not on the glory of the Law for its own sake but on the special relationship the giving of the Law creates between God and Israel. Therefore the litany of cosmic disturbances ends with the statement "All his creatures came together to see the LORD establishing a covenant with the sons of Israel" (32:8).

Part *g* ends on a note familiar to readers of the *Biblical Antiquities:* "And everything that the Most Powerful said, this he observed, having Moses his beloved as a witness" (32:8). God's title "Most Powerful" is common in this work, one of whose main themes is God's willingness to use that power for Israel. The declaration that God did everything God said is typical of Pseudo-Philo. The theme of witness runs throughout the *Biblical Antiquities.* That Moses is God's witness in this case is appropriate since he mediates those words and witnesses their fulfillment, partially in his own life and more completely in his visions (32:9; 19:10–16).

Part *h* (32:9) concerns a brief vision given to Moses before he died. Pseudo-

26. See LAB 11:5; 23:10; and our analysis of those passages.
27. For examples, see *1 En.* 1:4–8; Mic 1:3–4; Ps 97:1–5; *As. Mos.* 10:1–7.

Philo already described a predeath vision of Moses in chapter 19. This one is not merely a repetition, although nothing contradicts chapter 19. In each case, the vision is pertinent to its narrative context. In 32:9, God erects a platform from which Moses can see and shows him "what we now have as witnesses." God says, "Let there be as a witness between me and you and my people the heaven that you are to enter and the earth on which you walk until now. For the sun and the moon and the stars are servants to you." In Deuteronomy, earth and heaven are witnesses to God's covenant with Israel mediated by Moses (4:26; 30:19; 31:28). Here heaven becomes the place that Moses is about to enter and earth the place he has lived until the present. Moses is shown that the sun, moon, and stars are his servants. This fits the present context in that the stars have just finished fighting for Israel in chapter 31 (see below, 32:11), and the sun and moon are said in 32:10 to have fought on Joshua's side. The gist of Moses' vision is that the all-powerful God has a special relationship with Israel and will enlist the help of all creation in protecting it. This is essential to the foundation and identity of Israel and is attested to by the experience of the most important leader in its history, Moses.

Part *i* (32:10) supplies immediate evidence that Moses' vision was true. The sun and moon proved themselves to be authentic servants of Israel when they fought on its behalf at the time of Joshua. The episode alluded to is in Josh. 10:12–14. Pseudo-Philo recalls that Joshua was fighting his enemies when night approached. As in Judges 10, Joshua commands the sun and moon to stand still so that he can finish the battle against the Amorites. In the Bible, the prolongation of daylight was the full meaning of the event. Pseudo-Philo adds the detail that the sun and moon simultaneously gave light to Israel and darkness to their enemies, reflecting that God's creatures and elements of the universe are beneficial to the righteous and inimical to God's enemies.[28] God is again called the "Most Powerful," a title that fits the theme of this hymn, God's mighty acts for Israel.

Part *j* (32:11) summarizes the salvation wrought by God for Israel in the victory over Sisera. It stresses God's action, for it was God who "commanded" the stars to help Israel. God's motive is to reveal the divine power, a motive that matches the repeated use of the title "Most Powerful" in this chapter.

Part *k* (32:12) introduces the determination to praise God. It begins, "So we will not cease singing praise, nor will our mouth be silent in telling his wonders *[mirabilia]*." The first person plural indicates that it is still Deborah, Barak, and all the people who sing. The word *mirabilia* occurs frequently as a designation of the Lord's works for Israel. The hymn says the people will praise God "because he has remembered both his recent and ancient promises and shown his saving power to us." This is one of the most important themes of the *Biblical Antiquities*. Thanks is given for Jael's victory.

Part *l* (32:13–17) is the lengthiest portion of the hymn. It is an instruction to various persons and elements of the universe to praise God, supplying moti-

28. See our comments on 4:5. See also Wisd. 16:7–29.

vation for that praise. The form is known elsewhere in Jewish tradition.[29] It begins, "Go, earth; go, heavens and lightnings; go, angels of the heavenly host; go and tell the fathers in their chambers of souls and say, 'The Most Powerful has not forgotten the least of the promises that he established with us, saying, "Many wonders *[miracula]* will I do for your sons"'" (32:13).[30] Since a central point is to prove God's faithfulness to the promises to the fathers, important witnesses (angels, earth, heaven, lightning) are sent to the dead fathers to assure them the promises have been kept, as in LAB 21:9. Again, there is a series of nested quotations serving to prove that God kept a promise. Here, a generalized prediction is made based on God's miracles for Israel: "And now from this day on let it be known that, whatever God has said to me, he will do; these things he will do, even if man delays in praising God" (32:12). Since God has proven faithful, the divine words are reliable. Their reliability is underscored by the additional notion that God fulfills the divine promises regardless of human behavior.

In 32:14, Deborah herself is addressed; she is told to praise God and let the Holy Spirit awaken in her. In Judges, God's spirit often comes upon the judges to allow them to deliver Israel. That is not said of Deborah in Judges 4, neither is she said to be inspired by the Spirit when she sings in Judges 5. In Judges 4, Deborah is already judging Israel when the crisis arises. Pseudo-Philo makes up for the lack of reference to the Spirit in Judges 4–5 by attributing the Spirit to Deborah, but he does so in connection with her praise of God.

The hymn claims that the stars' intervention in the battle was a one-time event, not to be expected by Israel again, and that it happened at God's command. The hymn continues, "And from this hour, if Israel falls into distress, it will call upon those witnesses along with these servants, and they will form a delegation to the Most High, and he will remember that day and send the saving power of his covenant" (32:14). The stars will continue to be Israel's allies, but their role from now on will be to remind God of how much God did for Israel for the sake of the covenant, and this will spur God to defend the covenant. In 32:15, Deborah is addressed again, this time to instruct her to relate how she saw the stars fighting for Israel.

The earth is told to rejoice over its inhabitants because they know God. This must mean that since Israel has experienced God's power and understood it in terms of the covenant, it does indeed know the Lord.[31] The hymn praises the fact that God took Adam's rib from the earth (since Adam himself was

---

29. For example, see Psalm 148; Song of the Three Young Men. For an analysis of how the form was adapted in *2 Baruch* 10–12, see Murphy, *Structure*, 96–101.

30. This is the only occurrence of *miracula,* but it is clearly a synonym for *mirabilia* in the previous verse.

31. The designation of God as the one "that builds a tower among you" is unclear. Harrington (*OTP*, 347, n. p) chooses that reading over "burns incense" because of the reference to the tower in 32:1.

formed from the earth) to make Eve, because from Eve Israel descended. The hymn continues, "Your forming will be a testimony of what the LORD has done for his people" (32:15). Israel is the center of creation. The formation of the earth is yet another witness to God's action for Israel, perhaps a development of the idea that the earth is witness to the covenant, found in Deuteronomy and here.

In LAB 32:16, it is noted that night is approaching, threatening to put an end to the hymn. Day is told to tarry so that the hymn might be prolonged. This recalls that the day stopped to allow Joshua to finish his battle in Josh. 10:12 and LAB 32:10. The allusion to Joshua's battle is followed by an explicit reference to the Exodus. The coming night is compared to that on which God passed over the Israelites while killing all the firstborn of the Egyptians. Again, God's work for Israel forms a seamless web that spans all of history and involves the whole universe.

The hymn ends in the first person singular, so it is Deborah who says these words. LAB 32:17 brings together several themes found together elsewhere in Jewish tradition—creation, Passover, and the eschatological day.[32] Deborah says "then" she will cease her hymn, referring to the approaching night of 32:16. She will stop singing when night comes, "for the time is readied for his just judgments." The time frame has shifted from the historical situation of Jael's victory to the ultimate one—the end of the world and of all history. Jael's victory is of a piece with all of God's other salvific acts and should be seen in this ultimate framework. All salvation history is heading toward the ultimate consummation when God judges all according to how they have related to the divine saving activity.

At the time of the end, Deborah will sing a song to God "in the renewal *[innovatione]* of creation." In LAB 3:10, at the eschaton "there will be another earth and another heaven." In 16:3, God says that Korah and his band will be forgotten "until I remember the world and renew *[innovans]* the earth." The idea of a new or renewed earth is common in Jewish and Christian thought.[33] The hymn concludes, "And the people will remember his saving power, and this will be a testimony for it. And let the sea with its abyss be a witness, because not only has God dried it up before our fathers, but also he has diverted *the stars from their positions* and *attacked* our enemies" (32:17). The words in italics derive from Judg. 5:20. Pseudo-Philo emphasizes testimony and witness. The people will point to the concrete proof of God's saving power in the deliverance from Sisera. The sea, split at the Exodus, will be another witness. God's use of cosmic forces to save Israel stretches from the abyss to the heavens, as exemplified in salvation through the stars.

LAB 32:18 concludes the narrative of the victory over Sisera. Deborah goes up to Shiloh to sacrifice. Thus the attention is still on Deborah, as it was at the end of the hymn. Israel sacrifices and sings "to the accompaniment of

---

32. See SC 230, 175, which refers to *Tg. Ex.* 12:42–43, a reference that Perrot attributes to Le Déault (*Nuit*, 354, n. 50).

33. For example, see Isa. 65:17; Rev. 21:1.

the trumpets." Deborah comments, "This will be as a testimony of trumpets between the stars and their LORD" (32:18). Again the stress is on bearing witness to what the Lord has done.

Chapter 33: Deborah's Testament and Death

As Deborah is about to die, she calls the entire people to her to deliver her final speech. Her testament begins with an exhortation to listen and then reflects on death. There is a sapiential flavor to this chapter, both in Deborah's urging the people to listen and in the almost metaphysical treatment of death.[34] The sapiential tone is enhanced by Deborah's development of the fact that she is a woman. Although wisdom is more often presented in Jewish tradition as a lover than a mother, Deborah's accent on her womanhood connects with wisdom's portrayal in feminine terms. Deborah refers to herself as a "woman of God." Harrington comments that the phrase "seems to be the feminist counterpart of the common expression 'man of God.' "Deborah says that she "enlightens" the people "as one from the female race." She says, "Obey me like your mother and heed my words as people who will also die" (33:1). Motherhood is one female role in Pseudo-Philo's social setting that demands obedience. But the people must listen to her not only because she is their mother but also because they must all die one day, and she has insight into the nature of death itself, as becomes clear in her next words.

Deborah tells the people, "*Behold I am going today on the way of all* flesh" (33:2). The words echo those of Joshua in Josh. 23:14, but Deborah turns them into a reflection on what it means to die. She reminds the people that they also must come on the way on which she is about to embark. She exhorts, "Only direct your heart to the LORD your God during the time of your life, because after your death you cannot repent of those things in which you live" (33:2).[35] The state of the human heart is a constant concern to Pseudo-Philo.[36] The rest of Deborah's speech concentrates on the state of death, where humans have no ability to direct their own fate. Only decisions made in this life matter. At death, one's fate is sealed. One is incapable of morally significant actions after death. At death even the evil impulse ceases.[37] Death itself is God's agent, awaiting the command of God to bring humans forth for judgment.[38]

Having explained in forceful terms the necessity of correct decision during this life by asserting its impossibility in the next, Deborah creates an inclusion with the exhortation in 33:1–2 by repeating hers: "Now therefore, my sons,

---

34. The sapiential tone of the exhortation to listen is noted by Perrot (SC 230, 176).

35. For parallels, Perrot (SC 230, 176) points to *2 Bar.* 85:12, and Feldman ("Prolegomenon," cxix) notes *b. Šab.* 153a and *Midr. Qoh.* 1:15.

36. The phrase "direct your heart" is found only here. The nearest parallel is in 20:4, but instead of the verb *dirigere* the word *ponere* is found.

37. This idea is unique to Pseudo-Philo (*OTP*, 347, n. c).

38. See *2 Bar.* 21:23; 42:7–8 (SC 230, 176).

obey my voice; while you have the time of life and the light of the Law, make straight your ways" (33:3). In this concluding exhortation, the focus swings away from life after death to this life. Using language reminiscent of sapiential exhortations, Deborah tells the people to obey her. She defines life as the time when people can decide for or against God and as the period in which they have the light of the Law to guide them.[39] The "ways" of the people can be made straight by adherence to God's will expressed in Torah.

In 33:4, the people address Deborah as their mother. They recognize that at her death they will be leaderless, and that is dangerous.[40] They ask Deborah to pray for them after her death. This occasions another reflection by Deborah in 33:5, this time about the relation between the dead and the living. Just as morally meaningful decisions can be made only in this life, not the next, so also prayer on behalf of someone else or even thinking about them must cease at death. The dead cannot pray for or even know about the living.[41] Then Deborah says, "Therefore do not hope in your fathers. For they will not profit you at all unless you be found like them." Frequently the reader sees God helping Israel despite its unworthiness because of God's promises to the fathers. Yet here Deborah tells the people not to hope in their fathers. Harrington's comments are helpful here: "What is being disputed is the power of the dead to intercede for the living. See also 2Bar 85:12. Elsewhere in Ps-Philo (e.g. 35:3) the merits of Israel's fathers have power."[42] His point deserves development. The *Biblical Antiquities* attests throughout that God's relationship with Israel is permanent. The covenant is based upon promises to the fathers that will never be annulled. But that does not mean any individual Israelite or a specific Israelite generation will be in God's graces. The book advocates a fairly strict moral causality demanding that sins be punished. The tension between God's unconditional commitment to Israel and this moral causality informs the *Biblical Antiquities* as a whole. Individual Israelites and even whole generations can be punished, but that will never mean the end of Israel. Given this interpretation, Deborah's statement that the people cannot look to the fathers' intercession does not contradict the idea that God has a special relationship with Israel because of the fathers. Both are true, but in any given instance only being like the fathers can bring success. Deborah goes on to mention eschatological rewards for emulation of the fathers: "Then you will be like the stars of the heaven, which now have been revealed among you" (33:5). The idea that the righteous will join the stars is common in Jewish

---

39. Note the similarity in thought and language to John 11:9–10.

40. The interaction between Deborah and the people in 33:4–5 recalls similar interactions between Ezra and the people in 4 Ezra, and between Baruch and the people in *2 Baruch*. See 4 Ezra 12:40–50; *2 Bar.* 46–47; 77:11–17. The similarity in *2 Baruch* is especially close, since there the people are upset that Baruch is about to die and in the *Biblical Antiquities* they weep at the thought that Deborah is about to die.

41. Ginzberg (*Legends,* vol. 5, 160–61, n. 60; 419, n. 118; vol. 6, 199, n. 91) shows that the idea that the dead cannot intercede for the living is rooted in rabbinic literature (noted in Feldman, "Prolegomenon," cxix). For a full discussion, see SC 230, 177.

42. *OTP,* 348, n. d.

literature.[43] This depiction of the bliss of the righteous ties the chapter closely to chapter 32, where the stars' participation in the battle against Sisera is referred to repeatedly.

In 33:6, Deborah dies and is mourned by the people for seventy days. She is gathered to her fathers, those same fathers to whom she referred several times in the past four chapters. The people's lament, quoted directly by Pseudo-Philo, takes up Deborah's status as mother of Israel. She is called "holy one" and her role as leader is stressed. The lament is a celebration of her perfect leadership of Israel; its effect on Israel is summed up in the declaration "She firmed up the fence about her generation" (33:6).[44] Her leadership resulted in the protection of the people. Van der Horst concurs with Feldman's judgment that Deborah is "a mother in Israel fully comparable to the matriarchs, to the patriarchs, and to Moses."[45] Deborah dies, and the land is at peace for seven years.

43. The stars are often thought to be heavenly beings, sometimes angels. When the righteous are among the stars, they are in the heavenly places, close to God. See Murphy, *Structure*, 62; *2 Bar.* 51:10; Dan. 12:3; 4 Ezra 7:97, 125; *1 En.* 104:2; *2 En.* 1:5; Matt. 13:43.

44. For other instances of the same image, see SC 230, 178.

45. Van der Horst ("Portraits," 38) quoting Feldman ("Josephus'," 127).

8

From Aod to the Ascension of Phinehas: *Biblical Antiquities* 34–48

Chapters 34–48 cover the period between the first two great judges, Kenaz and Deborah, and Samuel. Of special concern in these chapters is the issue of idolatry. It is particularly evident in stories of Aod, Jair, and in the long complex involving Micah, the Levite's concubine, and the Israelite civil war (chaps. 44–47). Leadership is also important in these chapters, particularly in the stories of Gideon, Abimelech, and Jephthah. Samson's stories show the danger of mixed marriages. The chapters end with the ascension of Phinehas, marking the end of an era stretching from the desert period to the monarchy.

Chapter 34: Aod

This narrative is found nowhere else in Jewish tradition. Aod is a Midianite magician who leads the Israelites astray. Pseudo-Philo introduces him here because in Judges 4–5 the story of Deborah is followed by a description of Israel's oppression by Midian, a situation that provides the context for the story of Gideon. Judg. 6:1 says, "The Israelites did what was evil in the sight of the LORD, and the LORD gave them into the hand of Midian seven years." Pseudo-Philo takes this opportunity to insert an incident reflecting on Israel's seduction by foreign idolatry.

Chapter 34 features a conversation between the Israelites and Aod. It ends with God's anger at Israel's idolatry. The chapter is paradigmatic in that it presents in brief form an important theme of Pseudo-Philo—Israel is led into idolatry and abandonment of God through foreign influence. Foreign religion, here portrayed as magic, is seductive to the Israelites, who see it as embodying a power greater than that found in the Torah. But that power is shown to be deceptive and Israel is punished by God.

The initial exchange between Aod and the Israelites lays out the idolatry issue. "He said to Israel, 'Why do you pay attention to your Law? Come, I will show you something other than your Law.' And the people said, 'What will you show us that our Law does not have?'" (34:1). The temptation to idolatry is present here exactly as in chapter 25. The Israelites suspect that there is power in foreign religion not present in their own. They mistrust the power of Torah and so are unfaithful to God. Being unsatisfied with what the Law brings them and seeing the advantages of the religious secrets of the Gentiles, they let their curiosity get the better of them.

Aod answers the people's question about what he has to offer by asking them if they have ever seen the sun at night.[1] The people respond, "No," so Aod offers to show it to them "in order that you may know that our gods have power and do not deceive those who serve them" (34:1). The people say, "Show it." They are swayed by Aod's proposition, showing that they doubt God's power and suspect that God deceives them, particularly in the divine promises. There is irony in that Aod does accomplish the feat he promises, but only through magic, a term connoting trickery and falsehood. The readers see how he operates behind the scenes, while the people see only the results. The irony is complete when the narrator says in 34:5, "And the people of Israel were deceived and began to serve the gods of the Midianites." Promised a revelation of gods who have power and do not deceive, the Israelites accept the trickery that supports those empty promises. In 19:7, God predicts that when the people enter the land they will be deceived and led astray by graven images. This incident is but one fulfillment of that prediction.

The readers see the origin of Aod's power (32:2–3). Aod worships the angels in charge of magic and so is enabled to perform his tricks. The narrator explains that those angels were condemned and their power was not given to others, lest through the irresponsible disclosure of such secrets even the eschatological age be destroyed. This passage is in the tradition of angelic revelation of forbidden knowledge to humans and the punishment of those angels.[2] Pseudo-Philo does not deny some power to Aod, but the power comes through rebellious angels who were condemned and had their power curtailed. They will be allowed to exercise their influence only "until the age without measure comes" (34:3). The Israelites do not know the source of Aod's power as do the readers. They observe the sun shining at night and exclaim, "Behold how much the gods of the Midianites can do, and we did not know it" (34:4). They are fooled by Aod's tricks. In 34:5 the narrator reveals that God was testing Israel, allowing them to go their own way. God says in 34:5, "I will deliver them into the hands of the Midianites, because they have been deceived by them." This leads into Gideon's story and so rejoins the narrative of Judges.

---

1. James ("Biblical Antiquities," 180) finds a parallel in *Ascension of Isaiah* 4:5, where it is said concerning the Antichrist, "And at his word the sun will shine at night." Feldman ("Prolegomenon," cxx) notes that Dietzfelbinger (*Pseudo-Philo,* 285, n. 321) disagrees with James's reference to the Antichrist, but instead sees Pseudo-Philo as polemicizing against sun worship as found in the cult of Mithra (see Apuleius, *Metamorphoses* 11:23). Feldman rightly comments, "LAB's attack is not on sun-worship but on wizardry." See Ginzberg (*Legends,* vol. 6, 199, n. 93), referred to by Feldman in the same note, who refers to *Sipre Deuteronomy* 84, where the false prophet makes the sun and moon stand still, thereby testing Israel.

2. See, for example, *1 Enoch* 7–8; SC 230, 178–79.

Chapter 35: Gideon's Commission

Chapters 35–36 are structured by the narrative of Judges 6–8. Pseudo-Philo passes over the extensive description of Israel's situation (Judg. 6:2–5), as well as God's sending a prophet to explain to the people that they are being punished (Judg. 6:6–10). Instead, Pseudo-Philo goes directly to Gideon's encounter with the angel (Judg. 6:11–27). The encounter is highly developed. Pseudo-Philo uses the characters' words, especially those of the angel, to develop important themes.

The angel calls Gideon mighty in Judg. 6:12, 14, although it is clear that Gideon is in fact fearful. In 6:15 Gideon says he is the weakest in his family and his clan is the weakest in his tribe. That claim is not disputed by the angel. Judges 6–8 shows that God does not work through human strength but uses the weak to defeat the strong so that divine power might be known for what it is. The angel's ironic address to Gideon mocks human strength. Pseudo-Philo develops a different element of Judges 6, that of the blame for Israel's situation and its implications for God's faithfulness to the promises. Pseudo-Philo omits the distracting irony in the angel's interaction with Gideon. In 35:1, the narrator identifies Gideon as the "most powerful man among all his brothers," information that contradicts Judg. 6:15. Gideon's objection in Judg. 6:15 is rewritten in LAB 35:5 so that his weakness is not the issue. In the *Biblical Antiquities,* Gideon asks more generally about the appropriateness of choosing his family to rescue Israel. In Judg. 6:12, the angel greets Gideon with "The LORD is with you, you mighty warrior," but in Pseudo-Philo the angel just asks Gideon where he has come from and where he is going. The irony is removed from the encounter so that Gideon is a more credible challenger of God's justice. This throws the angel's response to him into greater relief.

In Judges, Gideon replies to the angel's greeting by challenging him to explain Israel's plight. Gideon asks why Israel is oppressed and where God's wonderful deeds are. In Pseudo-Philo, Gideon's challenge to the angel is essentially the same as in Judges, but Pseudo-Philo's Gideon is more aggressive, as he accuses God of wrongdoing by not fulfilling the divine promises. In Judg. 6:13, Gideon asks where are God's wonders that were recounted by the fathers. He then quotes the words of the fathers, "Did not the LORD bring us up from Egypt?" Pseudo-Philo's Gideon also quotes the fathers, but his quotation is, "The LORD has chosen Israel alone before all the peoples of the earth" (35:2). What is implied in Judges is explicit in the *Biblical Antiquities:* Gideon says Israel's plight contradicts what the fathers said about God's special relationship with Israel. Gideon's challenge is still stronger with his next words. Judg. 6:13 records him as saying, "But now the LORD has cast us off, and given us into the hand of Midian." In LAB 35:2 he says, "*And* behold now *he has delivered us up* and forgotten the promises that he told our fathers." He says that Israel would prefer to be destroyed all at once rather than through slow oppression, implying that God's ultimate intention is to destroy Israel.

In Judges 6, this interchange is followed by the angel's commission of Gideon to save Israel. In the *Biblical Antiquities,* the angel's commission is preceded by a speech in which he blames Israel for its predicament (35:3–4). Israel's own "schemes *[adinventiones]*" have brought about its distress.[3] Israel has "abandoned the promises" that it received from God. Gideon accused God; the angel accuses Israel. Abandonment of the promises is defined by the angel as Israel not being mindful of God's commandments revealed by its ancestors. It is ironic that Israel is guilty of the very forgetfulness of which Gideon accuses God. Nonetheless, the angel says, "He will have mercy, as no one else has mercy, on the race of Israel, though not on account of you but on account of those who have fallen asleep." The angel's revelation recalls Deborah's words in 30:7, when she tells Israel that God will have mercy on it even when it sins, not because of Israel but because of its fathers.[4]

Pseudo-Philo adds an explanation of God's decision to free Israel by Gideon's hand: "For the LORD says these words: 'Even if Israel is not just, nevertheless because the Midianites are sinners, though I recognize the wickedness of my people, I will forgive them and afterward I will rebuke them because they have acted wickedly. But for the present I will take my vengeance upon the Midianites' " (35:4). The reasoning is rather convoluted. God knows that Israel is unrighteous yet will deliver it, even as God punishes Midian for its unrighteousness. God forgives Israel in advance of any remorse on their part. God removes the Midianites' oppression from Israel before rebuking Israel, even though that very oppression is Israel's punishment. The preservation of the covenant is more important to God than the punishment of Israel's sin.[5]

In Judges, Gideon reacts to the angel's commission by protesting that he and his family are weak. The angel then promises to be with him. Pseudo-Philo rewrites Gideon's protest so that he questions the propriety of using him to rescue Israel. Then the angel launches into a short speech that recalls the principle voiced by Balaam in 18:3, "The plan of God is not like the plan of man." In 35:5, the angel says, "Perhaps you think that as the way of men is, so the way of God is. For men look for the glory of the world and riches, but God for the straight and good and for meekness." The angel's words about the ways of God and men build on the theme in Judges 6–8 that it is God who conquers Israel's enemies, a theme supported by the fact that Gideon is weak. Pseudo-Philo goes beyond the simple factors of strength and weakness into considerations of the world's vainglory and illusory wealth as opposed to goodness, uprightness, and humility.[6] This suits Pseudo-Philo's interest in morality.

---

3. The use of the term *adinventio* ties this passage in with Pseudo-Philo's general theme of the evil of human plans; see Murphy, "Divine Plan," and chapter 11 (this volume) under "Plans and Plots, Human and Divine."

4. See 2 Macc. 8:15.

5. See Murphy, "Eternal Covenant," 52.

6. Such themes are common in sapiential literature.

The angel underscores the divine initiative for the choice of Gideon to save Israel. He tells Gideon to prepare for battle, "for he has chosen you to take vengeance upon his enemies as he commanded you" (35:5).

In Judg. 6:17, Gideon requests a sign. He then prepares a meal for the angel and the angel burns it up with a touch of his staff. This signals to Gideon that he is dealing with God (6:19–24). Later in Judges 6, Gideon asks for additional signs (6:36–40). Pseudo-Philo telescopes these two requests. The motivation for requesting a sign is more respectful of God in the *Biblical Antiquities* than in Judges. In Judg. 6:36, Gideon says that he wants a sign "in order to see whether you will deliver Israel by my hand, as you have said." Pseudo-Philo rewrites this. Gideon justifies his request by citing the precedent of Moses, "the first of all the prophets."[7] If Moses, the greatest of the prophets, needed a sign, then of course Gideon would need one also. Gideon is anxious to avoid presumption: "But who am I, unless perhaps the LORD has chosen me? *May he give me a sign* so that I may know that I am being guided" (35:6). Gideon is a pious server of God, awaiting God's direction.

The sign bestowed by the angel is more impressive than any of the signs in Judges 6 (LAB 35:7). God's control of nature is manifest in the transformation of water into fire and blood. Although they are mixed together, the blood does not extinguish the fire nor does the fire burn the blood. The other signs of Judges 6 are briefly referred to but not narrated. The narrator explains that there is no need to tell of all the signs, for "are they not written in the Book of Judges?" Once again it is clear that the author expects his audience to know a broader story.

Chapter 36: The Rest of Gideon's Story

The rest of Gideon's story is abbreviated. Pseudo-Philo states simply that Gideon had three hundred men with him, omitting the explanation of how they were chosen (Judg. 7:1–8). There is no explicit mention in chapter 36 of the holy-war theme that God conquers many with few, a theme central to Judges 7. Gideon and his men approach the Midianite camp and hear them speaking, but the interaction between Gideon and God leading to that event and the detailed description of the foe's dream are absent. Instead, they hear each man in the Midianite camp speaking with his neighbor, saying they are about to be destroyed by Gideon's sword because God has delivered them into his hands. Pseudo-Philo adds, "He is about to destroy us utterly, that is, even mother along with children, because our sins have reached full measure as even our own gods have shown us and we did not believe them" (36:1). Even the Midianite gods witness that God is just and the disaster about to overtake Midian is fair. This notion is absent from the biblical text.

In 36:2, Gideon and his men take heart from what they hear from the

7. See LAB 53:1. For Moses as prophet, see SC 230, 180.

Midianite camp and the battle ensues. All hints that the battle is won by tricks are erased. The Israelites kill a huge number of Midianites and the rest flee. Pseudo-Philo bypasses the dense detail of the biblical narrative. He concentrates on the victory over the Midianites through God's power, a victory that punishes the Midianites for their sin. That the victory is really God's and not Gideon's is underlined by the rewriting of Judg. 7:20. In Judges, Gideon's men cry, "A sword for the LORD and for Gideon!" In the *Biblical Antiquities,* the cry is transferred to the lips of the Midianites, who shout, *"The sword of the Lord is upon us"* (36:2). The Midianites supply a powerful witness to God's action.

In 36:3–4, the narrator concludes Gideon's story. Gideon gathers the people and says, "Behold the LORD has sent me to fight your battle, and I have gone as he commanded me." These seemingly pious words express Gideon's recognition that he has merely done God's will and the victory is God's. Ironically, they introduce the story of Gideon's fashioning of the idolatrous ephod (Judg. 8:24–27). Judges records Gideon's idolatry but does not condemn it. Pseudo-Philo rectifies that. In LAB 36:4, the readers find out why God does not punish Gideon in this life, because they hear God's thoughts. God is unwilling to punish Gideon in this life because people will think Baal is avenging himself on Gideon for the destruction of his altar. God quotes people who said, *"Baal will avenge himself"* (36:4). God reasons, "Now if I should chastise him because he has acted wickedly against me, you may say, 'Not God, but Baal has chastised him, because he sinned against him first.'" God decides to let Gideon live and die of natural causes but promises that he will be punished after death. Having explained the situation, the narrator can conclude, *"And Gideon died at a good old age and was buried in his own city"* (36:4).

Chapter 37: Abimelech

Pseudo-Philo reduces Abimelech's story (Judges 9) to a version of Jotham's parable (Judg. 9:7–15) with a brief narrative introduction and conclusion. Pseudo-Philo's version of the parable is not really a parable, nor does it appear on Jotham's lips. It is an account of the plants talking to one another about Abimelech's ambitions.[8] It is ironic that nature knows better about the impossibility of Abimelech's leadership than he does. The plants also realize that they themselves are not destined for leadership, so they know themselves bet-

---

8. Feldman ("Prolegomenon," cxxi) thinks there is material missing from this chapter, and that originally this was a parable as in the Bible. James (*Biblical Antiquities,* 185) also thinks material has dropped out here. Feldman notes that Spiro ("Samaritans") bases much of his argument about the anti-Samaritan polemic in the work on this passage. Feldman rightly argues against this. Harrington (SC 229, 20–21) also sees material missing here, noting the absence of the judge Tola, the lack of identification of Jair in the next chapter, and discrepancies among the manuscripts. Perrot (SC 230, 184–85) argues for intentional omission of some details from Judges by Pseudo-Philo.

ter than Abimelech knows himself. The rewriting found in LAB 37 puts the emphasis firmly on the inappropriateness of someone seeking leadership on his own initiative.

LAB 37:1 summarizes Judg. 9:1–6: "And he had a son by a concubine. Abimelech *killed all his brothers,* for he wished to be leader of the people." The problem is that Abimelech seeks to be leader of the people, yet he has-killed his brothers. This is not how leadership in Israel is supposed to function. God chooses and appoints leaders, and those leaders should bring harmony to Israel under God. In 37:2–4, the trees of the field discuss the situation. In Judges, as each tree is asked to reign over all the trees, it indicates it would prefer its present life to that of a king. In the *Biblical Antiquities,* it is clearer that the reason each tree turns down the kingship is not just a matter of its preference but is due to the inappropriateness of its being king. This is manifest in the answer of the first to be offered the position, the fig: "Was I born for kingship or *rulership over the trees?* Or was I planted so as to reign among you? And so as I cannot reign over you, so Abimelech will not get a long tenure in his rule" (37:2). The fig knows it cannot rule, for that was not why it was planted. The same applies to Abimelech. One cannot become king by wishing it.

The vine says it was planted to yield sweetness to humans. Wine recalls blood, and the vine goes on to predict the shedding of Abimelech's blood. The apple tree knows its purpose is to produce apples, and predicts Abimelech's death by stoning. (Perhaps apples evoke the idea of throwing.)

The bramblebush is the final plant to be asked to reign, and its reply is the lengthiest of all. It first reminds its hearers that it has a long and important history. It begins, "When the thorn was born, truth shone forth in the form of a thorn." The incident to which the text refers is unknown. It is clear that the thorn stands for truth and this becomes the requirement for leadership later in its speech. The bramble recollects that Adam's sin led the earth to bring forth thorns and thistles and that God spoke to Moses through "a thicket of thorns," the burning bush of Exodus 3. The bramble uses this brief review of its history to prepare for its present declaration: "And now it will be that the truth may be heard by you from me." Then the *Biblical Antiquities* rejoins the text of Judges in the idea that those who ask the bramble to rule must dwell in its shade, that is, acquiesce in the consequences of its rule, or be destroyed by it.

There follows a brief insertion in which allegorical interpretations are given to the apple tree symbolizing the "chastisers," the fig signifying the people, and the vine symbolizing "those who were before us." Finally, the bramble-bush is explicitly likened to Abimelech. Perrot sees the trees in search of a king to be the people of Shechem, the apple tree to be the punishers of Abimelech, the fig tree to be those who oppose him, and the vine Gideon's murdered sons.[9] The similarity between the bramble and Abimelech is in the spirit of Jotham's parable, for which Abimelech's reign is like the fire that comes

9. SC 230, 183–84.

from the bramble to destroy the trees. The allegorical interpretation of the first three trees may have been a later addition to round out the interpretation.[10] Abimelech is identified as the one who "killed his brothers unjustly and wishes to rule among you" (37:4).[11] The key to the interpretation lies in the next sentence: "If Abimelech be worthy of them whom he wishes to rule for himself, let him be like the bramblebush that was made to rebuke the foolish among the people" (37:4). Any leader of Israel must be the one to correct the people. Abimelech himself is the epitome of foolishness, so he cannot possibly fulfill the requirements of a good leader.

In 37:4, fire goes forth from the bramble to destroy the trees, whereas in Judg. 9:15 only the possibility of this is mentioned. Pseudo-Philo is always concerned with moral causality and divine retribution. God deals not just in warnings but in concrete punishments. The narrative ends in 37:5 with a brief mention of Abimelech's ignominious end.

Chapter 38: Jair

Pseudo-Philo bypasses Tola's judgeship (Judg. 10:1–2) and goes directly to that of Jair (Judg. 10:3–5).[12] Jair is a minor judge about whom little is known. Pseudo-Philo makes him a paradigm of the bad leader. Jair builds a sanctuary and commands all to worship Baal under penalty of death. This sets up a narrative like that of LAB 6, where Abraham risks death by refusing to participate in building the tower of Babel. In LAB 16, the same sort of story is told, but with the difference that the judge (Moses) is righteous and the defendant (Korah) evil. These stories recall the trial scenes in Daniel 3 and 2 Maccabees 7.

In the analysis of LAB 6, attention was drawn to the following elements present in both LAB 6 and Daniel 3: (1)Someone reports to a leader (or leaders) about those who disobey the leader's commands; (2) the leader interrogates the offenders; (3) the offenders stand firm in their position and demonstrate awareness of the terrible punishment awaiting them; (4) the leader angrily passes sentence; (5) the sentence is carried out; (6) some of those who carry out the sentence are killed by the very punishment meant to consume their victims; and (7) the victims are miraculously saved. LAB 38 follows essentially the same structure with minor adaptations. In a section that corresponds to part 1, the narrator reports that seven men will not worship Baal and gives their names. The succeeding passage shows that the information has indeed been given to Jair. There is no direct equivalent of part 2, but Jair's command to worship Baal leads to the arraignment of the resisters before him, so he must interrogate them. In part 3, the resisters stand firm, making a speech about the foolishness of sacrificing to Baal. In part 4, Jair passes sentence. In

10. See SC 230, 183, which notes that the order of the trees is different in the interpretation.
11. Perrot (SC 230, 181, 184) sees this as a possible allusion to the Herodians of the real author's time.
12. There is perhaps a lacuna here. See SC 230, 184–85.

part 5, the sentence is carried out. In parts 6 and 7, an angel miraculously saves the resisters and burns the executioners, and then Jair is killed by the fire.[13]

Pseudo-Philo shows a characteristically pessimistic view of Israel in that only seven men refuse to participate in Jair's idolatry. The resisters' speech at their trial (39:2) shows them to be following the commandments given by "those who were before us and Deborah our mother." As usual, Pseudo-Philo highlights Israel's ties to its own past and its fathers, and in this case its mother. The resisters say that if Baal is God, he should speak as God. The *Biblical Antiquities* is full of God's words, and those words always affect the life of the people. The seven are thrown into the fire. The angel Nathaniel extinguishes the fire, burns Jair's servants, and saves the seven men, blinding the people so that no one can see them escape. Then Jair appears. The text continues, "And before he burned him up, the angel of the LORD said to him, 'Hear the word of the LORD before you die. And these words the LORD says: "I have raised you up from the land and appointed you leader over my people, but you rose up and corrupted my covenant, and deceived them and sought to burn up my servants with the flame because they chastised you' " (38:4). The nested quotations make clear that the readers hear God's authentic words and therefore get the proper interpretation of events. Jair is a legitimate leader in a way that Abimelech is not. Whereas Abimelech wished for himself to be leader, Jair was chosen and raised up by the Lord. But while a true leader teaches the people truth (37:4), Jair deceived the people by leading them into idolatry, the ultimate deception. The central purpose of Israelite leadership is to preserve the covenant, but Jair corrupts it.

God bestows the designation *servus* on the resisters and thus emphasizes the enormity of the crime of wanting to execute them. Jair wants to kill them precisely because they are true to the covenant and chastise him for abandoning it. God says that Jair will perish by "corruptible fire," as the servants were made alive by "a living fire." Jair will dwell in the fire. Thepunishment fits the crime, as Jair is tormented by the fire he prepared for God's servants. It also illustrates the idea that the very things that serve as punishment for the wicked bring benefit to the righteous.[14]

Chapter 39: Jephthah

Chapter 39 is in two parts; the first concerns the persuasion of Jephthah by his brothers to accept the leadership of Israel, and the second describes his work as leader. Both parts contain extensive dialogue. In 39:1, Israel is being attacked by the Ammonites. The narrator says twice that the Ammonites have captured Israelite cities, a detail not mentioned in Judges 10–11 that is stressed again later in the story2. They bemoan the fact that God has abandoned them and say, "There is no leader who may go in and go out before us." They

13. For the angel's name, see Feldman, "Prolegomenon," cxxi–cxxii.
14. See our comments on LAB 4:5.

recognize the importance of leadership to their well-being. Then they decide to take the initiative: "Now therefore let us see whom we may appoint over us to fight our battle." Such initiative should arouse apprehension in readers who have seen repeatedly that actions taken without God's command or approval usually end in disaster.

In 39:2, Pseudo-Philo omits any mention of the fact that Jephthah was the son of a prostitute and attributes his being driven into the land of Tob to his brothers' envy of his strength as a warrior. In Judg. 11:6, his brothers, faced with a superior enemy, come to him for help and ask him to be their commander. Pseudo-Philo expands their request with the following words: "For who knows if you have been kept safe to these days or freed from the hands of your brothers in order that you may rule your people in this time?" (39:3). This sentence is full of irony. The very brothers who unjustly drove him out now speculate on God's possible intentions at work in their unjust actions. They admit that Jephthah needed to be rescued from them and they now look for him to rescue them. Further, they confess no one knows whether God has chosen Jephthah to lead Israel.

In 39:4, Jephthah expresses skepticism about his brothers' request. His ironic question about whether their hate has really turned to love is added by Pseudo-Philo. The brothers tell Jephthah that God has freed Israel in the past in spite of their sins and Jephthah should do likewise in the face of Israel's distress. Jephthah retorts that God "has the time and place where he as God may restrain himself out of his long-suffering," but that Jephthah is unable to demand vengeance in a future life (39:5).[15] Jephthah articulates a motif that permeates the *Biblical Antiquities:* God's retribution is inexorable and extends to the afterlife. Gideon's story has just shown that one cannot judge God's retribution by looking at a person's fate in this life only. The brothers use the image of the dove, who, when her young are taken from her, puts the misfortune behind her. They point out that Israel has been compared to the dove.[16] Jephthah should act as does the dove. Finally, Jephthah comes with them.

Jephthah's first act is to gather the people to speak to them, following a general pattern in the *Biblical Antiquities.* What the leader has to say to the people is at least as important as what he or she does for them. Jephthah's speech falls well within Pseudo-Philo's point of view. He begins, "You know that, while our leaders were still alive, they warned us to follow our Law" (39:6). Jephthah is still reticent about his own leadership, since he speaks of "our leaders." He numbers himself among the people, not setting himself apart from them. The leaders obey "our Law," the Law that gives Israel its identity. Jephthah says that the Ammonites have led Israel astray to serve their gods, who would destroy Israel. Contact with foreigners causes Israel's downfall because it leads to idolatry. Jephthah's plan for action is praiseworthy

15. Feldman ("Prolegomenon," cxxii) says, "The notion that God has time and place to repose Himself of His long-suffering is unique with LAB within the Jewish tradition."

16. Perrot (SC 230, 187) points to rabbinic and pseudepigraphical parallels (*b. Ber.* 53b; *Cant. Rab.* 2:14; 4:1; 4 Ezra 5:26). See also LAB 21:6; 23:7.

and appropriate given Pseudo-Philo's viewpoint: "Now therefore set your hearts on the Law of the LORD your God, and let us beg him together, and so we will fight against our enemies, trusting and hoping in the LORD that he will not deliver us up forever. Even if our sins be overabundant, still his mercy will fill the earth" (39:6). Israel's hope is based on God's mercy, a divine trait emphasized throughout the *Biblical Antiquities*. Jephthah's speech is not presumptuous. He does not assume that God will save the people but hopes for it. Meanwhile, he encourages the people to do what pleases God.

The people pray according to Jephthah's instructions, requesting God's help on the basis of Israel's election. The prayer echoes Moses' in chapter 12. Both prayers use the image of Israel as a vine planted by God; both refer to Israel as God's "inheritance." The prayer in chapter 39 adds the elements of God's gift of the land, since Israel is now settled there, and the plea that God not hand Israel over to those who hate God. Oppression of Israel is equated with hatred of God.

The second part of chapter 39 opens with 39:8. It begins, "And God repented of his wrath and strengthened the spirit of Jephthah." God finally enters the action and helps Jephthah. Jephthah is not a leader like Abimelech, who desired the leadership for himself, or like Moses, who was chosen by God from the beginning. He is chosen by the people and seems to prove himself a good leader by his interaction with them.

Jephthah sends an emissary to the Ammonite king named Getal.[17] As in the Bible (Judg. 11:12–28), there is a verbal interchange between the two messengers, but Pseudo-Philo subtly refocuses the conversation. In Judges, Jephthah asks why the Ammonite king is making war against Jephthah's land. The king answers that it is because the Israelites took his land. Jephthah responds that Israel took the land only of those who forcefully resisted its passage through their land, that is, the Amorites under Sihon, so they deserved to lose their land. In the *Biblical Antiquities,* Jephthah asks not why Getal is warring against Israel but why Getal is taking Israel's cities (39:8; see 39:1). Judges contains no such accusation. Jephthah reminds Getal that Israel did not dispossess Getal's people. Jephthah demands that the cities be returned lest Getal taste his anger. Jephthah threatens to repay the Ammonites not just for their present injustices but also for "past offenses." He says he will "repay your wickednesses on your own head." He also reminds Getal of the Ammonite deception of Israel when Israel first approached Canaan. In 39:9, Getal answers with indignation, attacking Israel's estimation of its own status and claiming it thinks so highly of itself because it has stolen Amorite lands. He quotes Israel as saying it will take other Ammonite cities if Getal persists.

Pseudo-Philo's rewriting of Judges shifts the ground of debate between Jephthah and Getal. It is no longer clear that Getal is warring against Israel because Israel stole his land. Jephthah is the first to raise the issue of stealing,

17. Harrington (*OTP,* 352, n. e) says, "Perhaps this is 'Zenon, surnamed Cotylas, who was ruler of the city of Philadelphia' (Ammon) in Josephus' *Ant.* 13.8.1 § 235 (also *War* 1.2.4 § 60)." See Chapter 1 (this volume) under "Place and Date."

and it is the Ammonites who have stolen Israelite cities. Pseudo-Philo also adds other charges against the Ammonites, citing past offenses and deceptions not recounted in the Bible or in the *Biblical Antiquities*.[18] The effect of the rewriting is to make Ammon appear wrong and Israel right. This is the function of Jephthah's speech in Judges, too, but Pseudo-Philo's more succinct version of Jephthah's speech makes the case clearer and adds the accusation of the Ammonites' theft of cities.[19]

Jephthah tells Getal that God will destroy Getal unless he relents. He continues, "For they are not gods, as you say they are, who have given you your inheritance that you possess; but because you have been deceived by following after stones, fire will come after you for vengeance" (39:9). This changes Judg. 11:24, in which Jephthah says, "Should you not possess what your god Chemosh gives you to possess?" Judges does not question the existence or power of Chemosh. Pseudo-Philo, true to the sustained polemic against idolatry, uses this to strike at idolatry again. The text borrows a traditional Jewish polemic against idols, alluding to them as mere "stones."[20]

In 39:10, Jephthah prepares for battle, but as in the Bible he makes a rash vow: *"When the sons of Ammon have been delivered into my hands and I have returned, whoever meets me* first *on the way will be a holocaust to the Lord."* In Judg. 11:30–31, these words occur in a prayer. Pseudo-Philo softens the shock a bit by making them simply a declaration, not a prayer. Jephthah is a character tailor-made for one of Pseudo-Philo's themes—that people can be well-intentioned and foolish.

A striking difference between the Bible and Pseudo-Philo in what follows is God's enhanced role in the action. The readers immediately experience God's reaction to Jephthah's rash vow (39:11). The narrator says that God is angry and then quotes the divine words. God is angry because Jephthah's vow could result in something inappropriate, such as a dog being sacrificed.[21] God decrees that Jephthah's vow will "be accomplished against his own firstborn." What the readers can know from the Bible, that Jephthah's vow led to his daughter's death, is now unambiguously attributed to God's decision. God concludes, "But I will surely free my people in this time, not because of him but because of the prayer that Israel prayed" (39:11). Usually the liberation takes place not because of the merits of the people but because of the promises to the fathers. Here Pseudo-Philo makes clear that Jephthah's leadership was ineffective but that God rescued Israel anyway. Israel's prayer (39:7) argued from the fact of its election and implied that God's well-being was tied to Israel's welfare. That sort of prayer is often successful in Jewish tradition.[22]

18. Perrot (SC 230, 188) suggests Deut. 23:4–5.

19. This may reflect events close to the real author's time. Who controlled what cities in Palestine was an ongoing issue in the Second Temple period.

20. See Isa. 44:9–20; Jer. 10:1–16; Ps. 135:15–18; Wisdom 13–14; Romans 1.

21. For rabbinic references to such an objection, see SC 230, 188.

22. See our comments on LAB 12:8–10.

Chapter 40: Seila, Jephthah's Daughter

In 40:1, Jephthah's victory over Ammon is described.[23] As he comes home, women come out to greet him with song and dance. In Judg. 11:34, only his daughter comes forth. In both Judges 11 and LAB 40, Jephthah is grief-stricken when he sees his daughter. In Judg. 11:35, Jephthah's words leave ambiguous who is to blame for the misfortune: "Alas, my daughter! You have brought me very low; you have become the cause of great trouble to me. For I have opened my mouth to the LORD, and I cannot take back my vow." Josephus (*Ant.* 5.7.10 § 264) has Jephthah blame his daughter. LAB 40:1 places the blame more squarely on Jephthah by removing the first two sentences of Judg. 11:35.

Jephthah reveals his daughter's name to be "Seila," whereas she is unnamed elsewhere in Jewish tradition. Jephthah declares her to be aptly named since she is to be offered in sacrifice. Her name could mean "asked for" in Hebrew.[24] Jephthah says that he does not know whether joy at his victory or sadness at his daughter's death will prevail in him. Pseudo-Philo shows more interest in Jephthah's inner conflict than does the Bible. As in the Bible, Jephthah asserts that he cannot undo his vow.

In Judg. 11:36–37, Seila responds to her father in two sections separated by the editorial phrase "And she said to her father" at the beginning of 11:37. Pseudo-Philo follows Judges' division of Seila's speech into two parts. In the first section of the daughter's words in Judges, she tells her father to carry out his vow, since he has been given victory. In LAB 40:2–3, she also tells her father to perform his vow, but her words are developed. She firmly decides for her father in his wavering between joy and sadness, bravely declaring that the joy of Israel's liberation outweighs the sadness of her death: "Who is there who would be sad in death, seeing the people freed?"[25] To prove her point, Seila recalls the sacrifice of Isaac, emphasizing the willingness of both Abraham and Isaac to make Isaac a holocaust.[26] She claims that Abraham was actually rejoicing when resolving to sacrifice his son, a model Jephthah does not follow. This happened "in the days of our fathers," the foundational and paradigmatic time. This is the third time (see LAB 18:5; 32:1–4) Pseudo-Philo uses Isaac's sacrifice to make a point, despite the fact that it is not narrated in its proper chronological spot (LAB 8). Seila ends this first part of her speech by telling her father to carry out his vow, lest by his reluctance to perform his vow he should "annul everything" he vowed (40:3).[27] Seila's comparison of her death to the Aqedah is remarkable. The importance of the

---

23. For studies of Seila, see Philonenko, "Iphigénie;" Alexiou and Dronke, "Lament;" Bogaert, *"Antiquités."*

24. *OTP,* 353, n. b; SC 230, 189.

25. Josephus (*Ant.* 5.7.10 § 265) attributes the same attitude to Jephthah's daughter.

26. On parallels to this view of the Aqedah, see Feldman ("Prolegomenon," cxxiii) and Perrot (SC 230, 190).

27. The wrong attitude could invalidate a sacrifice (SC 230, 189–90).

Aqedah to Pseudo-Philo is evident; it is mentioned three times. P. S. Alexander says, "One feels that the sacrifice of Seila had a deep significance for the author of *LAB:* it has become the feminine counterpart of the *aqedat yizhak.*"[28] Van der Horst says, "What we have here is in fact a second Aqedah, completely on a par with the first, but this time it is a woman who is the protagonist."[29]

In Judg. 11:37, Seila asks to be allowed to go to the mountains for two months with her companions to bewail her virginity. In LAB 40:3, she requests time for lamentation but does not mention the figure of two months. She later seems to take only as much time as is needed to utter her lamentation of 40:5–7, leaving no room for suspicion that she is stalling her fate. In LAB 40:3, Seila explains her motivation for going to the mountains. She declares that she weeps only for her youth and virginity and is willing to do her part for Israel. After telling of her plans to lament and to include all nature in her tragedy, she says, "For I am not sad because I am to die nor does it pain me to give back my soul, but because my father was caught up in the snare of his vow; and if I did not offer myself willingly for sacrifice, I fear that my death would not be acceptable or I would lose my life in vain." Pseudo-Philo plays upon the poignancy of Seila's death but presents her, like Isaac, as one who places Israel's good above her own. The tragedy of her lost youth underlines her piety and willingness to sacrifice all for Israel. She follows a pattern supplied "in the days of our fathers" by Isaac and exhorts her father to complete the picture by emulating Abraham.

Seila receives permission to go to the mountains to lament. Pseudo-Philo says that the wise men of the people could not say anything to her. The readers hear God's thoughts on what is happening: "Behold now I have shut up the tongue of the wise men of my people for this generation so that they cannot respond to the daughter of Jephthah, to her word, in order that my word be fulfilled and my plan that I thought out not be foiled" (40:4). If the wise men were allowed to speak, they might put a stop to the proceedings. Harrington notes, "A rabbinic tradition says that Jephthah's daughter was sacrificed because the scholars forgot that his vow was invalid."[30] But the plans of God must be fulfilled. The strategy of allowing the readers to hear God's pronouncements directly makes the connection between God's plans and actual events unmistakable. God goes on to praise the wisdom of Seila, leaving no doubt that not only is she courageous but also in tune with God's will. God says, "The virgin is wise in contrast to her father and perceptive in contrast to all the wise men who are here" (40:4). Only she sees God's will clearly. That entails her death, but the framework of the *Biblical Antiquities* goes beyond this life; her reward will be to have her death appear precious in God's sight, and to "fall into the bosom of her mothers." This last is a striking phrase. Harrington comments, "The phrase 'bosom of her mothers' seems like a fem-

---

28. "Retelling," 110.

29. "Portraits," 41.

30. *OTP,* 353, n. g; Feldman ("Prolegomenon," cxxiii) points to *Gen. Rab.* 60:3 and *Lev. Rab.* 37:4 for this view.

inist counterpart to the more usual 'bosom of his fathers'; see also 'woman of God' in 33:1."[31]

LAB 40:5–7 contains Seila's lament, lacking in the biblical text. Perrot notes the careful structuring of the hymn.[32] In the lament, there is tension between the moving depiction of Seila's loss of her youth and potential womanhood and the need to fulfill Jephthah's vow. Pseudo-Philo presents the tension in the strongest terms, stressing the overriding importance of the fulfillment of God's plans and Jephthah's vow. The hymn dwells on the real cost to Seila of her obedience to God's will. It is not just death but the loss of the potential of her young life that is in question, yet she is most insistent on the inevitability of her sacrifice.

Seila's lament is in three sections. First, she declares she is being put to the test. Second, she argues that her death is not in vain. Third, she shows that her birth has been in vain. Seen this way, the hymn is built on the tension between the usefulness and the tragedy of Seila's death. It illustrates the ambivalence of divine–human interaction, yet insists on the necessity of God's will being fulfilled. She grapples with the same mixed emotions her father has and so is tested. In part 1, she invites nature to "be witnesses" of her dilemma, evoking the witness theme of the book. But as shown by her words to Jephthah and God's comments about her, she courageously takes the position dictated by wisdom. The hymn gives the readers a close look at her pain so that her obedience is deeply appreciated.

Part 2 of the hymn is summarized in its introductory words: "But not in vain *[non in vano]* will my life be taken away" (40:5). *Vanus* is a favorite word of Pseudo-Philo. What is or is not in vain is an abiding concern of the book. Then Seila says, "May my words go forth in the heavens, and my tears be written in the firmament!" (40:5). These lines stress the hymn's tension. The reason she proffers for the usefulness of her death is that it represents Jephthah's honoring of his vow and that such is the obligation of "a ruler," despite his role as "a father" (40:5).

Part 3 of the hymn appears to contradict part 2. It begins, "But I have not made good on my marriage chamber," and proceeds to develop that in emotional terms. In the body of the development is the statement "O Mother, in vain have you borne your only daughter" (40:6). That a woman is born only for the purpose of being married is, of course, a cultural assumption. What is remarkable about Pseudo-Philo is the explicit and developed tension between this expectation and the will of God that Seila be in the mold of Isaac. The hymn directs attention back to nature, which is now asked to join in the lament for her loss. Nature is capable of bearing witness to the rightness of her choice and death, and at the same time sharing in the sorrow that death creates.

LAB 40:8–9 brings the story of Jephthah and Seila to a close. It narrates Seila's return to her father, which apparently takes place immediately after her lament, implying that she is anxious to proceed. As in the Bible, it is

31. *OTP*, 354, n. i.
32. SC 230, 191.

claimed that a festival in her honor is instituted in Israel, but Pseudo-Philo goes further by stating that the lamentation at her death extended to all the people: "And the children of Israel made a great lamentation" (40:8). LAB 40:9 notes the death of Jephthah but ignores the brief account of the war within Israel that occurred during his judgeship. To narrate that event would detract from Seila's powerful story.

Chapter 41: Abdon and Elon

Pseudo-Philo reduces the number of judges between Jephthah and Samson to two (Judges has three). As in the Bible, they are minor, but Pseudo-Philo embellishes their stories. LAB 41:1 contains the story of Abdon. The Moabite king accuses Israel of taking his cities. Abdon retorts, "Have you not learned from what happened to the sons of Ammon, unless perhaps it is so that the sins of Moab have reached full measure?" Abdon voices the moral causality that fills the book. There is then a brief account concerning the Israelite army of twenty thousand that kills twice its number of the enemy and returns in peace. As elsewhere in the *Biblical Antiquities,* sacrifice is suitable to thank God.

LAB 41:2 summarizes Elon's judgeship, saying only that he took twelve cities from the Philistines. LAB 41:3 says that after Elon's death the Israelites "forgot the LORD their God and served the gods of those inhabiting the land; and on account of this *they were handed over to the Philistines* and served them *forty years."* Pseudo-Philo adopts the scheme of Judges, where the people fall into idolatry because of their leader's death and the attraction of the native gods. Pseudo-Philo uses the stock phrase "inhabitants of the land" for those who lead Israel astray. LAB 41:3 tightens the connection between Israel's sin and its punishment by saying that serving foreign gods is punished by serving the Philistines.

Chapter 42: The Announcement of Samson's Birth

LAB 42 rewrites Judges 13.[33] Pseudo-Philo considerably expands the short introduction to the story in Judg. 13:2. As usual, names are added to the text. Samson's mother's name is Eluma (found nowhere else in Jewish tradition) and there are genealogies for Manoah and Eluma.[34] Particularly striking is the

---

33. Harrington (*OTP,* 355, n. a) notes the elements common to the story of Samson's birth here and that of John the Baptist and Jesus in Luke—"a genealogy not derived from the OT, sterility, prayer in seclusion, the angel's appearance, the name announced." This does not indicate literary dependence but represents a style of narrating the birth of important personages current in the first century C.E. He also refers to LAB 9. See also Winter, "Proto-source;" Perrot, "Récits."

34. Feldman ("Prolegomenon," cxxiv) notes that the genealogies make Samson's ancestry noble, while rabbinic sources denigrate it.

effort to explain Eluma's sterility. Eluma and Manoah argue over who is at fault for their childlessness.[35] Because of the book's presuppositions concerning moral causality, it is assumed that one or the other of the parents is to blame. After mutual recriminations in 42:1, Eluma resorts to prayer in 42:2, asking that the guilty party be made known. She says that whoever is guilty should repent, and that if both are guilty they should be made aware of it so they will stop arguing and bear their guilt silently.

In 42:3, the angel's words from Judg. 13:3 are recrafted. His announcement to Eluma that she will bear a son is joined with the information that she is to blame for her barrenness, but that her coming pregnancy answers her prayer. Both elements are absent from the biblical text. As is typical of Pseudo-Philo, 42:3 stresses God's action in relieving her of childlessness: "The LORD has heard your voice and paid attention to your tears and opened your womb." Eluma is told to name the child Samson, *"for* this one *will be dedicated* to your LORD." In Judg. 13:24, it is the mother who names the child; here God takes the initiative. This makes the story more like other stories of illustrious births, and it also reinforces Pseudo-Philo's usual insistence on God's action.[36] In the Bible, the angel says that Samson is to observe Nazirite vows and that he is to deliver Israel. The two facts are simply juxtaposed. Pseudo-Philo omits direct reference to Samson's Nazirite status and transfers the command to avoid wine and unclean foods, directed to Samson's mother in Judges, to Samson. The narrator then says that he is to live his abstemious lifestyle *"because* (as he himself has said) *he will free Israel from the hands of the Philistines"* (42:3). A direct connection is drawn between his lifestyle and his saving Israel. God's guiding role in the action is reinforced by the interpolation "as he himself has said."[37]

In 42:4, Eluma admits her guilt to her husband: "I am placing my hand upon my mouth, and I will be silent before you all the days because I have boasted in vain and have not believed your words." Eluma embodies the good person who admits her faults and holds herself accountable for them. Manoah does not believe his wife and prays, lamenting his apparent unworthiness to have the angel appear to him. His unbelief furnishes a motive for seeking to clarify things further. Manoah's assumption that the angel did not appear to him because of his unworthiness may be based upon the cultural presumption that the angel should be talking to the man of the family, but it also presents him sympathetically since he shares the humility earlier displayed by his wife. As in the Bible, the angel again appears to Eluma, who fetches Manoah. The angel says, "Run and announce to your husband that God has accounted him worthy to hear my voice" (42:6). Moral status is at the forefront.

LAB 42:7 summarizes Judg. 13:11–14, avoiding repetition of information already given to Eluma. Then Manoah says to the angel, "See to it, sir, that *your word be accomplished* regarding your servant" (42:7). Feldman takes this

---

35. For other versions of their arguments, see Feldman, "Prolegomenon," cxxiv.
36. On the etymology of "Samson," see Feldman, "Prolegomenon," cxxv; SC 230, 195.
37. I agree with Harrington's (*OTP,* 356, n. h) identification of "he" as God.

as Manoah's continued suspicion of the angel.[38] If so, it is muted. One could read the ambiguous sentence as a prayer that God's will be done. In 42:8, Manoah asks the angel to eat with him and assures him he will later give him gifts to take along as sacrifices. The angel refuses the meal, lest not enough be left over for sacrifice. This provides motivation for the biblical version, where the angel simply refuses the meal and suggests the sacrifice without making a connection between the two. The angel is concerned that Manoah have enough for sacrifices, for he says, "If you offer *sacrifice* from what is not yours, I cannot show favor to you." This further clarifies the angel's motivation.

LAB 42:9 rewrites Manoah's sacrifice (Judg. 13:19–20), importing the element from Judg. 6:21 of the angel touching the sacrifice with his staff, causing fire to come forth from the rock and devour the sacrifice. LAB 42:10 repeats the couple's fear at having seen God face to face but goes further than the biblical text in having Manoah express anxiety at having been so bold as to ask the angel's name. LAB 42 did not include Manoah's question about the name, but it is assumed that the readers know Judges 13. Manoah demonstrates proper piety and fear of the divine. This presentation makes Feldman's observation about the suspicion expressed in 42:7 less likely. Chapter 42 ends with the narrator revealing the name of the angel, "Fadahel."[39]

Chapter 43: Samson

Chapter 43 condenses Judges 14–16. The stories of Samson are difficult to fit into Judges' neat scheme of leaders possessed by the Spirit who save Israel. They are popular tales of a local hero who did things of questionable moral value, but gets the best of the Philistines. Pseudo-Philo is not interested in the details of most of Samson's exploits. They are recalled briefly so that what is important about his story can be highlighted. Several of Pseudo-Philo's concerns emerge: moral causality; the danger of mingling with the Gentiles, especially women; and God's control of the action.

In Judges, Samson's clashes with the Philistines occur when he engages in questionable dealings with them. But in LAB 43, his story begins with his intention to attack them, revealed right after the narrator says that God was with Samson. This intention corresponds to the statement in 42:3 that Samson will free Israel from the Philistines. Samson sets out with no such intention in his cycle of stories in Judges. Since each of his exploits in LAB 43 grows out of this original intention, they look more honorable as a whole. Further, Pseudo-Philo omits many of Samson's exploits and concentrates on one event that shows his strength and closeness to God. In 43:2, when Samson tears up

---

38. "Prolegomenon," cxxv. Feldman points out that in Josephus (*Ant.* 5.8.3 § 281) Manoah's suspicion is quite clear.

39. See *OTP,* 356, n. o.

the gate of Ashdod and uses it as a weapon (Judg. 16:1–3), he says, "Behold now those fleas have locked me up in their own city, and now the LORD will be with me, and I will go out through their gates and attack them."[40] Feldman notes that Samson's speech displays "utter contempt for the enemy" and "militant faith in God." Pseudo-Philo makes him "almost a kind of superman."[41] Samson makes no such appeal to God in the biblical version.Indeed, the reason Samson is there according to Judg. 16:1 is to visit a Philistine prostitute, but Pseudo-Philo transfers that to later in the chapter. In LAB 43:2, he is in Ashdod because he is angry at its inhabitants, presumably for burning his wife (43:1). Pseudo-Philo enhances Samson's strength here by embellishing the story of Samson's fight. Judg. 16:1–3 says nothing of a battle. There Samson rips up the gate to escape the Philistine siege. The *Biblical Antiquities* describes a tremendous struggle in which Samson uses the gate of the city as a weapon and kills twenty-five thousand Philistines. Pseudo-Philo briefly refers to four other events in Samson's life, all of which demonstrate his strength and cunning, and refers the readers to the Book of Judges for more.

LAB 43:1–4 and the annunciation of Samson's birth in chapter 42 allow Pseudo-Philo to include Samson among God's agents. The rest of chapter 43 recounts his downfall. LAB 43:1 notes without comment that Samson took a wife from among the Philistines. This contrasts with Judg. 14:3, in which his parents argue with him over his choice. In Judges 14–15, the burning of Samson's wife by the Philistines is the result of a complicated story in which Samson's righteousness is not clear. Pseudo-Philo reduces this to the brief statement that the Philistines burn her because Samson had humiliated them, which can only be explained as a fulfillment of God's desire to free Israel through Samson (42:3) and Samson's resolution to fight the Philistines (43:1). The whole story assumes clearer moral lines.

In 43:5 Samson goes to a Philistine city and takes a prostitute named Delilah as his wife. This conflates the prostitute of Judg. 16:1 and Delilah from Judg. 16:4–22. Making Delilah the prostitute allows the narrator to present the good Samson in 43:1–4 and the bad in the rest of the chapter, thus explaining Samson's downfall.

God does not appear in Judges 16; the only reference to God is in Samson's prayer in 16:28. The case is otherwise in LAB 43:5–8. God makes a speech in 43:5 in which the divine reaction to Samson's marriage to Delilah is revealed and its consequences detailed. God says that Samson has been "led astray through his eyes, and he has not remembered the mighty works that I did with him; and he has mingled with the daughters of the Philistines." Contact with foreigners is his sin. That Delilah is a prostitute is not a source of scandal in the narrative. God takes Samson's consorting with Delilah as a desertion, for it means that Samson has forgotten God's deeds on his behalf. God recalls Joseph his "servant who was in a foreign land and became a crown for his brothers because he was not willing to afflict his own seed." This is a negative

---

40. In the Bible, this happens at Gaza, but Pseudo-Philo puts it at Ashdod.
41. "Prolegomenon," cxxvi.

example of an analogy between the narrative's present and Israel's past. Joseph acted so as not to harm Israel, which implies that Samson is putting Israel in jeopardy through his transgression. Mixed marriages endanger Israel.

God concludes by revealing the future: Samson will be punished because of his "mingling." The punishment fits the crime. Samson sinned through his eyes, so he will be blinded. But God discloses that at the moment of his death, Samson will be remembered by God and avenged "once more." The story unfolds as God foretells. LAB 43:6 condenses the biblical story of Delilah's pressuring Samson to reveal the secret of his strength. He tells her the secret, and she gets him drunk so that she can cut off his hair while he sleeps. In Judges 16, Delilah does not get him drunk.[42] In 42:3, Pseudo-Philo omits mention of Samson's Nazirite status and says that the command not to drink wine or eat unclean things, addressed to his mother in Judges, was really meant for Samson. Although Nazirite vows would include abstinence from wine, Pseudo-Philo's change in 42:3 makes Samson's negligence in getting drunk (43:6) that much clearer. He is captured, beaten, and blinded, and this happens "because he had made such a revelation." Samson is brought out during a Philistine feast to entertain them, as in the Bible. The most significant alteration of this scene is a clause added to Samson's prayer. He asks that he be allowed to punish the Philistines "because the sight that they took from me was given freely to me by you." In the Bible, Samson gets what he deserves. His trouble with the Philistines results from his unpraiseworthy dealings with them, not from his actions against them on behalf of Israel. Yet even in the Bible God returns Samson's strength to him so that he can have a final victory over his enemies. To justify this, Pseudo-Philo adds this clause to Samson's prayer so that God acts because of the outrage against the Deity and not because of the Philistines' opposition to Samson. The last addition by Pseudo-Philo is the number of Philistine dead in this incident—forty thousand, a number much higher than implied by Judg. 16:27.

Chapter 44: Micah

Chapter 44 extensively rewrites Micah's story from Judges 17 so as to advance Pseudo-Philo's anti-idolatry polemic.[43] It connects idolatry to the absence of leaders in Israel, a connection also made in Judg. 17:6: "In those days there was no king in Israel; all the people did what was right in their own eyes." Pseudo-Philo moves that verse to the beginning of the narrative so the readers know from the outset that lack of leadership leads to disaster (44:1). Pseudo-Philo also changes "king" to "leader" *(dux),* showing that leadership in general is in question in the *Biblical Antiquities,* not monarchy per se.

In Judges 17, Micah confesses to his mother that he has stolen silver from her and will return it. She takes the silver and has an idol made of it, thinking

42. This does happen in Josephus (*Ant.* 5.8.11 § 309).
43. For rabbinic parallels to this story, see Feldman, "Prolegomenon," cxxvii.

that she honors the Lord by doing so. Micah institutes a cult, appointing his own son as priest. When he later encounters an unemployed Levite, he hires him to be his priest, believing this will gain God's favor (Judg. 17:13). In Judges 18, some Danites lure the Levite away from Micah and steal his idol. The Danites then destroy a peaceful village and slaughter the inhabitants. Micah's story in Judges is ambiguous from a moral viewpoint. Nowhere is Micah condemned for his idolatry; the Danites look the worst. They are treacherous, murderous, and thieving. In Judges 17, Micah and his mother seek to please God, although they err in their efforts. There is no clear condemnation of Micah, his mother, or idolatry. The case is otherwise in Pseudo-Philo. Micah and his mother scheme to institute a cult from a base motive—profit. All hints that they are well intentioned but misguided are erased. The Levite's story is excluded since it attests to Micah's desire to please God. The actions of Micah and his mother are condemned absolutely by God. The Danites are omitted as distracting from the anti-idolatry thrust of the story. In chapter 45, Pseudo-Philo blames the war between the Benjaminites and the rest of Israel on the people's toleration of Micah's idolatry.

In Judges, Micah's mother orders the crafting of an idol, but it is Micah who institutes the cult. In LAB 44:2, the suggestion for the foundation of a cult comes from Micah's mother, Dedila, mother of Heliu, a name found only in Pseudo-Philo. Dedila's suggestion reveals her motivations as entirely blameworthy. She tells Micah to make an idol and to become its priest so that "you will make a name for yourself before death." The inducement to make a name for oneself inspired the builders of the tower of Babel in 6:1 and will discredit Saul's banishment of the wizards in 64:1. Dedila's words disclose the true motives for idolatry: deception for the sake of profit. In 44:3, Micah's mother continues to persuade her son, setting out specific prices for sacrifices and incense offerings. Idolatry can be lucrative. Micah will be wealthy and honored by the titles of "priest" and "worshiper of the gods." Micah is delighted with his mother's suggestions: "You have advised me well, Mother, on how to live. And now your name will be even greater than mine, and in the last days all kinds of things will be requested of you" (44:4). Micah's response is ironic. His mother has advised him terribly,showing him precisely the wrong way to live. Her advice sounds good to Micah because he shares her desire for fame and fortune, but neither of them knows that their fame will be of a sort they do not want. There is an implicit contrast drawn between Dedila, the mother who gives bad advice that her sons follow, and Deborah, the mother of Israel who gives her children good advice that they do not follow.

In 44:5, Micah does "everything that his mother had commanded him." The verb "to command" is frequent in the *Biblical Antiquities*. God is usually the subject. Here Micah is all too willing to follow the unwholesome commands of his mother. The rest of 44:5 supplies details of Micah's idolatry. People come to his cult to pray for wives, sons, riches, courage, servants, maids, and long lives. Each request is made through a different cultic figure—boys, calves, a lion, an eagle, a dragon, or a dove.[44] Pseudo-Philo summarizes Micah's activities with the statement "And his wickedness took many forms, and his impiety was full of trickery." Pseudo-Philo sees idolatry as deceptive and subtle, as emerges in the ambiguity of the motivations of the Transjordanian tribes in chapter 22 and the sinners' secrecy in chapters 25 and 27.[45]

Micah's idolatry leads to one of God's lengthiest speeches. The speech is in two major parts. In the first, God lays out the nature and depth of Israel's sin, and in the second God reveals the results of that sin. Each of these parts falls into two subsections. In section 1 of part 1, God recalls Israel's pledge at Sinai to obey the Decalogue, and in section 2 God demonstrates how Israel's idolatry violates each of the Ten Commandments. In section 1 of part 2, God predicts the specific punishments to come for the participants in Micah's idolatry. In section 2, God generalizes to show that all sin inevitably will be punished.

The narrative introduction to God's speech makes clear that Israel succumbed to Micah's idolatry and this amounts to "departing from the LORD" (44:6). God begins the speech with, "Behold I will root up the earth and destroy the whole human race." God says this will happen because Israel has transgressed. Pseudo-Philo's view of humanity is pessimistic. Abraham was chosen because, unlike the rest of humanity, he remained faithful to God (4:11, 16; 7:4). Now that Israel has shown itself to be no better than the nations, God contemplates annihilating the entire human race, along with the earth.

God recalls the theophany at Sinai and Israel's promise to obey the divine commandments. God goes through each of the Ten Commandments and insists that Israel pledged obedience to each.[46] Pseudo-Philo showcases the Ten Commandments here and elsewhere (11:6–13) as the epitome of God's covenantal commands to Israel. Israel's assurance that it would obey each command is stressed, since each was presented and accepted individually (44:6). After this enumeration of the Ten Commandments, God returns to the sin of idolatry, recalling that the Israelites were told not to make graven images (44:7). Traditional Jewish polemic against idols now makes its appearance, emphasizing that idols are human productions.[47] This aspect of idols is particularly relevant to Pseudo-Philo, who is primarily interested in human morality. In the latter half of 44:7, God shows in detail how idolatry violates each of the Ten Commandments. Idolatry is the root of all sin, and by committing it Israel has transgressed each of the Ten Commandments.[48]

The second part of the speech begins with a sweeping condemnation: "Therefore, behold I abhor the race of men, and I will cut away the root of

44. Efforts have been made to identify these cultic figures with a specific form of idolatry, the Mithras cult in particular, but they have not won general agreement. See Dietzfelbinger, *Pseudo-Philo*, 61–62; *OTP*, 358, n. a; Feldman, "Prolegomenon," xxxvi–viii, cxxvii–viii.

45. See Murphy, "Retelling," 283.

46. The order of the commandments here differs slightly from that in Exod. 20:13–15, but accords with Jer. 7:9 (Perrot, SC 230, 200).

47. See our comments on 39:9.

48. See Murphy, "Retelling," 279–81.

my creation" (44:8) because of the sin of the "house of Jacob" and the "impiety of Israel." Ever since Abraham's election, humanity's existence has hinged on Israel's relationship with God, one that the divine anger now considers broken. This is remarkable in view of Pseudo-Philo's consistent defense of the covenant's indestructibility. But one need only glance at the next chapter, indeed the next twenty-one chapters, to see that God does not make good on the threat. Although God does not explicitly relent in this chapter, the book as a whole proves that some change of heart must have taken place in God, for humanity does not cease to exist and God continues to honor the covenant. God asks the rhetorical question, "Can I not totally destroy the tribe of Benjamin, because they first of all were led astray after Micah?" (44:8). The answer is that since Benjamin violated the covenant, God can do whatever God wills. But the next chapter shows that God does not choose to destroy Benjamin, only to chastise it. Indeed, all Israel goes after Micah's idols, so God says, "And the people of Israel will not go unpunished. But this will be an everlasting scandal remembered for generations." God's prediction of punishment is fulfilled in LAB 46. Benjamin is singled out here because that tribe commits the sin against the Levite's concubine in the following chapter. Pseudo-Philo establishes a parallel between the two crimes, participation in idolatry and violating the concubine, so the former can be shown to be more serious than the latter.

In 44:9, God describes the punishment of Micah and his mother. The chapter has a chiastic structure, going from Micah's sin, to Israel's sin, to Israel's punishment, to Micah's punishment. Micah and his mother are punished in this life, so their hopes for fame and fortune prove false. They obtain the opposite of what they anticipate. The chapter is tied together still more tightly by the conversation between Micah and Dedila in 44:9, a conversation that contrasts with their earlier one in 44:2–4. In the earlier talk, each eagerly encourages the other to sin, listing the benefits of their unholy plans. Dedila holds before her son the hope of profit and reputation and Micah defers to her, insisting she will be even greater than he. All of that is turned on its head in 44:9. Subjected to the tortures of God's retribution, mother and son engage in mutual recrimination, each blaming the other for their predicament. Dedila says, "Behold what a sin you have committed!" and her son retorts, "And you have done even greater wickedness."

God then furnishes greater detail about Micah's punishment. Each cultic object he fashioned plays a specific role in his torment (44:9), an example of the maxim that the punishment fits the crime, a principle dear to Pseudo-Philo.[49] But the punishment is not restricted to the case of Micah; God generalizes it: "And I will not do this to Micah alone, but to all who sin against me" (44:10). God adduces examples of how sinners will be punished. Every sin is punished appropriately. The punishments highlight humanity's depen-

---

49. See our treatment of this principle in chapter 11 (this volume) under "Moral Causality."

dence on God for rain, life, posterity, and the answering of prayers.[50] The chapter ends as future sinners speak for themselves, bearing testimony to the accuracy of God's words. God says, "And when the soul is separated from the body, then they will say, 'Let us not mourn over these things that we suffer; but because whatever we ourselves have devised, these will we receive'" (44:10).

Chapter 45: The Levite's Concubine

Chapters 44–47 are a unit, for the narrative of the Levite's concubine in chapter 45 leads directly into that of the war against the Benjaminites in chapters 46 and 47, and then Micah's story and that of the concubine are brought together in God's reflections (47:3–8).[51]The story of the concubine is considerably streamlined so that the moral issues emerge more clearly. It contrasts the Benjaminites' sin in abusing the concubine with Micah's idolatry. God reveals that the Israelites judge each matter wrongly and so suffer the consequences in the civil war of chapter 46 (45:6). In chapter 44, the Israelites cooperate in Micah's idolatry, but in chapter 45 they are outraged at the violation of the Levite's concubine. Pseudo-Philo rewrites Judges 19 so as to make their outrage seem misplaced. First, the Levite giving his concubine to the townsmen to save himself is omitted. He does her no wrong in this version. This makes his later appeal for Israel's and God's help more plausible and makes the tribes' response more reasonable, although God later reveals that it is not reasonable from the divine point of view. Second, Pseudo-Philo strips the biblical story of its description of the tender relations between the Levite and his concubine and of the relationship between the Levite and his father-in-law. Third, the concubine is blamed for her own fate, claiming that she suffers retribution for transgressing against her husband by sinning with the Amalekites, a hated group in the Bible. The story of the Levite's concubine does little more in Pseudo-Philo than throw into greater relief the seriousness of Micah's sin and the Israelites' distorted moral judgment.

In the Bible, the Levite bypasses Jerusalem because it is inhabited by unfriendly Jebusites. Then he enters Gibeah, but receives no hospitality there except from an old man (not said to be a Levite). In LAB 45:1, he tries to enter Gibeah but is turned away by its inhabitants. Then he enters Nob and is offered no hospitality until a fellow Levite invites him into his house. The changes made by Pseudo-Philo serve several purposes. First, instead of having the Levite avoid a foreign city and then encounter trouble in the Benjaminite city of Gibeah, Pseudo-Philo has him encounter lack of hospitality in two Benjaminite cities, thus doubling the negative light cast on that tribe. Second, by having the Levite find trouble in the priestly city of Nob, the author may

50. See Feldman ("Prolegomenon," cxxviii) for rabbinic examples of sins that hold back the rain. See also SC 230, 201–2.

51. Feldman ("Prolegomenon," cxxix) notes that the rabbis also connect Micah's idolatry and the Benjaminites' sin.

be hinting at divisions within the priesthood or indirectly criticizing the priesthood for its lack of loyalty to fellow Israelites. Finally, because it is a fellow Levite who offers assistance to the travelers, the element of insiders versus outsiders is enhanced. In some sense both Levites find themselves in a foreign land even though their neighbors are fellow Israelites.

As usual, Pseudo-Philo uses direct address extensively. The kinship between the two Levites emerges when the one who lives in Nob (Bethac) says to the other, "Are you Beel from my tribe?" and the other answers, "I am" (45:2). Then Bethac tells Beel of the wickedness "of those who dwell in this city" and says they must hurry to his house, "and the LORD will shut up their heart before us as he shut up the Sodomites before Lot" (45:2).[52] This is another example of Pseudo-Philo's use of backward references to tie the narrative present to Israel's past. Once in Bethac's house, they are besieged by the inhabitants of the city, who demand that the travelers be brought out. Bethac pleads with them, using the argument *"Are not these our brothers?"* (45:3). In the Bible, the old man does not use this argument, though he addresses the attackers as brothers. The attackers reject the idea of brotherhood and so underscore divisions within Israel when they say, "It has never happened that the strangers gave orders to the natives."

The attackers force their way in, drag out the concubine, and abuse her sexually until she dies. Pseudo-Philo justifies their action by saying this happened to her "because she had transgressed against her man once when she committed sin with the Amalekites, and on account of this the LORD God delivered her into the hands of sinners" (45:3). Given Pseudo-Philo's stand against mixed marriages, her crime is worse because her infidelity is with Gentiles, Amalekites at that. This reinforces the idea of moral causality. The Levite calls on his fellow Israelites to avenge the wrong done to him. At the end of his appeal, he says, "If being silent pleases you, nevertheless the LORD judges. But if you wish to take revenge, the LORD will help you" (45:4). Pseudo-Philo adds the direct appeal to God's judgment and for God's help. These words put Beel into the category of such presumptuous characters as Joktan and the elders at the Red Sea. He thinks he knows God's will and rallies others to action. God's words in 45:6 and actions in chapter 46 make clear that Beel deludes himself and is to be seen in an ironic mode by the readers. Beel's appeal is also ironic in that he declares that if the people remain silent, God will judge them. Chapter 47 makes clear that God is particularly angry that the people were not silent about the Levite's concubine but let Micah's idolatry pass. Also ironic is the people's response to Beel. They rally to his side, crying, "If such *wickedness is done in Israel,* Israel will cease to be" (45:5). Israel does indeed place itself in jeopardy if it tolerates evil, but it did exactly that when it accepted Micah's idolatry. By reacting against the concubine's fate, Israel actually opposes God's judgment represented by that fate.

In 45:6, the readers hear the divine reaction. God speaks to "the adver-

---

52. Pseudo-Philo is unique in stating these two names (Feldman, "Prolegomenon," cxxviii).

sary," who is probably Satan, the heavenly prosecuting attorney as in Zech. 3:1–2 and Job 1:6–12.[53] The people were "foolish" because they were not disturbed "when Micah acted craftily so as to lead the people astray" (45:6). God continues, "Because they were not provoked to anger then, therefore let their plan be in vain; and their heart will be so disturbed that the sinners as well as those allowing the evil deeds will be destroyed" (45:6). The Israelites' plans will be thwarted by God, rendered "in vain" because they are out of step with God's plans.

Chapter 46: The Beginning of the Benjaminite War

Chapter 46 begins the account of the tribes' war against the Benjaminites. The war concludes at the end of chapter 47. Chapters 46–47 blame the war on the happenings in chapters 44 and 45. The people's determination to avenge the concubine gives God an opportunity to use their foolishness against them to punish their participation in Micah's idolatry. In the Bible, they confront Benjamin and ask that the sinners be handed over. They then consult God before initiating the campaign, asking only who should attack first. God picks Judah. God never says that they will be victorious, but merely answers the question asked. The people attack, are defeated, and then consult God, simply asking if they should attack again. God says to attack, again not promising victory, and they meet defeat a second time. Then they weep, fast, offer sacrifice, ask whether they should attack a third time, and the priest Phinehas himself also asks God this question. In Judg. 20:28, God tells them to attack a third time, this time saying that victory will be theirs.

In Pseudo-Philo, the people's words and God's response assume center stage. The people do not confront Benjamin until they go to God in the cult (Urim and Thummim). They say, "Let us ask the LORD first and learn if he will deliver our brothers into our hands; if not, let us desist" (46:1). They seem properly submissive to God. They are not guilty of presumption as was Beel. They do not assume that God will be on their side. They do not even ask Benjamin for the sinners before consulting God, as in the Bible. God's answer is unambiguous: *"Go up, because I will deliver them into your hands."*[54] The narrator adds, "But he led them astray so that he might fulfill his words" (46:1). God's words must always be fulfilled even if things must happen that are not justified according to human estimation. Here Pseudo-Philo does not shy from showing God using deception, unlike in Judges 20, to ensure fulfillment of the divine words. God's plan, overheard by the readers in 45:6 but unknown to the characters, must go forward.

53. Harrington (*OTP,* 360, n. G) remarks, "The Lat. *anteciminus* has been taken over from the Gk. *antikeimenos* (adversary), which is most likely the equivalent of the Heb. *śṭn.*" For other possibilities, see SC 230, 203–4.

54. Harrington prints these words in italics, signifying they have counterparts within Judges 20, but there they represent God's answer to the tribes' third question. The second time they ask God, God only tells them to go to battle (Judg. 20:23).

The initial confrontation between the tribes and Benjamin is presented with expanded direct address (46:2). The Benjaminites' answer stresses their brotherhood with the sinners, which prevents them from handing them over. At their first defeat, the tribes are "disturbed," a distress they should have suffered over Micah's idolatry (cf. 45:5, 6; 46:1) but did not. The description of their distress is fuller than in the Bible. They approach God at Shiloh and say, "Behold the LORD has delivered us before those dwelling in Nob, and now let us ask the LORD who among us has sinned" (46:3). The people know misfortune is not random. If they are losing battles, someone among them must have sinned. They share the view of moral causality espoused by the narrator.

God does not answer their question directly. In fact, the answer emerges slowly over this chapter and the next. God responds, "If you wish, *go up* and fight, and they will be delivered *into your hands,* and then it will be told to you why you have fallen before them" (46:3). Again the author has recrafted the story, this time in the interest of playing up God's deception. The people have not asked whether or not they should attack again, as they do in Judg. 20:21. God is the one who brings it up and volunteers the pledge that God will bring them victory, a pledge absent from God's second answer in Judg. 20:23. They are told to trust in this promise even before finding out why they were punished.

The people advance against Benjamin a second time and are defeated (46:3). Their reaction is more powerful than the first time: "Has God wished to lead his people astray? Or has he so established it on account of the evil that was done, that the innocent as well as those wicked deeds should fall together?" (46:4). The people accuse God of injustice, although the accusation is softened through the use of questions. The readers know full well that God has deceived them and might even sympathize with them here. But the people seem wrong in thinking that some of them suffer unjustly. Their sin was their complacency with Micah's idolatry (45:6). Of that sin all Israel is guilty. And their zeal in avenging the concubine cannot be condoned, because it is misplaced, as the readers know.

In chapter 46, as in Judg. 20:28, Phinehas prays. In Judges, he simply asks if Israel should attack Benjamin again. In Pseudo-Philo, he sides with the people and demands explanations from God. He asks why God has deceived the people and led them astray, why he did not make it known if Benjamin was right so that Israel could consider it, and why God has allowed Israel's defeat.

Chapter 47: God's Answer to Phinehas and the End of the Benjaminite War

LAB 47:1 continues Phinehas's prayer but begins anew: "And Phinehas added, saying." The tone of the addition is softer than that in the prayer in 46:4. Here he addresses God as "God of our fathers," a phrase that recalls

Israel's origin in terms characteristic of Pseudo-Philo. He calls himself God's "servant" *(servus)*. He suggests a divine motive for what has happened: "Perhaps the people have sinned and you were not willing to root out their evil deeds so as to correct those among us who have sinned against you" (47:1). These words place the blame on the people. God is not obligated to root out sin. By sinning, the people make themselves unworthy of a covenantal relationship with God. But the softer tone masks a strong challenge to God. Phinehas remembers the time in his own past when he attacked sinners in Israel's midst so as to root them out. He recalls that the rest of Israel tried to kill him, but God killed twenty-four thousand of them and "freed" Phinehas. This appeal to the past constitutes a potential criticism of God by an Israelite hero.

The challenge is clearer in Phinehas's next words. He describes what has happened in the Benjaminite war, which contrasts sharply with God's action in Phinehas's own past. He states that God sent the tribes up with the command to "go and kill them." They obeyed and were "delivered up." Phinehas tells God of the rumors circulating in Israel: "And now they say that your Urim and Thummim are telling lies in your sight" (47:2). Although Phinehas is not said to share this opinion, he is unable to answer it. His final plea is: "And now, LORD God of our fathers, do not hide from your servant but tell us why you have brought this wickedness against us" (47:2). Phinehas's words never lose their tone of respect, but his inquiry is insistent. His two references to the fathers that frame the second part of his prayer (47:1–2) are in themselves an argument, since God's relationship with Israel is unshakable precisely because of God's promises to the fathers.

The narrator says that God answered Phinehas because he "prayed earnestly before him" (47:3). God says, "I myself have sworn, says the LORD; if I had not sworn, I would not have remembered you in what you have said, nor would I have answered you today" (47:3). These words express a tension informing the whole of the *Biblical Antiquities*. God would frequently like to sever ties with Israel but cannot. God's words do not supply an indirect object for "swear," but given the context of the rest of the book, the most likely referent is the promise to the fathers. This is even more likely since Phinehas's prayer is framed by two references to God as LORD God of the fathers. God is restricted by the earlier divine promise that determines the overall course of history.

God tells a fable to reveal the real meaning of the events in chapters 44–47. It is introduced through nested quotations that attest to the authenticity of God's words. Paraphrasing somewhat, the "nest" runs: God said to Phinehas, "And now say to the people, 'Stand and hear the word of the LORD. These words the LORD says, "There was a certain mighty lion. . . ."' "[55] Most of the fable is explained plainly in 47:7–8. Unique to Pseudo-Philo, the fable is divided in two main parts. The first (47:4–5) deals with events up to the narrative present, the second (47:6) with things to come. Perrot offers a plau-

---

55. I have rearranged Harrington's (*OTP,* 361) quotation marks somewhat.

sible interpretation that is followed here in the main and is integrated into the paraphrase in the following paragraphs.[56]

Part 1 of the parable is in two subsections, the first (47:4) referring to Micah's idolatry and the second (47:5) to the murder of the concubine. There is a mighty lion (united Israel) in whom all other animals in the forest (the twelve tribes individually) trust for protection. "Wild animals" (Micah and Dedila) enter the forest and devour the young of the forest animals, "and the lion looked on and was silent." Israel's silence before Micah's idolatry is the cause of God's anger in these chapters. The individual tribes are also complacent: "And the animals were at peace, because they had entrusted the forest to the lion and did not realize that their own offspring had been destroyed." Neither on the level of national leadership nor on the level of the tribes did the people react to Micah's idolatry.

The second subsection of part 1 says, "And after a time there arose from those who had entrusted the forest to the lion a very small animal, and he ate up the small cub of another wicked animal. And behold the lion roared and disturbed all the animals of the forest, and they fought among themselves, and each attacked his neighbor" (47:5). From within the forest itself, "a very small animal" (the tribe of Benjamin) arises and devours the "small cub" (the concubine) "of another wicked animal" (Beel). Beel is wicked because of his presumption in rallying all Israel to his cause and assuming that God would be on their side.[57] The contrast between Israel's silence before Micah's idolatry and their disturbance over the concubine incident runs through chapters 44–47. It is Beel who actually rouses and disturbs Israel in 45:4, specifically saying that their silence will be judged by God. Because its cause is improper, their disturbance leads to civil war and the kind of chaos feared by the builders of the tower (6:1) and experienced by the Philistines (27:10).

God interprets (47:7–8) the parable's first part (47:4–5). Although 47:7–8 is not explicitly said to be an interpretation of the parable, it clearly is one. In 47:7, God recalls Micah's idolatry and claims that it made Israel rich. The seriousness of the idols is underlined by the hyperbole that Micah and Dedila created "wicked and evil things that no one before them had discovered." They came out of Micah's "craftiness," "graven images that had not been made until this day." God concludes the interpretation of the first section of part 1 with an accusation, "And no one was provoked but all were led astray, and you saw the fruit of your womb destroyed and you were silent like that wicked lion." God compares Israel to the lion, and condemns it for its "silence." It should have been provoked.

In 47:8, God passes to the story of the concubine, who, God says, "had done wicked deeds." At that the Israelites "were all disturbed." God admits having deceived the Israelites, and says, "Therefore I have deceived you and

---

56. SC 230, 207–8.

57. Perrot suggests that his wickedness is because he did not defend his concubine, but since Pseudo-Philo considers her wicked to begin with and nothing is said about his lack of action in the text, our proposal is more probable.

said, 'I will deliver them to you.' And now I have destroyed you, who were silent then.'" God generalizes, "And so I will take my revenge on all who have acted wickedly." What Israel will or will not tolerate in its midst is of the essence for its status before God (see chaps. 44–47). Israel's determinations will have consequences in its public life, its inner relationships (of particular concern in these chapters), and its relations with outsiders.

God does not interpret the fable's second part (47:6). "Another cub from another great forest" accuses the lion of the same things as God accuses Israel of in 47:7–8. The lion was "silent" at the first crisis and aroused the whole forest at the second. The new cub concludes, "And now you ought to be destroyed first, and so you will make the rest secure." The narrator says, "And the cubs of the animals heard this and killed the lion first, and they appointed the cub in its place, and so all the other animals were subject to one authority." Perrot offers three possible interpretations. He suggests first that this relates to the establishment of the monarchy, noting that the lion may refer to the "lion of Judah" from Gen. 49:9. That leaves the question of why the new cub comes from "another great forest." Perrot's suggestion that it may be to distinguish Saul (of the tribe of Benjamin) from David (of the tribe of Judah) does not solve the problem because he has already interpreted the first forest as Israel united. Perrot's second possible interpretation would make God the new cub. Tribal federation would then be replaced by theocracy. The precise referent of "another great forest" would still be unclear but could mean that God is outside of Israel. Finally, Perrot proposes that the new cub means foreign domination, which would make perfect sense of the other forest. There may be an interaction between the first and third interpretations at work in the parable itself. In the narrative, the monarchy will soon be established, but a native monarchy is not incompatible with foreign domination.

In 47:9–10, the Benjaminite war is finished. After hearing God's condemnatory speech in 47:3–8, the people simply turn and attack the Benjaminites again. They seem to understand that their punishment is accomplished and God will now honor the pledge to the fathers. The Benjaminites come out, thinking they will be victorious again. Judg. 20:34 says, "The Benjaminites did not realize that disaster was close upon them." Pseudo-Philo changes that to *"They did not know that evil* had reached full measure *against them"* (47:9). Moral causality is to the fore as the Benjaminites' sin is about to overtake them. LAB 47:9–10 summarizes the rest of the battle, depending heavily on Judges 20. Pseudo-Philo adds that after the battle the people returned to Shiloh with Phinehas. The return to the cultic center with the priest undermines any idea that Pseudo-Philo is anticult. Pseudo-Philo supplies a long list of names of surviving Benjaminites.

Chapter 47 concludes with the narrator's words: "And in that time the LORD repaid to Micah and his mother all that he had said. And Micah was destroyed in the fire and his mother was rotting away, just as the LORD had said concerning them" (47:12). God's words are absolutely reliable and must have their fulfillment.

Chapter 48: The Ascension of Phinehas

Chapter 48 describes the ascension of Phinehas and the procurement of wives for the Benjaminites. The chapter opens with Phinehas lying down to die and being told by God that he has exceeded the 120 years allotted to humans since the Flood (LAB 3:2). He is told to dwell on the remote mountain of Danaben until a distant time when he will be recalled and tested.[58] He will shut up heaven and reopen it with his word. Afterward he will be lifted up to where he will remain until the eschaton, at which time he and others with him will die. Perrot argues that the time of testing is the turbulent time described by LAB 44–47. Therefore, the interchange between Phinehas and God recounted here must be placed substantially before Micah. Indeed, Jewish tradition in general attributes an extraordinarily long career to Phinehas.[59] Pseudo-Philo has him present with Israel in the wilderness (LAB 47:1; cf. Num. 25:6), active during Kenaz's time (28:1), and at work here at the end of the judges' period. Perrot proposes that Phinehas's long sojourn at Danaben is invented by Pseudo-Philo to account for his inactivity during most of the period of the judges. His long career allows him to be a firm link in the priestly succession, connecting Eleazar the son of Aaron to Eli. Phinehas is the son of Eleazar and anoints Eli.[60] Phinehas's link with Eli is emphasized three times in the *Biblical Antiquities* (48:2; 50:3; 53:6).[61]

Perrot is surely right when he indicates the weight Pseudo-Philo places on the connection between Phinehas and Eli. But his identification of the testing undergone by Phinehas with the events of chapters 44–47 is less plausible. Perrot, like all commentators, observes that elements of Elijah's story have found their way into LAB 48:1. Like Elijah, Phinehas goes to a distant mountain where he spends some time, he returns to be tested, he shuts up heaven, he opens his mouth to speak to the people, and he ascends. Perrot stops short of seeing an identification between Phinehas and Elijah here,[62] but such an identification is made in later rabbinic literature.[63] To be sure, there is no explicit identification in the *Biblical Antiquities,* but if 48:1 assumes it, then the passage fits smoothly into its present context without a need to theorize that God is speaking to Phinehas at some earlier time. The opening words of

58. Danaben is unknown. For suggestions, see SC 230, 209.

59. For references, see SC 230, 209.

60. Spiro is probably right in detecting an anti-Samaritan polemic where the hated founder of Shiloh, Eli, is anointed by the Samaritan hero Phinehas (Hayward, "Phinehas," 28). He also sees (*Manners,* 238) an identification of Phinehas with Elijah and considers this part of the anti-Samaritan polemic, since the Samaritans denied Phinehas had not died. The connection of Phinehas with Shiloh would argue against the Samaritans' claim that he ministered at Gerizim. See the summary of his argument in Feldman ("Prolegomenon," cxxx), who also refers to Dietzfelbinger, *Pseudo-Philo,* 68–70. See also Spiro, "Ascension."

61. This refutes any notion that Pseudo-Philo is antipriesthood (SC 230, 209).

62. See also Harrington, *OTP,* 362, n. a.

63. See the numerous references cited by Hayward, "Phinehas." See also Feldman, "Prolegomenon," cxxix.

48:1, "at that time," tie the conversation between Phinehas and God firmly to their literary context. If Pseudo-Philo does indeed see Phinehas and Elijah as the same person, then the tight weave of Israelite history is again manifest. Phinehas fought the idolatry that entered Israel through foreign influence in the desert in Numbers 25 and again in the time of Micah. He will do so again during the monarchy when he appears as Elijah.[64]

In 48:1, Pseudo-Philo sees Phinehas (and so Elijah) in the category of Jewish heroes who were thought to have ascended to heaven.[65] In 4 Ezra 6:26, those who make it to the eschaton will see "those who were taken up, who from their birth have not tasted death."

In 48:2, the narrator says, "Now in those days when he anointed Eli as priest, he anointed him in Shiloh." "In those days" indicates that what this chapter recounts is all happening concurrently and so argues against Perrot's suggestion about when God's words to Phinehas are spoken.

LAB 48:3 concludes the Benjaminite incident. As in the Bible, the Benjaminites must procure wives to ensure continuation of the tribe. The tribes explain that they vowed in anger not to give their women as wives to Benjamin, but they do recognize Benjamin's need for wives. They tell the Benjaminites to seize wives by force. Pseudo-Philo omits the troubling detail that these were women of Shiloh.[66]

LAB 48:4–5 is a summary that crowns the whole period of the judges. LAB 48:4 corresponds to Judg. 21:25 and connects Israel's misfortunes to the lack of a good leader. Pseudo-Philo phrases the summary in a noteworthy way: "These are the commandments and judgments and testimonies and manifestations that were in the days of the judges of Israel" (48:5). Pseudo-Philo's major interest is in the will of God, how that guides history, how humans ought to respond to it, and the results of their actions. "Commandments" refers to God's direction of Israel. God is the most frequent subject of the words "to command." "Judgments" refers to God's reactions to events. The words "witness" and "testimony" are common ones in the work and imply that, read properly, all of history witnesses to Pseudo-Philo's worldview.

---

64. Hayward ("Phinehas," 28; following Spiro, "Ascension," 113) notes that Josephus said that Phinehas prophesied (*Ant.* 5.2.1 § 120). It is significant that Pseudo-Philo uses the priestly figure of Phinehas as the enemy of idolatry. The point is not that resistance to idolatry must come from the priests but that successful rejection of idolatry cannot occur without good leadership.

65. See SC 230, 210; possible figures include Adam, Enoch, Moses, Israel itself, possibly Samuel and Baruch, and Ezra.

66. Pseudo-Philo adds the detail that the feast when the Benjaminites took their wives was Passover. Later, he also says that the feast when Elkanah and his wives went to Shiloh was Passover (50:2).

9

From Samuel to David: *Biblical Antiquities* 49–65

As in the Bible, Samuel is a transitional figure between the time of the judges and the period of the monarchy. Pseudo-Philo's concern for leadership is very much to the fore in these chapters. Saul is paradigmatic for the bad leader, and David represents the potential for model leadership. As the book now stands, David's reign is not described, so his leadership abilities remain potential.

Chapter 49: Samuel's Father

Chapter 49 marks a new beginning for the *Biblical Antiquities*. The period of the judges is summed up in 48:4–5 and chapter 49 begins the story of Samuel, the transitional figure between the judges and the monarchy.[1] Chapter 49 is built on the image of the people reasoning among themselves, trying to discover how to do the right thing to improve their situation. As usual, they are seen in ambivalent terms, sometimes speaking the truth and making the right choice, sometimes not. They begin, "Let all of us cast lots to see who it is who can rule us as Kenaz did. For perhaps we will find a man who may free us from our distress, because it is not appropriate for the people to be without a ruler" (49:1). Casting lots puts the decision in God's hands and is a favorite mode of consulting God in the *Biblical Antiquities*. Kenaz is the ideal ruler. The people see their freedom as contingent on having the right ruler.

LAB 49:2 describes the initial failure of the people's consultation of God. The lots choose no one. Subscribing to the concept of moral causality, they assume that God does not answer because they are "unworthy." They try casting the lots by tribes, hoping that a group might find favor with God. They enunciate the following principle: "For we know that God will be reconciled with those worthy of him." What they "know" is supported by the book as a whole. Not even an entire tribe is found worthy. Finally the people give up

1. For parallels between the birth of Samuel and that of John the Baptist in Luke, see Winter, "Proto-source," 193, 198.

looking for divine guidance and decide to choose their own leader, saying, "For we know that God has hated his people and his soul has detested us." What the people "know" in this case is false, as becomes clear in the next section.

A man named Nethez (otherwise unknown) arises and disputes the people's pessimistic conclusion. He says,

> He does not hate us, but we have made ourselves so hateful that God should abandon us. And so, even if we die, let us not abandon him, but let us flee to him. We who have walked in our evil ways have not known him who created us, and so our plan will be in vain. For I know that God will not reject us forever, nor will he hate his people for all generations. And so strengthen yourselves, and let us pray again, and let us cast lots by cities. For even if our sins are many, nevertheless his long-suffering will not fail (49:3).

Nethez's words are confirmed: When the Israelites follow his advice and cast lots by cities, Ramathaim is chosen.

Nethez denies that God hates Israel but admits the people have surrendered every claim to God's love. That God does not hate Israel is testimony to the unshakable nature of divine love. Only God's devotion to Israel prevents calamity. But Nethez declares that disaster will not happen and proclaims that the people should trust in God even if they die. This echoes Kenaz's sentiments in 27:7 and Joshua's in 21:4. The deaths of individual Israelites or even of whole generations do not mean that God is unfaithful to Israel, so Israel should continue to trust in God. Nethez then plays on the idea of knowing, prominent in what the people have said. They think they "know" several things but are only partially right. Nethez asserts that Israel's lack of knowledge of their creator leads to their failure. He phrases this in a characteristic way—their plan is "in vain." Now Nethez says what he knows: God will not abandon Israel forever. He then tells the people to pray and to cast lots by city, reasoning that God's long-suffering does not allow the many sins of the people to nullify God's relationship with them.

In 49:4, the people conclude that Ramathaim is "more just" than other cities because it comes out in the lot, expressing their belief in moral causality. They decide to cast lots on individual men in that city, and the lot falls on Elkanah. They say to him, "Come, and be a leader for us" (49:5). Elkanah firmly declines, threatening suicide rather than being "defiled" by taking up leadership. He says, "For it is just that I should die only for my own sins rather than to bear the burden of this people."[2] Elkanah knows he is not to be the new leader, and subsequent events prove him right. He also knows that to assume leadership without God's approval is to fall out of God's favor, to be "defiled." He is willing to suffer retribution for his own sins, but he is not willing to go along with the people's misguided desires.

The rest of the chapter is a conversation between God and Israel. The people begin by accusing God of abandoning them at a time of distress; even the one chosen by lot does not obey the divine commandments. They see it

---

2. Note the echo of Moses' words in Num. 11:11.

as God's fault that Elkanah refuses to be their leader. They challenge the reliability of God's promises: "For if the ordinances that you have established with our fathers are true, saying, *'I will multiply your seed,'* and they will experience this, then it would have been better to say to us, 'I am cutting off your seed,' than to neglect our root" (49:6). As usual, Pseudo-Philo uses quotation to make a point. The people quote God's promise and then say that if God were unwilling to live up to the promise, God should have been more honest. They come close to calling God a liar.

God's response begins harshly: "If I were to pay you back according to your evil deeds, it would be necessary to pay no attention at all to your race" (49:7). Again the dominant theme of Israel's unworthiness is sounded, this time by the most reliable commentator of all. God wonders what divine action will be necessary to make Israel worthy to be associated with the divine name. In this pessimistic view, Israel cannot be counted upon to do anything to make itself more worthy. God must take action. God reveals that Elkanah cannot rule them, but his son will, and that hereafter and for a long time Israel will have rulers. God reveals that Elkanah's son, Samuel, will be both ruler and prophet. Samuel's role as prophet is stressed through repetition of the root for prophecy throughout the passage. The people ask which of Elkanah's sons will rule and prophesy, and God indicates the son of the sterile woman. God compares the divine love for Samuel with that for Isaac before him. The people look to the practical effects of all this: "Behold perhaps now God has remembered us so as to free us from the hand of those that hate us" (49:8).[3] The people expect God to liberate them from their enemies, but they couch this hope in tentative terms, having for the moment learned the lessons of presumption.

Chapter 50: Hannah

Chapter 50 rewrites 1 Sam. 1:1–18, emphasizing God's action and Hannah's worthiness.[4] In 1 Sam. 1:6–7, Peninnah taunts Hannah, but Peninnah is not quoted. The *Biblical Antiquities* does quote Peninnah.[5] In composing Peninnah's words, Pseudo-Philo takes a cue from 1 Sam. 1:5, where it says that Elkanah gave Hannah a double portion at the feasts "because he loved her, though the LORD had closed her womb." In LAB 50:1, Peninnah says that Elkanah's love is useless since Hannah is a *"dry tree."* Assessing her own standing, Peninnah asserts: "I know that my husband will love me, because he delights in the sight of my sons standing around him like a plantation of olive trees." Peninnah's words draw on Isa. 56:3 and Ps. 128:3 to prove the value of childbearing. She has biblical proof that a woman without children is truly

---

3. Note the similarity to Luke 1:71, 73–74.
4. See Callaway's treatment of Hannah's story (*Sing*, 35–57).
5. See Ginzberg (*Legends*, vol. 6, 261, n. 7) for rabbinic versions of her taunts.

unfortunate, for even the love of her husband becomes uncertain. What she "knows" will be disproved as Hannah is vindicated.

LAB 50:2 says that Peninnah was taunting Hannah daily, a time indication not present in the biblical text. The narrator then says that Hannah "had been fearing God from her youth." No such information is found in the Bible. Hannah's piety is important for Pseudo-Philo. Peninnah continues to provoke Hannah, even on Passover when they go to sacrifice.[6] Her provocation proceeds along the same lines as before. She asks what a woman may boast of and contends that beauty is not one of those things.[7] Children are the important thing. Without them, "love will be in vain." Jacob's love for Rachel would have been useless had not Rachel's barrenness been cured. There are a number of ironies in Peninnah's speech. She uses language typical of Pseudo-Philo, speaking of what is "in vain" twice. Like so many other characters, she reasons falsely and does not really know what is "in vain"—her own reasoning. Her appeal to biblical warrant is explicit in 50:2, while it was implicit in 50:1, so there is an intensification of the argument. Her recollection of Jacob and Rachel is ironic. Indeed, the cases of Hannah and Rachel are similar in that both women are especially loved by their husbands and both are barren. God will do for Hannah what was done for Rachel—open her womb. Ultimately the joke is on Peninnah, for the analogy with Rachel is truer than she suspects. LAB 50:2 juxtaposes Hannah's righteousness with her emotional state due to Peninnah's insults: She is sad and *"her soul grew faint and poured out tears."*

In 50:3, as in the Bible, Elkanah asks Hannah about her sadness. In the Bible, he asks whether he is not more to her than sons. In the *Biblical Antiquities,* he asks whether her "ways of behaving" are not better than sons.[8] Pseudo-Philo enhances Hannah's portrait as a righteous woman. It is her behavior that matters. Pseudo-Philo joins a debate about whether childbearing is indeed the most important value for a woman.[9] In passing, the author reinforces Eli's legitimacy, "whom Phinehas the son of Eleazar the priest had appointed, as had been commanded him."[10]

In 50:4, the readers hear from Hannah for the first time. Her prayer is quite different from the corresponding prayer in 1 Sam. 1:11. In 1 Samuel, she offers God a deal: If God gives her a son, he will be a Nazirite his whole life. In LAB 50:4, Hannah begins by declaring God's control and foreknowledge of all creation, including whether or not wombs are open. Then she speaks of her own righteousness: "Because you know my heart, how I have walked

6. The feast is unidentified in 1 Samuel. Pseudo-Philo says that it is Passover (see 48:3). Feldman ("Prolegomenon," cxxx) says this is an example of the application of the rabbinic hermeneutical principle of *gezerah shavah.* There is a similarity of language between 1 Sam 1:4 and Exod. 13:10, so the former is interpreted in terms of the latter.

7. The LXX develops the idea of boasting here (SC 230, 214).

8. Perrot (SC 230, 214) suggests that "ways of behaving" *(mores)* should be emended to "loves" *(amores).* The latter fits the biblical version of the story better but has no support in the manuscripts. "Ways of behaving" suits Pseudo-Philo's theme of moral causality.

9. See Wisd. 3:13; 4:1–11; Isa. 54:1.

10. See SC 230, 214, and Feldman, "Prolegomenon," cxxxi, for similar connections between Phinehas and Eli.

before you from the day of my youth." The narrator then explains why Hannah prayed silently; in 1 Sam. 1:13 this is not explained. Pseudo-Philo attributes her silence to piety. She reasons that she may not be worthy to be heard, then God will not answer her and she will have given Peninnah room for more insults. Her humility shows her innocent of presumption. She does not want to give her rival the opportunity to say, "*Where is your God* in whom you trust?" (50:5). Such taunts, insulting not only the pious but the God in whom they trust, are often uttered by skeptics.[11] This is made still clearer later in her prayer: "If they know that I am not heard in my prayer, they will blaspheme." If Hannah prays silently, "I will not have any witness except in my own soul." "Witness" continues to be a key concept.

Hannah voices a general principle: "And I know that neither she who has many sons is rich nor she who has few is poor, but whoever abounds in the will of God is rich" (50:5). There is a contrast between what Peninnah claims she "knows" in 50:1 and what Hannah really knows. Pseudo-Philo's interest in the truth or falsity of competing human opinions continues unabated here. Hannah's position shows her ability to penetrate the surface of things, in the tradition of Wisdom 4.

As in 1 Samuel, Eli takes Hannah to be drunk (50:6). In both the Bible and Pseudo-Philo, she explains herself. In Pseudo-Philo, her explanation plays upon the idea of drunkenness—she says she is drunk with sorrow.[12] Eli then asks Hannah why she is being taunted, although she has not given him that information (50:7). As becomes clear later, Eli knows her situation. Hannah tells him her story and he replies, "*Go,* because I know for what you have prayed; *your prayer* has been heard."[13] Who knows what is again at issue. Eli's claim to knowledge is a change from 1 Samuel, where Eli dismisses her with the prayer that her pleas be heard. The narrator explains, "Eli the priest did not want to tell her that a prophet had been foreordained to be born from her. For he had heard that when the LORD spoke concerning him" (50:8). The narrator confirms that Eli does indeed know God's plan and in passing stresses Samuel's role as prophet again.[14] Eli knows more than Hannah, and the readers know what he knows. The chapter ends with Hannah returning home consoled. She keeps quiet about her prayer, a reminder of her piety since her motive for it is to protect God's name.

---

11. See, for example, Ps. 42:3, 10; 79:10; 115:2; Dan. 6:20; Joel 2:17; Mic. 7:10; Mal. 2:17.

12. Perrot (SC 230, 215) notes that her answer displays "gentle irony."

13. The Latin text reads "you know" instead of "I know." Harrington (*OTP*, 365, n. i) emends it for sense. The emendation affects our interpretation only slightly.

14. Perrot (SC 230, 215) suggests that Eli is priest and prophet here.

Chapter 51: Samuel's Birth and Hannah's Song

When Samuel is born, his name is interpreted as " 'mighty one,' as God had named him when he prophesied about him" (51:1). This etymology is not in the Bible but fits Pseudo-Philo's emphasis on the strength of God.[15] Hannah brings the boy to the temple when he is weaned, and the narrator says, "The child was very handsome, and the LORD was with him." These attributes are not present in the biblical text but are common in infancy narratives.[16] Hannah presents Samuel to Eli, saying that this was what she had requested of God. She does not mention that she gives him to God in fulfillment of her vow: In the *Biblical Antiquities* no such vow is made. The child is a free gift from God, not something given in response to a promise of service. Eli replies that the boy is the answer not just to Hannah's prayer but to that of all the people. He fulfills a promise made to Israel. The prayer he alludes to may be in 49:1; God's promise is in 49:7. Eli says that Hannah (through Samuel) will "provide advantage for the peoples and set up the milk of your breasts as a fountain for the twelve tribes" (51:2). Harrington argues that the parallelism with "the twelve tribes" makes it unlikely that this is a reference to the Gentiles.[17] However, the parallelism need not be synonymous, and Hannah's song seems to claim that Samuel will make Torah known to the Gentiles. The idea that Hannah's breasts will supply milk to the twelve tribes suggests she is a mother of Israel as was Deborah.

Hannah now sings her song, as in 1 Samuel 2 (LAB 51:3–6). In Pseudo-Philo, she sings in response to the revelation just given her by Eli (51:2), whereas no such connection is made in 1 Samuel. Pseudo-Philo substantially reworks the song.[18] It can be broken down into the following sections:

a. Exhortation to the nations to listen (51:3)
b. Exhortation to Hannah's breasts concerning Samuel task (51:3)
c. Hannah's resolution to speak openly (51:4)
d. Address to the arrogant, connected with the vindication of the childless one (51:4)
e. Treatment of the Lord's retribution, connected with God's power over life and death (51:5)

15. Perrot (SC 230, 216) suggests that Pseudo-Philo sees "Samuel" as coming from the Hebrew *šmw 'l,* "His name is El," "El" meaning "mighty."

16. See SC 230, 216, which refers to Perrot, "Récits," 506, and LAB 43:1; 59:3. See Feldman, "Prolegomenon," cxxxi.

17. *OTP,* 365, n. e; Perrot (SC 230, 216) notes that *populi* (plural) often simply means Israel, but leaves open the possibility that it has a universal meaning here given Hannah's references to all nations in her song. See Feldman, "Prolegomenon," cxxxi, who sees *populi* as a translation of *gôyîm,* so that it means "nations."

18. Philonenko ("Paraphrase") considers this an Essene-style midrash with Gnostic elements. His hypothesis has not won general acceptance. For rabbinic paraphrases of the hymn, see Feldman, "Prolegomenon," cxxxii.

f. Exhortation to Hannah and Elkanah concerning Samuel as prophet and the fulfillment of prophecy (51:6)

g. Reference to the coming of the anointed one (51:6)

Parts *d*, *e*, and *g* correspond to points in Hannah's song in 1 Samuel, but the others do not. In part *a*, Hannah's summons to the nations to hear her voice is noteworthy given the lack of such universalistic elements in the biblical text, except for the idea that God will judge the ends of the earth in 1 Sam. 2:10. The phrases "all you nations" and "all you kingdoms" in LAB 51:3 mean Hannah's hymn has significance for more than just Israel. She claims she has been commanded to speak. Here as elsewhere in Pseudo-Philo, God is the one who does the commanding, so Hannah's words are reliable.

In part *b*, Hannah addresses her own breasts, drawing attention to her motherhood. In 51:2 her milk feeds all Israel. In part *b* of the hymn, it feeds Samuel in particular. The section stresses God's initiative in Samuel's birth, for her breasts have been commanded to give Samuel milk. This section also has universalistic overtones—through Samuel the people (Israel) will "be enlightened," but he will also "show to the nations *[gentibus]* the statutes."[19]

In part *c*, Hannah resolves to speak openly, for from her "will arise the ordinance of the LORD, and all men will find the truth."[20] God's ordinance is not just for Israel but is truth; as such, it must be proclaimed to all nations. This will happen through Hannah because she is Samuel's mother. Her words echo Isa. 51:4, where the prophet says, "A teaching will go out from me, and my justice for a light to the peoples." This verse from Isaiah finds several other echoes in the hymn.[21]

In part *d*, the song is closer to the biblical text. It quotes 1 Sam. 2:3, telling the arrogant not to utter proud words. In 1 Sam. 2:4, this is followed with the proclamation that God defeats the strong and raises the weak, but Pseudo-Philo replaces this verse with a statement of the themes that many possessions do not make one rich, neither do many children make one more of a mother.[22] Pseudo-Philo rejoins the biblical text at 1 Sam. 2:5, quoting it directly. This verse remarks upon the child given to the sterile one and the downfall of the one who had many children.

In 1 Sam. 2:6, Hannah says that God kills and brings to life. In 2:9 God protects the righteous and cuts off the wicked. Part *e* (LAB 51:5) joins these two elements, stating clearly that God's killing is due to the victims' wickedness and God's bringing to life is due to the merit of those brought to life. Moral causality is again affirmed. The section begins by attributing killing to God's judgment and God's bringing to life to divine mercy. Not even the just deserve life—it is always an expression of God's mercy. God condemns the

---

19. Harrington's (*OTP*, 365) translation of *terminos* as "statutes" is justified given that usage in 15:6, where it is from the Hebrew *ḥwqym*. See also 9:2.

20. Philonenko ("Paraphrase," 165) points to a parallel to this last clause in 1 QH 6:12.

21. See the margins of Harrington's translation (*OTP*, 365–66).

22. This theme recalls reflections such as those in Wisdom 4.

wicked to darkness and saves the light for the "just." Given Pseudo-Philo's propensity to associate the Law with light, an allusion to Torah is likely.[23] Death is the end for the wicked, but "when *the just* go to sleep, they will be freed."[24] Freeing is God's most characteristic act on behalf of the righteous. It often means rescue from an undesirable political situation. Here God frees from death itself. The section ends, "Now so will every judgment endure, until he who restrains it will be revealed." Judgment is inevitable. If judgment is not now evident, it is because God restrains it until its proper time.[25]

Part *f* begins with Hannah telling herself to sing a hymn about the miracles God has done for her. She displays proper humility and lack of presumption because she deems herself unworthy to be the mother of the prophet who is to be *"the light to the peoples."*[26] This last phrase quotes Isa. 51:4 and is universalistic. The light is not to be limited to Israel. Hannah tells Elkanah to "sing a hymn about the wonders of the LORD," for Samuel's birth is a fulfillment of Asaph's words in the wilderness, *"Moses and Aaron were among his priests, and Samuel was there among them"* (from Ps. 99:6).[27] Perrot sees this as claiming that Samuel is a priest.[28] Hannah's point is that Samuel's birth fulfills prophecy and is part of God's plan.

Hannah's song in 1 Samuel ends with a reference to the anointed one whom God will exalt. Pseudo-Philo's Hannah also speaks of an anointed one, also called king, in a rare reference to a kingly messiah (part *g,*) but there is no indication that the text means any other than the earthly Israelite monarch. Samuel's significance is that he is a light to the people until the king, probably David, comes. Hannah ends with the prayer that Samuel stay in the sanctuary and serve "until he be made a light for this nation." Perrot suggests that the "he" here is David, not Samuel. Samuel is Israel's light until David assumes that role.[29] God's guidance, be it through Torah or prophecy, is light to the nation.

The narrative resumes in 51:7. The people come rejoicing to Eli at Shiloh, bringing Samuel to him. Hannah already presented Samuel to Eli in 51:2, but Pseudo-Philo wishes to stress that this is not solely a matter between Hannah and Eli but involves the entire nation, just as Samuel's birth is not only a divine response to Hannah's prayer, as in 1 Samuel, but answers the prayer of the whole people and fulfills prophecy (50:8; 51:2, 6). The people "stood Samuel before the LORD, anointed him, and said, 'Let the prophet live among the people, and may he be a light to this nation for a long time!' " Pseudo-Philo

23. For Pseudo-Philo's extensive use of light imagery, see SC 230, 30.

24. This recalls a similar claim in Wisd. 3:2–9.

25. See 2 Thess. 2:6–7 (*OTP,* 366, n. j; SC 230, 219). So also Strobel, "Katechon-Parallele," 75–76; and Philonenko, "Paraphrase," 166. Feldman ("Prolegomenon," cxxxiii) questions whether God should be taken as the subject of *tenet* here.

26. The phrasing of Hannah's humble sentiment recalls that of Elizabeth in Luke 1:43.

27. The psalm is not attributed to Asaph in the Bible, but David has not yet entered the picture, and Asaph was a singer of psalms, for example, Psalms 80–83. Asaph and Elkanah are also associated by the rabbis (Feldman, "Prolegomenon," cxxxiii). See SC 230, 220.

28. See the parallels he adduces for this in SC 230, 220.

29. SC 230, 220.

confirms from the mouths of the people that Samuel is indeed God's prophet whom they accept, and that through the prophet true light comes, for true light is God's guidance.[30]

Chapter 52: Eli's Sons

This chapter opens with the statement that Samuel was very young and "knew nothing of these things." "These things" must refer to the revelations in chapters 50–51 about his own role. The statement may have been inspired by 1 Sam. 3:7, but instead of the biblical statement that Samuel was not yet experienced in the word of the Lord, LAB 52:1 claims Samuel's ignorance of his own role and fate. Therefore he can better serve as a model of one who, though not fully acquainted with God's plan, is open to whatever God wants.

Whereas the biblical text simply juxtaposes the statement about Samuel's service in the sanctuary (2:11) with the account of the sins of Eli's sons (2:12–17), Pseudo-Philo explicitly connects them temporally: "And while he *was serving before the Lord,* the two *sons of Eli* were not walking in the ways of their fathers" (52:1). Pseudo-Philo omits many of the details of the sons' sins from 1 Samuel 2, choosing instead to expand the interaction between Eli and his sons. Most significant is the omission of their sexual sins. The result is a sharper focus on their cultic sin: "taking their sacrificial offerings before they were offered as holy to the LORD." This is said to take place "near the house of Bethac," thus connecting this story to earlier ones (45:2). The interaction between Eli and his sons becomes a vehicle for Pseudo-Philo to reflect on sin and its consequences. The narrator comments that the sons "were not walking in the ways of their fathers." The fathers are seen as faithful.

In 1 Samuel, Eli disapproves of his sons' actions. Pseudo-Philo adds that the people and God shared his disapproval (52:2). Eli admonishes his sons, declaring that their sin is especially heinous since it is directed at God, adding that the sons are being untrue to their status in the priestly line designated by Phinehas. Eli asks his sons to consider the consequences when God asks for an accounting of their priesthood. If they repent, all will be well. If not, "you will destroy yourselves, and the priesthood will be in vain and what has been sanctified will be considered as nothing. And then they will say, 'Did the staff of Aaron spring up in vain or has the flower born of it come down to nothing?' " (52:2). The language is typical. Because God established the priesthood through the choice of Aaron and the designation through Phinehas of Eli's line, it should not be in vain. Eli holds out the possibility that human transgression can make it so. Pseudo-Philo supports the legitimacy of the priesthood and the centrality of the cult, but he sees a threat to the entire cultic establishment in its abuse. Eli's sons use their priestly position to rob God.

30. In 1 Sam. 3:20, all Israel accepts Samuel as a prophet.

Eli exhorts his sons to repent, claiming that those against whom they have sinned will pray for them if they do. This element is not in the biblical text and shows a hopeful attitude. If the leaders can refrain from sinning against the people, then the people will pray for the leaders and all may be well. Eli attempts to distance himself from his sons' transgressions and from their punishment. Nonetheless, the course of events follows that of the Bible, so Eli's entire line must bear the punishment brought on by the sins of his sons. Although individuals may be upright, the entire establishment fails if it violates God's will.

As in 1 Sam. 2:25, the sons do not repent because God has already decided they must die (52:4). To reinforce moral causality, Pseudo-Philo adds "for they had sinned" to the statement about God's decision. Then the narrator reveals that when Eli was admonishing them, they were reasoning to themselves that they would repent later.[31] But then the narrator observes, "And they who were warned by their father were not permitted to repent, because they were always rebelling and acting very unjustly in despoiling Israel" (52:4). Again Pseudo-Philo is concerned with proving God's justice. God is justified in resolving that the sons must die, for their actions were consistent and destructive. The chapter ends with the statement "The LORD was angry at Eli." Eli's attempts to persuade his sons are unsuccessful and he must bear the consequences of their actions. This accords with the biblical text and with the corporate responsibility of the priesthood.

Chapter 53: Samuel's Call

Chapter 53 rewrites 1 Samuel 3. Much of the rewriting has to do with explanation of features of the biblical text. The readers hear God's own deliberations. Pseudo-Philo begins this chapter with the statement from 1 Sam. 3:7 that Samuel had not yet heard the oracles of the Lord, a piece of information necessary for the rest of the narrative to make sense. Then the narrator says that Samuel was eight years old when the events of chapter 53 took place, a fact that will figure in God's thoughts in the next section.[32]

In 53:2, God wishes to reveal things to Samuel, and the readers hear the divine reflections on how to do so. God's thoughts both establish a parallel with Moses already hinted at in 51:6 and explain why Samuel did not at first recognize God's voice. God starts by saying that the young Samuel is beloved of God and that despite Samuel's not yet having heard the word of the Lord, he is "like my servant *[famulo]* Moses." This is high praise indeed, since *famulus* is applied only to Moses in the *Biblical Antiquities.* God observes that the divine apparition came to Moses when he was eighty years old, and he was

---

31. Perrot (SC 230, 221) notes that the rabbis assert that those who reason thus will not be allowed to repent; *b. Yoma* 85b; *m. Yoma* 8:9.

32. Josephus (*Ant.* 5.10.4 § 348) says that he was twelve.

afraid. God reasons that since Samuel is only eight years old, he will be still more afraid. God decides to approach Samuel with a human voice to begin with and then to "speak to him like God."[33]

In 53:3–4, Samuel hears God's voice and thinks it is Eli's. He runs to Eli and Eli says he did not call. Eli wonders whether an unclean spirit is calling Samuel, an element not present in 1 Samuel. He says that if the voice calls only twice it is an evil spirit, but if it calls three times it is an angel. In 53:5, the voice calls to Samuel again and this time Samuel thinks it sounds like Elkanah. Eli now recognizes that God is calling and knows that the next time the voice comes, it will sound like God's. In 53:6, Eli says, "Phinehas the priest has commanded us, saying, 'The right ear hears the LORD by night, but the left an angel.' "[34] Eli instructs Samuel that if he hears with his right ear, he is to say to God, "*Say* whatever you wish, *because I am listening,* for you have created me." If he hears with his left ear, he is to report back to Eli. Eli's instructions exalt God as the source and disposer of all.

When God speaks again, Samuel expresses humility by paraphrasing the words Eli instructed him to say: "If I am capable, speak; for you know more about me (than I do)" (53:7). Samuel's humility embodies the perfect attitude on the part of an Israelite leader—the opposite of presumption. Samuel is fully open to God's will. God makes a lengthy speech to Samuel (53:8–10). In the Bible, God simply discloses the impending destruction of Eli's house. In the *Biblical Antiquities,* God's speech is in three sections: recollection of Israel's history from Egypt to Sinai; remembrance of the establishment of the priesthood; and prediction of the priests' punishment. In 53:8, the speech's first section, it is said that at the beginning and end of Israel's history, from Egypt to Sinai, God "enlightened" Israel. Within that frame God remembers the choice of Moses as a prophet. This fits with Samuel's prophetic status and his similarity to Moses.

In the speech's second section (53:9), God alludes to the revolt against the Aaronic priesthood narrated in Numbers 16. God emphasizes the divine resolution of the revolt by using the word "command" twice. God commanded that all turn in their staffs and then commanded the ground to cause Aaron's staff to flower. This solution avoided destroying the rebels. Having recalled the divine efforts in establishing the priesthood firmly and without violence, God levels the accusation, "And now those who have flowered have defiled my holy things." This refers to the sacrilege committed by Eli's sons. In 53:10, God predicts punishment of the priests. Using the imagery of Aaron's flowering rod, God says, "I will trample on the flower that was born then and will stop them who transgress the word that I have commanded Moses my servant, saying, '*If you come upon a bird's nest, you shall not take the mother with young.*' So it will happen to them that mothers will die with daughters and

33. Note the similar musings of God before speaking to Moses in *Exod. Rab.* 3:1; 45:5. See SC 230, 222.

34. Feldman ("Prolegomenon," cxxxiv) notes the widespread favor for the right side in the ancient world. See SC 230, 222–23.

fathers will perish with sons." God quotes Deut. 22:6. The violations of Eli's sons are seen to transgress a divine command given through Moses. Their theft of Israel's sacrifices is a sin against all Israel, mothers and young together. In accord with the principle that the punishment fits the crime, God says the same thing will happen to them. This rationalizes God's punishment of Eli's entire clan for the sins of his two sons.

Naturally Samuel is reluctant to carry such bad news to Eli, who has been like a father to him. His reluctance is noted briefly in 1 Sam. 3:15, and Eli's persuasion of him is equally brief (3:17). Pseudo-Philo embellishes both elements, stressing Samuel's unpleasant obligations as a prophet (53:11–12). The readers witness Samuel's agonized thoughts. He laments that one so young should be forced to "prophesy the destruction of him who nourished me." He even questions the whole purpose of his mother's giving him to the service of the Lord. Samuel goes so far as to say, "How has he commanded me to announce evil as if it were good?" Pseudo-Philo presents Samuel as aware of the tragic aspects of God's relation with humans. Samuel's first prophetic task is a distasteful one with which he disagrees.

In 53:12, Eli reminds Samuel of who he is. Eli begins, "Listen now, my son. Behold before you were born, God promised Israel that he would send you to them and that you would prophesy." Eli relates Hannah's visit to Shiloh and his own encouragement of her based on foreknowledge of Samuel's mission. In accordance with God's plans for Samuel, God "guided your life." Even in the face of prophesying punishment for "the one who has brought you up," Samuel must perform his task. The idea of performing one's divinely appointed duty despite personal cost and social disruption is present in the biblical narrative, but Pseudo-Philo develops it substantially. The chapter ends with Eli's words of submission: God is the Creator and all comes from God's hands. God can take back whatever God has given. Eli justifies God's judgment with the final words, "Holy is he who has prophesied, for I am under his power." The one who has prophesied is God, whose control of everything Eli acknowledges. Eli is a tragic figure, but one who, even faced with punishment, testifies to the justice of God's ways. His testimony is poignant, and Pseudo-Philo makes the most of it.

Chapter 54: The Ark Captured, Eli Dies

Much of the rewriting of the capture of the ark (1 Samuel 4) allows the characters to speak for themselves. LAB 54:1 condenses 1 Sam. 4:1–3 but expands the Israelites' words after their defeat. In 1 Sam. 4:3, the people decide to bring up the ark "so that he may come among us and save us from the power of our enemies." Pseudo-Philo sharpens this until it is explicit that the people hope God will fight alongside them. Then he adds information about the ark: "In it are the tablets of the LORD that he established with our fathers on Horeb." This is part of the constant effort to link Israel's present with its past and to insist that Israel's identity rests on the covenant with the fathers.

In 1 Samuel, the Israelites shout when the ark enters the camp so that the whole earth resounds. Their shout is interpreted correctly by the Philistines as a signal that God has entered the camp. In LAB 54:2, the people's shout is replaced with God's own words, described as a thundering. In 1 Samuel, the readers must infer God's attitude toward the Israelites' decision to bring the ark to their camp. In Pseudo-Philo, the readers have direct access to God's own thoughts right from the beginning. God discloses the divine plan in advance, underscoring God's control over events. God begins the brief speech with another comparison of the present situation with the past, saying that in this instance the people have taken the ark without divine permission and that they did this before when they were in the wilderness. The earlier incident God refers to is not recorded in the Bible. God remembers that because they took the ark illicitly in the earlier episode, Israel experienced destruction. The sin in both incidents is presumption.

God says, "So also in this hour the people will fall and the ark will be captured in order that I may destroy the enemies of my people on account of the ark and correct my people because they have sinned" (54:2). Although God compares the present with the past, the two situations are different. In the past, God visited "destruction" on the people because of their presumption. In the present, it is the Philistines who will experience destruction. Indeed, the capture of the ark tricks the Philistines into giving God an excuse to destroy them. God welcomes this chance because the Philistines are the enemies of God's people. But in keeping with the author's strict deuteronomistic scheme of retribution, the people must also be "corrected." Nonetheless, God's words highlight the divine commitment to Israel.

LAB 54:3 rewrites 1 Sam. 4:10–11. In 1 Sam. 4:11, the deaths of Hophni and Phinehas are juxtaposed with the notice of the ark's capture, but no direct connection is drawn. Pseudo-Philo makes the connection explicit. He also adds the figure of Goliath, absent from the biblical story, in a dramatic scene. Goliath comes up to the ark, which Hophni and Phinehas are "holding onto." Then "Goliath took hold of it with his left hand and killed Hophni and Phinehas." It is unclear whether the priests hold onto the ark hoping it will protect them or in its defense. Given the motivation of the people in bringing up the ark, the former is more likely. The vivid scene in 54:3 graphically depicts the audacity of Goliath, the impotence of God's priests, and the central role of the ark, a role God has just explained.

In the Bible, an unnamed Benjaminite runs from the battle to report to Eli. Pseudo-Philo identifies him as Saul.[35] This is an instance of a tendency in the *Biblical Antiquities* to make connections between biblical stories through specific characters. Saul's flight from Goliath can be contrasted with David's conquest of Goliath in LAB 61. Saul's report differs in one significant aspect from the messenger's report in 1 Samuel 4. Like the messenger in 1 Samuel, Saul reports Israel's defeat, the death of Eli's sons, and the capture of the ark.

35. The identification was also made in some rabbinic texts. See SC 230, 224.

But Saul adds the interpretive clause "God has rejected Israel." The readers know that is false. God's words in LAB 54:2 make Saul's statement impossible.

In 1 Sam. 4:18, Eli falls down dead as soon as he hears about the ark's capture. Pseudo-Philo has him deliver a short speech. Eli recalls that his sons' and his own deaths were prophesied by Samuel, but notes that Samuel said nothing about the ark. This accurately reflects the biblical text, where Samuel did foretell the demise of Eli's house but said nothing about the ark. Eli's formulation may imply that Samuel must have known about the ark but did not see fit to mention it earlier. Eli ends by drawing a conclusion for Israel from the ark's capture: "Behold Israel departs from the truth, because the statutes have been taken away from it" (54:5). A variant reading for "departs from the truth" is "perishes utterly."[36] The variant reading would make Israel's very existence contingent on its possession of the Torah, suitable thinking for the *Biblical Antiquities.* Harrington's reading does not deny that Israel's existence is dependent on its possession of the Law, but it focuses on the necessity of the Torah for having "truth," proper understanding and perception of everything. This also fits Pseudo-Philo's outlook.

The narrative of Phinehas's wife in 54:5–6 is essentially the same as that in 1 Sam. 4:19–22, but in the Bible she makes no direct answer to the midwife who tells her not to be afraid since she has borne a son. In Pseudo-Philo she does answer, saying that although one person is born, four die—Phinehas, Hophni, Eli, and herself. She will not accept the midwife's consolation. As in 1 Samuel, she equates the capture of the ark to the departure of God's glory from Israel.[37] Pseudo-Philo ends the story more clearly than does the Bible: "And when she had said these words, she gave up her spirit" (54:6).

Chapter 55: The Return of the Ark

LAB 55:1–2 is a major insertion into the narrative of the ark. It consists mostly of a direct conversation between Samuel and God. LAB 55 opens with an explanatory section claiming that Samuel was unaware of the events of chapter 54 because God had sent him to inspect Ramathaim, where his home was to be. God is director of the action. The text does not say why God would want Samuel to be unaware of the preceding events, but his ignorance makes the interchange between God and Samuel possible. Samuel's reaction to the news of the ark's capture is despair. He begins to pray, "Behold now in vain has understanding been denied me, that I should see *[ut viderem]* the destruction of my people" (55:1).[38] Samuel means that if he had known what was happening, he might have prevented it. Because knowledge was denied him, he

36. See *OTP,* 369, n. d; SC 230, 224.

37. Harrington (*OTP,* 369, n. e) suggests that the reading "where is glory" mistranslates the Hebrew *'y kbwd, "no glory," as 'yh kbwd.*

38. Samuel's protest at being denied understanding is similar to that of Ezra in 4 Ezra, for example, in 4:12, 22. All manuscripts read *exercitium* ("army") here, but Harrington (*OTP,* 369, n. a) emends this to *exitium* ("destruction"), as does James (*Biblical Antiquities,* 225).

was unable to aid his people and they perished. This is a "vain" result. *Ut viderem* could indicate purpose or result. Samuel is accusing God at least indirectly, for it was God who sent him away, either with the result that the people perished, which makes God somewhat blameworthy, or for the purpose of destroying the people, which paints God in darker colors. But the sentence can be read on an ironic level. Samuel adopts the same assessment of events as that held by Saul—the ark's capture implies Israel's destruction. The readers know that to be false because of God's own words in 54:2, but Samuel shares Saul's ignorance.

Samuel continues his prayer in despair. Why should he go on living if the ark is captured?[39] In LAB 55:2, God reveals to Samuel that the ark will be returned and the Philistines punished. Samuel assumes God will wreak this vengeance only after some time has passed. He thinks he understands the divine ways and that God, being long-suffering, will not act immediately. Samuel expects that he and his contemporaries will be long gone before the ark is avenged.[40] He misjudges the situation; God responds that Samuel will see the vengeance against the Philistines before his death. The Philistines are characterized as God's enemies, as they were called Israel's enemies in 54:2. Israel's enemies are God's enemies.

Pseudo-Philo's rewriting of 1 Samuel 5–6 highlights the fact that the Philistines are punished for taking the ark. In 1 Samuel, the Philistines are convinced from the beginning that God is responsible for Dagon's fall (5:7). Only toward the end of the narrative is their conviction tested through the sign of the cows (6:9–12). But there is little suspense in the narrative, even on the part of the Philistines. Pseudo-Philo changes this. The Philistines' first reaction in LAB 55:3 is to blame their priests. They crucify them, but the next morning Dagon has again fallen before the ark, and "there was a great massacre among them." Opposition to God results in turmoil within the Philistine community. Thus Pseudo-Philo creatively fills the gap between Dagon's first and second fall (1 Sam. 5:3, 4).

The rest of LAB 55 is in a form familiar to the readers—people, this time the Philistines, discuss among themselves, trying to comprehend what is happening. The people now decide that Dagon has fallen and they have suffered because of God's ark (55:4). The Philistines' ignorance of the cause of their trouble, an ignorance not present in the Bible, is underscored by the idea that Dagon is falling "daily" before the ark and by their lament that that they have punished the priests "more than once" for this. They declare their actions to have been "in vain." In 55:5, their wise men suggest a test to discover the reason for their distress. The wise men do not advance an opinion at this stage. This contrasts with 1 Sam. 6:3, where the priests and diviners assure the people that they are correct in their assignation of the cause for their distress and tell

---

39. Similar plaints are heard from Baruch in *2 Baruch* and from Ezra in 4 Ezra in connection with the fall of the temple.

40. The same kind of protest is heard from Ezra in 4 Ezra 5:41 and from Baruch in *2 Bar.* 14:1–6.

them how to rectify the situation. Pseudo-Philo maintains the Philistines' indecision, leaving it for the sign of the cows to resolve. The alternative possibilities considered at the end of the biblical narrative are that God has caused the Philistines' troubles and that they have come about "by chance." Pseudo-Philo refines this second possibility by having the wise men suggest an "evil power" has come upon them "by chance" (55:5).

The wise men connect the test they propose to their people's punishment. In the Bible, nothing explicit is made either of the fact that milch cows are chosen to bring the ark back to Israel or that their calves must be separated from them (1 Sam. 6:7, 10). Neither is anything made of the cows' lowing as they proceed to Beth-shemesh. In the *Biblical Antiquities,* the wise men say that because pregnant and nursing women have perished and because sucklings and unborn children have died, milch cows should be sent with the ark.[41] The cows' willingness to leave their young to return the ark is a sign that the ark is the cause of their suffering. If they are unwilling to leave because of their longing for their calves, this will be a sign that the Philistines will be utterly destroyed. These signs are lacking in the Bible.

In LAB 55:7, the sign original to the biblical version is introduced. This biblical sign is brought in somewhat awkwardly through the new introductory formula "And some of the wise men and diviners answered." The Bible has the diviners say that if the cows go straight to Beth-shemesh, turning neither to the right nor the left, then it will be clear that Israel's God punished them. Pseudo-Philo develops "right" and "left," saying the cows should be placed where the left-hand road goes to Samaria, the road straight ahead goes to Ekron, and the right-hand one goes to Judah. That Judah is on the right-hand road may have something to do with the right side being the side of honor, whereas the left side, assigned to Samaria, is the side of dishonor.[42] The first sign, whether the cows are willing to leave their young, will tell whether the Philistines are doomed to destruction. The wise men and diviners now say that the second sign, which road the cows take, will reveal whether the Israelite God is the source of their troubles or whether it is "because now we have denied our own gods." Denial of their own gods is not an issue in 1 Samuel 6. Its presence here indicates Pseudo-Philo's abiding interest in idolatry and sets up the narrative to prove that the Israelite God is behind what happens to the Philistines. Their gods do nothing.

In LAB 55:8, the Philistines implement their plan. The cows, "even though they lowed and yearned for their calves," take the road to Judah. Pseudo-Philo uses the element of lowing from 1 Sam. 6:12, going beyond the biblical text. That the cows set off despite their reluctance to abandon their calves (shown by their "lowing") demonstrates the supernatural causation at work: "And then they knew that they were being destroyed because of the ark" (55:8). Pseudo-Philo waits until this moment for the confirmed result that God was responsible for these happenings so the assurance comes directly from

41. The tumors of the biblical version are omitted.
42. See comments on 53:6.

God. The Philistines' deliberations showcase this disclosure by illustrating that they are unsure until the end. This is more effective than the biblical narrative, where for most of the story they are already convinced that God is to blame. True to the ironic mode, they need revelation to understand what is happening.

In 1 Sam. 6:12, the Philistine lords follow the ark to the borders of Beth-shemesh. In accordance with his interest in Shiloh, Pseudo-Philo has them bring the ark there.[43] He adds that they went "with timbrels and pipes and dances," thus giving the impression that the Philistines were honoring God (55:9).[44] It is even said that "they consecrated the ark." How foreigners could possibly have consecrated the ark is left unexplained. Pseudo-Philo collapses the biblical notions that the Philistines made golden tumors because they had been afflicted by tumors and made golden mice because of the infestation of rodents into the notion that they made golden tumors because of the rodent plague. This was made necessary because the tumor problem was eliminated in favor of the affliction of babies and mothers earlier in the narrative.

The narrative is brought to closure in 55:10. The paragraph begins, "And on that day the destruction of the Philistines took place." This refers not to a destruction that occurred after the return of the ark but to the punishment already narrated, made clear by the explanation of the initial sentence. The deaths of pregnant women, sucklings, and nursing women are numbered. In addition, it is said that twenty-five thousand men died.

Chapter 56: The People Seek a King

In its account of the beginnings of the monarchy, the Bible uses sources embodying different views of those beginnings. There is a promonarchy and an antimonarchy source in 1 Samuel. Pseudo-Philo uses elements from both sources but weaves them into a whole that is against Saul's monarchy. Thus he explains the failure of Saul's kingship. Successful kingship cannot come until later.[45] In 56:1 the people ask for a king for the same reason as they do in 1 Sam. 8:4–5; Samuel is getting old and his sons are not worthy successors. Unique to Pseudo-Philo is the addition that the people base their request on a prophecy of Moses: "The word has been fulfilled that Moses said to our fathers in the wilderness, saying, '*Appoint from your brothers* a ruler *over you.*'" The people quote Deut. 17:15, which is not so much a prediction of monarchy as one of the restrictions to be placed on Israelite kingship once it is established. Samuel's and God's reactions show that the request is inappro-

43. See comments on 22:8–9.

44. Ginzberg (*Legends,* vol. 6, 224, n. 34) thought it wrong that the Philistines should bring the ark back, so he suggests changing *allophili* to *Israel* or *populi* (Feldman, "Prolegomenon," cxxxv).

45. The book ends before David's kingship is established. For how that might fit into the author's views of leadership and monarchy, see chapter 2 (this volume) under "Plot."

priate, so the people's interpretation of Deuteronomy cannot be correct. Even when they ground their reasoning in the words of Moses they are wrong.

Samuel's reaction to the people's request is striking (56:2). He knows that the monarchy was intended by God but does not think that it is time for it yet, nor is it time for the building of the temple.[46] Because it is not the predetermined time for a king, Samuel says, "But even if the LORD so wished it, it seems to me that a king could not be appointed." Samuel is wrong, as the subsequent narrative shows. Although God agrees with Samuel that it is not time for a king, God can appoint one. This is not the first time Samuel has been wrong (see 55:1). For Pseudo-Philo, even good leaders err. Their mistakes do not lead to disaster because of their lack of presumption and their openness to God's correction. But Samuel's opinion that God cannot change the divine plan does resonate for readers who have seen repeatedly that God would like to reject Israel. Over and over again God is unable to change concerning Israel's election. That commitment is irrevocable. In 56:3 God tells Samuel that a king will indeed be sent to Israel.

In 1 Samuel 9 is the promonarchy source's account of God's choice of Saul for king.[47] Saul comes to Samuel hoping that the seer can help him to find his father's asses. Before Saul comes, God tells Samuel that the one who is coming has been chosen to be king and to liberate Israel from its enemies. In LAB 56:3, God tells Samuel that Saul is to come the next day. But while in 1 Sam. 9:16 God says that Saul has been chosen to liberate Israel from its enemies, in LAB 56:3 God says, "I will send them a king who will destroy them, and he himself will be destroyed afterward." Pseudo-Philo rewrites 1 Sam. 9:16 under the influence of 1 Sam. 8:6–18, which is part of 1 Samuel's antimonarchy source.

Saul's appeal to Samuel to help find the asses is condensed in 56:4. Pseudo-Philo emphasizes Samuel's "seeing" function; the word *videre* occurs three times in this section. The next section (56:5) shows that Samuel's sight depends on his willingness to be directed by God's plans. The word *dirigere,* often connected with God's direction of the action, occurs twice in 56:5, and the related word *erigere* is used once in a sense synonymous with *dirigere.* At this crucial juncture in Israel's history, Samuel begins by misinterpreting God's capabilities and plans (56:2) but is corrected by God (56:3). Samuel's openness to God is demonstrated by the prayer with which 56:5 begins: "Direct your people, LORD, and tell me what you have planned for them." His words to Saul in 56:5 demonstrate faith that God controls all: "Behold may you know *that the Lord* has chosen *you as ruler for his people* in this time and has directed your ways, and your future will also be directed." The words designating God's direction of the action are added to the biblical story.

In 1 Sam. 9:21, Saul's response shows a humility common in the Bible for

---

46. For rabbinic views on how the foundation of the monarchy and the building of the temple ought to be related, see Feldman, "Prolegomenon," cxxxv.

47. Spiro ("Pseudo-Philo's") examines Pseudo-Philo's view of Saul. See Dietzfelbinger (*Pseudo-Philo,* 82–85) for criticism of Spiro (SC 230, 227; Feldman, "Prolegomenon," cxxxvi).

people chosen for a special task by God. LAB 56:6 couches that response in language taken from Jeremiah 1; Saul protests that he is too young for such a task. Samuel's reaction implies that if Saul were indeed to act according to his humble words, he would live a long life, because Saul's words are like those of Jeremiah.[48] The attribution to Saul of words like those of Jeremiah was inspired by the combination of his humble statement in 1 Sam. 9:21 with the idea that Saul was among the prophets in 1 Sam. 10:6–13. In 55:7, the people return to Samuel to demand the king he promised and Samuel informs them that Saul will come in three days. Saul's prophetic experience is passed over quickly by the statement that the fulfillment of Samuel's prediction to Saul (1 Sam. 10:6) is found in the "Book of Kings." Feldman notes Pseudo-Philo's silence about Samuel's anointing of Saul.[49] This may be so that Hannah's words in 51:6 might refer more clearly to David.

Chapter 57: Samuel Presents Saul to the People

LAB 57 rewrites 1 Samuel 12.[50] The chapter begins with Samuel summoning the people to present Saul. His words underline his disapproval of the new monarchy: "Behold you and your king. But I am in your midst as God commanded me" (57:1). Saul is the people's king, not Samuel's.[51] Samuel is present at the inauguration of the kingship only because God has ordered him there. Samuel continues his speech in a way based on 1 Sam. 12:1–3; he insists on the people's admission that he has ruled them fairly and has not taken from them anything that was not his (57:2–3). In the Bible, this constitutes Samuel's last formal speech, meant to state his record clearly. Although it takes place in the context of the institution of the monarchy, there is no explicit connection drawn between them. Pseudo-Philo draws this direct connection. Samuel makes this speech to compel the people to testify that they are not asking for a king because of his misrule (57:3).

Samuel's words in 1 Sam. 12:1–3 resemble those of Moses in Num. 16:15. In Numbers 16, Moses confronts the rebellion of Korah and seeks to prove that it is not for any misdeed of his own that he must face this revolt. He points out that he has not taken anything from the people. The similarity of Samuel's speech to that of Moses is not pointed out in 1 Samuel 12, but Pseudo-Philo says explicitly that the incident in LAB 57 is like the one in Numbers 16. History is of a piece and is controlled by God. In LAB 57:2, Samuel says that he speaks "before your king," thus reminding the people again that they approve this new monarchy but Samuel disapproves. He compares his words to those of "my lord Moses the servant of God" which he uttered "to your

48. The "because" in this sentence depends on taking the *tamen* of 56:6 in the sense of "seeing that" or "because," as does Perrot (SC 230, 227). Harrington takes it as meaning "nevertheless."

49. "Prolegomenon," cxxxv.

50. For rabbinic passages relevant to Pseudo-Philo's treatment of Samuel, see Feldman, "Prolegomenon," cxxxvi. Samuel is paralleled with Moses in 51:6; 53:2 (SC 230, 228).

51. See SC 230, 228.

fathers in the wilderness." Samuel honors Moses with the admission that he is his lord and with the phrase "servant of God." Samuel reminds the people of their fathers, as is usual in Pseudo-Philo. He then says that Korah and his company perished because they lied and claimed that Moses had taken things unjustly. This must refer to Moses' assignment of holiness to a new priestly caste and Korah's insistence that the entire people is holy (Num. 16:3). Samuel warns that if the people do not testify truthfully, they will suffer the same fate as Korah. If they admit that they are not asking for a king because he has mistreated them, God will be their witness (see 1 Sam. 12:5). This recalls Moses' calling God to witness in Num. 16:7. Samuel ends his speech as follows: "But if now the word of the LORD has been fulfilled, I and the house of my father are free from blame" (57:3).

In 57:4, the people answer, "We are your servants, but we have a king, because we are not worthy to be governed by a prophet." This emphasizes again that the king is theirs, not Samuel's. This response combines features of the people's answer in 1 Sam. 12:4, where they admit that Samuel has taken nothing, and 12:19, where they express fear that they have sinned in asking for a king. Pseudo-Philo turns this into an expression of respect for Samuel and an explanation for monarchy. The shift from rule by Samuel the prophet to monarchy is due to the people's unworthiness to be ruled by a prophet. This is a disparaging assessment of monarchy, seen as an inferior form of government made necessary by the people's flawed nature. This admission is even more powerful on the people's lips. Both people and king weep and acclaim Samuel with an acclamation not found in the Bible, "Long live Samuel the prophet!" The appointment of the king is accompanied by sacrifices to God. The chapter ends with a notice about Saul's military victories (57:5).

Chapter 58: Saul's Sin

In 1 Samuel, there are two different versions of Saul's fatal sin. In 1 Samuel 15, he spares Agag, king of the Amalekites, as well as some of the spoils, in violation of God's command. In 1 Samuel 13, he offers sacrifice before Samuel arrives although Samuel told him to wait for him. LAB 58 chooses the first sin as being the clearer example of disobedience. It is easier to assign a base motive, greed, for that sin than to assign fault for wanting to offer sacrifice before a battle that Saul could see slipping away from him. In 58:1, God condemns Amalek in terms reminiscent of 1 Sam. 15:3, Deut. 25:19, and Exod. 17:14. In 1 Sam. 15:1–3, Samuel tells Saul God's words, but in Pseudo-Philo the readers hear God speaking to Samuel. Pseudo-Philo strengthens God's injunctions to Saul. Whereas Deut. 25:19 ends with "Do not forget," Pseudo-Philo expands this to *"And do not forget* to destroy every one of them as has been commanded to you." The emphasis is on God's commands.

In 1 Sam. 15:8–9, Saul spares Agag and the best of the Amalekites' possessions. The text implies that Saul's motivation in keeping the best of the valuables was greed, though it does not say so outright. No motive is given for the mercy shown to Agag. Pseudo-Philo explains that Saul spared Agag because Agag told him he would show him hidden treasures. Saul's motivation is unambiguous: "On account of this *he spared him.*" Saul brings Agag to Ramathaim, home of Samuel, whereas in the Bible they go to Gilgal. The change is due to the central role of Samuel evident throughout these chapters.

In 1 Sam. 15:11, the readers hear God speak to Samuel directly, but God says only that God regrets making Saul king because he has disobeyed. Pseudo-Philo expands this considerably. God's words make Saul's motivation clear: "You have seen how in a short time the king has been corrupted with silver" (58:3).[52] Then God reveals a plan lacking in the biblical account. In 1 Sam. 15:32–33, Samuel kills Agag. The text implies that he acts according to God's will, though the readers never hear God say so. In LAB 58:3, God orders Samuel to let Agag and his wife live through the night so that Agag can have intercourse with his wife. The male child to be born from that intercourse "will become a stumbling block for Saul." Indeed in 65:4 it is Agag's son who kills Saul in fulfillment of God's prediction.[53] History is a tight web of prediction and fulfillment proceeding according to God's plan.

Only after God's lengthy instructions to Samuel do Samuel and Saul encounter each other (58:4). Saul opens the conversation by admitting that God gave Israel victory. Samuel says, "How much harm Israel has done because they demanded you for themselves as a king before the time came that a king should rule over them!" He condemns Saul for transgressing God's command, then he enumerates the consequences of Israel's and Saul's sins. Agag will die, his hidden treasures will not be revealed, and Agag's son will be Saul's stumbling block. The chapter ends with Samuel killing Agag.

Chapter 59: David's Anointing

As in 1 Sam. 16:1–3, the narrative of Samuel's anointing of David begins with a conversation between God and Samuel that discloses God's intentions (59:1). As in the Bible, God tells Samuel to go to anoint the next king. Pseudo-Philo adds God's reason for this command: "Because the time in which his kingdom will come to pass has been fulfilled." The stress is on God's control and foreknowledge of events. Saul's kingdom violated God's plan; it was "before the time." David's kingdom is now inaugurated in its proper time. Pseudo-Philo omits Samuel's grief over Saul. Samuel asks God directly whether God is "blotting out the kingdom of Saul," and God answers unequivocally, "I am blotting it out."

In 1 Sam. 16, Samuel does not know which of the sons of Jesse to anoint.[54]

---

52. Pseudo-Philo disagrees with the rabbis, who see Saul as too rich to need the spoils, and with Josephus, who spares Agag because he is handsome (Feldman, "Prolegomenon," cxxxvii).

53. Feldman ("Prolegomenon," cxxxvii) connects the idea that Agag's son kills Saul with traditions about Haman that make him an Amalekite.

54. This failure of Samuel caught the attention of Jewish commentators. See Ginzberg, *Legends,* vol. 6, 248, n. 19.

Pseudo-Philo has God reproach Samuel for his lack of vision. God reminds him that he introduced himself to Saul as *"I am the one who sees"* (1 Sam. 9:19; LAB 56:4). In 56:4 the word *videre* is used three times with respect to Samuel, laying the groundwork for God's reminder here. God tells Samuel that he should know whom he is to anoint since he is the "seer." God calls God's words to Samuel a reproach. In 1 Samuel 16, the scene concerning Jesse's sons is drawn out; Pseudo-Philo condenses it. As soon as he tells Samuel that the eldest son is not the one to be anointed, God tells Samuel to seek out "the least shepherd of all" and anoint him. This streamlines the narrative and focuses more sharply on the choice of David. In 1 Sam. 16:11, Samuel tells Jesse to send for David; Pseudo-Philo adds, "Because God has chosen him." After David's anointing, the biblical text says that the "spirit of the LORD" came upon him from that day forward. Pseudo-Philo changes "the spirit of the LORD" to "the LORD," thus bringing God closer to the action.[55]

David sings a psalm as soon as he is anointed.[56] His psalm begins in a manner similar to Psalm 61, also attributed to David. Here David says, "From the ends of the earth I will begin my song of glory," and in Ps. 61:2 he says, "From the end of the earth I call to you." The psalm in LAB 59 is remarkable in that it does not spend time on the significance of the institution of the monarchy or Davidic dynasty but rather interprets God's choice of David as divine protection of the least. As usual, an analogy is drawn from the past, but this time it is a negative one. When Cain was jealous of Abel, he killed him. This is unlike the present situation, for whereas the jealous older brother was allowed to wreak his revenge in the earlier episode, here God protects the younger brother, David. God assigned angels to protect David.[57]

There is no biblical record of jealousy on the part of David's brothers. This element may be imported from the story of Joseph in Genesis.[58] Neither is there any biblical record of David being neglected by his parents, as LAB 59:4 claims. The idea may be inspired by Ps. 27:10, a psalm attributed to David: "If my father and mother forsake me, the LORD will take me up." The ideas of brotherly jealousy and parental neglect are brought to bear on the story of 1 Samuel 16. They are used to explain the fact that when Samuel came to choose the messiah, David's family allowed him to remain in the fields: "And when the prophet came, they did not call to me. And when the anointed of the LORD was to be designated, they forgot me" (LAB 59:4). However, God had "mercy" on David. This interpretation of David's election as rescue by God is noteworthy.

In 1 Sam, 17:31–37, David offers to fight Goliath. When Saul expresses skepticism about his abilities, David says that in guarding his father's flock he

55. Josephus interprets the spirit of the Lord coming on David to mean that David prophesied (*Ant.* 6.8.2. § 166). Pseudo-Philo says nothing about prophecy.

56. For a list of David's extracanonical psalms, see SC 230, 230. There is another psalm of David in LAB 60. For a retroversion of the present psalm into Hebrew with comments, see Strugnell, "More Psalms."

57. Guardian angels are also seen in 11:12 and 15:5 (*OTP*, 372, n. e).

58. David's brother is angry with him in 1 Sam. 17:28, but this is not jealousy.

used to kill wild bears and lions. He says, "The LORD, who saved me from
the paw of the lion and from the paw of the bear, will save me from the hand
of this Philistine" (1 Sam. 17:37). Pseudo-Philo rewrites this. First, he allows
the reader to experience firsthand David's killing of a lion and a bear (59:5).
The animals appear on the scene at the conclusion of David's psalm. Before
killing them, David makes a short speech, declaring his impending defeat of
the animals a sign of his coming victory in battle.[59] He then kills them with
stones. Then God speaks directly to David and says, "Behold with stones I
have delivered up these beasts up for you. Now this will be a sign for you,
because with stones you will kill the enemy of my people later on" (59:5). This
combines several features of Pseudo-Philo—direct speech by God, God's prediction of the future, the similarity of one event to another signifying God's
control of things, and identification of specific elements of events (in this case
the stones) that ties them more closely together.

Chapter 60: David and Saul's Evil Spirit

LAB 60:1 condenses the narrative of 1 Sam. 16:14–23, concerning Saul's evil
spirit and David's playing the lyre to soothe him. Pseudo-Philo adds that David
plays at night, perhaps because the night is a special time for revelations.
David's song demonstrates his supernatural powers of perception.[60] This
becomes the occasion for another composition attributed to David,[61] this time
directed to the evil spirit and meant to exorcise it.

The first part of David's song (LAB 60:2) reworks the first five days of
Creation, paying special attention to the creation of the evil spirit itself.[62] By
demonstrating his knowledge of Creation and of the origin of the evil spirit,
David shows his power over the spirit.[63] Before Creation, there was darkness
and silence. Darkness comes from Gen. 1:2. Mention of God's word in Gen.
1:3 implies there was silence before that word was spoken.[64] (The idea of
primordial silence is common in ancient Judaism.[65]) In Genesis, God creates
light on the first day, and such a time scheme is implied here.[66] "Then your
[evil spirit's] name was pronounced in the drawing together of what had been
spread out." This happens on the second day of Creation, as 60:3 clarifies.[67]
The mention of the spirit's name denotes its creation. The drawing together

---

59. David's killing of the animals was seen as a sign elsewhere (see SC 230, 231).

60. See SC 230, 231; LAB 9:10.

61. For treatments of David's song, see Philonenko, "Remarques" and "Essénisme." I agree
with Perrot (SC 230, 231) that this hymn is neither Essene nor Gnostic. See Perrot's commentary
for a rebuttal of Philonenko's points. See also Feldman, "Prolegomenon," cxxxviii–cxl.

62. SC 230, 233.

63. An exorcist must have knowledge of the spirit to control it. See Mark 5:9. Mark 5:7 may
be an attempt of the spirits to counteract Jesus' power.

64. For numerous other parallels, see SC 230, 233.

65. The closest parallels are 4 Ezra 6:39; 7:30 and *2 Bar.* 3:7 since these are close to Pseudo-
Philo conceptually, chronologically, and geographically.

66. See Ps. 139:11–12.

67. Perrot notes that in *Gen. Rab.* 1:3, the creation of the angels takes place either on the

of what had been spread out refers to the restriction of the waters by means of the firmament to make heaven above and earth below (Gen. 1:6–8).[68]

David next mentions the creation of rain, which would be on the third day. Then the earth is ordered to bring forth nourishment for all living things on the fourth day. Finally, on the fifth day "the tribe of your [evil spirit's] spirits" was made. Perrot notes that in 60:2 God is depicted as the Creator of all, including evil spirits; no dualism is intended by Pseudo-Philo.[69]

At the beginning of 60:3, David commands the spirit to cease being "troublesome as one created on the second day." It is not clear whether this means that the spirit is to act properly as a creature of God, or that being created on the second day explains its nature as an evil spirit but it is to stop acting according to that nature.[70] David continues, "But if not, remember Tartarus where you walk." What this means is in doubt. Perrot suggests the following possibilities: (1) You are marching toward Tartarus; (2) if you do not behave well, you will return to Tartarus; (3) you live in Tartarus.[71] In any case, this is a further expression of David's knowledge of the spirit and he uses it to assert control. The exact meaning of the next sentence, in which David says that in what he sings to the demon *multis psallo,* is again unclear.[72] In any case David expects his psalm to make the demon behave. The next sentence again reminds the demon of its origins.

The final sentence of David's psalm is difficult to interpret: "But let the new womb from which I was born rebuke you, from which after a time one born from my loins will rule over you" (60:3). Harrington rightly dismisses a messianic interpretation of this sentence given Pseudo-Philo's lack of interest in a Messiah.[73] Instead he proposes that Solomon may be meant here since he was known for his power over spirits.[74] Chapter 60 ends as does 1 Samuel 16, with the observation that David's song was successful in relieving Saul of the evil spirit.

Chapter 61: David and Goliath

In LAB 61:1, David returns to tend his sheep in the wilderness. Pseudo-Philo mentions a battle with Midianites who come to take his sheep. In the battle,

---

second or the fifth day. Harrington (*OTP,* n. d) points out that in *2 En.* 29:1 evil spirits are created on the second day but that in *Jub.* 2:2 it is on the first day.

68. In 4 Ezra 6:41, God creates "the spirit of the firmament," and in *2 Bar.* 21:4 God "fixed the firmament by the word and fastened the height of heaven by the spirit." These two passages associate the creation of the firmament with a spirit, which fits the belief that the heavenly bodies either are angels or spirits or are controlled by them.

69. SC 230, 234.

70. Perrot (SC 230, 234) opts for the former, citing numerous parallels to support his point. However, since in some of those parallels the spirits are evil from their inception, the meaning remains ambiguous.

71. SC 230, 235.

72. For possibilities, see SC 230, 235.

73. *OTP,* 373, n. e.

74. For more possibilities, see SC 230, 235–36.

David kills fifteen thousand men. This incident is unique to Pseudo-Philo and enhances David's military prowess, decreasing the surprise at his victory over Goliath. Instead of being a young shepherd unfamiliar with battle, as in the Bible, David is an accomplished warrior.

In 1 Samuel 17, Goliath taunts Israel and dares them to send out any man to fight him. LAB 61:2 turns this into a personal taunting of Saul. Goliath reminds Saul that when he captured the ark and killed the priests, Saul fled. As usual, Pseudo-Philo ties the narrative together more tightly than does the Bible. This increases the ironic element in the story and reinforces the idea that there is a God-given significance to history. Goliath challenges Saul to fight, threatening to take him captive and make Israel serve the Philistine gods (61:2).[75] In 1 Sam. 17:9, Goliath threatens Israel only with servitude to the Philistines. Pseudo-Philo introduces idolatry here because of his abiding interest in the subject.

In 1 Sam. 17:16, it is reported that Goliath taunted Israel for forty days. Pseudo-Philo associates this with the forty days on Sinai: "According to the number of days in which Israel feasted when it received the Law in the wilderness, that is, forty days, so I will ridicule them and afterward I will fight them" (61:2). Goliath's taunt contains a threat of idolatry; his taunt is to last for as many days as it took for Israel to receive the Torah. The giving of the Torah and Goliath's ridicule both take place in the wilderness. Pseudo-Philo portrays this episode as a direct attack on Torah by an idolatrous foreigner and simultaneously casts it as a direct personal challenge to Israel's king. This contributes to Pseudo-Philo's general connection of idolatry to leadership.

In 61:3, David hears Goliath. He asks, "Is this the time about which God said to me, 'I will deliver into your hands by stones the enemy of my people?'" David makes clear that the action to come fulfills God's words. Further, David quotes God's words, a technique proving God's foreknowledge and control of events. Although David does not quote God's prediction of 59:5 completely accurately, the element of stones remains and the one to be killed is called "the enemy of my people," the same phrase used in 59:5. There is a brief interchange between Saul and David in 61:4 corresponding to 1 Sam. 17:31–37, where David informs Saul of his plans. In 1 Samuel, David tells Saul not to let anyone in Israel fear. In Pseudo-Philo, this is personalized to Saul; it is he who should not fear. This continues Pseudo-Philo's tendency to make Saul look worse. The rest of the passage is condensed, but Pseudo-Philo agrees with the LXX of 1 Sam. 17:36 when he includes David's assurance that God will take away reproaches from Israel. Unique to Pseudo-Philo is the assurance that God will remove hatred from Israel.[76]

In 1 Sam. 17:40, David chooses five stones for his sling. They become seven stones in LAB 61:5 and on them David writes the names of Abraham, Isaac,

---

75. *B. Soṭa* 42b makes the same connection (Feldman, "Prolegomenon," cxl).
76. See Luke 1:71.

Jacob, Moses, Aaron, himself, and God.[77] This symbolic act underlines Israel's very identity. Israel's relationship with its God is its very core. That relationship cannot depend on Israel's behavior, for it continually falls short of righteousness. Rather, it rests on God's covenant with the patriarchs, Abraham, Isaac, and Jacob. Moses is the best representative of the one who faithfully mediates between God and the people, so he is included. His inclusion is especially appropriate given Goliath's connection of his taunts to the giving of the Torah at Sinai. That Aaron is included shows a concern for cult and priesthood. David is included as God's chosen one. Ultimately, God brings the victory, so even God's name is written on one of the stones. In view of the context, it is fitting that God's title *Fortissimus* is used here. Finally, the readers are informed in advance that it is God who will bring the victory: "And God sent Zervihel, the angel in charge of might in warfare."[78]

The rest of chapter 61 describes the interaction between David and Goliath. David delivers a speech to Goliath in 61:6 centered on worship of God and of idols. David reminds Goliath that their "mothers" (which means "ancestors" here) were sisters.[79] Ruth, ancestor of David, was a Gentile. In the Book of Ruth she exemplifies the non-Israelite who forsakes her own people to belong to Israel, the people of God. Orpah, Goliath's mother, "chose for herself the gods of the Philistines and went after them," but Ruth, David's mother, "chose for herself the ways of the Most Powerful and walked in them." Those past choices explain the present situation, in which David, representative of an Israel whose identity is determined by its ancestors' choice to serve God, confronts Goliath, the one who seeks to reduce Israel to service to the Philistine gods and so destroy it. The contrast between Orpah and Ruth is not completely parallel; Orpah chooses and goes after the Philistine gods, but Ruth chooses the *ways* of God and *walks* in them. This formulation draws attention to the behavior demanded of God's people. David ends by insisting that the blood ties between him and Goliath are meaningless in view of the service of Goliath's people to the Philistine gods and of David's people to God. He predicts that he will also conquer Goliath's brothers and that Goliath will report to his mother that David has not spared their family.

In the Bible, David kills Goliath with a stone and then cuts off his head. There is no exchange of words between them. In LAB 61:7, the stone does not kill Goliath but merely fells him. David runs up and draws Goliath's sword. Goliath tells David to kill him quickly and rejoice. David orders Goliath to open his eyes and see who is really killing him (61:8). Goliath looks and sees the angel and confesses that David has not acted alone. Only then does David kill him. The narrative of David and Goliath ends in 61:9. The angel changes

---

77. Cohn points out that names are written on the five stones in *Midr. Samuel* 21. There the names are God, Aaron, Abraham, Isaac, and Jacob.

78. Harrington (*OTP,* 374, n. f) and Perrot (SC 230, 237) see this as the same angel as Zeruel, who helps Kenaz in 27:10.

79. The traditions seeing David and Goliath as born of common ancestors and connecting Goliath with the woman called Orpah here is detailed in SC 230, 237. See Feldman, "Prolegomenon," cxl.

David's appearance so that no one recognizes him, and Saul asks who he is. This explains why Saul did not recognize David after he killed Goliath even when speaking to him face to face (1 Sam. 17:55–58). Lack of recognition occurs several times in the *Biblical Antiquities*. It corresponds to the ironic mode in which the book is written. Humans do not see things as they are; God sees things accurately, and the readers share the divine viewpoint.[80]

Chapter 62: David and Jonathan

The biblical account of the souring relationship between Saul and David is summarized in 62:1, where it is said that Saul was jealous of David and wanted to kill him. David flees to Ramathaim and Saul pursues him. As in 1 Sam. 18:23–24, Saul falls into a prophetic trance. The Bible does not give the content of that trance. The trance supplies Pseudo-Philo with an opportunity to begin the chapter with a prophecy through a revelation to Saul. When Saul awakes from the trance, he remembers nothing of it. The revelation to Saul alerts the reader to what is to happen and to God's control of it, yet it does not disrupt the ironic mode. Saul remains ignorant of God's plan. The irony is deepened because Saul is unaware of what has come from his own mouth.

The prophecy begins, "Why are you led astray *[seduceris]*, Saul, and whom are you pursuing in vain?" (62:2). *Seducere* is common in the *Biblical Antiquities*. It is used to denote what happens to people who see things wrongly and so are disloyal to God in some way. To be so deceived leads to acting "in vain." Anything that is contrary to the plan of God is "in vain" and so is doomed to failure, as is Saul's intention to kill David. The prophecy continues, "The time allotted to your kingdom has been completed." God has predetermined everything and Saul cannot change that. Finally, the prophecy declares that Saul and his son will die and David's kingdom will appear.

The rest of chapter 62 consists of a conversation and the making of a covenant between David and Jonathan. David and Jonathan both make speeches. The biblical text supplies only a few phrases here; most of the section is Pseudo-Philo's composition. The key themes of the passage are David's innocence, the injustice of Saul's hatred of him, and the love between David and Jonathan. The love between the two men is contrasted with Saul's hatred for David and so serves to set that animosity into still greater relief. This section serves Pseudo-Philo's interest in leadership. It illustrates the unreasonable persecution of the righteous by the unjust leader, an unreasonableness that is underlined by the love Saul's own son Jonathan has for David. It makes David an example of the proper way to respond to such hatred—reliance on one's own innocence and trust in God.

David begins by suggesting to Jonathan that they make a covenant with one another before they are separated. Pseudo-Philo thus assigns the initiative for the covenant to David, whereas the biblical account gives the impression

---

80. See chapter 2 (this volume) under "Recognition."

that the covenant was Jonathan's idea (1 Sam. 18:3). Sounding the major theme of the speech, David declares that Saul is trying to kill him unjustly. The reference to Saul's plans fits Pseudo-Philo's constant attention to how human plans often run counter to those of God, and so are wrong and bound to fail. David's explanation of Saul's hatred—that Jonathan loves him and that David will take over the reign from Saul—fits the information narrated at the opening of the chapter that Saul is jealous of David.

David complains that he did only good to Saul, and Saul has paid him back with evil. In contrast, David does not retaliate but makes a covenant of love with Saul's son. Jonathan's plea that David maintain their relationship is sealed with their kiss, which ends the chapter (62:11). David and Saul are opposites. Were all this to remain on a human level, it would speak badly enough for Saul, but it involves God, too. David says, "When I killed Goliath according to the word of the Most Powerful, see the end that he [Saul] planned for me, for he determined to destroy my father's house" (62:4). In chapter 61, Pseudo-Philo made Goliath's challenge personal to Saul; therefore David's victory freed Saul in particular. At the same time, the good that David did for Saul was in obedience to God's command. So Saul's treachery is doubly reprehensible, and it all flows from jealousy. David tells Jonathan he would welcome impartial judgment of the issue.

In 62:5, David elaborates on his own innocence. He fears that if Saul kills him, then Saul himself will die. Feldman notes that this embodies the *ius talionis* and is absent from the biblical text.[81] This strengthens the idea of moral causality. David shares Pseudo-Philo's view of inevitable retribution for sin and here shows himself unselfish in that he is as concerned for Saul as he is for himself. This agrees with the biblical view that David continued to respect the anointed of the Lord even after Saul proved himself unworthy. In protesting his innocence David appeals to the fact that he has never shed innocent blood, a boast Saul could not make were he to succeed in his purpose.[82] His claim of being the least of his brethren is frequent in Davidic traditions.[83] Saul's envy is "in vain" also because David is so young. David contrasts the righteousness of his own father with the injustice of Jonathan's father, thereby deepening the contrast between the two.[84]

In the next section, David makes an argument *a maiore ad minus*. Even if David had sinned against Saul, Saul should forgive him in imitation of God.[85] If God, against whom no one should offend, is willing to forgive, how much more should a mere human be willing to forgive. But since David has done only good to Saul, so much the more should Saul treat him well. All of this makes Saul's persecution of David even more unjust. David's flight from Saul

81. "Prolegomenon," cxli.

82. Note the charge against Abimelech that he shed the blood of his brothers (37:4).

83. See SC 230, 239, which also draws attention to the theme of shepherding.

84. This is similar to David's contrast of his and Goliath's ancestors in chapter 61. On David's father's righteousness, see Feldman, "Prolegomenon," cxli.

85. The same argument is made in 39:4. See Matt. 6:12; 18:35.

should not be taken as an admission of guilt. David has not even complained to anyone except Jonathan and Jonathan's sister Michal (62:7).

David concludes his speech in 62:7–8. He suggests to Jonathan that the two of them go forth together "in truth," implicitly contrasting this with Saul, who lives a lie. David says that death in battle would have been preferable to death at Saul's hands, because in battle he was protecting Saul. The heinousness of Saul's injustice is emphasized: Saul seeks his protector's life. David ends by appealing to Jonathan to correct him if he is mistaken. This opens the way for Jonathan's words to David, which take up most of the rest of the chapter.

Jonathan's speech in 62:9–11 is in two parts, separated by David and Jonathan weeping and kissing one another. It begins with Jonathan's testimony to David's righteousness and then concentrates on their relationship and their grief that they must separate (62:9–10). The second part (62:11) appeals to David to remember not Saul's hatred but Jonathan's love. In part 1, Jonathan laments their impending separation but asserts that it happens because of their sins. There is nothing indicating that the narrator disagrees with this judgment, and Jonathan is a sympathetic character, so the readers are to conclude that Jonathan is correct. This fits with Pseudo-Philo's idea of moral causality. Saul's hatred is unjust, but if David and Jonathan suffer they must have deserved to do so because of their own sin. Nonetheless, although they are punished in this life, they will be rejoined and recognize each other in the afterlife.[86] Then Jonathan implies that history is predetermined by claiming David's earthly kingdom will come "in its own time."

The rest of part 1 of the speech elaborates on the grief that David and Jonathan feel because of the impending separation. They weep into a vessel and bury it as a monument to their pain. They call heaven and earth to witness their love and their covenant. Such language is borrowed from the Mosaic covenant (Deut. 30:19). The emphasis on the love of David and Jonathan is true to the biblical text but is thrown into still greater relief through this scene of almost melodramatic pathos and by excision of other aspects of the biblical narrative, such as the elaborate scheme for Jonathan to warn David of Saul's intentions.

In 62:11, Jonathan seeks David's assurance that when he becomes king he will remember his love rather than Saul's hatred, a hatred that was "in vain" because it was unjust and based on jealousy. In passing, Jonathan testifies that David's kingship comes through God's will. David's mercy to Jonathan's family constitutes his remembrance of the covenant sworn between the two men. The series of paired opposites contained in 62:11 is noteworthy: anger/covenant, hatred/love, ingratitude/table fellowship, jealousy/truth, lie/sworn oaths. This section is a structuralist's paradise. One must wonder whether there is a metaphor here for God's relationship with Israel. God had sworn to the fathers to uphold the covenant no matter what happened. Although God experienced

---

86. Harrington (*OTP*, 375, n. d) points to *2 Bar.* 50:3–4 as a parallel to the idea that the dead recognize each other at the Resurrection.

abandonment and even hostility at the hands of the people, he concentrated not on their failure but on God's covenant with the fathers.[87]

Chapter 63: Abimelech Dies

LAB 63 rewrites 1 Samuel 22. In 1 Samuel, the priests of Nob suffer unjustly at Saul's hands, but Pseudo-Philo has a theory of strict retribution. The priests must have done something to deserve their fate. The narrator claims that they "were profaning the holy things of the LORD and desecrating the first fruits of the people" (63:1). The only thing this could refer to in the biblical account is the giving of the holy bread to David and his men (1 Sam. 21:4–6), but Pseudo-Philo apparently does not mean that. The readers learn that the priests anger God, who says, "Behold I will blot out those dwelling in Nob, because they walk in the ways of the sons of Eli." The readers know how God feels and what God intends. The destruction of the priests becomes a fulfillment of God's prediction and a punishment not only for their own cultic sins but also for those of Eli's sons (see 1 Sam. 3:12–14; LAB 53:9–10; 54:5). The cultic sins of Nob's priests resemble those of Eli's sons (52:1).[88] Doeg the Syrian reports to Saul that Abimelech is helping David (63:2). LAB 63:3 reports subsequent events substantially as they occur in the Bible, except that Saul himself kills Abimelech rather than ordering his servant Doeg to do so.[89] As in the Bible, Abiathar escapes the massacre and reports to David.

In 63:3–4, Pseudo-Philo inserts two divine pronouncements into the narrative. In the first, God expresses indignation that the people protest Saul's plans to kill Jonathan (1 Sam. 14:43–46, unreported in the *Biblical Antiquities*) but remain silent when 385 priests perish (63:3). It is the same sort of accusation as that leveled against the Israelites in LAB 47:4–8, where God is angry that the people are aroused by the death of the Levite's concubine (chap. 45) but remained silent before Micah's idolatry (chap. 44). Ironically, Pseudo-Philo places the incident of the concubine at Nob although it takes place at Gibeah in Judges 19, thus drawing a subtle connection between the two events.[90] In 63:3, God predicts punishment for the people and their king at the hands of Israel's enemies. The prediction is fulfilled two chapters later. God's second pronouncement is against Doeg, Saul's servant who reported Abimelech's disloyalty to Saul (63:4). A fiery worm will enter Doeg's tongue and will cause him to rot away, and he will join Jair forever in "the inextinguishable

---

87. It is to be noted, however, that the word love is not applied to the relationship between God and Israel in the *Biblical Antiquities. Amare* is used only three times, of God's love for Moses (19:16), of Samson's love for Delilah (43:6), and of Jonathan's love for David. In 23:12 God calls Israel a "lovable flock" *(gregem amabilem).*

88. Josephus also sees the destruction of the priests of Nob as fulfilling God's curse of Eli's line but does not accuse the priests themselves (*Ant.* 6.12.6 § 260). The rabbis, in contrast, claim that the priests were righteous (Feldman, "Prolegomenon," cxli).

89. The MT says the priest's name is Ahimelech, but the LXX and Josephus agree with Pseudo-Philo in calling him Abimelech.

90. In 45:2, the incident at Nob is said to be like the one at Sodom involving Lot.

fire." This is another case of the punishment fitting the crime. Doeg offended with his tongue and will be punished through it.[91] For further information on Saul, especially his persecution of David, Pseudo-Philo refers the reader to "the Book of the Kings of Israel" (63:5).

Chapter 64: The Medium of Endor

Chapter 64 emphasizes that Saul's approaching death is determined by God. Pseudo-Philo rewrites it so as to enhance Saul's guilt. In 1 Sam. 28:3, it says that Samuel died and all Israel mourned him and buried him. Juxtaposed with this is the brief announcement that Saul had "expelled the mediums and the wizards from the land." LAB 64:1 substantially expands the notice about the mediums. The readers are privy to Saul's inner thoughts and so learn his true motivation: "Because I am to expel the wizards from the land of Israel, they will be mindful of me after my departure."[92] Saul's action is motivated not by loyalty to God but by desire for a good reputation after his death. Only after the readers hear Saul's thoughts does he expel the wizards.

As usual, the readers experience firsthand God's response to Saul's action, a response not explicit in the Bible. God says, "Behold Saul has not driven the wizards out of the land for fear of me, but to make a name for himself. Behold he will go to those whom he has scattered, to obtain divination from them, because he has no prophets" (64:1). God understands Saul's true motivation and characterizes it in language used of the builders of the tower of Babel (6:1) and of Micah and his mother (44:2–4). Desire for fame and good reputation drives Saul. God makes explicit the irony implicit in the biblical text: Saul must consult those whom he has banished. The readers of the Bible learn that there are no prophets available to Saul when he tries to find some (1 Sam. 28:6). In the *Biblical Antiquities,* the readers learn of the lack of prophets through God's words.

In the Bible, it is said simply that the Philistines had encamped against Israel (1 Sam. 28:4). In Pseudo-Philo, the readers hear the Philistines' reason for the campaign before they undertake it. They think now is the time to avenge the blood of their fathers because Samuel the prophet is dead, so there is no one to pray for Israel, and because "David, who fought on their behalf, is Saul's enemy, and he is not with them" (64:2). In 1 Sam. 28:5–6, the Philistine army frightens Saul and he tries to consult God and prophets. When this fails, he searches for a medium. Pseudo-Philo attributes Saul's fear to the fact that Samuel was dead and David was not with him. His fear is due to the same reasoning that led the Philistines to begin their latest campaign. Both the foreigners and the Israelite king recognize that the absence of a prophet to pray

91. *B. Sanh.* 106b proclaims that Doeg's soul will burn forever, and *Gen. Rab.* 32:1 and 38:1 say that he will never rise. See also *Deut. Rab.* 5:10; SC 230, 241–42.

92. This motivation for the expulsion is unique to Pseudo-Philo (Ginzberg, *Legends,* vol. 6, 235–36, n. 73). Josephus (*Ant.* 6.14.4 §§ 348–49) says that Saul confronted his own death bravely because he wanted fame after dying.

for Israel and the absence of the proper leader, David, make Israel vulnerable.[93] Saul tries to consult God and prophets, but God does not answer and no prophets appear. The latter has already been foretold by God in 64:1.

In 1 Sam. 28:7, Saul tells his servant to seek out a medium so that he can inquire of her. In Pseudo-Philo's narrative, Saul keeps the pronoun for the medium in the masculine so that the subsequent story does not influence his query (64:3). Pseudo-Philo also says that Saul wishes to inquire "what I should plan out," fitting with Pseudo-Philo's interest in human planning. The people tell Saul about the medium at Endor and give her a name unique to Pseudo-Philo, Sedecla. They say that she "is the daughter of the Midianite diviner who led the people of Israel astray with sorceries." "Midianite diviner" is an emendation; Harrington says, "Most MSS have 'Adod the Midianite,' who may be Aod of ch. 34."[94] The connection of the medium of Endor with Aod would be typical of Pseudo-Philo, who delights in drawing connections between different events and people in Israel's history. Even if the emendation is correct, Aod may still be meant by the phrase "Midianite diviner."

Pseudo-Philo's rewriting in 64:4 consists primarily of emphasizing that the diviner did not recognize Saul and revealing Saul's thoughts about that. When the woman fails to recognize him, "Saul said to himself, 'When I was king in Israel, even if the gentiles did not see me, they knew nevertheless that I was Saul.' " Lack of recognition is a common device in the *Biblical Antiquities;* here it accentuates Saul's fall from glory, presented forcefully in that Saul himself describes it. Saul's distress at not being recognized even though he has come in disguise and so is trying not to be recognized is amplified by his somewhat pathetic question, "Have you ever seen Saul?" The woman answers, "I have seen him often." This throws Saul into grief: "Saul went outside and wept and said, 'Behold now I know that my appearance has changed, and the glory of my kingdom has passed from me.' " The rest of what happens in the narrative is to some degree anticlimactic. Here Saul realizes his own fall from power and speaks of his kingly glory as already past.

When Sedecla calls up Samuel, she sees Saul with him and then recognizes Saul. She accuses him of treachery.[95] Saul commands her to describe her vision. Its otherworldly nature is underscored by her first words: "Behold forty years have passed since I began raising up the dead for the Philistines, but such a sight as this has never been seen before nor will it be seen afterward" (64:5). Sedecla's words may imply that the afterlife of faithful Israelites cannot be compared to that of idolatrous foreigners. Saul asks for details of the visionary person's appearance. In 1 Sam. 28:14, Saul knows that it is Samuel because of the robe in which he is wrapped. Saul does obeisance, a scene elaborated in LAB 64:6. In 1 Sam. 28:13, the woman says that the figure in the vision was a "divine being." In the following verse she says it is an old man. In Pseudo-

93. For intercession as the job of the prophet, see SC 230, 242.
94. *OTP,* 376, n. d.
95. In the MT, the woman sees Samuel; in some manuscripts of the LXX, she sees Saul; in Pseudo-Philo she sees both.

Philo, this becomes, "You are asking me about *divine beings*. For behold his appearance is not the appearance of a man" (64:6). The woman adds details not present in the biblical text: Saul wears a mantle in addition to a white robe and he is led by two angels, a sign of the honor in which he is held in the other world.[96] The narrator says that Saul realizes that the mantle worn by Samuel is the same as the one Samuel tore when he was alive. The tearing of the mantle was not narrated by Pseudo-Philo. Pseudo-Philo turns Saul's gesture of obeisance into the despairing gesture of pounding the ground.

Samuel's words occupy LAB 64:7–8. He first chides Saul for calling him up from the dead. He says, "I thought that the time for being rendered the rewards of my deeds had arrived." This reminds the readers and Saul of final retribution beyond death and shows Samuel's confidence that the Last Judgment will result in his reward for deeds performed in this life. Samuel's next words deny any real power to the medium. He declares that neither Saul the king nor the medium brought him forth, "but that order that God spoke to me while was still alive, that I should come and tell you that you have sinned now a second time in neglecting God. Therefore after rendering up my soul my bones have been disturbed so that I who am dead should tell you what I heard while I was alive" (64:7). God's foreknowledge is displayed in that even before Samuel's death he was told he would have to return to judge a sin that Saul would later commit. Saul's sinfulness did not cease with Samuel's death. Saul's actions described in chapter 64 amount to neglect of God. The only thing this could refer to in LAB 64 is Saul's decision to drive out the diviners not because of fear of God but for his own benefit.

Finally Samuel predicts the death of Saul and his sons (64:8): They and the people will be handed over to the Philistines. Samuel concludes, "And because your insides were eaten up with jealousy, what is yours will be taken away from you."[97] This refers to Saul's unjust jealousy of David, which occupied so much space in the narrative. Saul's response is to grow faint, to accept the truth of Samuel's predictions, and to express hope that his own death will atone for his sins.[98]

Chapter 65: Saul's Death

The last chapter of the *Biblical Antiquities* rewrites the account of Saul's death in 1 Sam. 31:1–4. It adds numerous remarks by Saul, and discloses the identity of Saul's killer. As in the Bible, Saul dies after the battle with the Philistines has gone badly. Pseudo-Philo adds Saul's words to himself: "Why are you

96. Harrington (*OTP*, 377, n. i) points to the parallel with Christ's resurrection in *Gos. Pet.* 10:39–40. For a discussion of the robe, see Feldman, "Prolegomenon," cxlii; SC 230, 243–44.

97. This may be another attempt to make the punishment fit the crime.

98. In *Pirqe R. El.* 33, Saul's death atones for his sins. That death might atone for sins is seen in LAB 25:7. Perrot refers to *b. Sanh.* 44b for the belief that death can atone for one's own sins (SC 230, 245). He refers to Isa. 53:4–10 and *b. Soṭa* 14a for the idea that one person's death can atone for another's sins.

strengthening yourself for life when Samuel has announced death for you along with your sons?" (65:1). Saul himself proclaims the futility of trying to escape a fate decreed by God through the prophet. The battle with the Philistines is foolish, for its outcome is foreordained. As in the Bible, Saul asks his armor-bearer to kill him, but he refuses. Saul tries to kill himself. In the Bible he is successful, but in the *Biblical Antiquities* he is not. This provides an opportunity for the narrative's final irony. Saul calls to a man running by to kill him but asks him to reveal his identity before killing him. The man says that he is "Edabus, son of Agag, king of the Amalekites." Saul declares, "Behold now the words of Samuel have come to pass upon me, because he said, 'He who is born of Agag will be a stumbling block for you'" (65:4). Samuel's prediction (58:4) and Saul's admission of it (65:4) are added by Pseudo-Philo to the biblical story. The fulfillment is emphasized by Saul's quotation of Samuel's prophecy.

In the last words of the *Biblical Antiquities,* Saul tells his killer to report his death to David. He is to say, "I have killed your enemy." Then he is to say, "Be not mindful of my hatred or my injustice." These final words of Saul echo Jonathan's plea to David to forget Saul's hatred and injustice. The *Biblical Antiquities* ends on a note of reconciliation between Israel's leaders, an end to hatred and jealousy, and an acceptance of God's just judgment.

III

Broader Perspectives on Pseudo-Philo

10

Major Characters: God, Humanity, Israel, Leaders, Other Major Figures

Most of the material in the next three chapters can be found scattered throughout the commentary of chapters 3 through 9. This chapter and the following ones do not repeat that analysis. They rather pull together the various strands of the narrative to arrive at a generalized picture of characters (this chapter), themes (chapter 11), and reflections of the author's real world (chapter 12). In most cases, the listing of passages that support a certain interpretation is illustrative rather than exhaustive. The full effect of the points made in these three chapters can be appreciated only in combination with the detailed investigations of the preceding chapters.

God

God is the most important character in the *Biblical Antiquities*. God is revealed by the divine words and actions, by how others relate to God and what they say about God, and by the narrator's comments. Analysis of God must consider other characters and must also look at plot. Since God as a character unifies the narrative, this leads to the following overview of the entire work.[1]

The *Biblical Antiquities* is a narrative theodicy, a defense of God's ways. It does not address a specific problem like the destruction of the temple, as does 4 Ezra or *2 Baruch*. Indeed, it was probably written before 70 C.E. Rather, Pseudo-Philo addresses a more general situation in which Israel is dissatisfied with its subjection to a foreign power, inadequate leadership, and a populace with conflicting ideas concerning what to do about the situation and what God wants. Pseudo-Philo exonerates God. God is as clear as can be throughout history. It is first humanity as a whole and then Israel in particular that is obtuse. Simply put, obedience to God brings success, disobedience brings disaster. All sin receives its punishment. Complete dependence on God leads to a perfect relationship with the Deity. God has done everything possible to make that a reality. History is a succession of events directed by God toward

1. Perrot discusses many of the following ideas in "La providence divine," SC 230, 49–52.

the end of establishing a proper relation with humans, but humans always ruin things either through wickedness or mistakes. God's mercy results in the continuation of history and points toward better things. Nonetheless, true resolution of the human condition will not take place until the afterlife, when everything lost through human sin will be restored to the worthy.

Only God is present in every part of the *Biblical Antiquities.* Divine words, actions, decisions, intentions, motivations, predictions, and reactions unify the work. God is extremely active, reacting in word and deed to practically everything human characters say and do. The designations for God are so numerous that it is not useful even to list all of them in the concordance. *Deus* occurs 248 times in the text, 186 of those instances in the nominative case. *Dominus* occurs 297 times, 115 in the nominative. There are also other titles used for God, of which the most common is *Fortissimus.* It appears 18 times, 8 in the nominative, and stresses God's active strength.

A brief review of some of the verbs most commonly predicated of God is a convenient way to summarize God's activity. God is often the subject of the verb "to say." God speaks frequently to the characters, but the readers are privy to an even fuller version of God's words and thoughts. God reveals many things, from the beginning and end of time, to the Torah, to specific things like who the sinners are in Kenaz's time. God makes the divine will known, utters curses and blessings, and predicts the future. God often "commands" and "sends." This demonstrates God's deep involvement in the plot. Much of what the good leaders do is in obedience to God's commands. God always acts on behalf of Israel. God most frequently "frees" them from political oppression. God "leads" the people out of Egypt, to Sinai, and to the promised land. God continually "directs" the people either directly or, since they are so obtuse, through leaders. God's words are never "in vain." God "fulfills" all of the divine predictions, promises, and statements. The word complex from the verb "to remember" is frequent in the *Biblical Antiquities.*[2] It is often God who does the remembering, but the people must also remember. This shows the orientation to the past. Past covenants and promises determine the present. When Israel remembers its past, it obeys and enjoys success. When God remembers the covenants with the fathers and the promises to them, Israel benefits.

God is defined through divine–human interaction. It is human history and the history of Israel in particular that occupies the narrative, not primarily God's relationship with the cosmos, which is taken for granted. The Creation is not even narrated, for example. Neither is God considered *in se* or in abstract terms. Harrington notes, "God is light (12:9; cf. 22:3) and life (30:6)," but those are not so much abstract qualities as distillations of what God does for humanity, giving them revelation and sustenance.[3] Pseudo-Philo enlightens the readers about God's ways through many narratives that share patterns and embody

2. See concordance under *memor, memoro, memoria.*
3. *OTP,* 300.

some of the same principles. There is an ongoing contrast between the divine and human realms.[4] On the one side is humanity in general and Israel in particular. Israel is often sinful, idolatrous, ignorant, unreliable, and disloyal. God represents the opposite qualities. Most striking is the utter constancy of God's faithfulness to the covenant.

The book begins not with the Creation stories but with the genealogies from Genesis 4–5. God appears for the first time in response to humans. In 1:16, 20, the individuals Enoch and Noah please God, though these positive statements are put in the context of a condemnation of general humanity for its evil deeds (1:20; 2:1, 8–10). This initiates a pattern wherein God is sometimes pleased with individuals but is almost never happy with groups, including Israel. Such a view is not far from 4 Ezra 3:36: "You may indeed find individuals who have kept your commandments, but nations you will not find." The first three chapters present humanity in its potential vastness (note the proliferation of names), with the two basic divine reactions to it—approval and disapproval—portrayed early. In Pseudo-Philo's rewriting, humanity's sinfulness is increased. As in the biblical story of the Flood, Pseudo-Philo's God regrets that humanity was created (3:3).

God is unfailingly faithful to the "covenants with the fathers." In 14:2, having completed the giving of the Torah at Sinai, God instructs Moses to assemble the people "until I fulfill all that I have spoken to their fathers and until I set them firmly in their own land; for not a single word from what I have spoken to their fathers will I renege on, from those that I said to them: *'Your seed will be like the stars of heaven in multitude.'*" At a covenant ceremony at Gilgal, the people solemnly declare, "He is the God who sent word to our fathers in the secret dwelling places of souls, saying, 'Behold the LORD has done everything that he said to us.' And truly now we know that God has established every word of his Law that he spoke to us on Horeb" (22:9). In 23:11, God again testifies to the divine faithfulness: "I fulfilled my covenant that I promised to your fathers." Deborah sings of all God did for Israel and sums up with "And everything that the Most Powerful said, this he observed, having Moses his beloved as a witness" (32:8).

God's fulfillment of promised progeny and land is a specific example of a general principle: God's words will never be in vain. Any human plans running counter to God's plan will be in vain.[5] Examples abound, but perhaps the most painful is the case of Seila, daughter of Jephthah. God recognizes Seila's goodness but refuses to allow her to be saved: "Behold now I have shut up the tongue of the wise men of my people for this generation so that they cannot respond to the daughter of Jephthah, to her word, in order that my word be fulfilled and my plan that I thought out not be foiled" (40:4). Her reward comes after death.

Numerous instances of prophecy and fulfillment punctuate the book, and show that history unfolds exactly as God predicts. As Kenaz declares in

---

4. For analysis of this contrast, see Murphy, "Divine Plan."
5. See Murphy, "Divine Plan."

ecstasy, "Hear now, you who dwell on the earth, just as those staying a while on it prophesied before me and saw this hour even before the earth was corrupted, so all of you who dwell in it may know the prophecies that have been fixed in advance" (28:6). A constant concern of the book is to show that all of God's words and plans will be fulfilled, whether they involve the promises to the fathers, the punishment of sinners, or the course of history, and whether they are spoken by God directly or mediated by such characters as Moses or Samuel. Indeed, all history is planned in advance by God. Pseudo-Philo speaks of the times being fulfilled in 3:9, 10; 19:15; 23:13; and 28:9. God goes so far as to deceive the tribes so that the divine words can be fulfilled in 46:1. The golden calf incident was foretold by God (12:3), the Exodus is an example of God fulfilling divine words (15:5), the conquest of the land is a fulfillment of God's words (21:9; 23:11), the people ask for a king because they think God has foretold it through Moses (56:1), Samuel says that in the decline of Saul the word of God is fulfilled (57:3), David sees in his impending fight with Goliath the fulfillment of God's prediction given to him earlier (59:5; 61:3), Amalek is destroyed as God said through Moses (58:1), Samuel rises from the dead as God told him he would (64:7), and Agag kills Saul as God said through Samuel (65:4). This list is by no means complete. Nothing happens that is not foreknown and controlled by God.

Pseudo-Philo finds many cases in which one episode of Israel's history recalls another, showing the divine rationality behind history.[6] Deborah says that God's glory is shown to her contemporaries as it was shown at the tower of Babel (32:1). The confession of the sinners under Kenaz is like that of Achan under Joshua (25:7). The building of the altar across the Jordan reminds Joshua of the golden calf (22:5). Moses' staff is a reminder of the Sinai covenant, just as the rainbow reminds God of the Noachic covenant (19:11). Aaron's rod that flowered is like Jacob's rods in Mesopotamia (17:3). The examples are numerous. The assumption is that history is of a piece. There is a plan behind it all, and that plan belongs to God.

God is the great revealer in the *Biblical Antiquities*. Although in places God imparts esoteric information to privileged persons, the essentials of that information are available to all. This makes the ironic mode of the narrative doubly ironic. The readers know more than the characters, but the characters should know almost as much as the readers. They simply do not listen properly to God. God does not demand more of humans than they can understand. Torah is the center of God's revelation, and esoteric revelation adds nothing essential to it.[7] Therefore leaders constantly exhort the people to study and remain close to the Torah. God says Torah is given so that humans will be without excuse when called to account for their actions (11:2). Joshua says, apparently with some annoyance, that the Transjordanian tribes could easily have avoided their mistake in building an altar if they had studied Torah

6. This is also a feature of rabbinic interpretation. See Eissfeldt, "Kompositionstechnik." See also chapter 2 (this volume) under "Plot."

7. This contrasts with such works as 4 Ezra and *1 Enoch.*

(22:5). Zebul tells Israel to "ponder nothing else except what belongs to the Law" (29:4).

The readers receive knowledge beyond the Torah. That knowledge does not surpass Torah but rather confirms its importance. The key to knowing why paradise was lost and the way to get it back are found in God's will as expressed in Torah. Esoteric revelations sometimes deal with the good things from which humans were separated at the Fall (19:10; 26:6, 14) that the righteous will receive back at the end of time (28:10). The readers experience esoteric revelation through characters such as Moses and Kenaz and experience the words, acts, and even thoughts of God firsthand. Nonetheless, what they learn serves only to reinforce the idea that obedience to Torah brings success, and disobedience brings disaster. This basic lesson is available to all Israel, hence the narrative's irony.

The readers are frequently treated to God's direct reaction to human behavior. They hear God speak, see God act, and sometimes even hear God think. God often explains history, divine motivations and plans, and things to come. The cumulative effect is to render a clear picture of how God thinks and acts and to convey an unambiguous understanding of how God relates to Israel. God responds to sin with anger and assures humanity that every sin will find its punishment (3:9–10; 44:10).[8] Indeed, most of God's interventions in the plot, even when salvific, also involve anger, because God often saves the people in spite of their unfaithfulness.[9] Pseudo-Philo has a rather pessimistic view of humanity and Israel, and God is continually frustrated with human failure to understand and to follow the divine will. Indeed, God borders on hatred of humanity for its wickedness. When humans try to build the tower of Babel, God says, "I will consider them like a drop of water and liken them to spittle," an allusion to Isa. 40:15 (7:3). In 26:14, Kenaz says, "And now today I know that the race of men is weak and their life should be accounted as nothing." When Israel commits idolatry in the Micah episode, God says, "Therefore, behold I abhor the race of men, and I will cut away the root of my creation" (44:8). Although God is usually unhappy with humanity and with Israel in particular, God never gives in to the temptation to call a halt to history. The promises to the fathers include Israel's eternal existence (4:11). God is a "round" character who suffers inner conflict caused by this contradiction between desire to destroy an intransigent humanity and faithfulness to the promises. The effect on the readers is twofold—to inspire confidence in God's faithfulness, but also to discourage presumption.[10]

Sin provokes God's anger, but God's mercy never fails.[11] The two terms often occur in the same passage. God's anger does not signify permanent abandonment of the people, although some characters in the narrative think it does. It does not jeopardize the covenant, although at times God's frustra-

---

8. See concordance under *ira, iracundia, irascor, iratus.*

9. See Murphy, "Eternal Covenant."

10. There are several characters who fall prey to presumption—Joktan in chapter 6, the elders in chapter 9, the Levite in chapter 45, and the eleven tribes in chapter 46, for example.

11. See concordance under *miseratio, misereor, misericordia, misericors.*

tion with the people's behavior reaches dangerously high levels. For example, because of Micah's deception of the people, God wants to destroy all of humanity but settles for declaring that every single sin will receive its proper punishment (44:10). Deborah says, "And behold now the LORD will take pity on you today, not because of you but because of his covenant that he established with your fathers and the oath that he has sworn not to abandon you forever" (30:7). When angry during the time of Phinehas, God says, "I myself have sworn, says the LORD; if I had not sworn, I would not have remembered you in what you have said, nor would I have answered you today" (47:3). God is pulled back and forth between the divine promises and frustrated anger.

Israel's history of suffering proves only that God punishes sins. The existence of the covenant is never really at risk, but God's justice is always preserved. Every sin finds its punishment.[12] Gideon, for example, who is not punished for his idolatry in the Bible, is punished after death in Pseudo-Philo (36:4). And the punishment fits the crime, as in the case of Saul meeting his death at the hand of the son of Agag the Amalekite (65:4). Further, what seem to be undeserved afflictions in the Bible are explained as the results of sin in the *Biblical Antiquities,* as is the case with the Levite's concubine (45:3; 47:8), the tribes' defeat by the Benjaminites in the same episode (45:6), and the priests of Nob who helped David (63:1). But God's mercy is evident in that the people are never totally extinguished. Indeed, the harshness of humanity is contrasted with God's mercy in the stories of Jephthah (39:4) and David (62:6). Not even Moses fully understands that God's anger is not the same as abandonment. Before his death, he prays, "Now you will correct them for a time, but not in anger" (19:9). God responds, "When they sin, I will be angry with them but I will recall your staff and spare them in accord with my mercy" (19:11). For God, anger and mercy are not incompatible.

Prayers often request mercy. A prime example is Moses' prayer in 12:8–9. Moses contends that Israel can survive only through God's mercy. He says, "If you do not have mercy on your vine, all things, LORD, have been done in vain, and you will not have anyone to glorify you" (12:9). At the end of the prayer, God replies, "Behold I have been made merciful according to your words" (12:10). Moses prays to God again at the end of the Moses cycle. He concludes his prayer: "Unless your patience abides, how would your heritage be established, if you were not merciful to them? Or who will yet be born without sin? Now you will correct them for a time, but not in anger" (19:9). Joshua picks up the theme two chapters later when he says, "And now let the fullness of your mercy sustain your people and choose for your heritage a man so that he and his offspring will rule your people" (21:4).

Moses' prayer in chapter 12 implies that to some degree God needs humans. Moses employs a form of persuasion in the prayer that is known elsewhere in the Bible and in Jewish tradition.[13] God needs human praise and must stand by Israel so that the nations will have proper respect for God. In

---

12. See chapter 11 (this volume) under "Moral Causality."
13. For this sort of prayer, see Murphy, *Structure,* 72–85.

the *Biblical Antiquities* as a whole, this is softened by the idea that God is less interested in the divine reputation than in being true to the divine purposes, but it is not so easy to separate those two things. In any case, God is not radically free. God is bound by past promises and in chapter 12 is influenced by what humans think.

Humanity

Pseudo-Philo's main interest is Israel, not humanity in general. But in writing Israel's story, Pseudo-Philo sketches a profile of the rest of the human race as well. Pseudo-Philo enhances humanity's sinful aspects found in the Bible. Chapters 1–8 are a preface to the history of Israel proper. They show that humanity has a corrupted heart, Abraham is an exception, and Israel's call is to follow Abraham's example. Pseudo-Philo preserves little of Genesis. Although a few individuals like Enoch and Noah are good, most of humanity is not. The genealogies introducing the *Biblical Antiquities* reverse those in Genesis 4–5. Notices about Enoch and Noah from Genesis 5 come in LAB 1, and LAB 2 deals with those from Genesis 4 who introduce sin into the world. Additions to the genealogy from Genesis 4 emphasize the sinfulness of humanity, such as the corruption wrought by Jobal's music, the idolatry caused by Tubal's technology, and the intensification of Lamech's ferocity (2:5–10). The impression is one of deterioration. Beyond the genealogies, which are expanded, Pseudo-Philo spends time primarily on the stories of the Flood and the tower of Babel, connecting Abraham's call to the story of the idolatrous tower. The genealogies make Israel's story central to world history.

Pseudo-Philo accents human responsibility. He seizes upon the Flood and the tower of Babel as two episodes that prove humanity's disobedient nature. Later, when Torah is given, human responsibility is again highlighted. Just before giving the Torah, God reasons: "I will give a light to the world and illumine their dwelling places and establish my covenant with the sons of men and glorify my people above all nations. For them I will bring out the eternal statutes that are for those in the light but for the ungodly a punishment" (11:1). God then says, "I have given an everlasting Law into your hands and by this I will judge the whole world. For this will be a testimony. For even if men say, 'We have not known you, and so we have not served you,' therefore I will make a claim upon them because they have not learned my Law" (11:2). It is unclear whether this means that God offered the Torah to non-Israelites. Pseudo-Philo may subscribe to the notion, known elsewhere in Jewish tradition, that the Gentiles did indeed have the opportunity to accept Torah and so are guilty.[14] Alternatively, the Gentiles can be held accountable because they began with a good relationship with God but ruined it through their rebellious nature. Israel's responsibility is unambiguous. In Kenaz's vision of

---

14. See *b.'Abod. Zar.* 2b and Sir. 24:5–7 (cp. *1 Enoch* 42), for example.

the whole of human history, the only thing mentioned about humans is that they sin against God (28:9).

Beginning from Israel's ancestor Abraham and continuing throughout the *Biblical Antiquities,* Israel differs from the nations because it worships God. The Gentiles are idolaters and so cannot please God. In chapters 6–7, all humans except Abraham and a few others participate in the building of the idolatrous tower. In chapter 9 the Israelite elders worry that if their female babies are given to Egyptian slaves as wives, then their own descendants will be idolaters. Amram reminds the elders that Tamar went so far as to seek fornication with Judah to avoid going to the Gentiles (9:5). In 18:13 and 30:1, contact with foreign women leads to idolatry and alienation from God. The people are tempted by the idols of the Midianite Aod (chap. 34). In Judg. 11:24, Jephthah says to the king of Ammon, "Should you not possess what your god Chemosh gives you to possess?" Pseudo-Philo changes that to "They are not gods, as you say they are, who have given you the inheritance that you possess" (39:9). Before killing Goliath, David says, "Were not the two women, from whom you and I were born, sisters? And your mother was Orpah, and my mother Ruth. And Orpah chose for herself the gods of the Philistines and went after them, but Ruth chose for herself the ways of the Most Powerful and walked in them" (61:6).

Humanity fails God. The *Biblical Antiquities* is punctuated with negative judgments on humanity (7:3; 26:14; 44:8). Given humanity's failure, it is urgent that Israel be faithful, lest God's work be utterly "in vain."

Israel

The tower episode shows that Israel has its origins in Abraham, the one who resisted human evil and trusted in God. The narrative then quickly gets Israel into Egypt by summarizing the Joseph story in a few lines, and it becomes detailed again only with the story of the Red Sea in chapter 9. The principle of selection among Genesis materials is the desire to place the birth of Israel in the context of humanity's evil. Pseudo-Philo also retains features of the biblical story that carry the history of Israel forward, such as getting the people to Egypt. It is concerned to present a coherent story of Israel, not just to illustrate themes.

Israel's conflict with external forces is the background for a good deal of the narrative. Foreigners continually oppress Israel and Israel must turn to God for liberation. The text's opposition to mixed marriages should be seen in this context.[15] Throughout the work, the question arises whether Israel will perish because of conflict with foreigners. The answer is no. God's promises to the ancestors are irrevocable. Outside forces are not a threat to Israel's existence or identity, because as long as Israel obeys God, those forces are powerless to overcome it. As Balaam tells Balak, "They will sin against their

15. 9:5; 18:13–14; 21:1; 30:1; 43:5; 44:7; 45:3.

LORD and fall into your hands; for otherwise you cannot fight against them" (18:13). Israel's fate is in its own hands. Obedience to God inevitably brings success and disobedience always brings punishment.

Threats to Israel's existence also arise internally. Two sources of the danger are Israel's foolishness and its iniquity. True to the ironic mode, the people usually know less than the readers. Ironically, they know all they need to know to please God. Israel is without excuse. Everything necessary to please God appears in Torah. Nonetheless, the people are often mistaken about God's will. They frequently assume they know it when they do not, or speculate about what God wants. Joktan creates a plan to rescue Abraham and his fellows and counts on God's help, but his plan is ignored by God (chap. 6). The elders react against Pharaoh's plan because they have a horror of idolatry, but they err in their calculation (chap. 9). The tribes debate on the proper course of action at the Red Sea and all of their suggestions are wrong (chap. 10). The Transjordanian tribes build an altar across the Jordan from good motives, but then are chided by Joshua for failing to study the Torah to see their error (chap. 22). Jephthah and his brothers have an argument about God's will and their proper course of action (chap. 39). The people misinterpret God's intentions as they look for a leader (chap. 49). David is unsure of God's plans (61:3). Samuel does not fully understand God or God's plans (55:1–2; 56:2). There are other examples. The people seem obtuse when it comes to understanding divine ways. Of course, the Gentiles are even worse. Balak thinks that a multitude of holocausts will buy God's favor even to the extent of making Israel's destruction possible (chap. 18).

Besides being obtuse, Israel also often proves itself iniquitous. It is more consistent in disobedience than obedience. Even some of Pseudo-Philo's heroes, like Abraham (6:11) and Kenaz (27:7), admit to sin. As a result, Israel seems constantly in jeopardy. God's statement in 49:7 is thematic for the entire narrative: "If I were to pay you back according to your evil deeds, it would be necessary to pay no attention at all to your race." In chapter 25, sinners are found among every tribe of Israel. Sinfulness spans Israel. The people's sins go beyond simple transgression of the Law to attacking its very foundation. In Judg. 2:10, it is said that a generation arose that did not know the acts of God. LAB 25:6 says they did not believe in them. Two main themes emerge from the enumeration of sins in chapter 25. One is that the sinners engage in idolatry, and the other is that they attack Israel's foundations. Idolatry is depicted as a search for knowledge and guidance. The people are attracted by the wisdom and magic of non-Israelites.

The interchange between the people and Aod shows that the people do not simply run to commit idolatry, but when confronted with what seems to go well beyond their own Torah, they cannot deny "fact" (chap. 34). They are skeptical of Aod's claims that he will show him what is not in their Law and demand evidence. Aod produces the "evidence," and so deceives the people. There is irony here. In the Kenaz chapters, the sinners are skeptical about the Torah and do not find enough supporting evidence in their own traditions. Here they take a bit of magic as good evidence and are convinced of the power

of Midian's gods. Also ironic is the use of the word "deceive," a word frequent
in the *Biblical Antiquities* as a description of idolatry. What Aod claims does
not deceive is the very thing that does deceive. The final irony is that the
people are convinced by a miracle in which they see the sun at night. That
miracle leads them to abandon the Law. Throughout Pseudo-Philo, the Law
is that which gives light. This chapter manages to make the idolatry of the
people somewhat understandable without exculpating them. The people also
come to Micah for information useful for their everyday lives (chap. 44). To
obtain a wife, riches, sons, courage, servants, or long life, Israelites consult
Micah's idols. Individual needs are not satisfied by their relation with God.

Pseudo-Philo conforms to the deuteronomistic pattern in seeing the people
as especially ready to fall away from the exclusive worship of God when they
are without suitable leaders.[16] From the time of the giving of the Law on Sinai,
the people succumb to idolatry. As in the Bible, they worship the golden calf
while Moses is absent. In 30:1, the narrator says, "Then the sons of Israel did
not have anyone to appoint for themselves as judge; and their heart fell away,
and they forgot the promise and transgressed the ways that Moses and Joshua
the servants of the LORD had commanded them, and *they were led astray after
the daughters* of the Amorites *and served their gods.*" In Deborah's first speech,
she says that when Moses, Joshua, Kenaz, and Zebul commanded the people,
"you showed yourselves as if you were serving your God; but when these died,
your heart also died" (30:6). In 39:6, Jephthah says, "You know that, while
our leaders were still alive, they warned us to follow our Law. And Ammon
and his sons turned the people from their way in which they walked, and they
served foreign gods who would destroy them." That the seduction by the
Ammonites occurs in the absence of an Israelite leader is clear in the words
of the people in 39:1: "There is no leader who may go in and go out before
us." In 48:4, the narrator echoes Judges when he says, "*They had no* leader
in those days, and each one did what was pleasing in his own eyes." Of course,
the mere presence of a leader does not guarantee adherence to Torah. Gideon
and Jair actually lead the people into idolatry. But without good leadership,
the people seem incapable of pleasing God.

A remarkable aspect of Pseudo-Philo is the understanding that the people
are not always fully culpable for idolatry when it is forced upon them. In the
golden calf story, Aaron is excused because the people force him (12:3). In
the aftermath of the golden calf incident, a lenient attitude is displayed toward
those who committed apostasy under duress. The people are made to drink
waters containing the remains of the golden calf. The result is the following:
"And if anyone had it in his will and mind that the calf be made, his tongue
was cut off; but if he had been forced by fear to consent, his face shone"
(12:7). Under Jair, too, the people are coerced into offering sacrifice to Baal
(chap. 38). There it is not said whether they are culpable, but no punishment
is mentioned for their sin.

Israel's failures are set in the context of the sinfulness of humanity as a

---

16. See chapter 11 (this volume) under "Idolatry," and Murphy, "Retelling."

whole. The contextualization of Israel's sinfulness is featured prominently in Pseudo-Philo, being found, for example, in two prayers of Moses. Moses prays,

> You gave them the Law and statutes in which they might live and enter as sons of men. *For who is the man who has not sinned against you?* And unless your patience abides, how would your heritage be established, if you were not merciful to them? Or who will yet be born without sin? Now you will correct them for a time, but not in anger (19:9).

Moses is saying, in effect, "Now Israel knows what it should do. Of course, Israel will disobey the Law because no one is perfect. Nonetheless, I am confident that you will overlook their transgressions." In an earlier prayer, he says, "Before you took the seed from which you would make man upon the earth, was it I who did establish their ways? Therefore let your mercy sustain us till the end, and your fidelity for length of days; for unless you had mercy, who would ever be born?" (15:7). Here Moses borders on blaming God for the sinfulness of humanity, as does Ezra in 4 Ezra 3. In chapter 12 Moses tells God that without divine mercy, there will be no one left willing to worship. In a sense, God depends on humanity. Joshua echoes Moses' arguments, reminding God that God created humanity, and could create a pure heart for humans: "And now, LORD, give to your people a wise heart and a prudent mind; and when you will give those orders to your heritage, they will not sin against you and you will not be angry at them" (21:2). The discussion of the pure heart is related to the concept of the evil yetzer, alluded to in 33:3 and 3:9.[17] When Kenaz is dealing with Israel's involvement in Amorite idolatry, he says, "Behold how much good God has made for men, but because of their sins they have been deprived of all these things. And now today I know that the race of men is weak and their life should be accounted as nothing" (26:14).

Pseudo-Philo's characterization of Israel is not complimentary. Were it not for the covenants and promises God made with the fathers, God would have given up on Israel many times in its history. Israelites are not a good deal better than their Gentile neighbors. Nonetheless, they do have Abraham, Amram, Moses, Joshua, Kenaz, and Deborah in their past, and for the sake of such individuals God has chosen Israel and remains eternally faithful to the covenant. However, every sin will receive its recompense, and membership in the chosen people does not guarantee salvation, either in this world or the next.[18]

Leaders—Good, Bad, and In-Between

Nickelsburg provides the most detailed study of leaders in the *Biblical Antiquities*. He claims that most of the narrative additions to the biblical text concern

---

17. Joshua's speech to God sounds like Ezra's in 4 Ezra 3.
18. This view corresponds to what Sanders ("Covenant") calls "covenantal nomism."

leadership. Having examined briefly a large number of good and bad leaders, Nickelsburg reconstructs Pseudo-Philo's paradigm of leadership.[19] The central element of the leaders' portraits is trust in God. That trust is expressed in the good leaders' exhortations to the people to obey and trust in God for deliverance and in the leaders' willingness to risk death, trusting in God's deliverance. Nickelsburg notes that Pseudo-Philo's leaders are people of word and deed. Their devotion to God is expressed by both. The leaders' words concentrate on the deuteronomistic theme that obedience will be rewarded and disobedience punished. He says that the scheme sin, punishment, repentance, and deliverance is evident both in what the leaders say and do. Also central to their rhetoric is the idea that God will never abandon Israel. For Nickelsburg, action is integral to Pseudo-Philo's notion of trust. Each good leader takes bold action because of his or her trust in God. That action is often military. Pseudo-Philo develops each leader's profile by contrasting him or her with other characters. The bold action of a leader contrasts with the "fidgeting" of other characters.

Nickelsburg's portrayal of Pseudo-Philo's major figures is correct in the main. His observation that the leaders are often contrasted with other characters is crucial, but the central element of such contrast is not action as opposed to inaction, or military action as opposed to passivity. Trust in God is complete dependence on God, being fully in line with God's will. It usually means not taking action on one's own initiative, even if that action is based on belief that God will come to the rescue. It means avoiding presumption—belief that one already knows God's will and forging ahead with human plans that are well intentioned but do not have their origin in God. This is the central aspect of leadership that Pseudo-Philo consistently advances.

It is important to distinguish between major characters and leaders. In the present section we confine the appellation of "leader" to those who hold public and political authority, for example, as judges or kings. Characters whom Nicklesburg treats that are not treated as leaders here are Abraham, Amram, Aod, Samson, Micah, and the Levite. Even such characters as Aaron and Phinehas, important priests, are excluded here because Pseudo-Philo does not present them as wielding the kind of political authority as Moses, Joshua, Kenaz, or Deborah. Those characters receive their due in the next section of this chapter.

A rough indication of whom Pseudo-Philo considers to be a leader in this sense could be obtained by observing his use of the words *princeps, principare, dux, ducere,* and related words. Aside from some general usages (20:3; 30:5; 44:1; 39:1, 6; 48:4), *dux* is applied to Fenech, Nimrod, and Joktan in the pre-Sinai period (chaps. 5–7), and then to Moses and Joshua (24:6), Kenaz (21:5; 25:2; 27:13), Zebul (29:1), Jair (38:4), perhaps Jephthah (39:1), and Samuel (49:6). Abimelech is unworthy to be *dux.* Those called *princeps* are the three leaders of chapters 5–6, Joseph in Egypt (and Potiphar; 8:9), Pharaoh (9:12), Kenaz (21:5; 25:2), Joshua and Moses (25:3), Jabin king of Hazor (30:3), Jeph-

19. "Leaders," 60–62.

thah (40:5), the tribal leaders (47:11), Samuel (49:7), and Saul and (indirectly) David (56:1, 5). The text speaks of the *principatus* of Kenaz (49:1) and Moses and Joshua (20:5). In 37:2, the trees discuss Abimelech's unworthiness to have *principatus*. As subjects of *principari* appear Israel's enemies (19:2; 30:2), Joshua (20:5), Kenaz (21:4; 25:2), and Kenaz's sons, if he had any (29:1).

Perrot notes that Pseudo-Philo draws a clear distinction between "political" and "religious" leaders, and that God does not always approve of political leaders.[20] Perrot's distinction may be too restrictive, but it is noteworthy that the list of persons to whom "leader" applies constitutes those who would be considered political leaders. Samuel is the only exception, but even in the Bible his status goes beyond that of a prophet. Like Moses, he is both prophet and political leader. As in the Bible, his prophetic status allows him to reliably judge Israel's first kings.

Pseudo-Philo's leaders are somewhat "round" characters. Even the good ones are not always perfect, although they come much closer to perfection than do the people as a whole. At times they verge on lack of trust, but they always come through in the end. They are sometimes deficient in insight, but this is usually corrected in the course of the narrative.

One of Pseudo-Philo's most characteristic alterations to the biblical stories is the addition of direct address in the form of speeches, prayers, and dialogue. This is true of the treatment of the leaders. The good leaders' speeches are didactic and hortatory. Their speeches to the people and dialogues with God reinforce the important themes of the *Biblical Antiquities:* God's justice and commitment to the deuteronomistic scheme, God's unfailing faithfulness to Israel because of the fathers, God's recurring anger with the people's sin or foolishness, the inadequacy of human plans as contrasted with divine plans, and so on. The following pages briefly review Pseudo-Philo's major leaders and show how they fit the paradigm elucidated here.

It seems simple common sense to include Abraham as the first leader in the *Biblical Antiquities.* Yet Abraham is not really a leader in Pseudo-Philo in the sense of holding any position of authority. The Shemite leader is Joktan. In LAB 6, Joktan is more active and military than Abraham. Joktan devises a scheme to save the resisters to the tower of Babel and then uses his soldiers to implement it. The narrator says that Joktan worships God, and the readers hear Joktan himself professing confidence in God's deliverance and exhorting the resisters to trust in God. But it is Abraham's refusal to do anything to save himself that truly exemplifies complete trust in God. The technique of contrast is complex in this chapter. Joktan contrasts favorably with Nimrod and Fenech because they actively promote idolatry, whereas he aids those who resist it, although he will not oppose it publicly, preferring to "work within the system." Abraham contrasts sharply with the idolaters since he rejects their plan, and he contrasts less sharply with his fellow resisters because his trust in God is more complete than theirs. Abraham also contrasts with Joktan. Joktan is a

20. SC 230, 46.

pragmatist who also trusts in God, while Abraham's trust is more absolute and leaves things completely in God's hands.

Moses is the most prominent leader in the *Biblical Antiquities.* As in the Bible, Moses mediates God's will to the people, both in the form of Torah delivered on Sinai (although very little legal material is explicitly dealt with) and through didactic and hortatory speeches. Moses also receives special revelation about protology and eschatology. This does not happen in the Bible but is common in noncanonical Second Temple Jewish tradition. Through Moses Pseudo-Philo reveals the whole sweep of creation, from beginning to end.

Especially noteworthy is Moses' role as intercessor. The fullest example of Moses' intercession occurs after the golden calf incident, where Moses contends that if God were to destroy Israel, no one would ever trust God again and no one would worship God (12:8–9). In the spies episode, Moses persuades God not to abandon Israel (15:7). Just before he dies, Moses asks God's mercy on Israel for the future (19:8–9). Moses' prayers in these chapters demonstrate the tension between divine mercy and anger. They argue eloquently to God to allow divine mercy to overcome the divine anger.

God's responses to Moses show that God does not always agree with him. God's impatient command to Moses at the Red Sea shows some imperfection in Moses' insight into God's ways (10:4–5). Before his death, Moses asks God not to be angry with Israel but to let the divine mercy rule (19:8–9). God responds that Israel will indeed feel the divine anger for its sins (19:11). Nonetheless, God will continue to protect and support Israel despite its sin. Not all of what Moses wishes can come to pass. The most important petition, that God allow Israel to exist, is granted, but that is practically a foregone conclusion anyway.

Korah is a bad leader (chap. 16).[21] He has a following of two hundred men and challenges Moses' leadership. His "platform" is anti-Torah; he sees no need for the "unbearable" law of tassels. He is a foil for those faithful to God's will who are willing to be tried and executed for it, such as Abraham in chapters 6–7 and the seven resisters to Jair's idolatry in chapter 38. His end is destruction and eternal misery.

Most of Joshua's biblical exploits are omitted. Nickelsburg notes that emphasis falls on his call, his interaction with the people, and his farewell address. Indeed, it is Joshua's words that receive the most attention. Like Moses, Joshua mediates between God and people. He asks God's mercy on the people and delivers lengthy didactic and hortatory speeches. His main concern is to know and convey the word of God to the people and to have them obey it. That he does not act on his own but is an agent of God is emphasized by the device of having his covenant speech transformed into a revelation from God revealed in a dream (chap. 23). Several details of Joshua's story show Pseudo-Philo's realistic touch. In Joshua's prayer in 21:2–6, he reasons in a way that shows his understanding of God's ways is not always

---

21. See Murphy, "Korah's Rebellion."

perfect but needs to be informed by God and by events as time goes on. In 21:2, he verges on accusing God for humanity's sinfulness because God created them as they are. Joshua remembers that he prayed in a similar vein during the Achan episode. He quotes a part of that prayer that shows he came close to despair then. In chapter 22, Joshua must confront the illicit altar erected by the Transjordanian tribes. Joshua admits his inability to discern human motivation and leaves ultimate judgment up to God. Joshua is not omniscient as are God and the narrator.

Kenaz's deeds are more important than his words. Kenaz emerges as God's perfect agent. His only desire is to know God's will and to follow it perfectly and without presumption. Kenaz does not take a single step without attempting to know for sure whether he is doing what God wants. He is the opposite of those who presume to know God's will. Kenaz discovers the sinners in Israel's midst by using lots, proof that it is God who reveals them. He disposes of the dangerous results of Israel's idolatry—magic stones, books, and the like—by carefully following God's instructions. Kenaz is curious about the idolatrous objects in chapter 26, but his inquisitiveness is not condemned. Rather it confirms that God's instructions must be followed. Kenaz's victory in chapter 27 is really God's victory. He consults God before undertaking the expedition, looks for signs during it, and receives an angel's help in the battle. Afterwards he confesses it is God's victory and demonstrates humanity's nothingness and God's greatness. In chapter 28, Kenaz humbly yields the floor to the priest Phinehas so that he can announce the vision of his father Eleazar. Then Kenaz receives his own vision of the beginning and end of history and delivers a brief exhortation to the people to die to the present, corruptible world. Kenaz is transparently a vehicle for the narrator to depict the perfect leader as God's instrument.

The next leader, Zebul, ensures that Kenaz's daughters receive an inheritance (chap. 29). Kenaz did not do it for himself because he did not want to appear "avaricious and greedy" (29:1). Zebul ends his brief career with an exhortation to the people to obey the Law.

Deborah is more prominent in the *Biblical Antiquities* than in the Bible, and her story takes up chapters 30–33. She balances Kenaz, whose deeds were more important than his words, because her words are more to the fore than her deeds. She addresses two long speeches to the people (chaps. 30, 33) and joins with others in a long hymn at the end of which she is the only one speaking (chap. 32). Deborah is a perfect leader. Her words embody Pseudo-Philo's point of view. She confirms the deuteronomistic worldview, but assures the people that God will save them because of their fathers although they do not deserve it. Her major point hinges on God's miraculous help to Israel under her leadership, as is especially well illustrated through the stars' action. She sees the deliverance wrought in her time as paradigmatic for all time (32:3).

Gideon's story occupies two chapters (34–35) and that of his son Abimelech one (36). Gideon is a mighty man of Israel who questions God's support of Israel. The angel uses the conversation to blame Israel for its own misfortune. The biblical emphasis on Gideon's reluctance to help save Israel is short-ened into a brief but emphatic exchange in which Gideon questions the appro-priateness of his election and the angel points out that the way of God is not like the way of humans (35:5). The story of Gideon's victory is rewritten to stress that God, not Gideon, wins the battle. Gideon's idolatry goes unpun-ished in the Bible, but Pseudo-Philo lets the readers hear God thinking about the fact that Gideon is to pay for his sin in the afterlife. Gideon does not speak for Pseudo-Philo's ideological point of view; he is too ambivalent a character. He does turn out to be an instrument of God through whom God accomplishes a limited purpose, and he is a good foil for the angel since he does not under-stand God's ways. He is a convenient character to restate the idea that human and divine ways differ.

Abimelech tries to become king of Israel because of his ambition. Pseudo-Philo condenses the story so that it consists mostly of Joram's parable, pre-sented not as a parable but as a straightforward account of actual happenings. The fig tree, the vine, and the apple tree all recognize their own inability to rule over the trees, and they condemn Abimelech. The bramblebush claims that truth is to be heard from it. It recalls Abimelech's fratricide and says that a real ruler corrects the foolishness of the people. Both because of his sowing of discord in Israel and because of his general wickedness, he cannot be a good leader. He exemplifies a would-be ruler who has none of the proper qualifi-cations and all of the wrong ambitions.

Jair is the most uncomplicatedly bad leader in the *Biblical Antiquities* (chap. 38). He forces the people into idolatry and is thus the opposite of what an Israelite leader should be. He should bring truth to the people, but instead he deceives them. Pseudo-Philo employs a trial scene to show that Jair, who used the judicial system to enforce his hideous sinfulness, experiences the very punishment he planned for the seven dissenters. The shocking aspect of the narrative is that whereas the trial scene usually involves righteous Israelites bearing witness before foreign rulers, here a legitimate Israelite ruler is in the position of the wicked judge. The angel's reproach of Jair shows that it was indeed God who made him leader (38:4). Native Israelite rulers can be every bit as bad as foreign despots.

Jephthah is a tragic character. He exemplifies unguided human reason gone wrong. The interaction between Jephthah and his brothers typifies the sort of discussion common in Pseudo-Philo between fellow Israelites about the right way to proceed. Jephthah appears to be a good leader with the right message of obedience to the Law and trust in God's deliverance in 39:6. God gives him the victory. But his idea that he should sacrifice the first being who meets him on his return home is completely misguided and angers God by its recklessness. Jephthah's anguish over the results of his stupidity is portrayed in 40:1. It is something over which he now has no control. The foolish leader must not only pay the price for mistakes but must also see others pay as well. A leader's decisions affect all Israel.

In chapter 49, the people seek a new leader. They know that "it is not appropriate for the people to be without a ruler" (49:1). They hope God will give them a ruler like Kenaz to "free us from our distress." From the people's point of view, the important thing about a ruler is that he or she will free them from suffering. They do not mention the other side of rulership—the ruler will correct them and make them conform to God's will. The lot falls on Elkanah, Samuel's father. Elkanah knows he is not to be a leader, and he forcefully rejects the people's attempts to make him one. God reveals that Elkanah's son, Samuel, will be leader.

As in the Bible, Samuel combines the qualities of judge and prophet. He is a transitional figure between the periods of the judges and the monarchy. He certainly exercises the kind of political power that defines leadership as the term is used here. The narrator discloses that Eli knows from the Lord that "a prophet had been foreordained to be born from" Hannah (50:8). Pseudo-Philo amplifies the idea that Samuel is God's gift to Israel, as all true leaders are. Samuel was "promised previously to the tribes" (51:2) and Eli has heard of his career from God. Hannah's hymn provides content for the word "prophet": "The people will be enlightened by his words, and he will show to the nations the statutes" (51:3). Hannah sings that the "ordinance of the LORD" and "the truth" will come through her since Samuel is to be born to her (50:4). Samuel is called the *"light to the peoples"* of Isa. 49:6; 51:4, and a "light for this nation" (51:6). Light comes from God. To be enlightened is to know God's ways, as the parallelism between enlightenment and statutes in 51:3 shows. All of this shows that Samuel embodies to a high degree a quality to be expected of all leaders: He conveys God's will to them and teaches them what God wants.

In chapter 53, God speaks to the child Samuel in the sanctuary at Shiloh. Eli teaches the child how to distinguish between God's communications and those of demons. As in the Bible, when Samuel receives word about the fall of Eli's house, he is reluctant to convey this distressing news to his mentor. In 1 Sam. 3:17, Eli simply insists that Samuel not hide anything from him and even threatens him should he do so. In LAB 53:12, Eli instructs Samuel at length about his mission and duties. Samuel has been guided by the Lord and has been born for the divine purpose of being prophet to Israel. He must convey God's word to Eli even if it is unpleasant. Samuel then tells Eli the news and Eli submits obediently.

Chapters 54–55 stress that God controls the action and Samuel is God's instrument. When Israel brings the ark of the covenant to the battle and the Philistines capture it, Samuel is unaware of those events because God has sent him away. God manipulates the characters for divine purposes. Samuel is portrayed as less than perfect in understanding in the following chapters. In 55:1, he thinks incorrectly that the ark's capture means Israel's destruction. In 56:2, he thinks that God cannot appoint a king before the time, but he is wrong. In 59:2, God chides him for his lack of vision in not seeing that God chooses David as the new king. Even after his death Samuel is not omniscient. When the witch Sedecla conjures him up for Saul, Samuel thinks it is the time for the Last Judgment but then remembers that God foretold he would have to come back to prophesy to Saul once again (64:7). Despite his deficiencies in understanding, Samuel is always open to God's guidance and correction. He listens to whatever God says and fearlessly conveys it to Israel and its leaders and so is himself a good leader.

The stories of Saul and David bring the *Biblical Antiquities* to a close, as the work ends with Saul's death. David is anointed in chapter 59, but nothing of his kingship is narrated, at least in the book's present form. David is the innocent victim of Saul's jealousy and is grateful to God for God's favors to him, but he never really acts out his role of leader in this book. Instead the book ends on the dissonant note of Saul's failure as king. In chapter 2 (this volume), this was compared to the ending of the Gospel of Mark. As Mark's ending leaves readers dissatisfied with the disciples' performance and places on them the burden of doing better in following Jesus, Pseudo-Philo's ending leaves readers unhappy with native Israelite leadership but hopeful that leaders to come, if they are chosen by God and faithful to God's ways, can bring good fortune to Israel again. The *Biblical Antiquities* provides the recipe for success.

Saul is a model of the bad ruler. The origins of his monarchy are inauspicious since he is appointed only because the people demand a king before the proper time. Indeed, the very institution of kingship is seen by the people as inferior to rule by a prophet, of which they are unworthy (57:4). God foretells that Saul will destroy the people and then will be destroyed himself. When he learns of his election, he reacts with humility (56:6), citing his youth. Samuel seems to hold out a bright future to him when he says that God will guide Saul and compares Saul's words to those of Jeremiah. Saul's first year is marked by victory over the Philistines.

Pseudo-Philo holds to the notion of moral causality so that Saul's downfall must be attributable to his own guilt and not just to the people's illicit demand for a king. The story of Saul keeping some of the booty from the defeat of Amalek and sparing the Amalekite king Agag is rewritten so that God explains Saul's motivation as greed. Later he is driven by jealousy of David and wishes to murder his fellow Israelite. The extensive conversation between David and Jonathan in chapter 62 highlights the injustice of Saul's vendetta against David. The slaughter of the priests of Nob in chapter 63 is rewritten so that the priests deserve their fate, but God still finds Saul guilty for it (63:3). The one constructive thing that Saul did during his reign, driving out mediums and wizards from the land, is presented in LAB 64:1 as done simply for fame. The readers hear Saul's thoughts on this matter and then immediately hear God pronounce Saul's motivation bad. Saul is told by Samuel (raised from the dead) that his fate is sealed, and hopes that his death will be his atonement (64:7–9). In the end Saul knows his death is inevitable and does not resist it (65:1).

David will become leader after the narrative ends. The nature of his leadership is left open, but the signs are good. David is chosen by God and anointed by Samuel at the proper time (chap. 59). His psalm shows him to be properly thankful to God (59:4). He looks for signs of God's will (61:3) and knows that his victory over Goliath is God's work (63:8). He makes peace with his enemy's son and wishes love and mercy rather than hatred and vengeance to characterize his relations with Saul's house (chap. 62). Indeed, Saul's last words hold out the hope of reconciliation within Israelite ranks. As he dies, Saul sends word to David, saying, "Be not mindful of my hatred or my injustice" (65:5). As the narrative ends, there is the potential that Israel will be at peace and governed by a good leader.

Other Major Figures

There are numerous other characters who stand out as individuals but strictly speaking are not leaders. They are both Israelites and non-Israelites. The following brief review highlights only the traits that bear directly on Pseudo-Philo's main themes.

Abraham does not act as a political leader in the *Biblical Antiquities,* so his story should be told here. However, it is so intertwined with that of Joktan that it was related in the previous section.

Noah is a significant character in that he represents a new start for humanity (chap. 3). He is a fairly flat character. As in the Bible, God chooses him because of his righteousness, a point that accords well with Pseudo-Philo's interest in moral causality. God dominates chapter 3 and Noah is fairly passive. He simply follows God's commands.

Joseph is mentioned only in passing, but he is an ideal figure from the past for the *Biblical Antiquities* just as he is in the rest of Jewish tradition. He is a model of forgiveness leading to brotherly harmony in 8:10. In 43:5, he contrasts with Samson, who goes to ruin because of his marriage to a Gentile woman. God says that Samson should have paid attention "to Joseph my servant *[puerum]* who was in a foreign land and became a crown for his brothers because he was not willing to afflict his own seed." Good Israelites bring concord to Israel.

In LAB 9, the Israelites face the crisis of the Egyptians' decision that male Hebrew babies be killed and the female babies be given to Egyptian slaves as wives. It is the elders, not Amram, who propose action. Amram intends to carry on as before and have intercourse with his wife. Nothing he says either changes previous behavior or violates Pharaoh's decree. His action assumes that God will save Israel, but this is not presumption because it does not lead to the implementation of a plan whose origin is not God. The elders' suggestion, to cease intercourse, is based on the belief that God will eventually act to save Israel. But it is their plan that involves action, for instead of continuing as before they would change their behavior. That change would hinder Pharaoh's plans, but it would also violate God's command to be fruitful and multiply and would in itself endanger Israel's survival. The elders fall prey to presumption, but Amram does not. The narrator does not claim that Amram convinced the rest of Israel, but because of Amram's trust God saves Israel.

Balaam is a non-Israelite whose story is told in chapter 18. The chapter stresses the impossibility of destroying Israel. If Israel sins, it can be conquered, though the rest of the book shows that even its defeat will be temporary. Balaam is a sympathetic character in that he knows Israel's status with God and even becomes a spokesman for that superior position before the Moabite king Balak, who is completely obtuse in his reasoning. Balaam finds himself in an impossible situation because although he would like to avoid conflict with Israel and God, he is pushed into it by God's command to go with Balak's messengers. In the end he does provide Balak with the information necessary to harm Israel. Balaam emerges as an ambivalent character. Perhaps the message is that even seemingly sympathetic Gentiles can turn on Israel.

Jael is a Gentile woman who kills Sisera in chapter 31. The story follows the main outline of the one in Judges 4 but is rewritten to underscore Jael's complete dependence on God. In her killing of Sisera, she proceeds cautiously, looking for God's approval each step of the way. Not much is made of her being a Gentile. The focus is on how Sisera's punishment, death at the hands of a woman, fits his crime, the desire to steal Israelite women. Although she is a Gentile, Jael's motivation is pure; she attacks the one who attacked God's chosen people.

Aod is a Gentile. Pseudo-Philo often associates idolatry with the Gentiles, and here a temptation to idolatry comes through this "Midianite magician." Aod is depicted as deceptive (34:5). The readers can see the full scope of his deception because they know the source of his power and just how fragile and circumscribed by God's judgment it is (34:2–3). Aod's power comes from an unholy alliance with angels who lost their real power and who face a final judgment to come. The people see only the appearances and take the power to be real, far beyond anything God has shown them. Pseudo-Philo uses Aod's story to portray both the seductiveness and the emptiness of the power of the Gentiles' gods. Aod is a real salesman of that power—in modern terms, a con man.

Seila willingly allows herself to be sacrificed for Israel's welfare (chap. 40). She contrasts with her erring father Jephthah in that she has a clearer concept of God's will and acts on this knowledge fearlessly. Her hymn reveals the depth of anguish that this causes her, but God divulges her ultimate fate—to be joined with her mothers in the afterlife. The strength with which Seila commits herself to God and the high cost this involves contrasts sharply with Israel's general tendency to treat its relationship with God cavalierly.

Samson is an ambiguous character, just as he is in the Bible. In the Book of Judges he does not really fit the mode of the other judges, and the same is true of his portrait in Pseudo-Philo. He does not wield political power in the same way as do Moses, Joshua, Kenaz, Deborah, Samuel, and others. But God does decide to free Israel through him (42:3). Samson acts alone. He does not lead an army or influence Israel's leaders. As in the Bible, his great strength is displayed in his exploits against the Philistines. Pseudo-Philo adds the comments of God in 43:5 that accuse Samson of lust and of "mingling" with the Gentiles. Those sins lead to his downfall, making him a tragic figure.

Micah appears as the same sort of con man as Aod, but this time the deceiver comes from within Israel. He and his mother discuss idolatry as a good way to make money and achieve fame. Their confident conspiracy is related in detail (44:1–4). At first it is very effective, and all Israel flocks to Micah for what his idols seem to be able to give. God angrily intervenes and punishes Micah and his mother in ways suited to their crimes. The characterizations of Micah and his mother stress their dishonest character and comment on the true nature of idolatry and the true motivations of the people who "sell" it.

Chapters 45–46 tell the story of the Levite's concubine and the consequent war of the tribes against Benjamin. The Levite stands out as a character because he takes it upon himself to call Israel to war against the sinful Benjaminites. He says that if they keep silent, "the LORD judges," but if they go to war to avenge the concubine's death, "the LORD will help you" (45:4). Events, interpreted by God's own words (see especially 45:6), make clear that the Levite is presumptuous. He dares to assume a leadership position in Israel and to claim God's sanction for his own vengeful aims. The narrator has already divulged that the concubine deserved what she got and God says that Israel's wrath over this incident compares unfavorably with its silence over Micah's idolatry (45:6).

Elkanah, Samuel's father, appears as a prudent man who knows his place (chap. 49). Although the lot falls on him for the leadership of Israel, he is not tempted by power. He professes himself willing to suffer for his own sins but refuses to allow the people to "defile" him by imposing this improper burden on him. Earlier in this same chapter, an enigmatic Nethez tells Israel its conclusion that God has abandoned it is false, and so he shows himself wise in the ways of God. Nothing more is said about him.

Hannah's picture is redone so that it is clear why she is chosen to bear Samuel. She possesses the qualities of humility and piety. Her hymn is rewritten so that she knows the significance of the one to whom she gives birth. As in 1 Samuel 2, she acknowledges the power of God over all people.

Eli the priest is a tragic figure. He himself is a good man. He knows God's plans for Samuel and slowly discloses them to Hannah in chapters 50–51. He tries to dissuade his sons from their iniquity in chapter 52. He patiently teaches Samuel about secret revelations in chapter 53. In chapter 54, he admits that he did not know God's plans concerning the ark, and he laments its loss and what this means for Israel. Eli and his sons suffer because of the sons' sins. Eli's line is cut off and the sin of his sons becomes paradigmatic (63:1).

Phinehas is a figure that spans many chapters in the *Biblical Antiquities*. He first appears in chapter 28 at the death of Kenaz. There he interrupts Kenaz's testament with the account of a revelation made to his father Eleazar that foretells Israel's unfaithfulness. In chapter 48, he is painted in the colors of Elijah, as his ascension is foretold by God. He is more of a symbol than a real character. There is no extended story about him; he merely appears from time to time to be "the priest" in the story. His most important function is to supply continuity to the priesthood. He is Eleazar's son and anoints Eli.

11

Major Themes

Just as plot, character, point of view, literary style, and so on are intimately tied together in this work, so the themes discussed here are closely bound up with the characters analyzed in the previous chapter and with the plot analyzed throughout this book. Topics broached here are relevant to Pseudo-Philo's characterizations, and significant themes that are not discussed here are the focus of attention in our treatment of characters and in the narrative analysis. This chapter is not the last word on Pseudo-Philo's themes but is meant to give some appreciation of the topics most interesting to Pseudo-Philo, as a general entrée to the work.

Covenant

God's covenant with Israel is one of the central symbols of the *Biblical Antiquities*.[1] The word *testamentum* occurs fifty-one times in the book. Related to the theme of covenant is that of witness. *Testimonium* occurs nineteen times, *testis* sixteen times, *testare* three times, and *testor* once. Usually witness is either to God's faithfulness to the covenant or Israel's neglect of it. Almost a century ago, Leopold Cohn focused on covenant.[2]

> In all the speeches the same idea recurs again and again: God has chosen the people of Israel and has made his covenant with them for ever; if the children of Israel depart from God's ways and forget his covenant, he delivers them for a time into the hands of their enemies; but God is ever mindful of his covenant with the patriarchs; he always delivers the Israelites through leaders of his choice, and he will never entirely abandon them.

"Covenant" denotes God's special relationship with Israel. Because Abraham resisted humanity's idolatry and trusted in God, God established a special relationship with him and his seed. This relationship is predicted in 4:11, and God makes a solemn pronouncement of it in 7:4: "And before all these I will choose my servant Abram, and I will bring him out from their land and will

1. See Murphy, "Eternal Covenant," on which this section is based.
2. "Apocryphal Work," 322. See also SC 230, 43–47.

bring him into the land upon which my eye has looked from of old." God goes on to say that the chosen land was spared in the Flood. Then God says, "There I will have my servant Abram dwell and will establish my covenant with him and will bless his seed and be lord of him as God forever." The essentials of Pseudo-Philo's idea of covenant are here. God creates an unconditional relationship with Abraham and his posterity in which God gives them land and blessings forever.[3] Covenant can be somewhat fluid, in that sometimes the focus is on the specific covenant with Abraham, but frequently it means the covenant with the fathers. Many other times it focuses on Sinai or on the covenant sealed by Joshua. More generally, it means God's relationship with Israel that began with Abraham and stretches to the eschaton.

The symbol of covenant so permeates the *Biblical Antiquities* that it is impossible to review all occurrences of the term here. Due note was taken of them in the commentary. The occurrences of the phrase "covenant with the fathers" and similar expressions are an index of how the symbol is used. In 9:4, 7, Amram recalls the covenant with the fathers as proof that Pharaoh's decree cannot destroy Israel. The covenant implies Israel's eternal existence. In 10:2, the people, terrified by the approaching Egyptians, wonder what is to become of the covenant with the fathers. They assume that Israel's destruction means an end to the covenant. In 13:10, the covenant with the fathers implies that God will send rain and make the earth fruitful. In 19:2, Moses is confident that no matter how angry God is, God will always preserve the people because of the covenant with the fathers.

The Joshua cycle is crucial in making explicit that the covenant with the fathers issues in a covenant with their sons and daughters. In 22:7, Joshua addresses God as the "God of our fathers" and then goes on to pray for God's mercy "on your covenant with the sons of your servants." In 23:2, Joshua says, *"Hear, O Israel.* Behold I am establishing with you a covenant of this Law that the LORD established for your fathers on Horeb." Later in the same chapter, God says to Israel, "I brought you into this land and gave you *vineyards. Cities that you did not build* you inhabit. And I fulfilled my covenant that I promised to your fathers" (23:11). This echoes the words of the people in 21:9: "Behold our LORD has fulfilled what he said to our fathers: '*To your seed I will give the land* in which you may dwell, *a land flowing with milk and honey.*'" The people say that word was sent to the departed fathers, "saying, 'Behold the LORD has done everything that he has said to us.' And truly now we know that God has established every word of his Law that he spoke to us on Horeb." The covenant centers on Israel's possession of the land.

Kenaz prays to the "LORD God of our fathers" for God to send him one of the "wonders that you are ready to do by reason of your covenant in the last days" (27:7). Kenaz expects God to be faithful to the covenant until the end of time. The eschaton will witness divine mighty deeds for Israel. What God does for Israel in Kenaz's time is a prolepsis of the eschaton. Just as Kenaz hopes for victory as a present benefit of the covenant, so do the people.

---

3. See Rom. 11:29 for Paul's view on the irrevocability of the covenant.

In 54:1 the people bring the ark of the covenant to the battle with the Philistines, saying, "Perhaps he may fight along with us, because in it are the tablets of the LORD that he established with our fathers on Horeb."

This brief survey of the phrase "covenant with the fathers" shows that God's association with Israel stretches back beyond Sinai to Abraham and concerns God's promise to him of land and eternal blessing for him and his seed. The covenant is consummated in the giving of the Law and the land. It implies that God will never abandon Israel to its enemies, although the book is replete with instances of God temporarily punishing the people. As in the cases of Amram and Moses with the Egyptians, Joshua with the inhabitants of the land, Deborah with the Amorites, or the people with the Philistines, God's commitment to Israel means protection from its enemies.

God's commitment to the covenant falls under a larger category examined in the previous chapter concerning God as a character in the narrative. God is absolutely reliable. Pseudo-Philo writes to prove that in detail. God's words are never in vain, divine predictions always come true, and God's promises are always fulfilled. This is the rock-solid basis of everything that happens in the *Biblical Antiquities*. God's covenant with the fathers, often portrayed as God's promises to them, will never fail. This is witnessed to even by a Gentile. In 18:10, Balaam says, "It is easier to take away the foundations and the topmost part of the earth and to extinguish the light of the sun and to darken the light of the moon than for anyone to uproot the planting of the Most Powerful or to destroy his vine." "Vine" is used numerous times for Israel in the book, signifying God's particular concern for Israel.

Pseudo-Philo conceives of the covenant as unconditional.[4] This is especially striking in that Pseudo-Philo does not emphasize the notion of repentance found in Judges, the source of much of the *Biblical Antiquities*. For example, repentance plays no role in the stories of Gideon and Jephthah despite the versions in Judges.[5] Indeed, Israel's prayers for help would go unheeded if God did not already have an obligation to help them. As God says to Phinehas, "I myself have sworn, says the LORD; if I had not sworn, I would not have remembered you in what you have said, nor would I have answered you today" (47:3). In 30:7, Deborah tells the people that God will never abandon them, "not because of you but because of the covenant that he established with your fathers and the oath that he has sworn not to abandon you forever." This borders on making the actions of the people ultimately irrelevant. They may affect the fate of a particular individual, group, or generation, but God's covenant with Israel will always endure.

---

4. In this Pseudo-Philo concurs with the priestly view of covenant. See Anderson, *Understanding,* 455; Gottwald, *Hebrew Bible,* 471–72.

5. See Murphy, "Eternal Covenant," 52.

Moral Causality

Moral causality is a strict application of the deuteronomistic idea that good is rewarded and evil punished. The term "moral causality" with reference to the *Biblical Antiquities* is taken from Perrot's commentary.[6] Pseudo-Philo subscribes to this view completely. The concept so permeates the book that every story illustrates it to some degree. It is impossible to discuss every example of it here, but the commentary does so throughout. The next paragraphs point out some instances in which moral causality causes Pseudo-Philo to make alterations to the biblical story.

The terrible fate of the Levite's concubine in Judges 19 is undeserved, but Pseudo-Philo does not believe such a fate could happen unless the person deserved it. The narrator explains that the concubine suffers "because she had transgressed against her man once when she committed sins with the Amalekites, and on account of this the LORD God delivered her into the hands of sinners" (45:3). The biblical story of Gideon ends with his idolatry, which goes unpunished. Pseudo-Philo adds God's own thoughts on the matter (36:4). God says that Gideon cannot be punished in this life lest people think he is being punished by Baal. God plans to punish Gideon in the afterlife. The story of the biblical Samson is told without moral judgments. Pseudo-Philo has God say that Samson must die because of his lust and his "mingling" with Gentiles. In Judges 20, the tribes suffer defeat twice when they fight with the sinning Benjaminites. Pseudo-Philo gives readers access to God's mind in 45:6, revealing that the tribes are defeated because they did not resist Micah's idolatry.

The principle of moral causality is enunciated repeatedly by the narrator and by reliable characters. God lays down the rules for history toward the beginning of the book (3:9–10). Every sin will receive its punishment in this life and the next. The speeches of every reliable character—Moses, Joshua, Kenaz, Zebul, Deborah, even Jephthah, and so on—are imbued with the deuteronomistic viewpoint. In 44:10, God says categorically that every human being will receive the fruit of his or her doings. At the end, those being punished will admit, "Let us not mourn over these things that we suffer; but because whatever we ourselves have devised, these will we receive" (44:10). Pseudo-Philo has little room for ambiguity on this point. One wonders whether he ever read the Book of Job or wrestled with the problems of doubt and suffering that Job addresses.

Pseudo-Philo believes in an ultimately rational universe that is controlled by God. The rationality of the universe expresses itself in moral causality. The most striking corollary of this is that the punishment always fits the crime.[7] In 31:1, God declares that because Sisera desired to take Israel's most beautiful

6. SC 230, throughout.

7. Feldman ("Prolegomenon," cxxviii) cites Dietzfelbinger (*Pseudo-Philo*, 227) in listing the following parallels for this idea: Matt. 7:2–3; Mark 4:24; Acts 7:41–43; Rom. 1:22–32; 2:1. The principle is stated in Wisd. 11:15–16 and illustrated in the rest of that book. See also Ps. 7:15–16; Heb. 7:2; *Jub.* 4:32 (SC 230, 201).

women, he will be defeated by a woman. In 38:4, God condemns Jair to the very fire he had prepared for those who resisted his idolatry. In 43:5, Samson, who sinned with his eyes, will be punished by being blinded. God says in 44:10 that at the Judgment the sinners themselves will admit that they have received what they themselves devised. Micah and his mother suffer quite specific torments that correspond to the precise forms of their idolatry (44:9). In 53:9–10, Eli's sons sin against all Israel and are said to violate the law in Deut. 22:6 against taking the mother bird with the young. For this reason the father Eli and his sons perish together. Saul takes forbidden booty and spares King Agag (chap. 58). God allows Agag's wife to live long enough to give birth to a son who later kills Saul (65:4). Doeg the Syrian, who sinned by informing Saul about the priests of Nob, suffers from a fiery worm in his tongue (63:4).

Pseudo-Philo shares the idea found in Wisd. 16:1–4, 24, that the same element is a benefit to the righteous and a punishment to the wicked. In 4:5 water is needed for fertility and showers down when humanity obeys, but the Flood of chapter 3 destroys the iniquitous. In 11:1, the Torah is a light to the good but retribution to the bad. In 23:6 fire is a revelation to the just but punishment to the wicked.

Pseudo-Philo's moral universe is not completely polarized. Good characters are capable of sin, and several characters fall somewhere between being entirely good or bad—for example, Joktan, the elders, and the Levite. Most striking is that both Abraham and Kenaz explicitly admit that they are sinners. In 6:11 Abraham refuses Joktan's help, saying, "If there be any sin of mine so flagrant that I should be burned up, let the will of God be done." Before his battle with the Amorites, Kenaz prays, "Even if I be handed over to death, I know that the LORD has not heard me because of my faults and has handed me over to my enemies" (27:7). A similar thought is expressed by Samuel's father Elkanah in 49:5 when the people try to persuade him to accept leadership: "If my sins have caught up with me, I will kill myself so that you may not defile me. For it is just that I should die only for my own sins rather than to bear the burden of this people."

Plans and Plots, Human and Divine

A frequent theme in Pseudo-Philo is that humans are constantly thinking about what to do and making plans, but that their plans are almost always evil, mistaken, or ill-advised.[8] Human plans, often said to be "in vain," are frequently contrasted with God's plans, which can never be "in vain." Human plans that challenge God's plans are futile. The only remedy is complete submission to God's will and plans as expressed in the Law, through prophecy, and by means of good leaders. Pseudo-Philo frequently uses the words *consilium* (and *consilari*), *cogitatio* (and *cogitare*), and *adinventio* (and *adinvenire*)

---

8. See Murphy, "Divine Plan."

to indicate acts of thinking and planning by both God and humans. A survey of these terms illustrates Pseudo-Philo's interest in the contrast between divine and human plans.[9]

Consilium (or *consiliari*) is used in several ways—negatively, neutrally, and positively. Its negative use is most prominent, designating plans that contravene the will of God. It appears several times in the story of the tower of Babel to denote the evil plans of the builders (6:4, 9, 13 [twice]). It also is used for Pharaoh's plan against Israel (9:1), Korah's plan against Moses (16:4), the plans of Balaam and Balak against Israel (18:13), Micah's mother's advice (44:4), and the tribes' plans against the Benjaminites (45:6). In 5:2 the leaders of the three divisions of humanity decide *(fecerunt consilium)* to take a census. Analysis of chapter 5 suggests that Pseudo-Philo sees the census, undertaken without instructions from God, as another apparently neutral human act leading in the wrong direction. In 10:3, the tribes caught between the Red Sea and the advancing Egyptians propose three courses of action *(tres divisiones consiliorum)*, all of which turn out to be wrong. In 18:11, it is said that no one should think *in consilio suo* that God will allow the chosen people to be destroyed. *Consilio* in the rest of Pseudo-Philo usually implies concrete plans, so here it may mean that God will not allow plots against Israel to succeed.

A positive use of *consilium* occurs in the story of Tamar, whose plan to have intercourse with her father-in-law Judah is defended (9:5 [twice]). The plan made by David and Abimelech must have been good given Pseudo-Philo's positive view of David (63:2). In 40:4, the word *consilium* is applied to the plan of God concerning Seila, daughter of Jephthah. *Consilium* is used ironically in the tower story when Joktan publicly calls the resisters' plan evil although he secretly sympathizes with it (6:9). Joktan, the resisters, and the readers are aware of the deception.

The only remaining use of *consilium* is in the story of Balaam (chap. 18). A sentence is placed on the lips of Balaam that fully expresses Pseudo-Philo's theme as it has emerged from our study of the term elsewhere in the book. Speaking of Balak, who wishes Israel to be cursed, Balaam says, "He does not know that the plan of God is not like the plan of man *[non ita est consilium Dei sicut consilium hominis]*" (18:3). Contrast between divine and human plans underlies every occurrence of the use of *consilium* and *consiliari* examined here.

The majority of the occurrences of *cogitatio* and *cogitare* are negative, and most of the positive ones have God as subject. Just as 18:3 contains what amounts to a general statement or principle using the word *consilium,* there are several principlelike statements using *cogitatio* and *cogitare* that sum up how Pseudo-Philo uses the term. LAB 16:3 says, "And now the thoughts *[cogitationes]* of men are very corrupt." Another principle appears in 21:4, where Joshua says about humanity that it "cannot place *[excogitare homo ut proponat]* one generation before another." Joshua tells God that he knows God

---

9. These are not the only words Pseudo-Philo uses to speak of human and divine plans. *Verbum,* for example, is another.

will make the divine word live even if humans, who cannot reason as God does, think that God has canceled previous plans and destroyed the chosen people. There is a contrast between God's understanding and humanity's, a contrast common in Jewish literature and prominent in Pseudo-Philo.[10]

Humanity before the Flood failed to live up to God's demands, and *"they were plotting evil [iniquitatem cogitantibus] all their days"* (3:3). Harrington's translation of *cogitantibus* as "plotting" rather than "thinking" is true to the thrust of Pseudo-Philo, which emphasizes humanity's concrete plans to contravene the will of God or to destroy God's people. The story of the tower of Babel is replete with the terms *consilium, consiliari, cogitatio,* and *cogitare.* In 6:9, Joktan assures the resisters, "I know that the evil plan *[consilium iniquitatis]* that they have agreed *[consiliati sunt]* to carry out will not stand, because their plot is foolish *[vana est cogitatio eorum]*." Chapter 7 begins by saying that the builders "were not turned from their malicious plottings *[a cogitationibus suis malignis]*" by the rescue of Abraham (7:1). LAB 7:5 says that the plan *(cogitatio)* of the builders "was frustrated." In chapter 18, *cogitare* is used twice in the context of possible action against Israel. In 18:6, God asks Balaam whether he proposes *(cogitare)* to curse Israel and in 18:12 Balaam himself declares that anyone plotting *(hec cogitaverunt)* against Israel will be punished. *Hec* refers to Balak's attempts to destroy Israel.

Joshua thinks *(cogitans)* that Moses is still alive. God reproaches him for that (20:2). Kenaz seeks out Israelites who do not have pure hearts and discovers that a large number have committed idolatry. Looking back on this discovery, he says, "When we were seeking out all those who planned evil deeds *[excogitabant mala]* craftily against the LORD and against Israel, God revealed them to us according to their works" (26:5). Kenaz then finds out that the Amorites "were planning *[cogitantes]* to come and fight against Israel" (27:6). In 49:3, the people search for a leader through the use of lots but have no success. Nethez declares, "We who have walked in our evil ways have not known him who created us, and so our plan *[cogitatus]* will be in vain."

Another negative use of the term *cogitare* is found when Jael says that Sisera "has made a plan *[cogitavit]* and said, 'I will go and punish the flock of the Most Powerful One'" (31:5). Later Saul is guilty of evil thoughts several times. In 62:3, 6, Saul plans *(cogitare)* to kill David. In 64:1 he decides *(cogitavit)* to expel the wizards from the land of Israel, but he does so to win earthly glory. In 64:3 Saul commits the ironic sin of going to one of the mediums whom he had previously expelled to *"inquire of him* what I should plan out *[quod cogito]*."

God is the subject of *cogitare* in 9:8, where God says that God thought of Moses from days of old. In 15:5 God angrily refuses to let the people's reaction to the report of the spies sent into Canaan interfere with the divine plan *(cogitatio)* to plant the people there. In 40:4, God thinks of Jephthah's daughter *(cogitavit super eam)*. God refuses to allow Israel's wise men to interfere with Seila's sacrifice "in order that my word be fulfilled and my plan that I thought

---

10. See the *Hodayot* of Qumran, and numerous instances in the Wisdom literature.

out *[consilium meum quod cogitaveram]* not be foiled." Before approaching Samuel at Shiloh, God gives it careful thought *(cogitavit),* comparing the appearance to Samuel to the one to Moses in the burning bush (53:2). In 56:5, Samuel asks God to reveal what he has planned *(cogitare)* for his people.

The terms for thought occasionally can be positive when applied to a few humans. The narrator says that "the strategy that Amram thought out *[quod cogitavit]* was pleasing before God." God says that what "Amram thought out *[cogitatio Amre]* is pleasing to me" (9:7). Amram says of Tamar, "Her intent *[consilium]* was not fornication, but being unwilling to separate from the sons of Israel she reflected *[recogitans]* and said" (9:5). He continues, "Her intent *[consilium]* saved her from all danger" (9:5). Joshua decides *(cogitavit)* to send spies into Jericho (20:6). He does not follow instructions from God, but he is really redoing what Moses did earlier (chap. 15). His move turns out to be a good one. Hannah thinks *(cogitavit)* before praying at Shiloh (50:5). Hannah is viewed sympathetically by the narrator, and her thoughts have good results. Zebul's exhortation in 29:4 epitomizes the theme that human thought is almost always in error unless it is dependent entirely on God's will: "Just as a wave understands *[intellegit]* nothing except what is in the sea, so let your heart ponder *[cogitet]* nothing else except what belongs to the Law."[11]

Another word used for human planning is *adinventio (adinvenire).* In 3:10, God promises to return to each the "fruits of his own devices *[adinventionum]*" at the Last Judgment. In 25:7–8, the word *adinventio* describes the schemes of the Israelite sinners discovered by Kenaz, and in 25:11 the idolatrous nymphs of the Amorites are what "seven sinful men devised *[adinvenerunt]*" after the Flood. In 26:5, Kenaz curses the Israelite sinners "who would plot *[adinvenerit]* to do such things." When Gideon bemoans Israel's miserable lot, the angel says, "Your own schemes *[adinventiones]* have done these things to you." In 44:7, God says, speaking of Micah's idols, "Imagination has invented *[adinvenit]* them." In 44:10, God predicts that at the Judgment people will admit, "Whatever we ourselves have devised *[adinvenimus],* these we will receive." In the same verse God says that humans will not make God jealous with their "inventions" *(adinventionibus).* In 47:7 God says that idols like Micah's were never "made" *(adinvenit)* before. In 52:2 Eli pleads with his sons to abandon their wicked schemes *(adinventiones).* This survey confirms what was found above: Pseudo-Philo has a pessimistic view of human thought and plans. Complete submission to God is the only answer.

This survey of the terms *consilium, consiliari, cogitatio, cogitare, adinventio,* and *adinvenire* demonstrates something already observed in numerous instances in the analysis of preceding chapters. A major theme of Pseudo-Philo is that humans on their own tend to go wrong. Any human thoughts or plans are fated to be mistaken or downright evil unless they are in complete dependence on God and on divine guidance. By far the majority of instances

---

11. *Intellegere* always refers to understanding the ways of God: 18:12; 20:3, 4; 29:4; 32:3, 7; 53:2, 5; 55:1; 56:6. Thus, the exhortation to understand nothing but the ways of God is embodied in the Latin by not using the word "understand" for anything but God's ways.

of human thought and planning fall into the category of evil, opposed to God. A few can be called misguided, such as Joktan's plan to save Abraham and the other resisters of the tower of Babel. When thought or planning is used in a positive way, it most often refers to divine thoughts and plans. This theme is but one more way to state that God is the center of human existence and history.

Idolatry

Pseudo-Philo shows a particular interest in idolatry.[12] Pseudo-Philo enhances the element of idolatry when it appears in the biblical text and often inserts it in contexts where it is not originally present. Service to God and resistance to idolatry should be the hallmarks of Israel's existence but often are not. Israel's contact with Gentiles can lead to idolatry. Good leaders keep the people from idolatry and bad leaders do not.

The note in Gen. 4:22 about Tubal-cain's metalworking is transformed by the addition of the words "Those inhabiting the earth began to make statues and to adore them" (2:9). In 4:16, everyone except Abraham's family engages in astrology. In chapters 6–7, Abraham and eleven others refuse to participate in the idolatry of the tower of Babel, saying, "We know the one LORD, and him we worship" (6:4). Although there are twelve resisters, only Abraham fully trusts in God to deliver him. As a result God initiates an eternal covenant with Abraham and his seed (7:4).

For the rest of the story, Israel vascillates between faithfulness to and abandonment of God. The latter predominates, so that God often wishes to reject the people altogether but cannot because of the promises to the fathers. Good leaders, such as Moses, Joshua, Kenaz, and Deborah, keep the people away from idolatry and preach against it. Bad leaders, such as Jair or Gideon at the end of his career, either encourage idolatry or fail to keep it in check. In the golden calf incident of chapter 12, Moses' absence and Aaron's weakness lead to idolatry.

Idolatry symbolizes the essence of sin—abandonment of God and of God's claims on the people. This is especially evident in two passages. In the first, God is angry that the people flock to Micah's idolatrous shrine. God reviews the Ten Commandments, showing that idolatry violates each of them. The following paragraph from my earlier study on idolatry in Pseudo-Philo shows that this is the case.[13]

> Idolatry is the root of all evil. In a speech in 44:6–10 God recalls Sinai and the people's acceptance of the Ten Commandments. He lists each of the commandments beginning with the first, rephrased in the following way: "I said that they should not make idols, and they agreed not to carve out the images

12. See Murphy, "Retelling." This section depends on that study.
13. Murphy, "Retelling," 279–80. On idolatry as the root of all evil in rabbinic thought, see Sanders, *Paul,* 113, 134–35, 174.

of gods." Every commandment is broken by the making of idols (44:7). Worshiping idols is equivalent to giving God's name to them and so takes God's name in vain. Idolatry defiles God's sabbath. Dishonoring the Creator relates to dishonor of father and mother. Idolatry is the same as thievery. To seduce others (*seducere,* in this case meaning "to lead into idolatry") is the same as killing. Idolatry is adultery. Idolators accept false testimony. The connection between lust for foreign women and idolatry is implicit here but explicit throughout Pseudo-Philo. To commit idolatry is to commit every other possible sin at the same time.

When Kenaz discovers the sinners in the midst of Israel's tribes in chapter 25, he makes them confess their sins in public. The degree to which idolatry underlies all of their sins is noteworthy.[14]

Pseudo-Philo associates idolatry with the land and with Gentiles. The association with the land is shown in the reason adduced for Moses' being barred from the chosen land. The reason is unique to Pseudo-Philo and is put into God's mouth: "Now I will show you the land before you die, but *you will not enter it* in this age lest you see the graven images with which this people will start to be deceived and led off the path" (19:7). In the golden calf incident, the paradigm of idolatry, God says, "If they had entered that land, even greater iniquities would have been done" (12:4).

The elders are upset that their female descendants will be given to Egyptian slaves as wives because this means they will worship idols (9:2). In LAB 12:2, the people ask for false gods so that they can be like the other nations. All of chapter 34 is devoted to describing how the Midianite magician Aod leads the people into idolatry. In 30:1, the narrator says, "*They were led astray after the daughters* of the Amorites *and served their gods.*" However, the association of idolatry with the Gentiles is not firm. For example, the people (18:14) and Samson (43:5) sinfully consort with Gentiles without idolatry being mentioned explicitly. Tamar (9:5) avoids going to the Gentiles, but avoidance of idolatry is not mentioned as her motivation.[15] Further, idolatry can also enter Israel through its own citizens. The best examples of this are the golden calf (chap. 12), Gideon (chap. 36), and Jair (chap. 38).

Pseudo-Philo introduces the issue of idolatry into biblical stories where it is not present. When Jephthah confronts the Ammonite king in Judg. 11:24, he says that the Ammonite god Chemosh has given Ammon to the Ammonites. Pseudo-Philo changes this so that Jephthah challenges the existence of Chemosh, saying, "They are not gods, as you say they are" (39:9). Just before David kills Goliath, he attributes his success and Goliath's failure to his own worship of God and Goliath's idolatry (61:6). The story of the Levite's concubine is connected to that of Micah's idolatry by Pseudo-Philo, whereas they are unconnected in the Bible. The defeat of the tribes as they war against Benjamin because of the abuse of the Levite's concubine is attributed to their failure to oppose Micah's idolatry (47:7–8).

14. Murphy, "Retelling," 280.

15. Thus I must qualify the somewhat closer association between Gentiles and idolatry I posited in my earlier study ("Retelling," 277–78).

In several places Israelites seem to be fascinated with the power and wisdom of foreign gods. This is especially clear with the sinners under Kenaz (chap. 25), the Israelites misled by Aod (chap. 34), and those who go to Micah (chap. 44). Even the good leader Kenaz appears curious about the power of the Amorites' secret stones and books (chap. 26).

Slaves and Servants

The words *servus* and *servire* are prominent in the *Biblical Antiquities,* used sixteen and twenty-five times, respectively. The related word *servitutis* appears four times. In almost every case, the words denote service either to God or to idols. *Servus* occurs with the meaning "servant of God" as a term of high praise restricted to a few: Abraham (6:11); the fathers (15:5); Balaam (18:4); Moses (20:2); the fathers (22:7); Kenaz, Eleazar, and the elders (25:6); Kenaz (27:7, twice); resistors of Jair's idolatry (38:4); and Phinehas (47:1, 2). *Servus* can be used in other contexts as well. In 6:10, the eleven resisters of the tower call themselves servants of Joktan, but, as the analysis of that passage makes clear, their self-description as servants of Joktan is contrasted with Abraham as servant of God. In 57:4 the people style themselves servants of Samuel, but in the context of their failing to be full servants of God. Only in 9:1 is the word *servus* used of Israelites when it means slaves of others, in that case the Egyptians. In that context, the Israelites are made to suffer by Pharaoh even though they have done nothing to deserve such punishment. This is quite unusual in the *Biblical Antiquities,* where suffering is usually caused by sin.

The uniqueness of Israel's subjection to the Egyptians is underlined by Pseudo-Philo's use of the word "servitude" *(servitutis).* It is used only four times in the *Biblical Antiquities;* three of those refer to the period of slavery in Egypt. The first time is in 9:3, when Amram explains Israel's bondage since the time of Abraham (and so including the time in Egypt) by recalling God's prediction of that bondage to Abraham (see Gen. 15:13). In 11:6, *servitutis* refers to the Egyptian bondage from which God liberated Israel, as in Exod. 20:2. In 18:11 God asks Balaam indignantly whether he intends to curse Israel and reminds him of "what he sent upon Pharaoh and his land because he wished to reduce them to slavery *[servitutem]."*

The final occurrence of *servitutis* is in 34:5. God says that because Israel "began to serve *[servire]* the gods of the Midianites," he would "deliver them into the hands of the Midianites." The narrator then informs the reader, "And he *delivered them into* their *hands,* and the Midianites began to reduce Israel to slavery *[servitutem]*" (34:5). There is a wordplay here in the Latin that would also be present in the Hebrew. Just as the words being examined in this section are all from the same Latin root, so in Hebrew they would be from the single root *'bd.*[16] The idea is that service to idols or their worshipers results in slavery. Just as the words *servire* and *servitutis* are related, so is service to

16. See, e.g., Gen. 15:13–14 (cp. LAB 9:3); Exod. 20:2 (LAB 11:6).

idols and servitude. The converse is that service to God results in liberation and freedom.

Both sides of the theme that service to idols brings slavery and service to God brings freedom are prominent in the *Biblical Antiquities*.[17] A clear statement concerning service to idols is found in 41:3: "But the sons of Israel forgot the LORD their God and served *[servierunt]* the gods of those inhabiting the land; and on account of this *they were handed over to the Philistines* and served *[servierunt]* them *forty years.*" To serve *(servire)* idols issues in serving *(servire)* the worshipers of those idols. Conversely, service to God results in freedom. That is expressed in the relationship of the words *servire* and *liberare* in several passages. In 6:11, there is irony when the eleven resisters expect liberation to result from their subjection to Joktan. They express their gratitude to the Shemite leader by calling themselves his servants. Ironically, liberation comes because Abraham is a servant of God, as Joktan unwittingly suggests when he addresses Abraham as *serve Dei*. Nonetheless, Joktan informs Abraham that he will be saved *(liberaberis)* only by following Joktan's plans.

In 27:7 Kenaz identifies himself through his servanthood to God when he asks God to free the people to show that God saves *(liberat)* not by means of a large army. Kenaz expects a "sign of deliverance *[signum salutis]*." In 38:4, God tells Jair that those who resisted Jair's idolatry are divine servants *(servos meos),* and so they were delivered *(liberati sunt)* from Jair's punishing fire. In 47:1 Phinehas styles himself a servant of God, and recounts the time that God saved him *(me liberasti)* from the hands of his enemies.

The idea that service and faithfulness to God result in salvation from all evil surfaces continually throughout Pseudo-Philo. The point of this section is that a close examination of the root *serv-* points to the sustained contrast in the *Biblical Antiquities* between service to idols or their adherents, which results in slavery, and service to God, which results in liberation. Other passages in which God is the object of *servire* are: 6:6; 9:7; 11:2; 19:7; 22:3, 7; 23:14; 24:1 (three times); 30:6. Passages where idols are the object of that verb are: 9:2; 12:2; 18:12; 30:1; 34:1, 5; 39:6; 41:3; 61:2. The Egyptians are found as the object of *servire* in 9:1; 10:3; and 15:5, but in 9:2 there is a clear connection drawn between service to the Egyptians and worship of their gods. In 41:3, service to the gods of the people of the land results in servitude to the Philistines. The only time the word *servire* appears outside service to God, idols, or idol worshipers is in 26:3, where the only water that can blot out the writing of the magical books is water that has not "served" humans.

It is clear that servanthood is an important theme of the *Biblical Antiquities* and that there is a sustained contrast between serving God and serving idols. The former results in liberation, the latter in servitude.

---

17. For a similar comparison of these two sorts of service, see Romans 6.

Protology and Eschatology

Perrot produced an excellent synthesis of Pseudo-Philo's thought on these topics, and the present section owes much to his study.[18] Perrot observes correctly that Pseudo-Philo shows no interest in protology or eschatology for its own sake. He claims that Pseudo-Philo is more accurately a pastor who subscribes to the ideas of the period and brings them into the narrative to support his pastoral points than a teacher whose purpose is to impart doctrines. Perrot's distinction between pastor and teacher may be somewhat overdrawn and in need of qualification in terms of the author's cultural milieu, but his basic insight is sound. Pseudo-Philo is less concerned to convey ideas about the afterlife than to engender obedience.

Although Pseudo-Philo does not narrate the Fall, he assumes that there was a time when humankind lived a paradisal existence. This is shown through revelations made to Moses and Kenaz. In 13:8, God shows Moses "the place of creation and the serpent," clearly referring to Eden. God says that Adam could have remained there had he not sinned. The text continues, "The LORD continued to show him the ways of paradise and said to him, 'These are the ways that men have lost by not walking in them, because they have sinned against me'" (13:9). During Kenaz's conversations with God concerning the secrets of the Amorites, Kenaz proclaims, "Behold how much good God has made for men, but because of their sins they have been deprived of all these things" (26:14). After his vision in 28:6–9, which goes from Creation to the eschaton, Kenaz declares, "If the repose of the just after they have died is like this, we must die to the corruptible world so as not to see sins" (28:10). Coupled with 26:14, this implies that humans will regain what they lost if they do not sin.

The fullest description of the eschaton occurs in 3:10 on God's lips. Its narrative setting is significant. It comes after the story of the Flood, wherein most of humanity proved itself sinful. The main thrust of 3:9–10 is that every sin will receive its punishment in this world and the next, although the positive results of judgment for the just are also mentioned (3:10). In 3:10 God discloses that at the eschaton light and darkness will cease, meaning that the present creation will pass away. There will be a universal resurrection at which God renders "to each according to his works and according to the fruits of his own devices." The world will go out of existence, death will cease, and hell will "shut its mouth." Then the earth will cease being sterile, the good will be rewarded, and "there will be another earth and another heaven, an everlasting dwelling place." The function of this passage is to state in strong terms the idea of moral causality. It is placed toward the beginning of the narrative at the world's new beginning represented by the aftermath of the Flood. It sets the "ground rules" for the rest of the book. All of the *Biblical Antiquities* should be read with the awareness that this is what awaits humanity at the

---

18. SC 230, 53–57; the present section does not reproduce all of his detail.

end of time. The frequent references to the afterlife that follow, whether the hope entertained by Moses, Kenaz, or Deborah, or the terrible fate in store for Gideon or Korah, assume that the description in chapter 3 is true.

In the speech conveyed to the people by Joshua at the covenant-making ceremony at Shiloh, God tells of bestowing a vision upon Abraham at the sacrifice described in Genesis 15. God says, "I sent upon him *a deep sleep* and encompassed him with *fear* and set before him the place of fire where the deeds of those doing wickedness against me will be expiated, and I showed him *the torches of fire* by which the just who have believed in me will be enlightened" (23:6). Fire is an important image in Pseudo-Philo. Here it means salvation to the just and punishment for the wicked and so is an instance of the idea that creation can both be a benefit for those who obey God and work against those who oppose God.

Pseudo-Philo emphasizes the significance of this life—it seals one's fate in the next. One cannot sin in the next life; even the evil impulse goes away (33:3). The people ask Deborah to intercede for them after her death, but she says, "While a man is still alive he can pray for himself and for his sons, but after his end he cannot pray or be mindful of anyone" (33:5). The real point here is that the dead cannot help the living. Deborah's additional point that they cannot even be mindful of the living must be qualified by several passages in which messages about the living are brought to the dead. After death, individuals join their fathers and mothers. Pseudo-Philo seems to believe that one is judged at death and that such judgment endures until the end time (51:5). Presumably, then, when the Israelite fathers receive word of Israel's fate they are already enjoying their afterlife bliss (21:9). God says that if the people obey, "at the end the lot of each one of you will be life eternal, for you and your seed, and I will take your souls and store them in peace until the time allotted the world be complete" (23:13). Evil humans who die are already being punished. As Jael kills Sisera, she tells him, "Go, boast before your father in hell and tell him that you have fallen *into the hands of a woman*" (31:7). For sinners, death brings one to a place of punishing fires and darkness (18:12; 23:6; 31:7; 36:4; 38:4; 63:4).

The function of eschatology in Pseudo-Philo is clear in Moses' words. In 19:4, Moses says, "God has revealed the end of the world so that he might establish his statutes with you and kindle among you an eternal light." Eschatology supports Torah. Perrot claims that 19:13–15 implies the end is near, though it is not stressed. This passage can also be read in the opposite way. That four-and-a-half times have passed and two-and-a-half remain might assume a time scheme in which the world lasts for seven thousand years, meaning there have been forty-five hundred years since the Creation and twenty-five hundred remain. Pseudo-Philo would then mean that the eschaton is sure and will come, but in the distant future. His idea that punishment and rewards follow upon death and that good and bad undergo their fate between now and the eschaton makes the dating of the eschaton less urgent. Perrot is certainly correct when he claims that Pseudo-Philo does not share the "eschatological fever" of some of his near-contemporaries.

Women

Pseudo-Philo gives a remarkable amount of attention to women.[19] Perrot notes that most of the women in the narrative, with the exception of Delilah and Micah's mother, are "honored."[20]

Deborah is one of the major leaders in the book. Her story occupies chapters 30–33. Pseudo-Philo gives Deborah much more to say than the Bible does. Deborah becomes an important teacher regarding the Torah, Israel's history and relation to God, the afterlife, and so on. She introduces her testament with these words: "Listen now, my people. Behold I am warning you as a woman of God and am enlightening you as one from the female race" (33:1). Harrington goes so far as to characterize "woman of God" as the "feminist counterpart" of the term "man of God." When Deborah dies, the people lament, "Behold there has perished a *mother from Israel,* and the holy one who exercised leadership in the house of Jacob" (33:6). Within the story of Deborah is that of Jael. Pseudo-Philo has embellished that story considerably, concentrating on Jael's dependence on God and bringing her action into line with God's will. Part of his strategy for doing so is to import various elements from the story of another Jewish heroine, Judith.

Perrot lists the following examples of women in the narrative. My comments on each of these figures should be consulted. In 4:11, Melcha, a female ancestor of Abraham, prophesies Abraham's future glory. Miriam receives the angel's annunciation of Moses' birth, and Eluma, mother of Samson, is told by the angel of Samson's birth (chaps. 9 and 42). The daughter of Pharaoh is guided by a dream (9:15). Dinah becomes Job's wife (8:8). Amram adduces Tamar as an example of proper action in a crisis (9:5). She receives the exalted title of "our mother," and thus matriarchal status. "Sons of Leah" is an appellation for Israel in 10:4. The well in the desert is associated with Miriam (20:8). Sarah is quarried from the same rock as Abraham and has her womb opened by God (23:4–7). Zebul ensures the honoring of Kenaz's three daughters, and it is said that husbands are given to them rather than vice versa (chap. 29). Women offer treasure to them in chapter 29. Seila is the epitome of willing acceptance of God's will, despite its tremendous personal cost (chap. 40). Her sacrifice is even compared to Isaac's. Hannah is also a major character for Pseudo-Philo, and her righteousness is enhanced. Important prayers are uttered by Deborah, Seila, and Hannah. All told, Pseudo-Philo's interest in women is truly noteworthy. Van der Horst concludes his treatment of Seila with, "It is clear, anyhow, that this procedure of aggrandizing the role and

19. See van der Horst, "Portraits." Cheryl Anne Brown has recently published a monograph examining the treatment of Deborah, Jephthah's daughter, Hannah, and the witch of Endor in Pseudo-Philo and Josephus. I did not receive her book in time to incorporate her insights into my analysis, but I now recommend it as an important study of Pseudo-Philo's treatment of biblical women.

20. In much of these paragraphs I follow Perrot's presentation of the women characters (SC 230, 52–53).

importance of women is not restricted to one isolated case. We can rightfully speak of 'the feminism of Pseudo-Philo.' "[21]

Israel's Inner Harmony

Pseudo-Philo's concern with Israel's inner harmony surfaces from time to time in the text. Abimelech's greatest sin is that he kills his brothers (37:1, 4). Joseph is a model of reconciliation with his brothers and is compared favorably with Samson because, unlike Samson, he did not betray the peace of his own people by consorting with a foreign woman (8:10; 43:5). Jephthah's brothers are jealous of him and drive him from the land (39:2). When they need his martial skills to help them, they approach him. Their conflict is settled when Jephthah finally gives in to their request to put their differences behind them and to help them against their enemies. He apparently accepts their exhortation to imitate God's forgiveness, although at first he argues against it (39:4–5).

The extended narrative of the relationships between David and Jonathan and between David and Saul is a parable of what relationships within Israel should and should not be. Chapter 62 is taken up mostly with speeches by David and Jonathan. Those speeches contrast David's righteousness and his unselfish service to Saul with Saul's jealousy, which tears apart their alliance. David says that even if he has committed some sin against Saul of which he is unaware, Saul should imitate God in forgiveness (62:6). This is the same argument Jephthah's brothers make to him in chapter 39. The love David and Jonathan have for each other is a foil to Saul's jealousy. Jonathan's last words read as a recipe for a harmonious Israelite community. He urges David to forget Saul's anger, hatred, ingratitude, jealousy, and lies, and to remember Jonathan's covenant with David and his love, table fellowship, faithfulness, and oaths (62:11).

In 64:8, Samuel tells Saul that because of his jealousy he and his sons will die and Saul will lose everything. Saul's last words, which are also the last words in the present form of the *Biblical Antiquities,* are words of reconciliation, signaling hope for Israel. He tells his killer, "Now go and tell David, 'I have killed your enemy.' And you will say to him, 'Be not mindful of my hatred or my injustice' " (65:5).

Saul's motivation is his own fame and profit. In 64:1, he drives out the wizards to make himself a name. In 58:3 God reveals that he spared Agag out of greed. All of his problems with David arise out of jealousy. Such motivations tear Israel apart. The same is true in the case of Micah. He and his mother establish their idolatry because of desire for fame and fortune (44:1–3). They lead Israel astray, and Israel remains silent in the face of their iniquities. The consequence is civil war (chaps. 46–47). A subtheme in chapters 44–47 is that Israel's silence in the face of iniquity in its midst leads to disaster. God levels

21. "Portraits," 42.

the same accusation of silence at Israel in 63:3, where Israel accepts Saul's slaughter of the priests of Nob.

Moses shows that lack of jealousy brings harmony to Israel. The people recall that Eldad and Modad prophesied that leadership would pass from Moses to Joshua and that Moses was not jealous when he heard the news (20:5). This paved the way for Joshua to divide the land "in peace" between the tribes. In another case, David sings that his brothers were jealous of him, but that God protected him from their jealousy (59:4). The kingship of David was thus made possible because God negated the kind of intramural jealousy that would have sabotaged it.

The speculation about God's ways and proper courses of action observed throughout the narrative commentary can be seen in the context of Israel's inner harmony. Amram and the elders argue over what they should do because of Pharaoh's decree (chap. 9). God sides with Amram. Faced with the crisis of the oncoming Egyptian forces at the Red Sea, the Israelites divide into competing factions (chap. 10). Their conflict is solved by Moses' appeal to God and God's intervention. The Shemites Abraham and Joktan disagree about the best way to react to the idolaters at the tower of Babel. God intervenes to vindicate Abraham (chaps. 6–7).

This analysis could be carried much further. Ultimately, the issue of harmony in Israel must be seen as subordinate to the idea that submission to God's will brings success. If all of Israel obeys God's Law, then harmony naturally results. It is because Israel is too foolish to know God's will or too wicked to follow it that it suffers.

Messianism

Pseudo-Philo has no concept of an eschatological Messiah.[22] Indeed the only reason to raise the subject here is its abiding interest to Christian scholars. It does not arise from the text. *Christus* occurs four times. It occurs in Hannah's song in 51:6, referring to the king that Samuel will anoint. The reference depends on 1 Sam. 2:10 and refers to David. The word occurs again in 57:3, where Samuel demands that the people judge his leadership before God and God's anointed, Saul. The reference depends on 1 Sam. 12:3. In chapter 59, Samuel goes to Jesse's family to find the new king. *Christus* appears in 59:2 in dependence on 1 Sam. 16:6 and refers to David. *Christus* in 59:4 is in David's psalm. David refers to himself here, and the passage does not depend on any specific biblical verse. This is Pseudo-Philo's only use of the word not taken directly from the Bible. No case for an eschatological Messiah can be made from these uses of *christus*.

In 21:5, Joshua pleads for a ruler from Judah in language drawn from Gen. 49:10. In some places outside the *Biblical Antiquities,* that verse is interpreted

22. See SC 230, 57–59.

messianically. In Pseudo-Philo, however, it seems to find its fulfillment in Kenaz (21:5).

The strongest argument against the idea that Pseudo-Philo expects an eschatological Messiah is that when the text speaks of the eschaton, no Messiah is present.

Angelology

Interest in angels is present in many documents from the Second Temple period.[23] Pseudo-Philo's angelology is like his eschatology in that he shares the ideas of his times but does not focus on this topic for its own sake. Angels appear numerous times but do not receive a great deal of attention. They underscore the fact that God is present and active in history. For example, Goliath is killed not just by David but also by an angel (61:5–8). An angel aids Kenaz in his fight with the Amorites (27:10). The angels are given names that sometimes have some correspondence with other Jewish traditions and sometimes do not. This follows the pattern found with Pseudo-Philo's addition of human names. It proves that the author understands how the universe works and who is in charge of what, but it is not really meant as freestanding information important for its own sake.

23. See SC 230, 59–63.

12

The Real Author in Historical Context

It is always difficult to move from story world to real world. Historical criticism often tries to use texts as windows onto the real worlds—social, political, religious, and so on—that produced them. Such an enterprise is valid, but it must be done cautiously. Placing a work like the *Biblical Antiquities* into its historical context is difficult. It certainly was not written at the time of the events it narrates or any time close to them. Neither is it an account of those events using trustworthy historical evidence independent of the author's main source, the Bible. Indeed, the *Biblical Antiquities* contributes nothing to knowledge about the preexilic period. Rather, as a rewriting of the sacred text of the Bible, it reveals more about the author's ideological point of view than about the events described. But this is itself historically important. If the consensus that the *Biblical Antiquities* was written in the first century C.E. is correct, then it provides access to the thought of at least one individual who lived at that time. If the work is the product of a group or represents the distillation of a community's storytelling over time, so much the better. Then it attests to views held by more than one person in the period in question. Of course, it is always debatable whether the interpretation of the previous chapters does indeed reflect an accurate understanding of the author's thought. This leads to theoretical questions about author, text, and reader that are very much under discussion at present and to which I have no theoretical contribution to make. Nonetheless, ancient texts to some degree reflect the thoughts, intentions, attitudes, and emotions of those who produced them, and the attempt to uncover those thoughts and intentions, no matter how problematic, is a worthwhile endeavor.

In previous chapters, I have bracketed specifically historical concerns in favor of a more literary approach. Observations about historical connections were kept to a minimum and relegated to the notes. The primary concern was to see the text as narrative and to see how it works, particularly in terms of plot, character, narrator's point of view, and ideological point of view. Strictly speaking, references to the "author" or to "Pseudo-Philo" (when that term meant the author as opposed to the text) meant the implied author, the author inscribed in the text. One might question whether the views of the implied author are the same as those of the real author. But the ideological point of view of the character God coincides with that of the narrator, and thus there is little reason to think that the real author's point of view is different. Indeed, the very idea of an unreliable narrator is a modern one and finds no counterpart in ancient literature.[1] I assume that the ideological point of view of the real author, the implied author, and the narrator are the same. Indeed, the text claims that such a point of view coincides with that of God.

This chapter ventures onto thinner ice by suggesting how such a narrative might reflect and speak to Jews of first-century Palestine. Taking account of what is known from other sources, the question becomes how Pseudo-Philo fits into the period. It can be said with certainty that Pseudo-Philo illustrates one way that the Bible, or part of it, was read in first-century Palestinian Judaism. The *Biblical Antiquities* attests both to the importance of sacred stories and to the freedom with which they could be retold. The precise purpose of the retelling is debatable, but it must be discerned in features of the text itself. Pseudo-Philo is clearly interested in connections between events. The text illuminates such connections, as in the numerous instances when one event is said to be like another from a very different period. One need not stretch very far to suggest that the real author expected the real readers to carry that process of analogy making into their own time. Readers should see that events, situations, and people from their own time are like those described in the narrative. Such recognition would cause readers either to reassess their own views and attitudes or to reaffirm them. The major concerns of the text are thus those that the author thinks need addressing in his own time. The author rewrote the Bible to make it speak to his own time, to actualize it. If so, then it is appropriate to review the principal themes of the *Biblical Antiquities* to see how they might relate to late Second Temple Judaism in Palestine.

A topic constantly addressed by Pseudo-Philo is the existence of Israel and its relationship with God. In the narrative, the people constantly find themselves facing enemies, usually from without, but sometimes from within. The crises often make characters question God's commitment to Israel, expressed through conversations between human characters, speeches, prayers, and interactions with God. Indeed, the sins of Israel frequently push God to the brink of canceling the covenant and allowing Israel to perish. But over and over again the narrative leads to a reaffirmation of God's relationship with Israel and the divine determination not to abandon it. Through God's words, those of reliable characters, even through the observations of foreigners like Balaam and Jael, and through the direction of the plot in which Israel always survives, the *Biblical Antiquities* consistently asserts the indestructibility of Israel and the covenant. No matter how evil or how neglectful of God's ways Israel gets, the covenant survives. It depends not on the people's deeds but on the promises to the fathers. This allows Pseudo-Philo to affirm two things and to hold them in tension: Israel will indeed suffer when it does not obey God, but this suffering does not mean that the covenant is at an end; and sin will always be punished, but God will never forsake Israel.

1. See Moore, *Literary Criticism,* 33, who agrees with Scholes and Kellogg on this point.

It is not hard to see how such a message would speak to Palestinian Jewish society of the first century. In recent years that period has been the subject of countless studies that reveal its turbulence and the problems of identity encountered by Israel because of foreign oppression and internal division. The existence of Israel did not always seem secure, neither could God's commitment to Israel have always gone unquestioned. The author's decision to give extensive treatment to the period of the judges may have been influenced by the fact that both during that era and during the first century, Israel found itself subject to foreign occupation, with unsettled leadership, and with foreign religious influences a danger. The rewriting of chapter 39, where who takes whose cities becomes an issue, may reflect the author's own times, when conflicting loyalties between cities was a concern.

Moses himself predicts Israel's future difficulties in its own land:

> I am to sleep with my fathers and will go to my people. But I know that you
> will rise up and forsake the words established for you through me, and God
> will be angry at you and abandon you and depart from your land. And
> he will bring upon you those who hate you, and they will rule over you, but
> not forever, because he will remember the covenant that he established with
> your fathers (19:2).

If the author intends readers to see in Moses' prediction a foreshadowing of their own time, this technique is similar to Moses' prediction of the exile at the end of Deuteronomy.[2] It is significant that LAB 19:2 does not predict exile but oppression of Israel within its own land by what must be Gentiles. That matches the actual situation of the work's author. Earlier in the work, God tells Moses that Israel will commit the worst offenses against God within the land of Israel (12:4). In 19:7 this is the reason Moses is not permitted to enter the land. All of this may well be a pointed criticism of the author's contemporaries, living in Israel but insufficiently devoted to God and suffering under foreign domination. In general, the author seems to see relations between Jews and Gentiles as problematic. There are few positive figures who are Gentiles. A notable exception is Jael, and Balaam is at least ambivalent. The text's opposition to mixed marriages probably reveals the real author's thought that such unions threatened Israel's identity in his own time.

The author's picture of internal divisions matches what we know from other sources of first-century Israel. The same is true of controversies surrounding leadership both in the text and in first-century Palestine. The issue of how to confront and handle crises raised by foreign hostility or by the people's neglect of Torah was as much a matter of debate in first-century Jewish society as it is in Pseudo-Philo's narrative. Specific details of the author's world cannot be read out of the narrative, but general observations about similar issues do reveal some things about how the author viewed contemporary events.

---

2. See also Jesus' prediction of the difficulties of the early church in passages such as Mark 13.

The *Biblical Antiquities* does not evince a disparaging attitude toward the priesthood. Perrot effectively lays out the issues here.[3] He notes the arguments of James, Cohn, Riessler, Delcor, and Le Déaut concerning an alleged lack of interest in priesthood, temple, and sacrifice, but finds those arguments successfully countered by other scholars such as Spiro, Feldman, Stow, and Jaubert. There are certainly instances in which the priesthood appears in a negative light. Aaron is incapable of stopping the Israelite idolatry at Sinai (chap. 12). Eli's sons sin and his entire line must suffer (chap. 52). The priests of Nob are found culpable of cultic sin (chap. 63). God levels a particularly pointed criticism at the priests in 53:9, saying they defiled the holy things. Nonetheless, the *Biblical Antiquities* is also full of support for priesthood, temple, and sacrifices. Sacrifice punctuates the book and is seen throughout as a legitimate way to thank God. There is a special concern with the cult at Shiloh and for what Perrot calls the unity of the cult over time.[4] The building of Solomon's temple is foretold to Kenaz (26:12–15). The priesthood's establishment by God is the subject of chapter 17. Phinehas is a particularly revered figure and his connection with Eli's line is emphasized, showing the author's concern with cultic continuity. Joshua warns against making sacrifices more important than Torah when the Transjordanian tribes transgress Torah by offering sacrifice in their own territory (22:5), and Balak holds the mistaken view that God can be bribed with sacrifices (18:7–8). Neither of these instances is an attack on cult. Both reflect a proper understanding of it. The author shares the critical attitude toward priestly abuses common in his time, but does not reject priesthood as such or display a lack of interest in cultic matters.

Leadership is a problem in the *Biblical Antiquities*. Good leadership is crucial to Israel's well-being. The narrative presents a variety of leaders, from good ones like Moses and Deborah, to bad ones like Jair, to ambiguous ones like Joktan. Joktan is particularly interesting because he tries to "work within the system." He wants to protect true worshipers of God while appearing to cooperate with idolatrous foreign rulers. The real author may well have known many such leaders in his own time.

The author does not write a narrative in which only one form of leadership is valid. One does not come away with the picture that monarchy is the only viable system, for example. A good leader is one who lets God's will guide him or her in everything. Action alone is not a value. Action that implements God's will is advocated. Once that will is known, the good leader will trust in God to the extent of leaving even his or her own physical safety in God's hands. The narrative shows that the discernment of God's will is not always easy. Centering on Torah is crucial, but that does not always provide specific answers to concrete crises. Pseudo-Philo presents a number of instances when Israelites with good intentions confront a crisis, take what seem to be reasonable steps based on good faith and trust in God, but that are wrong and not supported by God.

---

3. SC 230, 39–43.
4. See the incident of the Transjordanian altar in chapter 22.

Idolatry is a central concern of Pseudo-Philo, seen as a symbol of all disobedience to God. The story of Aod shows that Gentiles' power is associated with idolatry's seduction. Indeed, the Romans claimed that their military and political success was due to their piety, not just to their own gods but to all peoples' gods. Micah's story shows that foreign practices held out hope of handling one's daily needs more effectively. The sinners uncovered by Kenaz show an interest in magic and secret powers combined with skepticism about the divine origin of the Torah and the holiness of the temple. Perrot sees the list of sins in LAB 25 as proof that the author's community is not a closed one but one in close contact with outsiders, and so is tempted by their ways.[5]

Pseudo-Philo's answer to the problem of idolatry is to be expected and has a long tradition in Judaism. First, idolatry is always wrong and angers God. It must be avoided at all costs, even at the cost of one's life. Abraham is an example of this, as are those who resisted Jair's idolatry. Second, idolatry is deceptive. Foreign gods do not have the power they appear to have. Even if there is real power behind Gentile dominance, it is due to fallen angels and will be vanquished in the end.[6] Third, association with Gentiles leaves one open to idolatry. God demands complete loyalty, which cannot coexist with honoring other gods.

Pseudo-Philo writes in an ironic mode. The readers see that humans are typically unaware of God's will and of the proper course of action in any situation. Human plans are repeatedly contrasted unfavorably with divine plans. Even good people can become obstacles to the divine will. The answer for the people is meditation on Torah and submission to proper leaders. The answer for the leaders is to discern carefully between their own human outlook and that of God.

Perhaps the strongest single theme of the *Biblical Antiquities* is its advocacy of moral causality. The author believes firmly that good is rewarded and evil punished in this life and the next. It is an absolute rule that if Israelites suffer and are oppressed, it is their own fault, because those who suffer are by definition guilty. Abraham voices that sentiment clearly and it is repeated throughout the text. The strong insistence on moral causality could be taken as a theodicy, for it absolves God of any blame whatsoever for anything bad that has ever happened to the chosen people. One gets what one deserves. It is as simple as that. Were it not for God's mercy, Israel would perish. God treats them not as their sin deserves but as the promises to the fathers dictate. Seen this way, the continued existence of Israel accounts for the survival of the world in spite of its wickedness. Several times God speaks of humanity in general in strongly negative terms, accounting it as nothing and worthy of annihilation. God also speaks of Israel in similar terms. Abraham's loyalty and the resultant promises to the fathers prevent the world from being obliterated. Although the author holds to moral causality, he can be lenient when people

---

5. SC 230, 153–54.

6. This recalls 1 Cor. 10:14–22, where Paul accords the objects of idolatry power but insists that they are demons and not gods.

are forced to sin. In the golden calf incident, those who were forced to commit idolatry escaped unpunished (12:7). Since the author is so insistent on moral causality, it is likely that he was confronting fellow Jews who read their misfortunes as abandonment by God and not as their own doing. Such an attitude can be seen in the Ezra of the first three sections of 4 Ezra, for example.

One of the most interesting aspects of Pseudo-Philo is the extent to which it incorporates ideas current in Second Temple Judaism and takes them for granted. It is important when comparing Pseudo-Philo's views to those of others not merely to see if an idea is present in the *Biblical Antiquities,* but to ask what role it plays in the narrative. Critics of the synoptic Gospels are accustomed to making such distinctions, but there is still a tendency to be satisfied with noting the simple occurrence of a theme or idea in pseudepigraphal texts. For example, in his eschatology Pseudo-Philo assumes there will be an end to this world, a new earth will come into existence, the good will be rewarded forever and the evil will be punished by fire, hell will yield up those that it holds, and so on. But he assumes that the readers know these things. There is no extensive attention paid to them. They can be introduced to bolster the moral causality that the text spends much more time proving. The same is true of things like the Resurrection and angelology. Pseudo-Philo is not Pharisaic, Sadducean, apocalyptic, Essene, or anything else that we can determine exactly. The existence of the *Biblical Antiquities* shows that more restricted groups took up and emphasized elements taken for granted and used by Pseudo-Philo in a much less intensive way. Pseudo-Philo shows how things like the Resurrection and the end of the world could be incorporated into a worldview more suited to everyday existence, lived under the rule of God and not in the heat of imminent apocalyptic expectation.

A fascinating question about the authorship and social context of the *Biblical Antiquities* is raised by the prominence of women in the work. Van der Horst, at the end of his important article on women in Pseudo-Philo, has the following to say.[7]

> It can never be excluded that *LAB* is the writing of a female author. But even if we do not go that far, we surely have to establish that the portraits of a number of biblical women in *LAB* are of such a nature as to point in direction of an author who was concerned, among other things, to ascribe to women a greater and much more important role in Israel's history than they were accorded in the Bible, *sc.* as great and as important a role as the patriarchs and Moses had played. That he/she did this with an eye on his/her actual situation can hardly be doubted, and this is a point where further research is to be done. For if this author was a man, he was a rare bird in ancient Judaism.

Van der Horst does not see the complete reversal of traditional profiles of men and women in the *Biblical Antiquities* that he finds in the *Testament of Job.*[8] Nonetheless, Pseudo-Philo's rewriting of the role of women in Israel's past is remarkable and significant.

7. "Portraits," 45–46.
8. "Images."

We turn now to a comparison of the views of Pseudo-Philo with the *Zeitgeist* of first-century Judaism as recently depicted by Charlesworth.[9] (We do this to illustrate how important Pseudo-Philo's witness is to a particular outlook that uses elements of other outlooks but does not fully subscribe to their worldviews.) Charlesworth follows von Rad in seeing a major shift in Israel's perception of God's relation to history in the postexilic period.[10]

> History has been depleted soteriologically. Recent and contemporary events, namely the subjection of the sons of Israel to enslavement not to Yahweh but to foreign idolatrous nations, tended to falsify and to disprove the faithful recitation of confessions, recitals of history, and the Deuteronomic optimism in history. The salvation of the nation Israel, now assuredly seen as only a faithful remnant of it, must come from a cataclysmic event from the beyond, anticipated only through divine revelations obtained through apocalyptic trips to the heavens above, the world ahead, or in apocalyptic visions and dreams. The present is devoid of salvific movements; only the eschaton contains meaning, salvation, and the trifold unification of humanity with itself, humans with nature and animals, and created beings with the Creator. These characteristics permeated virtually all the writings of Early Judaism, whether they be apocalypses, testaments, wisdom tracts, or hymns and prayers.

What Charlesworth says can be applied to Pseudo-Philo only with qualification. Pseudo-Philo abounds in "salvific movements" in history. Pseudo-Philo is not directly describing its own times, it is true, but the complex web of forward and backward references that punctuate the text assumes a view of history that sees God as extremely active and in control. There is no indication that the real author sees that control as having come to an end in his own time. The behind-the-scenes view granted to Pseudo-Philo's readers supports this. Nor is the information given to the readers put primarily in the context of esoteric revelations through heavenly trips, visions, or any such means. Bogaert observes that the esoteric revelations to Moses, Kenaz, and others "are neither central nor essential."[11] They play a different role than in works such as *2 Baruch,* 4 Ezra, or the *Testament of Moses.* There is little indication that Israel is seen as but a remnant of the people in the *Biblical Antiquities.* Israel is not divided up as at Qumran or in some of the apocalypses.

Several pages later, Charlesworth mentions Pseudo-Philo in particular. He cites the lament of Jephthah's daughter Seila (chap. 40) as an example of a prayer with a "stinging ring of alienation" about it, suggesting that the Jews of this period were alienated from this world and longed for the next. He says, "In short the early Jew almost always thought in terms of eschatology."[12] But the lament of Seila, far from giving voice to alienation from this world, bemoans the fact that Seila must leave it. It is a longing not for the next world

---

9. *Prolegomena.* This work shows how the study of the Pseudepigrapha can aid in the study of the New Testament and earliest Christianity. See my review in *JBL* 107 (1988): 339–42.

10. *Prolegomena,* 64.

11. Feldman, "Prolegomenon," lv. See 19:10–13; 28:6–10.

12. *Prolegomena,* 67.

but for this one. So far as Seila is concerned, nothing is wrong with this world that a bit more prudence on the part of her father could not have amended.

The demonology described by Charlesworth as characteristic of Early Judaism is not prominent in Pseudo-Philo. "The Accuser" to whom God speaks in 45:6 is presumably Satan, but he is apparently still a member of the heavenly court and not prince of demons.[13] The reference to Saul's evil spirit comes straight from the biblical text. In chapter 25, the sinners from Issachar inquire of the demons of the idols but are not seduced by them or under their control. The following statements of Charlesworth are questionable for Pseudo-Philo: "The earth is full of *demons*. Humanity is plagued by them. Almost all misfortunes are because of the demons: sickness, drought, death, and especially humanity's weaknesses about remaining faithful to the covenant."[14] For Pseudo-Philo, humanity is responsible for its own misfortunes. To be informed about them they need only open the Torah.

Eschatology does play a role in the *Biblical Antiquities*. Feldman calls it an area of particular interest to the work,[15] but eschatology is not its focus. There is little interest in the future world for its own sake or in the events that inaugurate it.[16] The eschaton shows that rewards and punishments are just and inevitable. Alienation from this world and longing for the next is not really the effect of the eschatological sections. Eschatology underlines God's justice and encourages the people to obey the divine commands. Moses tells the people, "God has revealed the end of the world so that he might establish his statutes with you and kindle among you an eternal light" (19:4).

These observations about the *Biblical Antiquities* do not invalidate Charlesworth's synthesis. They might possibly support it indirectly, in that Pseudo-Philo could be opposing or at least qualifying parts of the worldview described by Charlesworth. Whether or not the reconstruction is indeed present in all texts of the time, the ideas were widespread. But although the reconstruction of a *Zeitgeist* is useful, each text must be examined in its own right to see to what degree it embodies the given worldview.

The *Biblical Antiquities* of Pseudo-Philo is a creative work that meant to reflect and influence its own day. It is the product of an author with strong faith in God's faithfulness to Israel, even though he sees Israel oppressed by foreigners without and doubt and misunderstanding within. The author finds hope in God's past actions, although some of his contemporaries do not believe in them. The work holds out the hope of good leadership and supplies general guidelines for it, but does not shrink from criticizing Israel's leaders,

13. See our comments on 45:6.

14. *Prolegomena*, 66.

15. "Prolegomenon," xlviii.

16. Although Pseudo-Philo believes in a new heaven and earth, there is no sense of urgency in this belief. In chapter 19, Moses receives a revelation concerning how much time the world has left. He is told, "Four and a half have passed, and two and a half remain" (19:15). If those numbers refer to millennia, then there are still twenty-five hundred years until the eschaton. Of course, the author's time is substantially after that of Moses, but one cannot build an imminent expectation on this verse.

priests and laymen alike. The book holds to the conviction of moral causality, but it also highlights God's mercy without denying God's anger. Pseudo-Philo's outlook is captured by Zebul's last words to Israel: "Look to the testimonies that our predecessors have left as witnesses, and do not let your heart be like the waves of the sea. But just as a wave of the sea understands nothing except what is in the sea, so let your heart ponder nothing else except what belongs to the Law" (29:4).

Bibliography

Abbreviations

SBLDS   Society of Biblical Literature Dissertation Series

SNTSMS   Society for New Testament Studies Monograph Series

BZAW   Beihefte zur Zeitschrift für die neutestamentliche Wissenschaft

WMANT   Wissenschaftliche Monographien zum Alten und Neuen Testament

RSR   *Recherches de science religieuse*

Alexander, P. S. "Retelling the Old Testament." In *It is Written: Scripture Citing Scripture,* 99–121. Cambridge: Cambridge University Press, 1988.

Alexiou, Margaret, and Peter Dronke. "The Lament of Jephta's Daughter: Themes, Traditions, Originality." *Studi Medievali, 3d Ser.,* 12 (1971): 819–63.

Alter, Robert. *The Art of Biblical Narrative.* New York: Basic, 1981.

Alter, Robert, and Frank Kermode, editors. *The Literary Guide to the Bible.* Cambridge, MA: Harvard, 1987.

Anderson, Bernhard. *Understanding the Old Testament.* 4th ed. by Englewood Cliffs, N.J.: Prentice-Hall, 1986.

Barnet, Sylvan, Morton Berman, and William Burto. *A Dictionary of Literary, Dramatic, and Cinematic Terms.* Boston: Little, Brown, 1971.

Bauckham, Richard. "The Liber Antiquitatum Biblicarum of Pseudo-Philo and the Gospels as 'Midrash.'" In *Gospel Perspectives III: Studies in Midrash and Historiography,* edited by R. T. France and D. Wenham, 33–76. Sheffield: JSOT Press, 1983.

Beardslee, William A. "Recent Literary Criticism." In *The New Testament and Its Modern Interpreters,* edited by Eldon Jay Epp and George W. MacRae, S.J., 175–98. Philadelphia: Fortress, 1989.

Berger, Klaus. *Die Gesetzesauslegung Jesu: Ihr historischer Hintergrund im Judentum und im Alten Testament.* Neukirchen: Neukirchener Verlag, 1972.

Bissoli, G. "La morte di Mosè nel *Liber Antiquitatum Biblicarum.*" *SBFLA* 34 (1984): 273–82.

Bloch, René. "Midrash." In *Approaches to Ancient Judaism: Theory and Practice,* edited by William S. Green. Vol. 1, *Brown Judaic Studies,* 29–50. Missoula, Mont.: Scholars, 1978.

———. "Note méthodologique pour l'étude de la littérature rabbinique." *RSR* 43 (1955): 194–227.

Bogaert, Pierre-Maurice. "Les *Antiquités Bibliques* du Pseudo-Philo à la lumière des découvertes de Qumrân. Observations sur l'hymnologie et particulièrement sur le chapitre 60." In *Qumrân: Sa Piété, Sa Théologie et Son Milieu,* edited by M. Delcor, 313–31. Paris: Duculot, 1978.

———. "La figure d'Abraham dans les Antiquités Bibliques du Pseudo-Philon." In *Abraham dans la Bible et dans la Tradition Juive,* edited by P.-M. Bogaert, 40–55. Brussels: Institutum Iudaicum, 1977.

———. "Les Antiquités Bibliques du Pseudo-Philon. Quelques observations sur les chapitres 39 et 40 à l'occasion d'une réimpression." *RTL* 3 (1972): 334–44.

Booth, Wayne C. *The Rhetoric of Fiction.* Chicago: University of Chicago, 1967 [1961].

Brown, Cheryl Anne. *No Longer Be Silent: First Century Jewish Portraits of Biblical Women.* Louisville: Westminster/John Knox, 1992.

Callaway, Mary. *Sing, O Barren One: A Study in Comparative Midrash.* SBLDS 91. Atlanta: Scholars, 1986.

Charlesworth, James H. *Jesus Within Judaism: New Light from Exciting Archeological Discoveries.* New York: Doubleday, 1988.

———.Charlesworth, James H., ed. *The Old Testament Pseudepigrapha.* Garden City, N.Y.: Doubleday, 1983–85.

———. *The Old Testament Pseudepigrapha and the New Testament: Prolegomena for the Study of Christian Origins.* Cambridge: Cambridge University Press, 1985.

Chatman, Seymour. *Story and Discourse: Narrative Structure in Function and Film.* Ithaca: Cornell University Press, 1978.

Clifford, Richard J., and Roland E. Murphy. "Genesis." In *The New Jerome Biblical Commentary,* edited by Raymond E. Brown, S.S., Joseph A. Fitzmyer, S.J., and Roland E. Murphy, O.Carm., 8–43. Englewood Cliffs, N.J.: Prentice-Hall, 1990.

Cohn, Leopold. "An Apocryphal Work Ascribed to Philo of Alexandria." *JQR, Old Ser.,* 10 (1898): 277–332.

———. "Pseudo-Philo und Jerachmeel." In *Festschrift zum Siebsigstage Geburststage Jakob Guttmanns,* 173–85. Leipzig: Gustav Fock, 1915.

Collins, John J. "The Testamentary Literature." In *EJMI,* 268–85.

Cross, Frank Moore. "The Contribution of the Qumran Discoveries to the Study of the Biblical Text." *IEJ* 16 (1966): 81–95.

———. "The History of the Biblical Text in the Light of Discoveries in the Judaean Desert." *HTR* 57 (1964): 281–99.

Culley, Robert C. "Exploring New Directions." In *HBMI,* 167–200.

Culpepper, R. Alan. *Anatomy of the Fourth Gospel: A Study in Literary Design.* Philadelphia: Fortress, 1983.

Daly, Robert. "The Soteriological Significance of the Sacrifice of Isaac." *CBQ* 39 (1977): 45–75.

Davies, Philip R., and Bruce D. Chilton. "The Aqedah: A Revised Tradition History." *CBQ* 40 (1978): 514–46.

de la Fuente Adánez, Alfonso. "Antigüedades Biblicas (Pseudo-Filon)." In *Apocrifos del Antiguo Testamento,* 4 vol., edited by A. Diez Macho et al., vol. 2, 195–316. Madrid: Ediciones Cristianidad, 1983.

Delcor, M. "Philon (Pseudo-)." In *DBSup,* vol. 7, 1354–75.

Delling, Gerhard. "Von Morija zum Sinai. Pseudo-Philo Liber Antiquitatum Biblicarum 32,1–10." *JSJ* 2 (1971): 1–18.

———. "Die Weise von der Zeit zu reden im Liber Antiquitatum Biblicarum." *NovT* 13 (1971): 305–21.

Dietzfelbinger, Christian. "Pseudo-Philo: Antiquitates Biblicae (Liber Antiquitatum Biblicarum)." In *Jüdische Schriften aus hellenistisch-römischer Zeit.* Vol. 2, *Unterweisung in erzählender Form,* edited by W. G. Kümmel. Gütersloh: Mohn, 1975.

———. *Pseudo-Philo, Liber Antiquitatum Biblicarum.* Ph.D. diss., Göttingen, 1964.

Dimant, Devorah. "Use and Interpretation of Mikra in the Apocrypha and Pseudepigrapha." In *Mikra: Text, Translation, Reading, and Interpretation of the Hebrew Bible in Ancient Judaism and Early Christianity,* edited by Martin Jan Mulder, 379–419. Minneapolis: Fortress, 1988.

Doran, Robert. "The Martyr: A Synoptic View of the Mother and Her Seven Sons." In *IFAJ,* 189–221.

Eissfeldt, Otto. "Zur Kompositionstechnik des Pseudo-Philonischen Liber Antiquitatum Biblicarum." In *Kleine Schriften,* vol. 3, 340–53. Berlin: Mohr, 1966.

Feldman, Louis. "Josephus' Portrait of Deborah." In *Hellenica et Judaica: Hommage à Valentin Nikiprowetzky,* edited by M. Hadas-Lebel A. Caquot and J. Riaud, 115–28. Paris: Peeters, 1986.

Feldman, Louis H. "Epilegomenon to Pseudo-Philo's *Liber Antiquitatum Biblicarum* (LAB)." *JJS* 25 (1974): 305–312.

———. "Josephus as a Biblical Interpreter: The 'Aqedah." *JQR* 75 (1985): 212–52.

———. "Prolegomenon." In *The Biblical Antiquities of Philo,* edited by M. R. James, vii–clxix. New York: Ktav, 1971.

Ferch, Arthur J. "The Two Aeons and the Messiah in Pseudo-Philo, 4 Ezra, and 2 Baruch." *AUSS* 15 (1977): 135–51.

Fishbane, Michael. *Biblical Interpretation in Ancient Israel.* Oxford: Clarendon, 1985.

Frei, Hans. *The Eclipse of Biblical Narrative: A Study in Eighteenth and Nineteenth Century Hermeneutics.* New Haven: Yale, 1974.

Fröhlich, I. "Historiographie et aggada dans le Liber Antiquitatum Biblicarum du Pseudo-Philon." *Acta Antiqua Academiae Scientiarum Hungaricae* 28 (1980): 353–409.

———. "Le manuscrit latin de Budapest d'une oeuvre historique hellénistique." *Acta Antiqua Academiae Scientiarum Hungaricae* 27 (1979): 149–86.

Frye, Northrop. *Anatomy of Criticism: Four Essays.* Princeton: Princeton University Press, 1971.

Gaster, M. *The Chronicles of Jerahmeel.* New York: Ktav, 1971.

Genette, Gérard. *Narrative Discourse: An Essay in Method.* Ithaca: Cornell University Press, 1980.

Ginzberg, Louis. *The Legends of the Jews.* 7 vols. Philadelphia: Jewish Publication Society, 1938.

Gottwald, Norman. *The Hebrew Bible: A Socio-literary Introduction.* Minneapolis: Fortress, 1985.

Groves, Joseph W. *Actualization and Interpretation in the Old Testament.* SBLDS 86. Atlanta: Scholars, 1987.

Gry, L. "La date de la fin des temps, selon les révélations et les calculs du Pseudo-Philon et de Baruch." *RB* 48 (1939): 337–56.

Hadot, Jean. "Livre des Antiquités Bibliques." In *La Bible: Ecrits Intertestamentaires,* edited by A. Dupont-Sommer and M. Philonenko, 1225–392. Paris: Gallimard, 1987.

———. "Le milieu d'origine du 'Liber Antiquitatum Biblicarum.'" In *La littérature intertestamentaire. Colloque de Strasbourg (17–19 Octobre 1983),* edited by A. Caquot et. al., 153–71. Paris: Presses universitaires de France, 1985.

Hanson, Paul. "Rebellion in Heaven, Azazel and Euhemeristic Heroes in 1 Enoch 6–11." *JBL* 96 (1977): 195–233.

Hardison, O. B., Jr. "A Commentary on Aristotle's Poetics." In *Aristotle's Poetics.* Englewood Cliffs, N.J.: Prentice-Hall, 1968.

Harrington, Daniel J. "Biblical Geography in Pseudo-Philo's *Liber Antiquitatum Biblicarum.*" *BASOR* 220 (1975): 67–71.

———. "The Biblical Text of Pseudo-Philo's Liber Antiquitatum Biblicarum." *CBQ* 33 (1971): 1–17.

———. "Birth Narratives in Pseudo-Philo's *Biblical Antiquities* and the Gospels." In *Festschrift Joseph A. Fitzmyer,* edited by M. P. Horgan and P. Kobelski. New York: Crossroad, 1988.

———. *The Hebrew Fragments of Pseudo-Philo's Liber Antiquitatum Biblicarum preserved in the Chronicles of Jerahmeel.* Texts and translations, Pseudepigrapha ser. 3. Cambridge, MA: Society of Biblical Literature, 1974.

———. "The Original Language of Pseudo-Philo's Liber Antiquitatum Biblicarum." *HTR* 63 (1970): 503–14.

———. "Palestinian Adaptations of Biblical Narratives and Prophecies. I. The Bible Rewritten." In *EJMI,* 239–58.

———. "Pseudo-Philo, *Liber Antiquitatum Biblicarum.*" In *Outside the Old Testament,* edited by M. de Jonge, 6–25. Cambridge: Cambridge University Press, 1985.

———. "Pseudo-Philo." In *OTP,* 297–377.

———. *Text and Biblical Text in Pseudo-Philo's Liber Antiquitatum Biblicarum.* Cambridge: Harvard University Press, 1969.

———. "The Text-critical Situation of Pseudo-Philo's Liber Antiquitatum Biblicarum." *RBén* 83 (1973): 383–88.

Harrington, Daniel J., and Jacques Cazeaux. *Pseudo-Philon: Les Antiquités Bibliques. Vol. 1, Introduction et Texte Critiques.* SC 229. Paris: Cerf, 1976.

Hayward, Robert. "Phinehas—The Same Is Elijah." *JJS* 29 (1978): 22–34.

Heinemann, J. "210 Years of Egyptian Exile." *JSJ* 22 (1971): 19–30.

Jackson, B. S. "Liability for Mere Intention in Early Jewish Law." *HUCA* 42 (1971): 196–225.

Jacobson, Howard. "Biblical Quotation and Editorial Function in Pseudo-Philo's *Liber Antiquitatum Biblicarum.*" *JSP* 5 (1989): 47–64.

———. "Marginalia to Pseudo-Philo *Liber Antiquitatum Biblicarum* and to the *Chronicles of Jerahmeel.*" *REJ* 142 (1983): 455–59.

———. "The 'Son of Man' in Ps.-Philo's *Liber Antiquitatum Biblicarum.*" *JTS* 34 (1983): 531–33.

James, M. R. *The Biblical Antiquities of Philo.* New York: Ktav, 1971.

———. "Notes on Apocrypha (Pseudo-Philo and Baruch)." *JTS* 16 (1915): 403–5.

———. "Transmission of an Old Text (Pseudo-Philo *Liber Antiquitatum Biblicarum*)." *Proc. Cambridge Phil. Soc.* 100–102 (1915): 9–10.

Jaubert, A. *La notion d'alliance dans le judaïsme aux abords de l'ère chrétienne.* Patristica Sorbonensia 6. Paris: Seuil, 1963.

Johnson, Marshall D. *The Purpose of the Biblical Genealogies: With Special Reference to the Setting of the Genealogies of Jesus.* SNTSMS 8. Cambridge: Cambridge University Press, 1969.

Kingsbury, Jack Dean. *Matthew as Story.* Philadelphia: Fortress, 1988 [1986].

Kisch, Guido. "The Editio Princeps of Pseudo-Philo's *Liber Antiquitatum Biblicarum.*" In *Alexander Marx: Jubilee Volume on the Occasion of His Seventieth Birthday,* edited by S. Lieberman, 425–46. New York: Jewish Theological Seminary, 1949.

———. "A Note on the New Edition of Pseudo-Philo's Biblical Antiquities." *Historia Judaica* 12 (1950): 153–58.

———. *Pseudo-Philo's Liber Antiquitatum Biblicarum.* Notre Dame, Ind.: University of Notre Dame, 1949.

———. "Pseudo-Philo's Liber Antiquitatum Biblicarum, Postlegomena to the New Edition." *HUCA* 23, pt. 2 (1950–51): 81–93.

Klausner, Joseph. *The Messianic Idea in Israel: From Its Beginning to the Completion of the Mishnah.* New York: Macmillan, 1955.

Knibb, Michael. "The Exile in the Intertestamental Period." *HeyJ* 17 (1976): 253–72.

Knierim, Rolf. "Criticism of Literary Features, Form, Tradition, and Redaction." In *HBMI,* 123–65.

Kolenkow, Anitra Bingham. "The Literary Genre 'testament.'" In *EJMI,* 259–67.

Kort, Wesley A. *Story, Text, and Scripture: Literary Interests in Biblical Narrative.* University Park, Pa.: University of Pennsylvania, 1988.

Le Déaut, R. "Miryam, soeur de Moïse et Marie, mère Du Messie." *Bib* 45 (1964): 198–219.

———. *La Nuit Pascale.* Rome: Pontifical Biblical Institute, 1963.

Leiman, Sid Z. *The Canonization of Hebrew Scripture: The Talmudic and Midrashic Evidence.* Trans. Conn. Acad. Arts Sc. 47. Hamden, Conn.: Archon, 1976.

Lewis, Jack P. *A Study of the Interpretation of Noah and the Flood in Jewish and Christian Literature.* Leiden: Brill, 1968.

Macdonald, John. *Memar Marqah: The Teachings of Marqah.* BZAW 84. Berlin: A. Töpelmann, 1963.

McKnight, Edgar V. *What Is Form Criticism?* Philadelphia: Fortress, 1969.

Moore, Stephen D. *Literary Criticism and the Gospels: The Theoretical Challenge.* New Haven: Yale, 1989.

Muñoz Iglesias, Salvador. "El Procedimiento Literario del Anuncio Previo en la Biblia." *EstBib* 42 (1984): 21–70.

Murphy, Frederick J. "Divine Plan, Human Plan: A Structuring Theme in Pseudo-Philo." *JQR* 77 (1986): 5–14.

———. "The Eternal Covenant in Pseudo-Philo." *JSP* 3 (1988): 43–57.

———. "The Exodus in Pseudo-Philo." Paper delivered to the task force on "The Theology of the Hebrew Bible/Old Testament," Catholic Biblical Association annual meeting, Washington, DC, August 1992.

———. "God in Pseudo-Philo." *JSJ* 19 (1988): 1–18.

———. "Korah's Rebellion in Pseudo-Philo 16." In *Of Scribes and Scrolls: Studies on the Hebrew Bible, Intertestamental Judaism, and Christian Origins,* edited by Harold W. Attridge, John J. Collins, and Thomas H. Tobin, S.J., 111–20. New York: University Press of America, 1990.

———. *The Religious World of Jesis: An Introduction to Second Temple Palestinian Judaism.* Nashville: Abingdon Press, 1991.

————. "Retelling the Bible: Idolatry in Pseudo-Philo." *JBL* 107 (1988): 275–87.

————. *The Structure and Meaning of Second Baruch.* SBLDS 78. Atlanta: Scholars, 1985.

————. "The Temple in the Syriac *Apocalypse of Baruch. JBL* 106 (1987): 671–683.

Neusner, Jacob, William S. Green, and Ernest Frerichs, eds. *Judaisms and Their Messiahs at the Turn of the Christian Era.* Cambridge: Cambridge University Press, 1987.

Nickelsburg, George W. E. "The Book of Biblical Antiquities." In Michael Stone, *Jewish Writings.*

————. "Good and Bad Leaders in Pseudo-Philo's *Liber Antiquitatum Biblicarum.*" In *IFAJ,* 49–65.

————. *Jewish Literature between the Bible and the Mishnah: A Historical and Literary Introduction.* Philadelphia: Fortress Press, 1981.

Olyan, Saul. "The Israelites Debate Their Options at the Sea of Reeds: *LAB* 10:3, Its Parallels, and Pseudo-Philo's Ideology and Background." *JBL* 110 (1991): 75–91.

Perrin, Norman. *What is Redaction Criticism?* Philadelphia: Fortress, 1969.

Perrot, Charles, and Bogaert Pierre-Maurice. *Pseudo-Philon: Les Antiquités Bibliques.* Vol. 2, *Introduction Littéraire, Commentaire et Index.* SC 230. Paris: Cerf, 1976.

————. "Les Récits d'enfance dans la haggada antérieure au IIe siècle de notre ère." *RSR* 55 (1967): 481–518.

Peterson, Norman. *Literary Criticism for New Testament Critics.* Philadelphia: Fortress, 1978.

Philonenko, Marc. "Essénisme et gnose chez le Pseudo-Philon. Le symbolisme de la lumière dans le Liber Antiquitatum Biblicarum." *Numen Sup.* 12 (1967): 401–12.

————. "Iphigénie et Sheila." In *Les Syncrétismes dans les religions grecque et romaine,* 165–77. Paris: Presses universitaires de France, 1973.

————. "Une paraphrase du cantique D'Anne." *RHPR* 42 (1962): 157–68.

————. "Remarques sur un hymne essénien de caractère gnostique." *Semeia* 11 (1961): 43–54.

Porton, Gary. "Defining Midrash." In *The Study of Ancient Judaism I,* edited by Jacob Neusner, 55–92. New York: Ktav, 1981.

Reinmuth, E. "Ps.-Philo, *Liber Antiquitatum Biblicarum* 33.1–5 und die Auslegung der Parabel Lk. 16.19–31." *NovT* 31 (1989): 16–38.

Rhoads, David, and Donald Michie. *Mark as Story: An Introduction to the Narrative of a Gospel.* Philadephia: Fortress, 1982.

Riessler, Paul. "Philo: Das Buch der Biblischen Altertümer." In *Altjüdisches Schrifttum Ausserhalb der Bibel,* 735–861. Darmstadt: Wissenschaftliche Buchgesellschaft, 1928/1966.

Rohde, Joachim. *Rediscovering the Teaching of the Evangelists.* Philadelphia: Westminster, 1968.

Saldarini, Anthony J. "Reconstructions of Rabbinic Judaism." In *EJMI,* 437–77.

————. *Pharisees, Scribes and Pharisees in Palestinian Society.* Wilmington: Michael Glazier, 1988.

Sanders, E. P. "The Covenant as a Soteriological Category and the Nature of Salvation in Palestinian and Hellenistic Judaism." In *Jews, Greeks, and Christians: Studies in Honor of W. D. Davies,* edited by R. Hamerton-Kelly and R. Scroggs, 11–44. Leiden: Brill, 1976.

————. *Jesus and Judaism.* Philadelphia: Fortress, 1985.

———. *Paul and Palestinian Judaism.* Philadelphia: Fortress, 1977.

Sanders, James A. *From Sacred Story to Sacred Text.* Philadelphia: Fortress, 1987.

Schaller, B. "Zur Überlieferungsgeschichte des Ps.-philonischen *Liber Antiquitatum Biblicarum* im Mittelalter." *JSJ* 10 (1979): 64–73.

Scheiber, A. "Lacrimatoria and the Jewish Sources." *IEJ* 25 (1975): 152–53.

Scholes, Robert, and Robert Kellogg. *The Nature of Narrative.* New York: Oxford University Press, 1966.

Smelik, K. A. D. "The Witch of Endor. 1 Samuel 28 in Rabbinic and Christian Exegesis Till 800 AD." *VC* 33 (1979): 160–79.

Sparks, H. F. D., ed. *The Apocryphal Old Testament.* Oxford: Clarendon, 1984.

Spiro, Abram. "The Ascension of Phinehas." *PAAJR* 22 (1953): 91–114.

———. *Manners of Rewriting Biblical History from Chronicles to Pseudo-Philo,* 173–248. Ph.D. diss., Columbia University, 1953.

———. "Pseudo-Philo's Saul and the Rabbis' Messiah Ben Ephraim." *PAAJR* 21 (1952): 199–237.

———. "Samaritans, Tobiads, and Judahites in Pseudo-Philo; Use and Abuse of the Bible by Polemicists and Doctrinaires." *PAAJR* 20 (1951): 279–355.

Steck, Odil H. *Israel und das Gewaltsame Geschick der Propheten.* WMANT 23. Neukirchen-Vluyn: Neukirchener Verlag, 1967.

Sternberg, Meir. *The Poetics of Biblical Narrative: Ideological Literature and the Drama of Reading.* Bloomington: Indiana University Press, 1985.

Stone, Michael. *Fourth Ezra: A Commentary on the Book of Fourth Ezra.* Minneapolis: Scholars, 1990.

———, ed. *Jewish Writings of the Second Temple Period: Apocrypha, Pseudepigrapha, Qumran Sectarian Writings, Philo, Josephus.* Philadelphia: Fortress Press, 1984.

———. "Lists of Revealed Things in the Apocalyptic Literature." In *Magnalia Dei: The Mighty Acts of God,* edited by F. M. Cross, W. E. Lemke, and P. D. Miller, 414–51. Garden City, NY: Doubleday, 1976.

Stow, Kenneth. *Pseudo-Philo, an Essene Work.* Ph.D. diss., Columbia University, 1968.

Strobel, A. "Eine Katechon-Parallele in Pseudo-Philo? Zur Interpretation von Cp. 51,5." In *Untersuchungen zum Eschatologischen Verzögerungsproblem auf Grund der Spätjüdischurchristlichen Geschichte von Habakuk 2.2 Ff.,* 74–77. Leiden: Brill, 1961.

Strugnell, John. "More Psalms of David." *CBQ* 27 (1965): 207–16.

———. "Philo (Pseudo-) or Liber Antiquitatum Biblicarum." In *EncJud,* vol. 13, 408–9.

Tannehill, Robert. "The Disciples in Mark: The Function of a Narrative Role." *JR* 57 (1977): 386–405.

———. "The Gospel of Mark as Narrative Christology." *Semeia* 16 (1979): 57–92.

Tannehill, Robert C. *The Narrative Unity of Luke-Acts: A Literary Interpretation.* Philadelphia: Fortress, 1986.

van der Horst, Pieter Willem. "Images of Women in the Testament of Job." In *Studies in the Testament of Job,* edited by M. A. Knibb and P. W. van der Horst, 93–116. Cambridge: Cambridge University Press, 1989.

———. "Portraits of Biblical Women in Pseudo-Philo's *Liber Antiquitatum Biblicarum.*" *JSP* 5 (1989): 29–46.

———. "'Seven Months' Children in Jewish and Christian Literature from Antiquity." *ETL* 54 (1978): 346–60.

Vermes, Geza. *Post-biblical Jewish Studies.* Vol. 8, *Studies in Judaism in Late Antiquity,* edited by Jacob Neusner. Leiden: Brill, 1975.

———. *Scripture and Tradition in Judaism: Haggadic Studies.* Leiden: Brill, 1973.

———. "The Torah Is a Light." *VT* 8 (1958): 436–38.

von Rad, Gerhard. *Old Testament Theology.* 2 vols. Trans. D.M.G. Stalker, New York: Harper and Row, 1962–65.

Wadsworth, Michael. "The Death of Moses and the Riddle of the End of Time in Pseudo-Philo." *JJS* 28 (1977): 12–19.

———. "Making and Interpreting Scripture." In *Ways of Reading the Bible,* edited by M. Wadsworth, 7–22. Sussex: Harvester, 1981.

———. "A New Pseudo-Philo." *JJS* 29 (1978): 186–91.

Winter, Paul. "Jewish Folklore in the Matthaean Birth Story." *Hibbert J.* (1954–55): 34–42.

———. "Philo, Biblical Antiquities of." In *IDB,* vol. 3, 795–96.

———. "The Proto-source of Luke I." *NovT* 1 (1956): 184–99.

Zeron, Alexander. "Einige Bemerkungen zu M. F. Collins, *The Hidden Vessels in Samaritan Traditions.*" *JSJ* 4 (1973): 165–69.

———. "The Martyrdom of Phineas-Elijah." *JBL* 98 (1979): 99–100.

———. "Erwägungen zu Pseudo-Philos Quellen und Zeit." *JSJ* 11 (1980): 38–52.

Concordance of Proper Names

This concordance lists names according to their spelling in Harrington's English translation, which uses usual biblical forms where they can be recognized. When the Latin spelling is different, it is listed in parentheses. Spelling is not always consistent throughout the Latin text. There are also times when several names seem to have been run together in the Latin. For example, *Deglabal* in 4:10 seems originally to have been *Diklah* and *Obal*. There seem to be other corruptions in the Latin. By comparison with the biblical text, Harrington has in several cases reconstructed the probable original names. I follow him in all these instances.

Multiple occurrences of a name in a section are not noted. Therefore, this concordance will not give the absolute number of occurrences of a specific name. Verse ranges indicate that the name appears in every verse in the range. For example, 1:1–5 means that the name is in 1:1, 2, 3, 4, and 5.

Aaron, 9:9; 12:2, 3; 17:2; 20:8; 22:9; 51:6; 52:2; 53:9; 61:5
Abac, 47:11
Abarim, 19:8
Abdon, 41:1
Abel, 1:1; 2:1; 59:4
Abiathar, 63:2
Abidan, 27:4
Abiel, 4:12
Abiesdrel, 38:1
Abimahel, 6:3
Abimelech, 37:2, 4, 5; 63:2
Abino, 32:1
Abiuth, 4:2

Abocmefec, 8:14
Abraham, 8:3; 9:3; 18:5; 23:4, 5; 25:9; 32:1, 2; 61:5
Abram, 4:15; 6:3, 11–13, 15–18; 7:4; 8:1–3
Accur, 4:12
Achan (Achiar, Achiras), 21:3; 25:7
Achaun, 1:17
Aculon, 4:10
Ada, 1:12
Adah (Ada), 2:6, 7, 10; 8:5
Adam, 1:1, 2; 26:6
Admah (Adama), 4:8
Aela, 4:2
Aendain, 4:6

279

Agag, 58:2–4; 65:4
Almodad (Elimodan), 4:10
Aluma, 1:19
Amalek (Amalech), 8:5; 58:1–3
Amalekite (Amalechitus), 45:3; 65:4
Amathin, 4:6
Amboradat, 4:2
Amibel, 47:11
Ammiel, 4:2
Ammon, 39:1, 6–10; 40:1; 41:1
Amorite (Amorreus), 18:1, 2; 20:2, 9; 21:3;
   24:1; 25:9, 10, 12; 26:4; 27:1, 6–11; 30:1;
   39:9
Amram, 9:3, 7, 9, 12, 14
Amuga, 1:19
Ana, 1:10
Anac, 1:14; 4:2
Anael, 27:4
Anaf, 27:4
Anah (Anan), 8:5
Anath, 1:3
Anaz, 1:17
Anazim, 27:4
Anuel, 47:11
Aod, 34:1
Araf, 47:11
Arafaz, 47:11
Aram, 4:9; 5:6
Arebica, 1:4
Armodat, 6:3
Arpachshad (Arfaxa), 4:9; 5:6
Arteman, 4:10
Asaph, 51:6
Asapli, 4:2
Ashbel (Esbel), 8:14
Ashdod (Azotum), 29:2; 43:2
Asher (Aser), 8:6; 10:3; 25:4, 10; 26:11
Ashkelon (Calon), 4:8
Ashkenaz (Cenez), 4:2
Asin, 1:4
Asshur (Assur), 4:9; 5:6; 38:1
Athac, 1:10
Aufin, 6:3
Auz, 8:5
Azat, 27:4

Baal, 36:4; 38:1–4
Babylon (Babilon), 6:1
Balaam, 18:2–4, 7–9, 13, 14
Balac, 47:11
Balak (Balac), 18:2, 3, 7, 8, 10–12, 14
Balinoc, 47:11
Ballana, 4:2
Bama, 56:4
Barak (Barach), 31:1, 2, 7, 9; 32:1

Basemath (Bassemeth), 8:5
Batuel, 15:3; 51:6
Beath, 4:2; 27:4
Beel, 45:2, 4
Beeri (Bereu), 8:5
Bela (Gela), 8:14
Belloch, 47:11
Belon, 47:11
Benin, 47:11
Benjamin (Beniamin), 8:6, 14; 10:3; 25:4, 13;
   26:11; 44:8; 46:2–4; 47:8–11; 48:3
Beor, 18:2
Beosomaza, 4:8
Berechap, 4:14
Beri, 15:3
Besac, 27:4
Besto, 4:4
Betaal, 8:12
Bethac, 45:2, 3; 52:1
Bethel, 59:2
Bethuel (Patuel), 8:4
Betul, 27:4
Bilhah (Bala), 8:6, 12
Boac, 27:4
Bosara, 4:2
Bosorra, 4:4
Brabal, 1:3
Bruna, 4:14

Cades, 45:4
Cain, 1:1; 2:1–4, 10; 16:2
Caleb (Caleph, Chaleb), 15:3; 20:6, 10; 25:2
Camoel, 4:14
Canaan, 4:6; 5:5; 8:1, 2, 7, 9, 10; 23:5; 25:11
Canaanites (Cananitides), 8:11
Cappadocian (Cappadox), 4:7
Carmi (Carmin), 8:11
Caruba, 4:4
Casluhim (Ceslun), 4:7
Catennath, 1:8
Cechar, 1:12
Cedema, 4:12
Ceel, 4:4
Cehec, 27:4
Celeth, 2:3
Cene, 4:14
Cenen, 15:3
Cere, 27:4
Cesse, 4:2
Chaldean (Chaldeus), 6:18
Chemosh (Chamos), 18:12
Ciram, 2:5
Citha, 2:4
Code, 47:11
Cush (Chus), 4:6, 7

Cusin, 4:6

Cuut, 2:5

Dabircamo, 4:8

Dabra, 15:3

Dagon, 55:3

Dan, 8:6, 12; 10:3; 25:9; 26:11; 42:1

Danaben, 48:1

David, 59:3–5; 60:1, 3; 61:1, 3–9; 62:1–3, 9, 11; 63:2, 5; 64:2, 3; 65:5

Dealma, 27:4

Debac, 47:11

Deberleth, 4:2

Deborah (Debbora), 30:5; 31:1, 2; 32:1, 14, 15, 18; 33:4–6; 38:2

Dedasal, 4:12

Dediap, 4:14

Dedila, 44:2

Defad, 4:2

Defal, 38:1

Deffaf (Deffap), 27:4

Degal, 4:4

Deli, 6:18

Delilah (Dalila), 43:5

Dema, 42:1

Demech, 47:11

Derisa, 4:12

Desac, 27:4

Desuath, 25:11

Diasat, 8:8

Dica, 4:13

Diffar, 8:8

Diklah (Deglabal; *see* Obal), 4:10

Dinah (Dina), 8:6, 7, 11

Doad, 4:2

Dodanim (Doin), 5:4

Dodanim (Dudeni), 4:3

Doeg (Dohec), 63:2, 4

Doel, 29:2

Doffo, 47:11

Duodenin (Iesca), 2:3; 4:4

Duzal, 27:4

Ebal (Gebal), 21:7

Eber (Heber), 4:9

Ecar, 27:4

Ecent, 27:4

Edabus, 65:4

Edoc, 42:1

Efal, 27:4

Effor, 27:4

Effrata, 41:1

Egypt (Egiptum), 8:9–11, 14; 9:1, 3, 11, 12; 11:1, 6; 12:1; 13:4; 14:1, 4; 19:5, 9, 10, 12; 23:9; 25:6; 32:6; 53:8

Egyptian (Egiptius), 9:1; 10:1, 2, 6; 16:3; 23:9; 32:16

Ekron (Accaron), 29:2; 55:4, 7

Elam, 4:9; 5:6

Elamiel, 1:3

Elas, 25:8, 9

Elat, 4:6

Elath, 25:11

Elaz, 4:2

Eldad (Eldat), 20:5

Eleazar, 22:8, 9; 24:4; 25:5, 6; 28:1, 3; 46:4; 47:10; 50:3

Eli (Heli), 50:3, 6–8; 51:2, 7; 52:1, 4; 53:3–6, 12; 54:3–5; 63:1

Eliab, 59:2

Elidia, 1:6

Eliel, 47:11

Eliesor, 27:4

Elifac, 8:8

Eliphat, 15:3

Eliphaz (Elifan), 8:5

Eliseel, 1:3

Elisefan, 29:2

Elishah (Elisa), 4:2, 4; 5:4

Elith, 1:17

Elkanah (Elchana), 49:5–8; 50:1, 7; 51:6; 53:5

Elon, 8:5, 11; 40:7

Eluma, 42:1, 4; 43:1

Emon, 15:3

Enath, 27:4

Endor, 64:3

Enoc, 4:2

Enoch, 1:13, 15, 16; 2:2–5; 8:11

Enoflasa, 47:11

Enosh (Enos), 1:5, 7

Ephraim (Effraim, Effrem), 8:14; 15:3; 24:6; 25:4, 13; 30:3; 56:4

Er, 8:11

Eriden, 42:1

Ermoe, 8:8

Esar, 6:3; 27:4

Esau, 8:4, 5; 23:9; 32:2

Esca, 4:14

Etha, 4:14

Ethema, 29:2

Eva, 4:2

Ezbaile, 47:11

Fadahel, 42:10

Fadesur, 42:1

Falacus, 4:10

Fallita, 4:2

Faltia, 4:10

Fanata, 4:2

Faruta, 4:2
Feed, 4:4
Feila, 29:2
Felac, 27:4
Feledi, 1:17
Felucta, 4:2
Fenech, 5:1, 4; 6:14
Feneth (Fanath), 4:2, 3
Fenoch, 47:11
Ferita, 4:12
Fienna, 47:11
Fimei, 4:2
Finon, 4:2
Fison, 26:1; 27:12
Fodde, 4:13
Foe, 1:8
Fonna, 1:6
Fosal, 2:4
Fretan, 47:11
Fua, 1:4
Futh (Phuth), 25:11
Futh, 4:4

Gabaon, 48:3
Gad, 8:6, 13; 10:3; 22:1, 3; 25:4, 10; 26:11
Gal, 15:3
Galifa, 15:3
Gatam (Getan), 8:5
Geluc, 4:6
Gemet, 47:11
Gemuf, 47:11
Genuth, 47:11
Gerar (Gerras, Gerara), 4:8; 43:5
Geresaraz, 47:11
Gershon (Getson), 8:11
Getal, 39:8, 9
Getalibal, 38:1
Getel, 27:4
Gether (Gedrumese, *see* Mash), 4:9
Gibeah (Gabao), 45:1
Gideon (Gedeon), 35:1, 5–7; 36:1–4
Gileadites (Galadites), 38:2
Gilgal (Galgala), 21:7; 22:8
Goda, 4:4
Goliath (Golia), 54:3; 61:2, 6–7; 62:4
Goloza, 4:2
Gomer (Domereth), 4:4
Gomer, 4:2; 5:4
Gomorrah (Gomorra), 4:8

Hadoram (Dura), 4:10
Hagar (Agar), 8:1
Ham (Cam, Cham), 1:22; 4:1, 6; 5:1, 5, 6
Hamor (Emor), 8:7
Hannah (Anna), 50:1–5, 8; 51:1–3, 6

Haran (Aran), 4:15
Havilah (Evila, Evilach, Evilath), 4:6, 10; 25:11
Hazor (Asor), 30:3
Heber, 31:3
Hebrew (Hebreus, Ebreus), 9:1, 12, 15; 27:11; 31:8
Helifaz, 4:10
Heliu, 44:2
Hezron (Asrom), 8:11
Hillel (Elel), 41:1
Hophni (Ofni), 52:1; 54:3, 5
Horeb (Oreb), 19:1, 7, 9; 21:9; 23:2; 26:12; 54:1
Hurrite (Correus), 8:7
Hushim (Usi), 8:12

Iaal, 47:11
Iabat, 27:4
Iebal, 1:12
Iebbat, 2:3
Iectas, 1:4
Ierimuth, 47:11
Ieruebemas, 8:5
Ietar, 1:14
Igat, 27:4
Inab, 1:19
Ingethel, 27:10
Ionadali, 37:2
Ioollam, 8:5
Iosac, 4:14
Isaac, 8:3, 4; 23:8, 9; 32:5, 6; 49:8
Issachar (Isachar), 8:6, 11; 10:3; 25:4, 9; 26:10
Ishmael (Ismael, Ismahel), 8:1, 5
Israel, 9:1, 3–5, 11, 16; 10:1–3, 6; 11:1, 5, 15; 12:1; 14:3; 17:3; 19:3; 20:5, 8; 21:6, 9; 22:1, 3, 7, 8; 23:1, 2; 24:6; 25:1, 2; 26:5, 12; 27:6, 8, 13; 28:4; 30:1, 3, 4; 31:1, 5; 32:8, 14, 15, 18; 33:6; 34:1, 5; 35:2–4; 36:3; 39:1, 3, 5, 8, 9, 11; 40:8, 9; 41:1–3; 42:3; 43:8; 44:1, 6, 8; 45:5; 46:1–3; 47:10; 48:3–5; 49:1, 2, 4, 6; 52:4; 53:2, 8, 12; 54:1, 3–6; 55:1; 56:1; 58:4; 61:1, 4, 6; 62:2; 63:5; 64:1–4; 65:1

Jabin (Iabel), 30:3
Jabis (Iabis), 28:1
Jachin (Iachim), 8:11
Jacob (Iacob), 8:4, 6, 7, 9, 11–14; 9:7, 12; 18:6; 21:5; 23:9; 32:5, 6; 33:6; 44:8; 50:2; 61:5
Jael (Iahel), 31:3–7, 9; 32:12
Jahel (Iahel), 26:12
Jahleel (Iaillel), 8:11
Jair (Iair), 38:2–4; 63:4
Jambres (Iambri), 47:1

Jamin (Iamin), 8:11

Japheth (Iafeth), 1:22; 4:1, 2; 5:1, 4

Jared (Iareth), 1:11, 13

Jephthah (Ieptan), 39:2–6, 8–11; 40:1, 4, 5, 8, 9

Jephunneh (Ieffone), 15:3

Jericho (Iericho), 20:6

Jerusalem (Ierusalem), 22:9

Jesse (Iesse), 52:2–3

Joash (Ioaz), 35:1

Job (Iob), 8:8, 11

Jobab (Iobab), 2:7; 6:3

Jobal (Iobal), 2:7

Jochebed (Iacobe), 9:12

Joktan (Iectam, Iectan), 4:9, 10; 5:1, 6; 6:6, 14, 16

Jonathan (Ionathas), 62:1, 9, 11; 63:3

Jordan (Iordanem), 22:1, 3

Joseph (Ioseph), 8:6, 9, 10, 14; 9:1; 10:3; 12:1; 15:3; 26:11; 43:5

Joshua (Ihesus), 15:3; 20:1–3, 5, 6, 9, 10; 21:1, 2, 7, 10; 22:1–3, 5, 7, 8; 23:1, 2, 4; 24: 1, 3, 4; 25:1, 3; 30:1, 5; 32:10

Judah (Iuda), 8:11; 10:3; 15:3; 21:5; 25:4; 26:10; 30:4

Kenan (Cainan), 1:7, 9

Kenaz (Cenez), 8:5; 20:6, 10; 25:2–7, 9, 10, 12; 26:1, 2, 5, 6, 8, 9, 12, 14, 15; 27:2–7, 9–16; 28:1, 3, 5, 6, 10; 29:1, 2; 30:5; 49:1

Kenite (Cineus), 31:3

Kish (Cis), 54:3; 56:4

Kittim (Cethim), 4:2, 4; 5:4

Kohath (Caath), 8:11

Korah (Chore, Coro), 8:5; 16:1, 4, 6, 7; 57:2

Lamech, 1:18, 20–21; 2:5–6, 10

Leah (Lia), 8:11; 10:4

Lebanon (Libanum), 26:11; 32:8

Leetuz, 27:4

Levi, 8:6, 7, 11; 9:9; 10:3; 14:3; 25:4, 9; 26:10; 45:1

Levites, 21:9; 45:2

Lot (Loth), 4:15; 6:3; 8:1, 2; 45:2

Manasseh (Manassen), 8:14; 22:1, 3; 25:4, 13

Manoah (Manue), 42:1, 5, 6, 8–10

Mash (Gedrumese, *see* Gether), 4:9

Mefiz, 47:11

Melcha, 4:11; 23:4

Melchiel, 8:13; 9:16

Melec, 47:11

Memihel, 38:1

Merari, 8:11

Mesopotamia, 8:4; 17:3; 18:2; 32:6

Metach, 47:11

Meturia, 47:11

Micah (Micha), 44:2, 4, 5, 7–10; 45:6; 47:12

Michal (Michol), 62:7

Midian (Madian, Mazia), 18:13; 34:1; 36:1

Midianites (Madianites), 34:4, 5; 35:1, 2, 4, 5; 36:1, 2; 61:1; 64:3

Miriam (Maria), 9:9, 10; 10:5; 20:8

Mizpah (Masphat), 39:1

Moab, 18:2, 10–12, 14; 27:4; 41:1

Modad (Modat), 20:5

Mofar, 8:13

Moses (Moyses), 9:16; 10:1, 2, 4–6; 11:2–4, 14, 15; 12:1, 2, 4, 5, 8; 13:1, 2; 14:3–5; 15:1, 5, 7; 16:4, 7; 17:1, 2; 18:1; 19:1, 3, 8, 14, 16; 20:2, 5, 6, 8, 10; 21:1, 7; 22:2, 5; 23:9; 24:3, 6; 25:3, 5, 13; 26:4, 12; 30:1, 2, 5; 32:8; 35:6; 37:3; 40:6; 47:1; 51:6; 53:2, 8, 10; 56:1; 57:2; 58:1; 61:5

Nahor (Nachor), 4:13–15; 6:3; 23:4

Namuel, 8:11

Nanubal, 8:14

Naphtali (Neptali, Neptalim), 8:6, 12; 10:3; 25:9; 26:11

Nathaniel, 38:3

Neemmu, 8:12

Nefelien, 15:3

Nefuth, 47:11

Nesach, 27:4

Netach, 47:11

Nethez, 49:3

Nimrod (Nembroth), 4:7; 5:1, 5; 6:14; 25:11

Noa, 1:12

Noac, 27:4

Noah (Noe), 1:20–22; 3:4, 5, 7, 8, 11; 4:1, 17; 5:2, 3, 8; 13:8; 19:11

Nob (Noba), 45:1, 4; 46:3; 47:10; 63:1

Nun (Nave), 15:3; 20:1, 2, 5; 23:1; 24:1, 3

Obal (Deglabal; *see* Diklah), 4:10

Obal, 27:4

Odihel, 29:2

Odon, 42:1

Og, 18:1

Ohad (Doth), 8:11

Oholibamah (Elibema), 8:5

Onan (Auna), 8:11

Ophir, 26:11

Opti, 8:12

Orpah (Orfa), 61:6

Pallu (Fallu), 8:11

Peccan, 47:11

Peleg (Falech), 4:9, 10

General Concordance

This concordance does not list the number of times a word occurs in any one verse, so it will not give absolute numbers of occurrences. The concordance is complete except that most numbers, conjunctions, pronouns, particles, and prepositions are not listed, and some words, such as *sum, Deus,* and *Dominus,* are so frequent that they are omitted.

Pseudo-Philo does not use classical Latin orthography, so many forms here do not appear precisely as they do in most Latin dictionaries. Harrington (*OTP,* 298) says, "Pseudo-Philo now exists in a Latin version whose idiom and style represent that vulgar Latin in which the Old Latin versions of the Bible were written." Forms in which words are found in dictionaries of classical Latin are often indicated in parentheses. Where alternate spellings exist within the *Biblical Antiquities,* they are usually indicated in parentheses by "also" plus the alternate spelling. Some words are latinized versions of Greek words. Words that are apparently from the Greek and are *not* contained in the *Oxford Latin Dictionary* (Oxford: Clarendon, 1968–82) or in *A Latin Dictionary* (Lewis and Short. Oxford: Clarendon, 1958) are often indicated by "Greek" in parentheses.

Verse ranges indicate that the word appears in every verse in the range. For example, 1:1–5 means that the word is in 1:1, 2, 3, 4, and 5.

abeo, 6:18; 27:12; 34:2; 35:6; 36:1, 3; 40:4; 47:9; 51:7; 53:4, 6; 56:7; 58:2; 61:6; 62:2, 11; 63:2; 64:4, 9
abhominamentum, 11:6; 29:3; 44:7
abhomino (abomino), 11:7; 49:2; 53:9
abicio, 9:1; 49:3

abnego, 26:6; 44:10
abscido, 11:15; 12:7; 19:4; 40:7; 49:6
abscondo, 6:9, 18; 9:5, 12; 24:6; 25:9, 10; 35:1; 47:2; 53:12; 58:2, 4
absolutus, 27:11
absorbeo, 18:10; 26:4

abstraho, 2:10; 45:3

abundantia, 28:5

abutor, 65:2

abyssus (also abissus), 3:5; 9:3; 11:5; 12:8; 15:5; 22:3; 23:10; 32:8, 17; 39:5

accedo, 11:2, 15; 13:3; 20:10; 36:2

accelero, 11:9; 19:13

acceptabilis, 18:5; 40:3; 59:4

accepto, 9:9; 32:3; 44:7

accido, 18:11; 39:4; 55:7

accingo, 27:12

accipio, 2:5, 6; 3:1, 4, 8; 4:4, 10, 11; 6:2, 3, 7–9, 12, 15, 16; 8:1, 4–8; 9:4, 5, 9, 12, 15; 10:3; 11:7, 15; 13:3, 7; 15:7; 16:5; 17:1; 18:7; 19:10, 12; 20:2–4; 22:5; 23:4–7, 13; 26:1–8, 12, 13, 15; 27:6, 11; 28:3; 29:1; 31:1, 5–7, 9; 32:15; 33:3; 35:3, 6; 36:1, 3; 37:2; 38:3; 39:1, 8, 9; 41:1, 2; 42:1, 8; 43:1, 5, 8; 44:2, 6, 7; 45:4; 49:5; 52:2; 53:10; 54:2; 55:6, 8; 57:2; 59:5; 61:2, 4, 5; 64:8

accipiter, 62:6

accuso, 40:5

achates, 26:11

actus, 21:6; 52:2

acutus, 27:9

adamas, 26:11

adduco, 6:4, 7, 8, 13, 15; 7:4; 10:4, 7; 15:6; 18:5, 10; 19:2, 9; 23:10; 25:3, 4, 7; 27:3; 31: 8; 39:9; 48:1; 53:8; 55:2; 58:2; 59:3; 60:1

adhuc (also adhoc), 5:2, 8; 9:4; 10:2, 6; 13:9; 14:3; 16:4, 6; 18:7, 12; 19:9, 14, 16; 20:2; 23:1; 27:11; 32:10; 33:5; 34:5; 42:10; 43:5, 7; 47:11; 49:3, 6; 52:3; 53:1, 2; 54:5; 55:1; 56:2; 59:5; 61:7; 65:3

adicio, 3:9, 11; 10:6; 13:9; 16:2, 3; 18:7; 21:6; 24:1; 25:1; 39:9; 42:6; 43:7; 47:1; 53:4, 7

adimpleo, 3:3; 14:2

adinvenio, 25:11; 26:5; 28:7; 44:7, 10; 47:7

adinventio, 3:10; 25:7, 8; 35:3; 44:10; 52:2

adiudico, 37:3; 44:10

adiuvo, 12:5; 16:6; 36:1; 43:2; 45:4; 62:5

admiror, 18:11

admoneo, 52:4

adoro, 2:9; 6:4; 18:9; 36:3; 38:2

adquiesco, 9:5

adsum, 25:8; 32:15; 51:6; 61:8

advena, 15:5; 45:3

advenio, 3:4; 10:2; 28:8; 47:4; 53:12; 54:2; 59:1; 62:9

adventus, 23:10

adversarius, 27:10

adverso, 52:4

adversum, 47:1

adversus, 9:1; 11:12; 27:2, 6, 15; 32:4, 7; 39:6; 57:2

affero, 7:5; 12:3; 13:7; 25:11; 26:8; 29:3; 57:4

affligo, 9:3; 10:1

affodio, 23:4

ager, 42:6, 7; 47:4

aggravo, 9:11

agnosco, 8:10; 9:5; 13:6; 20:4; 28:4; 61:9

agnus, 32:3

ago, 9:10; 20:5; 21:2; 25:6, 9; 27:12; 33:3; 44:9; 49:6; 50:6; 52:1, 4

albus, 17:3; 40:6; 64:6

alienigena, 19:7

alienus, 14:1; 21:1; 39:6; 42:8; 43:5; 44:7

aliquis, 33:5

aliquoties, 30:5

alius, 3:10; 12:9; 20:4; 26:3; 35:7; 42:1; 46:3; 47:4, 6; 55:3, 7; 56:4

allocutio, 51:3

altare, 22:1, 8

altarium, 42:9

alter, 2:6; 47:5; 50:1; 53:4

altercor, 9:14; 42:2

alteruter, 6:1; 25:10; 27:10; 43:2; 62:9

altissimus, 12:8; 32:14; 53:2

altitudo, 3:4; 30:5

altus, 32:1, 4; 51:4

amabilis, 23:12

amaritudo, 12:6; 25:5

amarus, 59:5

ambo, 2:10; 20:10; 42:2; 47:1; 62:7

ambulo, 4:16; 6:4; 11:6; 13:9, 10; 16:5; 20:4; 30:4; 32:9, 15; 39:6; 45:1; 49:3; 50:4, 7; 52:1, 2; 56:1, 4; 60:3; 61:6; 62:6; 63:1

amen, 22:6; 26:5

ametistus (amethystus), 26:11

amicus, 23:9; 24:3; 25:3, 5; 31:8

amigdalinus (amygdalinus), 17:3, 4

amigdalum (amygdalum), 17:2

amitto, 54:6

amo, 19:16; 43:6; 62:11

amplifico, 9:4; 49:3, 6; 55:4

amplio, 4:5

amplus, 9:12; 16:3; 29:1

anathema, 21:3; 26:2; 29:3

ancilla, 8:1; 9:15

angelus, 11:5; 15:5; 18:5, 6, 9; 19:5, 9, 12, 16; 24:3; 25:2; 26:4, 8; 27:10; 30:2, 5; 32:1, 13; 34:2, 3; 35:1, 3, 5–7; 38:3, 4; 42:3, 4, 6–10; 47:1; 53:4, 6; 59:4; 61:5, 8, 9; 64:6

angustia, 35:2; 49:6

anima, 3:10, 11; 8:11–14; 13:2, 6, 10; 15:5; 16:3; 21:9; 23:13; 28:3; 31:3, 4, 6; 32:3, 13; 33:4; 36:1; 40:1, 3–6; 43:2, 7; 44:10; 47:1; 49:2; 50:2, 5; 54:6; 58:1; 61:7; 62:5, 9; 64:7; 65:3

animal, 3:4; 31:5

animo, 23:10

animositas, 6:9; 22:4

animus, 12:2; 42:7

annuncio (annuntio), 9:7; 14:1, 5; 25:9; 32:3, 14; 43:6; 53:6; 56:4, 5; 62:7

annus, 1:2, 5, 7, 9, 11, 13, 15, 18, 20–22; 2:3, 4; 3:2, 6, 10; 4:12–15; 5:3, 8; 8:9, 14; 9:3, 8; 10:7; 11:15; 13:8; 14:1, 3–5; 19:5, 7, 8, 13; 22:8; 24:6; 27:16; 28:8; 29:4; 30:2; 32:5, 18; 33:3, 6; 37:5; 40:7–9; 41:1–3; 43:8; 48:1; 49:7; 51:1; 53:1, 2; 55:1, 10; 57:5; 63:3; 64:5

anteciminus (Greek), 45:6

antiquus, 9:8; 32:12

anulus, 9:5

anxio (ango), 50:6

aperio, 3:5; 9:15; 12:5; 16:6; 18:9; 23:7; 40:1; 42:3; 48:1; 50:4; 51:3, 4; 61:8

apex, 19:15

apparatus, 5:5

appario, 3:12; 4:5; 10:5; 15:5; 27:13; 28:4; 32:4; 60:2; 62:2; 64:3

appellatio, 44:7

appello, 60:2

appono, 10:2, 6; 18:7; 23:12; 42:4

apprehendo, 43:4, 8; 54:3

appropinquo, 5:2; 9:2; 19:13; 23:1; 28:1; 32:5, 10; 33:1; 59:4; 64:7

appropio (see appropinquo), 12:2; 27:6; 31:7

approximo, 7:3

aqua, 3:5, 7, 9, 11; 6:9; 7:3–5; 9:10, 14; 10:3, 5, 7; 11:5, 6, 15; 12:7; 15:5, 6; 16:3; 17:3; 18:10; 19:9–11; 20:8; 26:3, 6; 30:6; 31:4, 5; 35:6, 7

aquila, 24:6; 44:5, 9; 45:6; 48:1; 62:6

ara, 3:8; 32:4; 44:3

aranea, 28:8

arbitror, 7:3

arbor, 9:12; 40:7

arca, 3:4, 5, 7, 8; 4:1; 5:3; 11:15; 13:1; 19:11; 21:8, 9; 22:8, 9; 23:1; 26:12, 15; 46:4; 54:1–6; 55:1–6, 8, 9; 61:2

arcus, 3:12; 4:5; 19:11

ardere, 11:5, 14; 27:15; 28:7, 8

arefacio, 12:8

argentum, 2:9; 29:3; 44:2, 3; 58:3

arguo, 35:4; 60:3; 62:8

aries, 22:7; 23:6, 7; 31:5

arma, 5:4, 5; 10:3; 15:2

armo, 27:1; 39:10

aroma, 12:9

ars, 2:9; 16:5; 34:4; 44:7

artifex, 25:11

ascendo, 4:3; 11:2, 15; 12:8; 15:1; 16:5; 19:5, 8; 20:6, 7; 21:9; 22:5, 8; 25:1; 26:13; 27:1, 12; 28:8; 32:18; 34:1; 39:8; 42:2, 5, 9; 46:1–3; 48:2, 3; 50:2, 4; 51:1; 54:2; 63:4; 64:5

ascensus, 15:2

asina, 18:9; 43:4; 56:4

aspergo, 17:3

assimilo, 21:6; 23:7; 26:10, 11; 31:5; 39:5; 53:5; 56:6

assisto, 38:4

assumo, 27:11

asto, 22:4; 25:8; 50:1

astringo, 27:11

astrum, 4:16; 9:3; 11:5; 13:7; 15:2; 18:5; 19:13; 21:2; 31:1, 2, 4; 32:9, 11, 14, 15, 17, 18

astucia (astutia), 22:6

astutus, 25:6; 44:5, 9

attente, 47:3

audeo, 7:2

audio, 2:10; 7:3, 5; 15:4; 16:6; 19:4, 16; 20:6; 22:1, 5; 23:2; 25:3; 26:13; 27:3, 8, 10, 13, 15; 28:3, 6, 7; 29:1; 32:3; 33:1; 36:1, 2; 37:3; 38:4; 40:5; 42:5, 6; 44:2; 47:1, 3, 6; 50:2, 3, 6, 8; 51:3, 4; 52:2, 3; 53:1, 2, 5, 6, 11–13; 54:5, 6; 55:1; 56:2; 60:3; 61:2–4, 6; 62:4, 8; 64:7, 9

auditio, 52:2

auditus, 20:5

aufero, 7:1; 14:4; 16:3; 17:1; 20:4, 8; 25:10; 26:4; 31:9; 39:5; 43:3; 46:1; 50:6; 51:1; 53:13; 54:5; 55:2; 60:1; 61:2, 4, 8; 62:10; 64:1

aureus, 13:1; 25:10; 36:3; 55:9

auris, 19:4; 21:7; 26:13; 53:6, 7

aurum, 2:9; 12:9; 18:13; 29:3; 44:2, 3

autumnus, 3:9

avarus, 29:1

averto, 18:14; 36:3; 39:6

avis, 13:2

avoco, 6:9

azimus (azymus), 13:4

balsamum, 12:9

basis, 11:15; 13:1

beatitudo, 32:3

beatus, 30:4

bellum, 5:7

bene, 21:8, 9; 44:4

benedico, 7:4; 13:10; 18:6, 12; 19:5; 20:10; 21:10; 24:3, 4; 25:5; 26:6; 27:13; 31:9; 32:6; 62:6

beneplacitus, 20:10

berillus (beryllus), 26:11

bestia, 3:8; 6:11; 32:8; 40:3; 47:4

bibo, 17:3; 19:10; 31:4–6; 50:6

bis, 53:3, 4

bissinus (byssinus), 9:10

blasphemo, 38:3; 50:5

bonus, 25:3; 26:14; 31:3; 32:12; 35:5; 36:4; 50:2; 52:2; 62:4; 64:4

brachium, 27:10; 31:1, 2, 7; 43:4

brevio, 19:13

cacumen, 25:10
cado, 6:11; 26:6; 46:4; 54:2; 55:4; 63:3
calamus, 7:3
caleo, 27:11
calix, 50:6
calor, 3:9
caminus, 6:16–18
campester, 40:3
campus, 6:1; 7:3; 11:15; 27:12, 14; 32:8, 15;
    37:2–4; 40:3
candelabrum, 11:15
canis, 39:11
canticum, 40:1
capio, 2:3, 8, 9; 3:1, 5; 4:5, 8, 16; 7:2; 19:1;
    20:8; 26:13; 27:6, 10; 28:6; 30:3; 34:5; 36:2;
    39:1; 40:5; 43:1; 48:3; 49:1; 52:1; 54:2; 59:4;
    63:3
capra, 13:2; 23:6, 7
captivitas, 15:4; 54:5; 55:3
captivo, 54:6; 61:2
caput, 6:1, 11; 15:5; 31:9; 39:8; 43:6; 46:4;
    54:4; 61:8
carbunculus, 26:10
carcer, 6:9; 25:4; 27:3, 15; 43:6
carnalis, 3:2
caro, 3:10, 11; 9:8, 13, 15; 25:9; 33:2; 42:2, 9;
    62:6
castigo, 30:5; 36:4; 37:3; 38:4; 44:9; 53:12
castrum, 5:4, 5, 7; 11:4; 16:3; 27:6, 7, 10;
    32:11; 36:1; 54:1, 2, 4; 61:2
cataclismos (cataclysmos), 3:7; 5:8
cataracta, 3:5
cathedra, 11:8
catulus, 24:6; 47:4–6
cecitas (caecitas), 27:10; 38:3
ceco (caecare), 43:5
cecus (caecus), 25:12
cedo, 4:5; 27:10; 42:10; 43:8; 46:2–4; 49:7;
    54:5; 55:3
cedrinus, 3:4; 13:3
cedrus, 13:7; 32:8
celebro, 13:4
celer, 9:3
celo, 9:12
celum (caelum), 3:4–6, 10, 12; 6:1, 14; 7:2;
    10:7; 11:5, 6, 8, 9; 14:2; 15:6; 18:5; 19:4, 10,
    13; 23:10; 24:1; 32:9, 13; 33:5; 40:5; 44:10;
    48:1; 53:3, 5; 60:2; 62:10
cesso, 7:5; 32:12; 59:4
ceterus, 9:9; 12:2; 20:6; 30:4; 34:3; 47:4, 6,
    11
chaoma (Greek), 60:3
cherubin, 26:12
chorus, 21:8; 40:1; 51:7; 55:9
christallinus, 25:11

christus, 51:6; 57:3; 59:2, 4
ciatus (cyathus), 19:15
cibus, 3:11; 31:3
cidaris, 13:1
cilicium, 30:5
cinara, 21:8
cingo, 35:5; 36:2
cinis, 27:15; 46:4; 54:4
cinnamum, 12:9
circa, 14:5; 21:4; 22:1; 29:2; 43:8; 55:7
circueo, 35:2; 43:2
circuitus, 43:8; 50:1
circumdo, 19:7; 23:6
circumiacens, 4:8
circumsto, 6:17
citius, 23:8
cito, 63:3, 4
citona (Greek), 13:1
civitas, 2:3; 4:8; 7:1, 2, 5; 8:7; 13:8; 20:7; 23:7,
    11; 33:6; 36:4; 39:1, 8, 9; 40:1; 41:1, 2; 43:2,
    5; 45:1–4; 46:2; 47:10, 11; 49:3, 4; 62:11
clamo, 10:1, 2; 42:6, 7; 53:2–5; 59:4; 65:3
clarus, 50:5
claudo, 3:10; 15:1; 32:4; 43:2; 48:1; 50:4
coacto, 12:7
coangusto, 39:1
coccinus, 13:3
cocus (coquus), 8:9
cogitatio, 6:9; 7:1, 5; 9:7; 15:5; 16:3
cogitatus, 49:3
cogito, 3:3; 7:3; 9:7, 8; 18:6, 12; 20:2, 6; 27:6;
    29:4; 31:5; 40:4; 50:5; 53:2; 56:5; 62:3, 6;
    64:1, 3
cognatio, 61:6
cognomino, 6:18; 9:16
cognosco, 2:2; 7:3, 5; 8:3, 10; 11:2, 14; 12:1, 8;
    18:11; 21:9; 27:7, 12, 15; 28:6; 35:4; 43:6;
    50:5; 53:3; 61:9; 62:3, 9
cogo, 62:9
coinquino, 3:10
colligo, 22:2; 25:3; 30:4; 39:6; 45:5; 54:1; 64:2
collis, 11:5; 40:3, 5
colloco, 21:6
color, 26:10
coluber, 13:8
columba, 13:2; 21:6; 23:6, 7; 39:5; 44:5, 9;
    45:6
columna, 10:7; 20:8; 38:4; 43:7, 8; 44:3
comburo, 6:6, 12, 13, 17; 26:1–3, 6, 8; 27:15;
    38:3, 4
comedo, 6:11; 37:3, 4; 40:6; 42:3; 47:4–6;
    50:3
comforto, 43:7
commemoratio, 19:11
commendo, 7:3; 33:4; 47:4, 5; 62:10

comminor, 10:5

commisceo, 9:5; 21:1; 35:7; 43:5

committo, 47:7

commixtio, 43:5

commoror, 28:6; 39:2; 52:1

commotus, 20:3; 32:7, 8

commoveo, 6:17

compaginatio, 60:2

compago, 32:7

compareo, 35:7

comparo, 44:3

compesco, 53:10

compleo, 3:9; 4:10; 9:5; 12:3; 13:6; 15:5; 19:8, 15; 20:6, 10; 21:9; 23:11, 13; 24:6; 29:4; 40:4; 46:1; 58:1

completus, 3:10; 9:6; 12:4; 13:1; 28:9; 36:1; 47:9; 56:1; 57:3; 59:1; 61:3; 62:2

complico, 24:5

compono, 13:1; 18:5

comprehendo, 6:4; 27:11, 15; 49:5, 6

concedo, 42:2

concido, 6:18; 9:3; 50:3

concipio, 2:2; 8:1, 3, 4; 9:5, 12; 42:3, 4; 43:1; 51:1

concludo, 23:5, 7; 32:5; 40:4; 42:1; 45:2; 50:7; 51:5

concordo, 12:4

concrematio, 6:17

concremo, 6:7, 14–17; 25:3, 6; 26:2, 3, 5; 38:4

concubina, 8:6; 27:2; 31:1, 8; 37:1; 45:3, 4; 47:8

concubo, 18:13

concupiscentia, 43:5

concupisco, 11:13; 44:6, 7, 10; 56:1

concutio, 43:3

condo, 2:3; 62:10

confectio, 40:6

confidenter, 14:2

confido, 6:9, 11; 39:6; 50:5

configo, 25:11

confirmo, 21:5; 25:11

confiteor, 25:6, 7; 27:15; 28:2

conflatilis, 12:3; 44:2

conflatio, 44:7

conflictus, 20:5

conflo, 30:6; 44:2

conforto, 12:6; 20:5; 39:8; 65:1

confringo, 12:5, 7; 20:4; 21:9

confugio, 49:6

confundo, 7:5; 32:1

confusio, 7:5

confusus, 42:5

congregatio, 17:3; 28:4

congrego, 6:1, 13; 9:2, 14; 11:5; 12:2; 15:6; 21:7;23:1,2,4;24:1,6;25:5;26:2;28:4;29:1;

31:2; 33:1; 36:3; 39:1, 2; 43:2; 55:9; 56:1; 57:1; 64:1

congressus, 54:1

coniungo, 6:4; 16:7

conscientia, 32:15

conscindo, 42:9

consecratio, 25:11

consentio, 6:4, 5; 12:7; 27:15; 40:2; 44:6

consequi, 10:7; 64:1

conservo, 7:4; 11:8; 24:3; 51:5

consideratio, 5:4

considero, 5:2, 3, 8; 10:3; 27:10; 28:6, 7

consilior, 6:9, 13; 18:13; 44:4

consilium, 5:2; 6:4, 6, 9, 13; 9:1, 5; 10:3; 16:4; 18:3, 11; 40:4; 45:6; 63:2, 2

consimilo, 26:10

consisto, 57:4

consonantia, 15:2

consono, 60:3

conspectus, 5:4, 5, 7; 6:17; 7:3, 4; 9:7; 10:2; 13:4, 5; 14:4; 15:6; 18:2, 5; 19:11, 13; 21:3, 9; 22:4, 7; 23:1, 2, 7; 24:1; 25:4; 26:1, 12; 27:2; 30:5; 32:4, 17; 39:1, 4, 7; 40:4, 5; 41:1; 44:1, 9, 10; 45:2, 4; 46:2–4; 47:1, 3; 49:8; 50:1, 2, 4, 7; 51:2, 7; 52:1; 53:1, 2; 55:4; 57:2, 3; 58:3; 59:5; 60:3; 61:2; 62:6; 65:1

conspicio, 15:1

constabilio, 19:9

constituo, 2:1; 5:1; 9:2; 12:2; 13:4, 5, 7, 8; 14:2; 15:7; 17:4; 21:2; 22:8; 25:2; 27:12–14; 29:1, 3; 30:1; 32:3; 40:8; 41:2; 44:6; 46:4; 47:6; 48:1, 2; 51:2; 56:1; 62:4

constitutio, 51:4

construo, 6:16

consulo, 44:5; 58:3

consummatio, 7:4; 55:2

consummo, 6:9; 36:1

consumo, 6:5, 11; 20:9; 28:2; 45:6

contamino, 2:8; 9:2; 16:3; 25:1, 3, 13; 26:4; 49:5; 63:1

contemno, 29:1

contero, 27:2; 31:2

contineo, 6:9; 12:9; 52:2

contingo, 6:18; 9:3; 18:11; 40:1; 41:1; 53:10; 55:1; 63:2

continuus, 31:5

contradico, 18:5; 20:3; 32:2; 40:2; 52:2

contribulo, 15:1, 5

contrio, 19:7

contristo, 19:12; 30:5; 31:9; 39:8; 42:2; 43:5, 7; 44:10; 50:2; 52:3; 56:2, 3

conturbatio, 22:2

conturbo, 11:5; 15:4; 22:1; 29:3; 31:1, 2; 45:5, 6; 46:1, 3; 47:5, 8; 64:7

conululo, 40:7

convalesco, 55:4

convenio, 5:1, 2; 7:1; 22:8; 32:8; 37:2; 40:8; 45:3; 51:6; 52:1; 55:5; 58:3

converso, 27:6

converto, 7:1; 12:4; 21:6; 47:10; 53:7; 55:6

convirginalis, 40:3, 4

convirgo, 40:6

convoco, 16:4; 20:6; 29:4

cooperio, 10:6; 12:1

coopero, 27:10

cor, 3:9; 9:3; 10:2; 12:2; 15:1; 19:3; 20:4, 6; 21:2, 9, 10; 22:3, 6, 7; 23:12; 25:1, 3; 26:2, 8, 13; 28:3, 7; 29:3, 4; 30:1, 6; 31:2; 33:2; 38:2; 39:6; 40:1; 43:6; 45:2, 6; 46:2–4; 50:3, 4; 51:7; 53:2, 11; 56:2; 59:2; 62:6, 11; 65:1

coram, 9:1; 12:2; 16:6; 21:2; 39:4, 7; 42:2; 47:2

cornu, 51:3, 6

corona, 13:1; 40:6; 43:5

corpus, 6:14; 15:5, 6; 16:3; 27:12, 14; 31:7; 43:7; 44:9, 10; 45:4

corrigo, 52:3

corripio, 54:2

corrumpo, 2:8, 10; 3:6, 9, 11; 12:2, 4; 13:10; 19:4; 20:4; 21:4, 10; 22:2; 23:10; 25:5; 28:4, 6; 38:2, 4; 39:7; 40:6; 44:7; 47:6, 7; 58:3

corruptela, 44:7

corruptibilis, 28:10; 38:4

corruscus (and coruscus), 26:3; 27:9

cortex, 9:12

coruscatio, 13:7; 15:2; 31:1

corusco, 11:4

costa, 32:15

costum, 12:9

crastinus, 11:2; 26:9; 56:3; 58:3, 4; 64:8

creator, 44:7

creatura, 13:6; 15:6; 32:17; 60:3

credo, 9:10; 12:9; 14:4; 20:5; 23:5, 6, 12; 25:6; 42:4, 5

cremo, 45:3

creo, 49:3; 60:2

cresco, 3:8, 11; 9:1; 43:1

crinis, 43:6

crisolitus (chrysolithos), 26:11

crisoprassus (chrysoprasos), 25:11; 26:10

cristallus, 26:10

crucifigo, 55:3

cubitum, 3:4

culpa, 52:3

cultiva, 29:2

cultor, 12:8; 32:1; 44:3

cupiditas, 33:3

cupidus, 29:1

cura, 25:9

curo, 62:11

curro, 19:13; 35:6; 42:6, 7; 53:3, 5; 61:7; 65:3

currus, 10:6; 30:3; 31:1; 55:6, 8

cursus, 18:12; 23:10; 31:1; 32:7

custodio, 11:6; 15:5; 21:9; 28:3; 32:1, 8, 11; 44:6, 7; 47:4; 59:4; 62:8

custos, 11:12; 22:5; 59:4

cynera, 2:8; 51:7

cythara (cithara), 2:8; 60:1

dealbo, 21:7

debeo, 29:1; 45:6

debitum, 3:10

decido, 26:6; 40:4

decimatio, 14:4

decimus, 19:7; 26:11; 47:11

declino, 19:9; 26:2; 30:1; 38:2

decoriatus, 17:3

deduco, 6:9; 10:7; 18:12; 23:10; 64:6, 7

deficio, 6:11; 9:2; 11:9; 20:4; 21:5; 49:3, 7

defluo, 6:9

defraudo, 26:14

defunctus, 20:1–3, 8; 21:3; 28:10; 30:6

deglutio (degluttio), 16:2, 3, 6; 57:2

deicio, 15:6

deinceps, 25:10; 37:2

delecto, 50:1; 51:4

deleo, 3:3; 24:2; 26:3, 6, 8; 48:3; 59:1; 63:1

deliquo, 27:7; 36:4

demergo, 19:9

demitto, 37:5

demolior, 38:4; 19:7

demon (daemon), 25:9

demonstratio, 22:8, 9; 25:5; 46:1

demonstro, 19:7; 27:11; 30:6

dens, 18:12; 26:10

denudo, 10:5

depono, 12:4; 25:9, 10, 12; 33:3; 43:3; 52:2

deporto, 15:1

deposco, 7:5

deprecor, 39:6

deputo, 26:14; 52:2

derelinquo, 13:10; 15:6; 19:2; 21:1; 25:9, 13; 27:6, 11; 28:2; 30:4; 31:1; 32:10; 47:11; 49:6; 50:4

descendo, 4:5; 6:18; 7:4; 8:10, 11, 14; 9:15; 11:15; 12:1, 5; 13:1; 14:3, 5; 15:6; 20:8; 21:7, 8; 23:9, 10; 27:6, 7, 10; 31:1, 2; 32:6, 11, 18; 36:2; 43:5, 8; 48:1; 51:7; 52:2; 53:7; 61:1, 2

descensus, 23:10

desero, 30:7

deservio, 22:9; 52:1; 53:1

desiderium, 18:11; 23:12; 51:2

desidero, 51:2; 55:6

designo, 26:9

desino, 20:8; 24:5

desipio, 3:9

despero, 54:5

despumo, 28:9

destruo, 22:7; 40:3, 4

desuper, 25:11

deterius, 12:3

determinatio, 62:4

determino, 9:4; 62:4

detineo, 11:15

detractio, 27:15

detractor, 27:3

devasto, 61:6

devio, 19:7; 22:7

devoro, 37:3; 42:9

devoveo, 40:5

dexter, 25:3; 27:11; 38:2; 39:7; 43:3; 53:6, 7; 55:7, 8; 59:4

dextralia, 36:3

diatris, 25:12

didragma (didrachma), 44:2, 3

dies, 2:4; 3:3, 5–9; 4:9, 11; 5:8; 6:1, 6, 9, 12, 13, 17, 18; 9:8; 10:7; 11:2–4, 8, 9, 15; 13:4, 10; 15:6, 7; 16:6; 18:11; 19:3, 7, 11, 13, 16; 20:5, 9; 21:1, 6, 10; 22:6, 8, 9; 23:1, 2, 14; 24:1, 3; 25:6; 26:5, 7, 15; 27:1, 2, 7, 9, 16; 28:1, 10; 29:1, 3; 30:3–5, 7; 32:1, 10, 11, 13, 14, 16; 33:1, 6; 38:2; 39:3; 40:2, 6, 8; 41:1, 2; 42:4; 43:1, 7; 44:1, 4–7; 45:2; 46:3; 47:1, 7; 48:2, 4, 5; 49:8; 50:2, 4; 51:1; 52:3; 53:4, 9, 10; 54:1, 5; 55:1, 3; 56:3, 5, 7; 58:3; 59:3, 4; 61:2, 3; 62:5, 9; 63:3, 4

differentia, 25:8

diffidens, 16:4, 5

diffusus, 26:15

dignifico, 32:3

dignor, 24:2; 42:6

dignus, 25:2; 37:4; 42:5; 49:2; 50:5

dii (pl. of deus), 24:1; 25:9; 30:1; 34:1, 4, 5; 36:1; 39:6, 9; 41:3; 61:2; 64:6

diiudico, 3:2, 9; 8:10; 56:1

dilectio, 39:4; 50:2; 62:11

diligo, 11:6, 9; 19:8; 32:5, 8; 44:7; 49:8; 50:1, 2; 53:2; 62:3, 4

diluvium, 3:5, 9, 11; 4:17; 5:3; 7:4; 13:7; 16:3; 19:11; 25:11

dimergo (demergo), 21:3

dimidius, 22:1, 3

dimitto, 18:6; 22:7; 24:3; 27:11; 42:1; 63:2

dinumero, 14:3

diplois, 64:6

directe, 18:3

directus, 27:9; 34:5; 35:5

dirigo, 20:3, 4; 24:4; 32:12; 33:2, 3; 35:6; 52:2; 53:12; 55:7, 8; 56:5

diripio, 47:10; 52:4; 59:5

dirumpo, 7:4; 43:4

discedo, 8:2; 19:2; 28:2; 30:7; 32:11; 64:1

discerno, 44:10

disco, 21:5; 46:1

disperdo, 3:4, 9; 22:6; 30:4; 32:4; 39:8, 9; 44:8; 47:1, 8; 53:9; 58:1; 62:4

dispergo, 3:9; 4:3; 6:1; 7:3, 5; 64:1

dispono, 3:4, 11, 12; 7:4; 8:3; 9:3, 4; 10:2; 11:1, 3; 13:8, 10; 19:2, 4, 7, 11; 20:1; 23:1, 2; 24:3; 26:2; 28:2, 4; 30:5, 7; 32:8, 9, 13; 49:6; 54:1; 56:2; 62:1, 3; 63:2

dispositio, 11:8; 18:5; 21:2; 31:1; 32:11, 17; 49:6, 8

dispositus, 9:7; 62:11

disrumpo, 6:9; 15:5; 54:4; 64:6

dissipo, 9:7; 12:9; 20:6; 23:10; 31:2; 36:4

dissolutio, 18:12

dissolutus, 31:4, 7; 46:4; 47:12; 50:2; 53:11; 64:9

dissolvo, 4:11; 20:6; 27:11; 31:5; 54:6

distinctio, 26:10

distinctus, 25:11

distraho, 12:9

dito, 47:7; 50:5

diversus, 12:9; 26:10

dives, 51:4

divido, 4:3, 9, 17; 5:8; 6:1; 7:3, 5; 10:3; 17:3; 19:1; 20:5; 23:1; 31:1, 5; 45:4

divinatio, 4:16; 64:1

divinus, 55:7; 64:3

divisio, 10:3

divitie (divitiae), 35:5; 44:5

divulgo, 22:5

do, 1:20; 6:6, 9, 14; 8:3; 9:1; 10:2; 11:1, 2, 5; 12:3, 4, 8; 13:7, 10; 14:4; 16:2; 18:3; 19:3, 9–12; 20:5, 8–10; 21:2, 9, 10; 23:5, 7–11; 26:12; 29:1, 2; 31:6; 32:1, 5; 34:3; 35:6, 7; 36:3; 38:3; 39:9; 40:1, 4; 42:2, 8; 43:7; 44:3; 47:9; 48:3; 49:8; 50:2; 51:6; 52:4; 53:9, 11, 13; 56:6, 7; 63:2

doceo, 2:7; 13:8; 15:6; 16:5; 22:5, 6; 25:9, 13; 41:1

dogma, 18:11

dolatura, 23:4

doleo, 40:3; 52:3

dolor, 12:5; 31:7; 50:6, 8; 55:1

domesticus, 28:2

dominatio, 55:5

dominor, 7:4; 11:11; 26:6; 30:2, 4; 31:2

domo, 6:7–9; 8:11; 9:7; 11:6; 25:3; 26:13; 27:2; 33:6; 39:4; 40:1; 42:6; 44:3; 60:3; 62:6

domus, 11:13; 12:4, 9; 16:6; 21:6, 9; 22:9; 24:1; 26:12; 27:12; 35:5; 42:4, 8; 43:8; 44:6, 8; 45:1, 2; 50:3, 8; 53:7, 8; 56:2, 6; 57:3; 58:4; 62:4; 63:2

dono, 10:3; 32:2; 62:6

donum, 42:8

dormio, 3:10; 6:15; 11:6; 19:2, 6, 12, 13; 27:12; 28:10; 31:3, 5, 7; 33:6; 35:3; 51:5; 53:2–4, 6

dormitio, 19:12

draco, 44:5; 45:6

dragma (drachma), 44:2

ducatio, 5:4–7

ducator, 31:5

ducatus, 5:4; 9:10; 20:5; 33:6; 49:6

duco, 6:8; 20:2; 25:4; 32:7; 45:1

ductor, 5:4

dulcis, 2:8; 11:15

duritia, 30:6

durus, 15:2

dux, 5:1; 6:4–7, 11–13, 15, 16; 7:1; 20:3; 21:5; 24:6; 25:2; 27:13; 28:3; 29:1; 30:5; 37:1; 38: 4; 39:1, 6; 44:1; 48:4; 49:5, 6

ebdomas (hebdomas), 13:5, 8

ebrius, 50:6

ebullio, 11:5; 6:17; 28:8

ecclesia, 11:8

edificator (aedificator), 7:5

edifico (aedifico), 2:3; 3:8; 4:8; 6:1; 7:1, 3, 5; 12:3, 4; 18:10; 21:7, 10; 22:1, 6, 9; 23:7, 11; 26:12; 38:1; 42:9; 44:3; 48:3; 56:2

edo, 3:11

edoceo, 39:5

educo, 3:8; 6:9; 10:2, 7; 11:6; 15:6; 23:10; 32:7

efficio, 11:7; 14:2; 55:6

effigies, 7:5; 19:16; 44:5, 6, 9; 45:6

effigio, 12:3

effodio, 7:3; 22:6

effringo, 6:9

effugio, 35:1

effundo, 3:11; 26:8; 35:7; 40:3, 6; 62:5

egeo, 50:5

egredior, 43:2

eicio, 7:4; 11:1, 4; 23:10; 25:6; 32:1; 39:2, 4; 44:9; 45:3; 51:4

elatus, 18:10

electio, 17:1; 19:8

elevo, 14:1; 15:4; 19:10; 32:7; 48:1; 64:4, 5, 7

eligo, 3:1; 7:4; 18:5, 6, 11, 13; 20:4; 21:4; 23:12, 13; 26:11; 27:5; 28:4; 30:2; 31:5; 32:1; 35:2, 5, 6; 39:7; 41:2; 44:6, 7; 49:2, 4; 53:8, 9; 56:5; 59:3; 61:6

elocutio, 53:7

eloquium, 53:1

eloquor, 51:4

emendo, 19:9; 47:1

emitto, 12:8; 32:1

emo, 8:10; 18:11

emundo, 25:12

enarro, 9:10; 12:6; 14:3

enitor, 8:6

eo, 9:5; 20:10; 24:6; 25:12; 26:3–5, 8; 27:12; 31:1–3, 5; 32:13; 39:2; 47:2

epomes (and eppomes; ephod), 11:15; 13:1; 26:4

epulatio, 23:14; 26:7; 27:9; 40:1

epulor, 26:7; 40:2; 49:8; 61:2

equalis (aequalis), 25:1

equaliter (aequaliter), 46:4

eques, 10:6; 27:6, 7

equus, 12:2; 27:5; 31:3

eradico, 12:8; 18:10; 44:6, 8

eramentum (aeramentum), 2:9

erigo, 3:10; 56:5; 61:9

eruo, 3:4; 6:11; 8:10; 12:9; 23:5; 60:2

esca, 3:4; 4:14; 6:11; 8:10; 12:9; 60:2

estimo (aestimo), 12:4; 27:10; 47:9

estivus (aestivus), 35:1

eternus (aeternus), 7:4; 9:7; 11:5; 12:8; 23:13

evacuo, 51:4

evado, 6:11, 13

evagino, 27:7, 9; 61:7

evanesco, 15:6

evangelizo, 53:11; 65:1

evenio, 54:4

everto, 32:17; 55:2

evigilo, 32:14

evincio, 47:9

evolo, 19:7; 24:6

exagito, 47:6

exalto, 51:3

exardesco, 11:5; 31:6

exaudio, 4:5; 10:1; 15:5; 19:3; 27:7; 31:5; 32:7; 39:10; 42:3; 43:7; 44:10; 49:2; 50:5–7

excavo, 26:11

exceco (excaeco), 43:6

excelsus, 4:11; 11:1, 10; 19:16; 23:10; 26:11; 44:6

excido, 12:10; 26:11

excipio, 27:11

excito, 19:12, 13; 27:12; 28:8; 53:3

exclamo, 4:5; 10:4, 5; 13:2; 32:7, 11; 47:5; 64:5

excogito, 21:4; 26:5

excusatio, 22:7

excuso, 57:3

excutio, 35:1

exemplar, 11:15

exeo, 3:8; 4:1, 7; 6:9, 11; 8:1, 7; 10:2; 11:10; 12:3; 13:4; 15:5; 19:11; 20:1; 25:2, 3, 7; 27:5, 13; 28:3; 30:6; 31:3, 8, 9; 37:3, 4; 38:3; 39:1, 10; 40:1; 42:9; 44:9; 45:2–4; 46:2, 3; 47:9; 49:2, 4; 51:4; 54:1, 3; 55:3; 58:4; 59:5; 61:2; 62:1; 64:4; 65:1

exfero (effero), 28:6

exhorresco, 44:8; 49:2

exileo, 6:17

existimo, 49:5

exitium, 54:2; 55:1

exitus, 5:3; 16:3; 55:3

exoratio, 64:9

exoro, 13:2; 33:5; 40:3

exosus, 49:3

expavesco, 53:2

expecto, 6:12; 18:3, 8; 23:3; 27:6

expedio, 57:5

expello, 16:2

expergefacio, 6:15; 27:14; 28:7, 10; 31:5, 6; 32:8; 53:3

experimentum, 42:1

experior, 26:6

expio, 23:6

explorator, 15:1; 20:6

exploro, 15:1; 20:1

expono, 12:2; 32:16

exprimo, 26:11

exprobatio (exprobratio), 59:2

exprobro, 63:1

expugno, 6:1; 18:2, 13; 20:7; 23:12; 27:1, 7, 8; 30:3; 31:1; 32:10, 11, 14, 17; 39:1, 3; 40:1, 5; 41:1, 2; 43:1, 2; 46:3; 47:5; 48:3; 54:1; 58:2; 61:1, 2, 4; 64:2; 65:1

exquiro, 22:4; 26:5; 37:2; 44:4

exsculpo, 26:8, 10; 44:5

exsolvo, 27:11

exspecto, 21:6

exsplendeo (exsplendesco), 25:12

exsurgo, 12:6, 7; 19:6; 27:12; 28:4; 32:10; 36:2; 38:4; 47:5, 7, 9; 48:1; 51:4, 6; 53:5, 9; 58:3; 61:6; 63:3; 64:2

extendo, 12:8; 36:3

extensio, 60:2

exterminatio, 55:10

extermino, 7:4; 18:10; 21:3; 22:2; 44:7; 47:4, 6; 55:4, 7–9; 56:3

extero, 52:2

extinguo, 3:2, 10; 15:2; 18:10; 23:10; 26:6; 28:9; 35:7; 38:3; 55:2

extollentia, 20:4

extra, 5:7; 6:3

extremus, 36:1

exulto, 51:7; 61:7

exuo, 27:12

exurgeo, 11:9; 20:4; 26:12; 35:7

exuro, 26:2; 32:7

fabrico, 7:2

fabula, 22:5

facies, 4:5; 7:5; 12:1; 15:5; 19:9; 27:10; 36:3; 42:5, 10; 54:4; 55:3, 4; 61:9; 62:6

facilis, 18:10

facio, 2:3, 4, 9; 3:1, 3–6, 8, 9, 11; 4:3, 5, 11, 16; 5:2, 4–6, 8; 6:1, 5–9, 11, 17; 7:1, 2, 4, 5; 8:8–10; 9:1, 2, 4–7, 9, 10, 12, 14, 16; 10:2, 5, 6; 11:3, 4, 6, 8, 15; 12:1–3, 5–7, 9, 10; 13:1, 3, 5; 14:3, 4; 15:6, 7; 16:6, 7; 17:2, 4; 18:5, 9, 13, 14; 19:4, 11, 16; 20:3, 4, 10; 21:1, 4, 9; 22:1–7; 23:6, 10, 14; 24:3; 25:3, 4, 6, 7, 9, 12; 26:2, 5, 6, 8, 13, 14; 27:2, 4, 6, 7, 10–14; 28:1, 4, 10; 29:1; 30:4, 6, 7; 31:5, 7; 32:1–3, 6, 10, 13, 15; 33:1; 34:2, 3; 35:3–5, 7; 36:3; 37:3, 4; 39:3–5, 7, 11; 40:1–3, 6, 8; 42:1–3, 5–7, 9; 43:1, 5, 7; 44:1–3, 5–7, 9, 10; 45:1, 3–5; 46:1–4; 47:1, 2, 7, 9; 48:2–5; 49:3, 6–8; 50:2; 51:1, 6, 7; 52:3; 53:2, 8, 12; 54:2, 6; 55:2, 9, 10; 58:3, 4; 60:2; 61:2, 3; 63:2, 4, 5; 64:1, 5

facula, 23:6

fallo, 34:1; 43:6; 47:8

falsus, 11:12; 44:6, 7, 10

fames, 3:9; 6:11; 8:10

famulus, 30:2; 47:1; 53:2, 8, 10; 57:2; 58:1

fastigium, 18:10; 28:7

fel, 24:5

femina, 3:4; 9:1; 29:3; 32:5

femineus, 33:1

femur, 21:5

fero, 8:1; 17:3; 18:10; 26:8; 29:3; 42:8; 64:1

ferrum, 2:9; 15:1, 2; 21:7; 26:3, 6; 30:3, 6

ferus, 6:11; 7:3; 40:7; 47:4–6; 59:5

festino, 12:4, 5; 13:1, 10; 16:2; 18:9, 10; 19:13; 31:2; 32:4, 7, 16; 42:7; 45:4; 51:4; 61:7

festinus, 45:2

festivitas, 13:4–7

feto, 21:6

fetus, 3:10

ficus, 37:2, 3

fidelis, 13:10; 23:12; 27:13; 53:13

figura, 3:9; 12:3

filia, 1:1, 2, 4–15, 17–19; 2:4, 5; 3:1; 4:10–14, 16; 8:4–8, 11, 13; 9:9, 15; 18:14; 25:13; 29:1, 2; 30:1, 31:8; 40:1, 2, 4, 5, 8; 42:1; 43:5; 48:3; 51:6; 53:10; 64:3

filius, 1:1, 2, 5–9, 11, 13, 15, 17, 18, 20, 22; 2:3, 4, 10; 3:1, 4, 5, 8, 11; 4:1–4, 6, 9, 10, 12–14, 16; 5:1, 4–7; 7:2; 8:1, 5–9, 11–14; 9:1–5, 9, 11, 14–16; 10:2–4; 11:1, 5, 6, 9, 15; 12:1; 14:3; 15:3; 16:2, 4–6; 18:2, 5, 6, 8; 19:3, 9; 20:1, 2, 5, 6, 8, 10; 21:6, 9; 22:1, 3, 5–9; 23:1, 2, 7–9; 24:1, 3–5; 25:1, 9, 13; 26:6; 28:1–4; 29:1; 30:1, 4; 31:8, 9; 32:1–6, 8, 10, 13; 33:3–5; 35:1; 36:1; 37:1; 39:1, 5, 6, 8–10; 40:1, 2, 8, 9; 41:1, 3; 42:1–4; 43:1; 44:2, 5, 6, 9; 46:2–4; 47:4, 6, 8–10; 48:3, 4; 49:1, 7, 8; 50:1, 3, 5; 51:1, 4, 6; 52:1, 3, 4; 53:3, 10, 12;

54:1, 3, 5; 55:6, 8; 56:1, 4; 59:2, 3; 62:1, 2; 63:1, 2; 64:8, 9; 65:1, 4

fimbrie (fimbriae), 16:1

finio, 20:8; 54:2; 55:1

finis, 7:3; 15:7; 19:2, 4, 5; 21:4; 23:13; 30:7; 33:5; 39:6; 49:3; 56:6; 59:4; 62:4

firmamentum, 16:6; 18:5; 19:10; 32:7, 9; 40:5

flamma, 6:17; 11:5; 23:5, 10; 28:7, 8; 30:6; 31:4; 32:7; 35:7; 38:4; 42:9

fletus, 50:6

floreo, 17:1; 53:9; 55:1

flos, 17:2; 52:2; 53:10

fluctus, 3:11; 29:4; 32:7, 8

flumen, 9:1, 12, 15; 23:4; 27:12

fluo, 15:4; 21:9

fluvius, 19:10

fluxus, 10:6

fons, 3:5; 7:4; 51:2

foras, 45:3; 64:4

forma, 26:9

fornicaria, 43:5

fornicatio, 9:5

forsitan, 20:4; 24:2; 35:5; 45:1; 49:1, 8; 52:3; 54:1

fortasse, 27:15

forte, 11:14; 18:7; 25:5; 35:6; 41:1; 47:1, 4; 50:5; 55:1

Fortis (title for God), 11:8

fortis, 6:9; 22:5; 44:9; 51:1

Fortissimus (title for God), 16:5; 18:10, 11; 20:4; 31:5; 32:4, 8, 10, 13; 61:5, 6; 62:4

fortissimus, 21:7; 35:1; 59:5

fortiter, 11:4; 16:3

fortitudo, 44:5

fragilis, 26:14

fragmentum, 37:5

frango, 6:14; 22:2; 26:6

frater, 2:1; 4:9; 6:1; 7:3, 5; 8:1, 9, 10; 12:1; 20:6; 22:3, 4, 6; 26:5; 27:12, 14; 32:1; 35:1; 37:1, 4; 39:2, 3; 43:5, 8; 45:3; 46:1, 2; 56:1; 59:3, 4; 61:3, 6; 62:5, 8, 9, 11

fraudo, 18:12; 42:2

frequenter, 64:4

frequento, 11:5

frigus, 3:9

fronio, 40:6

frons, 61:7

fructus, 3:10; 9:2, 5, 6, 14; 11:9; 12:8; 13:5, 7, 10; 14:4; 15:1; 20:8; 22:3; 28:4; 32:2, 4, 8; 37:2; 39:11; 42:1–3; 44:10; 47:4, 6, 7; 50:2, 7; 55:4

frux, 15:1

fuga, 38:3

fugio, 6:9, 11, 13; 27:11, 15; 31:3; 36:1, 2; 41:1; 47:10; 49:3; 54:4; 61:2; 62:1, 6; 65:1

fulgur, 11:5; 18:12; 19:16; 32:7, 13

fundamentum, 10:5; 16:6; 18:10; 28:7–9; 32:7

fundibulum, 61:7

fundo (-are), 18:4; 35:7

fundo (-ere), 35:6

fungor, 32:14

furor (noun), 6:9; 12:9; 16:6

furor (verb), 21:3; 44:6, 7

gaudeo, 6:18; 20:5; 40:2; 51:7

gemitus, 40:6

generatio, 4:11, 17; 5:8; 8:11–13; 11:6; 13:8; 14:4; 19:3; 20:1, 3; 21:2, 4; 31:5; 32:3, 4; 33:6; 40:4; 44:8; 49:3; 50:4

genero, 4:10; 8:14; 32:6

genicium (gynaeceum), 40:6

geno (gigno), 1:1, 2, 5, 7, 9, 11, 13, 15, 18, 20, 22; 2:4, 5, 7, 9; 4:7, 9–15; 8:1, 4, 5, 8; 9:7; 12:2; 16:5; 19:10; 23:4, 8; 26:6; 33:1; 35:3; 47:11

gens, 4:11, 17; 9:5; 11:1; 12:2; 15:5; 16:3; 20:4; 21:5; 27:7; 30:4; 32:1; 39:7; 51:3, 6, 7; 64:4

genuinus, 25:12

genus, 9:3, 4; 12:4; 17:1; 18:4; 19:8; 26:14; 44:6, 8, 10; 49:7; 53:9

germino, 3:3; 25:5

gero, 22:4; 25:8; 33:6; 35:4; 36:4; 45:6; 47:8

glacies, 26:8

gladius, 3:9; 8:7; 26:6; 27:11; 43:3; 47:10; 58:4

gloria, 6:1; 9:7; 11:15; 15:5; 17:1; 19:16; 23:8; 30:2; 32:1; 35:5; 51:7; 54:6; 64:4

gloriatio, 51:4

glorifico, 11:1, 8; 12:9; 19:12; 59:4

glorior, 31:1, 7; 32:5, 12; 42:4; 50:2; 64:7

gloriosus, 9:16; 12:1

glutio (gluttio), 16:7

grandis, 6:17; 28:4

grando, 10:1; 30:5

gratia, 3:4; 6:10; 32:14

gratificor, 42:8

gratis, 43:7

gratulor, 32:15

gravis, 27:12

grex, 17:4; 19:9; 23:12; 28:5; 30:5; 31:5; 59:3

gusto, 42:3; 48:1

gutta, 17:3; 19:15

gyrus, 16:7; 18:8; 29:2

habeo, 6:9; 9:1, 5; 11:13; 12:2, 7, 9; 18:4, 7; 22:3; 23:5; 24:6; 25:9, 12; 29:1, 3; 30:1, 3; 32:5, 8, 9; 33:3; 34:1; 35:1; 36:3, 4; 37:1; 38:4; 39:5, 7; 43:3; 44:2, 3, 6; 49:3, 6, 8; 50:7; 53:4; 55:4, 10; 58:4; 62:5, 11; 64:1

habitabilis, 11:5; 39:7

habitaculum, 3:10; 21:10

habitatio, 4:11; 10:5; 16:3; 32:8; 38:4; 55:1; 63:4

habito, 2:1, 7–10; 3:3, 4, 6, 10, 12; 4:3, 5, 16; 5:2; 6:1; 7:3; 8:1, 2, 7, 9, 14; 9:3, 8; 10:2; 11:9; 12:4; 14:5; 15:6; 18:1, 2; 19:12, 13; 20:9; 21:1; 22:1, 2; 23:4, 5, 11; 24:1; 25:9; 26:13; 28:6, 8, 9; 30:4; 32:6, 15; 41:3; 45:1, 2, 4; 46:3; 48:1; 63:1; 64:3

habundantia (abundantia), 51:4

habundo (abundo), 50:5

haurio, 11:5

hedus (haedus), 17:3

hereditas, 12:9; 18:11, 12; 19:8, 9; 21:2, 4, 10; 23:9; 24:3; 27:7; 28:2; 30:4; 32:3; 39:7, 9; 49:6

heredito, 15:1; 18:1; 32:3

heremus (eremus), 10:7; 11:1, 8, 15; 14:5; 15:5, 6; 18:9; 19:9; 20:3, 6; 21:3; 22:2, 5; 25:9; 26:4; 39:8; 51:6; 53:8; 54:2; 56:1; 57:2; 61:1, 2; 62:11

hesternus, 19:13; 55:3

heu, 53:3

hilaritas, 21:10

hodiernus, 22:8; 25:6; 26:5, 15; 27:9; 30:7; 32:13; 45:2; 53:4

holocaustoma (Greek), 3:8; 4:5; 11:15; 13:1; 18:5, 7; 22:8; 26:7; 32:2, 18; 40:8; 41:1; 42:9

holocaustum, 18:7; 26:7; 39:10; 40:2

homicidium, 44:6

homo, 2:9; 3:1–4, 9, 11; 6:13; 7:2; 9:8, 16; 11:1, 2, 14; 12:4; 13:8, 9; 14:4; 15:2, 7; 16:2, 3, 6; 18:3, 4, 7, 10; 19:9–12, 16; 20:8; 21:4; 22:3, 7; 25:5; 26:2, 3, 5, 6, 13, 14; 27:12; 28:4, 8, 9; 32:1, 3, 13; 33:5; 34:3; 35:5; 37:2; 39:4; 44:6–8, 10; 45:6; 48:1; 49:1; 50:5; 51:4; 53:2, 4; 61:8; 64:6

honorifico, 18:2; 44:6

hora, 12:6; 18:12; 25:11; 27:5; 28:6; 31:2; 32:14, 16; 37:4; 43:5; 45:6; 54:2; 56:3

hortus, 37:2

humiliatio, 9:6

humilio, 8:7; 9:11; 19:16; 23:9; 30:4; 43:1

hymnizo, 21:8; 32:12–14, 17; 51:3, 6; 59:4; 60:3

hymnus, 18:6; 19:16; 32:1, 17; 59:4; 62:6

hypocrisis, 37:3

iacinctinum (hyacinthus), 40:6

iacto, 31:7; 43:8

iaspis, 26:10

idolon, 9:2; 22:5; 25:9, 11; 26:4; 29:3; 36:3; 44:2, 6, 7

ieiunium, 13:6

ieiuno, 13:6; 22:7; 30:4, 5

igneus, 63:4

ignis, 3:9; 4:16; 6:2, 4, 5, 7, 11–14, 16–18; 10:7; 11:5, 14; 12:3; 15:5; 18:10; 20:7; 23:6, 10; 25:3, 6, 8, 13; 26:1–3, 5, 6; 27:15; 30:6; 32:1, 7; 35:7; 37:3, 4; 38:3, 4; 39:9; 42:9; 43:1; 44:7, 9; 45:3; 47:12; 53:2; 63:4

ignitus, 19:9

ignorantia, 22:6

ignoro, 32:4; 53:12; 55:1

illudo, 43:7; 64:5

illumino, 11:1, 2; 12:2; 18:4; 19:6; 23:6, 7, 10; 30:2; 33:1; 37:3; 51:3; 53:8

imaginor, 4:16

imago, 3:11; 16:5; 28:8; 50:7

imitor, 9:9; 20:6; 25:9

immemor (and inmemor), 39:4, 8; 40:2; 43:5; 60:3

immineo, 35:1

immobilis, 31:1

immolo, 4:5; 13:2; 22:1; 25:9; 34:2

immortalis, 19:12

immundus, 42:3; 53:3

immunis, 52:3

immuto, 20:2

impedio, 31:1

impello, 31:7

imperitus, 37:4

impero, 45:3

impietas, 44:8

impius, 11:1, 6

implano, 19:7; 34:5

impleo, 3:11; 9:3; 26:13; 39:6

impono, 6:7, 8; 38:3; 44:7; 45:4; 46:4; 54:4; 55:8

improperium, 50:7

impropero, 50:1, 2, 5; 61:2

impunis, 44:8

impunitus, 57:3

imputo, 22:3

inapparentis, 28:7

inaures, 12:3

incendo, 6:2, 16; 9:8; 12:8; 15:6; 19:4; 20:3, 7; 31:2; 32:11; 38:3, 4; 43:1; 44:3; 47:10

incensus, 11:15; 13:1; 44:3

inchoo (incoho), 4:16

incido, 9:10; 15:4; 18:13; 26:3; 27:15; 31:1, 2, 7; 32:14; 35:2; 61:6; 62:5, 8

incipio, 14:1; 19:7, 10, 12; 23:7; 24:4; 27:9; 30:7; 32:14, 15; 36:1; 53:5; 59:4

incisio, 23:4

inclino, 15:6; 23:10; 40:7

includo, 6:7, 9, 12–14; 15:5; 25:4; 27:3, 4, 15; 39:1; 43:2; 45:4; 55:6, 8

inconveniens, 49:1

incredulus, 15:6

increpo, 23:10

incubo, 65:3

indiatrius, 25:11

indico, 43:6

indigeo, 26:13; 27:14

indignatio, 25:3

indignor, 2:8; 19:14; 28:4; 35:6; 52:4; 63:1

indignus, 57:4

indissolubiliter, 27:11

induco, 15:4; 21:9; 23:11; 39:7

induo, 20:2; 27:9; 36:2; 64:4

induro, 46:2

indutus, 27:10

inebrio, 43:6

inestimabilis, 25:12; 36:1

inextinguibilis, 63:4

infans, 9:12, 16; 51:1; 52:1; 62:10

inferior, 28:8, 9; 60:2

infernus, 3:10; 16:3; 21:4; 31:7; 33:3; 40:6

infero, 21:7

infirmus, 18:12; 31:1

infundo, 26:11

ingemisco (ingemesco), 42:2

ingratus, 62:11

ingredior, 3:4, 5; 8:7; 9:4; 10:6; 12:4; 14:2;
   16:5; 19:7; 22:2; 25:12; 31:3, 5, 6, 9; 32:9;
   35:1; 39:1; 42:7, 8; 45:1–3; 47:1; 62:11

inhabitabilis, 3:9; 11:1, 8

inhabitatio, 19:12

inhabito, 3:9; 7:4, 5; 18:2, 8; 21:9; 39:8; 45:3;
   48:1, 3

inhonorifico, 44:7

inicio, 2:8; 65:2

inimicus, 9:2; 10:2–4; 11:10, 11; 15:5, 6; 19:7,
   9; 20:9; 21:3, 9; 22:2; 23:1, 9, 12; 26:13;
   27:2, 7, 9, 16; 30:2, 4, 5, 7; 31:2, 9; 32:7,
   10, 11, 14, 17; 35:5; 39:1, 4, 6; 43:2, 5; 49:6;
   53:8; 54:2, 5; 55:2; 58:4; 59:5; 61:3; 62:8;
   63:2, 3; 64:2; 65:5

iniquitas, 1:20; 3:3, 6; 6:9; 12:4; 19:3; 22:3, 7;
   23:6; 28:4; 30:4; 32:3; 34:5; 35:4; 39:4, 9;
   44:5, 8, 9; 45:5; 46:1, 2; 47:2, 6; 52:1, 3;
   62:5, 6, 8; 64:9

iniquus, 2:8, 10; 19:4; 33:3, 3; 35:4; 36:4; 45:6;
   46:4; 47:7, 8; 49:3; 51:5; 52:1, 4; 60:1

initio, 2:7; 4:7; 7:5

initium, 1:1; 7:4; 13:6; 26:13; 39:7; 47:6; 55:7,
   8; 59:5; 62:9

iniuria, 39:5

iniuste, 32:15; 37:4; 47:6; 52:4; 62:3

iniusticia (iniustitia), 65:5

inmaculatus (immaculatus), 3:4; 4:11

inmensurabilis (immensurabilis), 9:3; 32:3;
   34:3

inmitto (immitto), 23:6; 27:12

inmundus (immundus), 3:4

innovatio, 23:14; 32:17

innovo, 16:3

innoxius, 22:4; 46:4

innubilo, 3:12

inpedio (impedio), 23:10

inpono (impono), 40:2

inportunus (importunus), 39:8; 43:6,

inprimis (imprimis), 16:2; 53:2; 59:4

inquieto, 64:7

inquiro, 46:1; 52:2

insidie (insidiae), 47:9

insilio, 28:6

insipiens, 45:6

insipientia, 22:5

insisto, 14:2

inspeculor, 50:4

inspergo, 12:9

inspicio, 4:16; 5:2, 4, 6; 14:1, 2; 18:8; 19:10;
   20:6, 7; 55:1

inspiratio, 10:5; 32:8

instituo, 62:11

insto, 16:6

instruo, 22:8

insufferibilis, 16:1

insula, 4:3

insulto, 50:2

insuper, 21:9

insurgo, 32:11; 47:1

intellectus, 32:7; 55:1

intelligentia, 20:3

intelligo, 18:12; 20:4; 29:4; 32:3; 53:2, 5; 56:6

intendo, 2:10; 33:1; 34:1; 35:5; 38:2; 39:7;
   40:5; 42:3; 43:5; 46:4; 49:7; 51:3; 53:6; 56:6;
   61:2

intenebresco, 18:10

intenebrifico, 32:10

intercisus, 7:5

interfector, 61:8

interficio, 2:1; 8:7; 9:1, 5; 15:6; 18:1; 27:10,
   11; 32:4; 41:1; 43:3, 4, 8; 47:6, 10; 49:5;
   54:3, 4; 58:3, 4; 59:5; 61:2, 7, 8; 62:3, 5, 6;
   63:2, 3

interim, 48:4

interimo, 27:1

interpres, 18:2

interpretor, 6:18; 51:1

interrogo, 18:11; 22:8; 25:1, 5, 6, 8–10, 13;
   27:14, 15; 35:2; 42:10; 44:3, 5; 46:1, 3; 54:4;
   55:3; 56:4; 61:9; 64:3, 4, 6

intexo, 40:6

intono, 54:2

intro, 16:5; 19:9; 47:1

intueor, 27:12

invalesco, 9:11; 20:9

invenio, 1:16; 3:4; 5:5, 6; 6:1, 10–15; 9:3; 10:2;

25:4, 6, 9, 10, 12; 26:1, 2, 4, 5, 9; 31:9; 33:5; 35:3; 36:3; 45:4; 47:10; 49:1, 2; 51:4; 55:3, 4
investigo, 21:2
invetero, 40:7
invicem, 44:9; 62:3, 7, 9, 11
invideo, 32:1; 62:5
inviscero, 30:7
invisibilis, 12:1; 27:10; 28:7–9
invoco, 25:11; 32:14; 49:7
ira, 6:9; 7:4; 9:4; 10:5; 15:5; 19:9; 22:6, 7; 26:1; 39:5, 8, 11; 47:2; 48:3; 62:11
iracundia, 6:9; 25:3; 29:3; 39:8; 52:1
irascor, 12:8; 19:2, 11; 21:2; 28:4
iratus, 6:5; 16:2; 30:2; 39:11; 43:2
irreligiositas, 44:5
irrigatio, 19:10
irrigo, 19:10
irruo, 18:10
isopum (hyssopum), 13:3
iter, 18:9; 28:2
iterum, 2:7; 7:1; 12:4; 27:12; 49:6; 52:2; 55:4
iubeo, 7:5; 9:1; 19:13
iubilo, 21:9
iucunditas, 21:10; 51:7
iucundor, 13:4
iudex, 3:10; 19:3; 22:6; 30:1; 35:7; 41:1, 2; 43:4; 48:5
iudicium, 9:8; 11:15; 12:2, 4; 51:5; 62:4
iudico, 11:2; 15:5; 29:4; 32:18; 34:3; 37:3; 40:9; 41:1, 2; 43:8; 44:10; 45:4; 57:4
iumentum, 6:7, 8; 10:1
iungo, 55:6, 8
iuramentum, 30:7; 62:11
iuro, 39:7; 47:3; 48:3; 62:11
iusticia (iustitia), 9:8; 11:15; 12:2, 10
iustificatus, 3:10
iustus, 3:4
iuventus, 3:9

labium, 10:4; 51:3
labor, 12:9; 14:4; 19:5; 29:1; 32:11
laboro, 18:11; 19:5; 27:14; 28:4, 5; 29:1
labrum, 11:15; 13:1
lac, 15:4; 21:9; 31:5, 6; 51:1, 2; 62:10
lacrima, 40:3, 5; 42:3; 50:2, 5; 62:10
lactens, 2:10; 30:4; 39:7; 55:6, 10
lacto, 51:1, 3; 55:4, 6, 8, 10
lacus, 35:6
lamina, 13:1
lampas, 11:14; 19:16
lancea, 62:6
lapideus, 12:10
lapis, 6:2–6, 16; 7:5; 11:15; 12:9; 13:1; 18:13; 21:7; 25:10–12; 26:2–13, 15; 30:5; 37:2; 39:9; 59:5; 61:3, 5, 7

largior, 21:2
latitudo, 3:4
latus, 6:2, 16; 9:11; 32:1, 18; 44:9; 53:7; 60:3
laudo, 28:4; 32:14
laus, 11:8
lavo, 9:15; 27:12
lectulus, 24:4
lectus, 24:5; 31:3, 7
legatio, 32:14
legatus, 39:8
lego, 21:7; 26:1
leo, 24:6; 43:4; 44:5, 9; 45:6; 47:4–7; 59:5
lepra, 13:3
leprosus, 13:3
lesura, 6:17
levis, 18:12; 24:6; 54:4; 62:6
levo, 10:1; 18:5, 8; 21:8, 9; 22:8; 24:2; 28:5; 33:4; 38:4; 43:3; 51:1; 54:1
lex, 11:2, 5; 12:2; 13:2, 3; 16:1, 5; 19:1, 6, 9; 21:7, 9; 22:5, 6; 23:2, 10; 25:3, 13; 29:4; 30:5; 33:3; 34:1; 38:2; 39:6; 42:1; 61:2
liber, 25:13; 26:1–3, 6–8; 35:7; 43:4; 56:7; 63:5
liberatio, 18:11; 32:12, 14
libero, 6:9, 11; 9:6, 16; 10:1; 19:9; 20:4; 23:9, 12; 27:7; 31:3; 32:1; 35:4; 38:4; 39:3, 4, 11; 40:2; 42:3; 47:1; 49:1, 8; 51:5; 59:5; 63:2
ligirium, 26:11
lignum, 3:4; 11:15; 12:9; 13:3, 7; 37:2–4; 40:3; 50:1
ligo, 32:4; 43:7
ligula, 44:2
lingua, 4:17; 6:18; 7:2, 3, 5; 12:7; 32:1; 40:4; 63:4
liquefacio, 6:16
liquor, 25:11; 26:11
locus, 6:11, 18; 7:5; 9:12; 12:1, 10; 13:8; 15:6; 16:7; 18:14; 19:7, 8, 10, 13; 21:6; 22:3; 23:4, 6; 26:4, 8, 13, 15; 28:7–9; 30:5; 32:1; 38:4; 39:5; 47:9; 48:1; 49:6; 52:2; 55:1; 62:2
locusta, 10:1
locutio, 53:2
logion, 11:15; 13:1; 26:4
longanimitas, 19:8, 9; 39:5; 49:3; 55:2
longevus (longaevus), 23:10; 56:6
longitudo, 3:4; 15:7; 44:5
longus, 11:15; 51:7
loquor, 6:5, 12; 9:3, 4, 14; 11:2, 6, 14; 12:1, 3, 9; 13:2, 7; 14:2; 15:2, 4, 5; 16:1, 2, 4; 17:1; 18:3, 5; 19:1, 2, 4, 6; 20:1, 2, 4, 6, 10; 21:3, 9, 10; 22:2; 23:2, 3, 13; 24:5; 27:2, 9, 11, 13, 15; 28:3, 10; 31:1; 32:15; 33:4; 36:1, 4; 38:2; 42:3, 6; 44:9; 46:1; 47:6, 12; 51:3, 4; 53:2, 7; 58:1, 4; 59:5; 60:2; 61:3, 4; 62:10, 11
luceo, 9:8; 10:7; 14:5; 15:2; 19:16; 25:12; 32:10
lucerna, 9:8; 13:1; 15:6; 19:4; 25:12

lucrificatio, 13:10
luctor, 18:6
luctus, 9:2
lugeo, 19:12; 20:2; 43:7; 46:3
lumbus, 12:6; 20:2, 3; 31:1; 35:5; 51:6
lumen, 3:10; 9:8; 11:1, 9; 12:1, 9; 18:10, 12;
    19:13, 16; 22:3; 25:12; 26:13, 15; 28:3, 8;
    33:3; 51:4–7
lumino, 30:5
luna, 11:6; 12:1; 18:10; 19:13; 26:13; 32:9, 10
lutum, 6:2
lux, 28:9

machera (machaera), 65:3
magicia (magice, magicus), 34:2
magis, 9:1; 12:9; 40:4; 49:7; 62:6
magister, 53:5
maior, 12:4; 16:2; 44:9
maledico, 3:9; 16:2; 18:2, 6, 12; 26:5; 32:4
malefacio, 47:1
maleficium, 34:2–4; 64:3
maleficus, 34:1; 64:1
malicia (malitia), 39:8, 9; 45:2; 46:2; 47:9
malignitas, 3:3
malignor, 8:10; 32:7
malignus, 7:1
malleus, 31:7
malo, 35:2
malus, 1:20; 12:6; 18:7; 20:1, 6; 21:4; 26:5;
    27:2; 35:3; 37:2, 3; 45:3; 46:4; 47:7; 49:7;
    53:11; 55:1; 57:3; 62:4, 11
mamilla, 2:10; 51:2, 3
mando, 11:6, 15; 13:8; 15:5; 16:5; 18:2; 21:9;
    23:12; 25:3; 26:4; 28:3, 4; 30:1, 2, 5; 31:9;
    35:3; 39:8, 9; 44:10; 48:1, 5; 49:6; 53:10
manduco, 19:5; 20:8; 25:9; 42:8; 62:11
mane, 9:10; 18:7, 8; 23:4; 42:3; 45:2, 4; 46:1;
    53:12; 55:3; 56:4, 5
maneo, 16:7; 18:11; 42:2; 45:1, 2; 51:6; 62:2
manifestatio, 47:2; 48:5
manifesto, 18:12; 19:1; 21:7; 25:8, 9, 13; 26:5;
    32:4; 33:5; 39:9; 42:1, 4; 43:6; 53:9
manipulus, 35:1
manna, 19:10; 20:8
mansueto, 23:10
mansuetudo, 35:5
manubrium, 27:11
manufactus, 22:5
manus, 3:2; 6:6, 10; 11:2, 10; 12:5; 18:13; 19:7,
    16; 20:2; 21:3; 22:7; 23:10; 24:4–6; 25:11;
    27:4, 6–9, 11–13; 30:7; 31:1, 7, 9; 32:2, 12;
    34:5; 35:2, 4; 36:1–3; 39:3, 10; 40:1; 42:3, 4;
    43:2, 3; 44:7; 45:3; 46:1, 3; 47:1, 8; 49:8;
    51:1; 54:3; 55:3, 4; 58:4; 61:3, 6; 62:5, 6, 8;
    63:3; 64:3, 6, 8; 65:2

marcesco, 18:11; 40:6; 44:9; 47:12
mare, 4:3; 10:2–7; 11:8; 15:5; 21:2, 3; 23:10;
    26:4, 8; 29:4; 32:8, 17
maritus, 42:1
masculus, 3:4; 9:1, 12; 58:3
mater, 9:5, 16; 11:9; 31:3, 8, 9; 32:5; 33:1, 4,
    6; 36:1; 38:2; 40:4, 6; 44:2, 4–7, 9; 47:7, 12;
    51:4; 53:10–12; 59:4; 61:6; 62:10
maxilla, 43:4
mechor, 11:10; 25:10; 44:6, 7
mediator, 9:8
meditatio, 22:5
meditor, 22:6
medius, 10:2, 6; 19:1; 23:12; 28:8; 35:7; 37:5;
    47:4, 9; 53:3; 55:7; 57:1; 59:3
mel, 15:4; 19:15; 21:9
melior, 9:2, 5, 14; 10:3; 21:3; 24:2; 26:13; 50:3;
    62:8
melotis, 9:5
memor, 10:4, 13:6, 7; 24:3; 26:13; 28:4; 31:3,
    5; 32:14, 17; 33:4, 5; 35:3; 38:2; 39:5; 47:1,
    3; 49:8; 53:3; 62:9, 11; 64:1; 65:5
memoria, 3:12; 4:5; 14:4; 26:12; 32:4; 44:8
memorialis, 13:4
memoro, 3:7; 11:1; 16:3; 18:12; 19:11; 23:9;
    32:12; 39:4; 43:5; 48:1; 53:2; 54:5; 60:3; 64:6
mendacium, 62:11
mens, 20:3; 27:12
mensa, 11:15; 13:1; 62:11
mensis, 9:5, 12; 11:1; 19:7; 23:2, 8; 37:5; 40:8
mensura, 19:10; 33:3
mentior, 44:10; 47:2; 57:2; 62:11
merces, 18:7; 64:7
meridies, 53:4
metra (Greek), 23:7, 8; 32:1, 5; 42:1, 3; 50:4,
    7; 51:2; 60:3
metus, 10:3
miles, 19:16
militia (and milicia), 19:2; 23:10; 27:7; 32:1,
    7, 13
minimus, 30:4; 32:13; 40:3; 47:5; 59:2; 62:5
minister, 7:5; 30:1; 32:9, 10, 14; 42:10; 50:5
ministro, 22:8; 34:3; 44:7; 51:6
minor, 16:2; 46:1; 61:2
minoro, 47:6; 50:5
minuo, 3:7; 9:3; 14:2
minute, 18:5
mirabilis, 9:7; 12:2; 14:4; 20:4; 26:5; 27:7;
    28:1, 2; 30:5, 7; 32:12; 35:2; 51:6
miraculum, 32:13
miror, 27:12
mirre (and Myrra; Marah), 11:15; 20:8
mirre (myrra), 12:9
misceo, 31:6
miseratio, 19:8; 21:4

misereor, 12:9; 13:10; 15:7; 19:9; 22:7; 25:7;
   27:15; 31:2; 35:3
misericordia, 3:4; 11:6; 13:6; 15:7; 19:8, 11,
   14; 22:5; 24:3; 28:5; 39:6; 51:5; 59:4
misericors, 12:10; 22:6
mitifico, 50:8
mitto, 3:9; 6:4–6, 9, 12–14, 16; 8:10; 9:15;
   10:1, 3, 4; 11:15; 12:3, 7; 15:1; 16:4, 6; 18:2,
   7, 11; 19:9; 20:6, 10; 21:10; 23:1, 9; 24:3, 4;
   25:1–3, 9, 10; 26:3, 6; 27:2, 6, 7, 10, 12, 15;
   28:1; 29:4; 30:2, 5, 6; 31:1, 3, 8, 9; 32:4, 6,
   14; 33:1; 35:4; 36:3; 39:8; 41:1; 42:3, 5, 9;
   43:6; 45:4; 46:2; 47:1, 2; 49:2–5; 53:12; 55:1,
   4, 5; 56:3; 57:1; 58:1, 4; 59:3; 60:1; 61:4, 5,
   7; 63:2
modicum, 6:17; 14:2; 18:11; 22:5; 31:4
modus, 7:2; 12:8; 13:7; 18:2; 20:10; 21:9; 25:7,
   11, 12; 35:2; 53:2; 62:9
moles, 25:9; 37:5
molestus, 60:3
mollis, 62:5
momentum, 19:15; 58:3
moneo, 30:6; 33:1; 39:6
mons, 6:11; 11:5, 14, 15; 12:2, 8; 15:6; 18:10;
   19:8, 9; 21:7; 23:10; 24:6; 25:9, 10; 26:3, 4,
   7, 9, 11; 28:7; 30:3, 4; 32:7; 35:1; 40:3–5;
   43:3; 44:6; 48:1; 56:4; 59:5
monstro, 34:3
montanus, 6:7–9, 11, 12, 18; 27:11
morior, 6:9, 11; 9:2, 5, 14; 10:3; 11:14; 16:3;
   19:7; 21:1; 23:1, 10; 24:2; 25:7, 8; 27:15;
   28:1, 3, 4, 10; 29:4; 31:7; 32:9; 33:1, 4; 36:4;
   37:2; 38:1, 4; 40:2, 3; 42:1, 10; 43:7; 44:8;
   45:3, 6; 48:1; 49:3, 5; 50:4, 7; 52:3, 4; 53:10;
   54:6; 55:2, 6; 58:3, 4; 61:6, 8; 62:2; 63:2;
   64:9; 65:3
moror, 32:13
mors, 3:9, 10; 10:1; 11:11; 13:8; 19:3, 16; 21:4;
   24:3; 25:1, 8; 27:7; 33:1–3, 6; 35:2; 37:3;
   40:3, 4; 42:10; 43:5; 44:2, 10; 48:1; 52:3;
   61:6; 62:5, 9; 63:2; 65:1
mortalis, 39:4, 5; 44:7
mortalitas, 10:1
mortifico, 14:4; 47:1; 51:5; 63:3; 65:2–4
mortuus, 2:4; 3:10; 5:8; 10:1; 13:6; 14:1; 18:8;
   19:16; 21:3; 25:7; 30:6, 7; 31:9; 33:6; 36:4;
   37:5; 40:9; 41:1, 2; 45:4; 47:8; 51:5; 54:5;
   55:10; 64:1–3, 5, 7
mos, 26:6; 50:3
motus, 23:10; 28:8; 31:2
moveo, 3:11; 6:11; 11:5; 16:6; 23:10; 32:7, 8;
   47:6
mox, 36:2
mugio, 55:8
mula, 63:2

mulgeo, 31:5
mulier, 2:1, 2, 5, 6, 10; 3:4, 8; 4:11; 5:4, 5, 7;
   8:1, 4–6, 13; 9:2, 4, 5; 11:2; 12:3, 5; 13:8;
   14:4; 15:4; 18:13; 23:1, 2, 4, 5, 7, 8; 25:10;
   27:2; 30:2, 4; 31:1, 3, 7, 9; 32:5, 12; 33:1;
   37:5; 39:7; 40:1; 42:1, 2, 5, 7, 10; 43:1, 6, 8;
   44:7; 47:10; 48:3; 50:1, 2, 7; 54:6; 58:3; 61:6;
   64:3–5, 7
multiformis, 44:5
multiplico, 3:1, 8, 11; 4:11; 9:1; 23:7; 27:9;
   44:8; 45:3; 50:5; 51:4; 52:1; 55:3
multitudo, 3:11; 10:2; 14:2, 4; 19:14; 23:7, 10;
   27:6–8, 11, 12, 14, 15; 49:2; 62:4
multus, 11:9, 15; 18:2, 11, 12; 21:1, 9; 32:13;
   34:2; 39:1; 47:6; 60:3
mulus, 45:1, 4
mundus, 1:1; 3:4, 8; 9:3; 11:1
munus, 18:11, 12; 51:1
murmuratio, 17:1
murmuro, 27:15
murus, 15:5; 43:3
muto, 7:5; 19:16; 27:12; 28:8, 9; 64:4
myrtus, 13:7

nabla (nablia), 21:8; 51:7
narro, 32:12; 35:2; 40:4
nascor, 3:1; 4:9, 11; 9:1, 3, 10, 13; 13:6; 16:2;
   17:3; 19:9; 21:2, 6; 23:4, 7; 30:5; 32:3, 5, 15;
   37:2, 3; 44:7, 8; 49:7, 8; 50:4; 51:4; 52:2;
   53:10, 12; 54:6; 58:3, 4; 60:3; 61:6; 65:4
natio, 14:1
nativitas, 1:20; 32:7
navis, 4:3
nebula, 11:15; 19:13
necessarius, 25:12
necessitas, 49:2
neglego, 49:6; 59:4; 64:7
nego, 44:6; 55:7
nemo, 6:18; 35:3; 38:3; 40:4; 47:10; 49:5; 61:9
neo, 40:6
nequam, 25:5
nequiter, 25:8
nequitia, 25:7
nescio, 12:1; 18:3, 8, 10; 28:10; 47:9; 53:1;
   55:1; 59:2; 63:2
nidus, 53:10
nihil, 15:6; 21:4; 26:14; 29:4; 52:1, 2; 63:3
nimis, 46:3
nimius, 18:2
nimpha (nympha), 25:10, 11; 27:8, 9
nobismetipsis, 6:1
noceo, 39:5, 9; 52:2; 57:2; 58:4; 62:6; 64:4
noctu, 6:14; 27:6; 28:4; 34:1; 40:4; 43:2; 53:3;
   56:3; 62:9; 64:4
nolo, 6:3, 4, 11, 13; 9:5; 11:14; 32:16; 33:5;

38:1; 39:10; 43:5, 7; 47:1; 50:5, 8; 51:4, 6; 52:3; 53:9, 12; 55:2, 6; 56:3; 60:3; 64:5, 7; 65:2

nomen, 1:3, 6, 8, 10, 12, 14, 17, 19; 2:1, 3, 4, 6; 4:9, 10, 12–14; 6:1–3, 18; 7:5; 8:3, 8, 11; 9:9, 16; 10:4; 11:7; 15:3; 20:4; 21:10; 23:4; 25:8, 11; 26:2, 4, 8, 10–12; 27:4; 28:4, 9; 29:2; 32:4; 38:1; 40:1, 8; 42:1, 3, 10; 43:1, 5; 44:2–4, 6, 7, 10; 45:2; 47:11; 49:3, 7, 8; 50:1; 51:1; 54:6; 56:6; 58:1; 60:2; 61:2, 5; 64:1, 3

nomino, 23:12; 26:10; 28:4; 54:5; 59:4

nosco, 6:4; 9:1; 18:3; 19:2; 53:7

novus, 6:1; 8:8; 13:10; 22:8, 9; 23:8; 26:3, 7; 27:7; 28:1; 30:7; 32:1; 44:4; 55:6, 8; 60:3

nox, 3:5, 9; 6:7–9, 15; 9:10; 10:7; 11:15; 13:7; 18:3, 4, 8, 11, 12; 22:6; 23:2, 3, 7, 13; 25:12; 26:8; 27:5, 12; 32:16; 34:4; 38:2; 42:2; 45:2; 53:3, 4, 6; 58:3; 60:1

nubes, 3:12; 4:5; 10:7; 11:5; 13:1, 7; 15:5; 19:10, 11; 20:8; 23:10; 26:3, 8; 30:5; 32:7

nudus, 18:13

nullus, 14:2; 19:12; 27:5; 45:1; 47:7; 49:2, 8; 50:8

numero, 14:3; 21:2

numerus, 5:4–8; 8:13; 13:6; 14:2–4; 16:3; 19:10; 25:4; 27:5; 31:2; 43:8; 44:8; 47:11; 55:10; 61:2

nuncio (nuntio), 8:10; 14:4; 32:13; 64:7; 65:4

nuncius (and nuntius), 27:6; 39:8; 41:1; 46:2

nuptie (nuptiae), 32:5; 40:6

nurus, 54:6

nusquam, 35:7

nutrio, 9:16; 12:8; 48:1

nutritor, 53:11, 12

nutrix, 40:6

obaudio, 9:14; 12:3; 20:4; 23:12; 24:1; 30:5; 33:1, 3; 44:9; 52:4; 64:3

obdormio, 24:5; 29:4; 31:5, 6

obduro, 10:2, 6; 23:10; 33:6

obeo, 28:4; 39:7; 62:11

oblatio, 13:5, 6; 18:5, 7, 10; 19:10; 22:3; 32:3

obliviscor, 9:4; 13:10; 19:6; 21:6; 30:6; 39:5; 58:1

obprobrium (opprobrium), 61:4

observatio, 2:10; 11:15

obsorbeo, 26:8

obstetrix, 54:6

obumbro, 18:11; 23:12

obviam, 11:4; 27:13; 31:2, 3, 8, 9; 40:1; 46:2; 47:9; 54:3; 58:4

obvio, 6:18; 13:4; 35:1; 39:10, 11; 53:10, 11; 56:7; 61:1

occasus, 19:13

occido, 10:3; 11:11; 13:3; 16:2; 19:1; 30:5;

31:5, 7; 32:2, 4, 12; 36:2; 37:1, 4; 43:4; 44:7; 45:1, 4; 59:4, 5; 61:1, 8; 62:1, 4, 8; 65:5

occisio, 32:3

occultus, 21:9; 22:3; 27:10

oculus, 6:10; 7:4; 9:5; 18:9, 11; 20:10; 22:4; 24:4, 5; 25:12; 26:9, 13; 27:11, 12; 28:7; 29:1; 40:5; 43:5; 44:9; 48:4; 61:8; 62:8

odi, 8:9; 19:2; 49:3, 8; 62:4, 5, 11; 65:5

odium, 27:11; 32:5; 35:3; 39:4; 49:3; 61:4

odor, 3:8; 32:3; 37:2; 40:6

offero, 3:8; 4:5; 13:2; 18:7, 10; 22:3, 7–9; 26:7; 30:1; 32:2–4, 13, 18; 35:2; 39:11; 40:1–3, 8; 41:1, 3; 42:8, 9; 46:1; 51:7; 52:1; 59:4

officium, 32:10

oleum, 13:1; 40:6

olivetum, 29:2; 50:1

ometocea, 9:2

onichinus (onychinus), 26:11

operatio, 11:8

operio, 13:1

operor, 2:8, 10; 4:5; 11:8; 12:4; 17:3; 18:5; 27:2, 10; 34:3; 44:7, 9

oportet, 18:11; 28:10; 47:6; 49:7

opprimo, 54:4

opus, 1:20; 3:3, 4, 6, 10; 9:11; 11:8; 17:3; 20:4; 22:2, 7; 23:6; 25:5, 6, 11; 26:5, 13; 27:13; 32:5, 8, 14; 34:5; 44:7; 64:7

oratio, 31:5; 32:7; 39:11; 40:3; 44:10; 50:4–7

orbis, 11:2, 8; 13:6; 19:4, 13, 16; 21:5; 23:12

ordior, 28:8

organum, 2:7, 8; 21:8

oriens, 6:1

orior, 52:2

ornamentum, 11:6; 31:3

orno, 12:9; 18:13; 31:3

oro, 12:8; 19:3, 8; 22:7; 25:6; 27:7, 8; 33:4, 5; 39:7, 11; 40:3, 8; 42:2, 5; 43:7; 46:4; 47:3; 49:3, 6; 50:4–8; 51:2, 3; 52:3; 53:12; 55:1; 64:2

oromas, 23:3

ortigometra (ortygometra), 10:7

os, 3:10; 8:7; 9:12; 11:2, 14; 12:2; 16:6; 19:16; 25:3; 27:11; 28:3; 32:4, 12; 40:1; 42:4; 47:10; 48:1; 51:3, 4; 64:7

osculor, 24:3, 4; 62:11

ostendo, 2:9, 10; 9:8; 11:15; 13:1, 6, 8, 9; 14:1; 16:5; 17:1; 18:5, 11, 14; 19:7, 10, 13, 14; 22:8, 9; 23:6, 8; 25:2, 11; 26:2, 5, 6, 11; 27:7, 11, 13; 28:1; 30:5, 6; 32:1, 9, 12; 34:1, 4; 36:1; 44:6; 51:3; 58:2, 4

ostento, 25:11

ostium, 6:9

ovis, 13:2; 17:4; 19:9; 30:5; 44:3; 61:1; 62:5

pacificus, 5:2; 21:8, 9; 26:7; 49:8

palma, 13:7

palus, 31:7

pammixia (Greek), 10:1

panis, 10:7; 13:4, 5; 19:5; 42:8

par, 11:2, 3; 27:5; 31:1; 40:2

parabola, 18:10

paradisus (and paradysus; Greek), 13:9; 19:10; 26:8; 32:8

parateces (Greek), 3:10

parco, 2:2, 7; 8:1, 3, 6, 11–14; 19:11; 23:8; 28:2, 5; 40:6; 43:1; 46:2; 51:1, 4; 58:2; 60:3; 61:6

pareo, 9:10, 12; 11:6; 17:3, 4; 23:7; 42:1, 3, 4; 51:4, 6; 54:6; 58:3

pariter, 16:3; 36:2

pars, 4:3; 12:5; 14:1, 4; 18:10; 26:2; 29:1; 35:7; 45:4

parturio, 12:5; 42:3

parturitio, 9:6

partus, 4:11

pascha (Greek), 48:3; 50:2

pasco, 2:7; 19:9; 59:4; 61:1; 62:5

passer, 62:6

passio, 8:8

pastor, 19:3, 9; 28:5; 59:2

patefacio, 9:8

pater, 2:7; 4:11; 8:10; 9:4, 7; 10:2, 4; 11:9; 12:4; 13:6, 10; 14:1, 2, 4; 15:5; 16:5; 18:2, 5; 19:2, 6, 12; 20:4, 6; 21:3, 5, 9; 22:3, 5, 7; 23:2, 4, 9, 11–13; 24:4, 5; 25:6; 27:7; 28:3, 4, 10; 29:1, 4; 30:2, 4, 7; 31:7; 32:1, 3, 4, 6, 13, 17; 33:5, 6; 35:2, 5; 39:4; 40:1–5, 8, 9; 43:7, 8; 44:6, 7; 47:1, 2; 49:6; 52:1, 2, 4; 53:3, 5, 7, 10; 54:1, 6; 56:1, 4, 6; 57:2, 3; 59:4; 61:5; 62:3–6, 8, 11; 63:2; 64:2

patior, 7:2; 9:2; 25:5; 44:10; 54:1; 55:6; 62:5, 7

patria, 47:11

paucus, 30:5

pausatio, 49:6

pauso, 6:9; 11:8; 26:1; 28:9; 32:17, 18; 33:3; 39:8; 45:5; 46:1

pavor, 11:4, 14; 23:6

pax, 19:12; 20:5; 22:7; 23:13; 40:1; 41:1; 63:2

peccator, 8:2; 25:8, 11; 35:4; 39:4, 5; 45:3, 6

peccatum, 6:11; 11:6; 13:10; 16:7; 19:3, 9; 22:5; 25:3, 4; 26:13, 14; 27:15; 28:2, 10; 36:1; 39:6; 41:1; 42:2; 44:9, 10; 45:3; 46:1; 49:3, 5; 58:3; 62:6, 9

pecco, 3:9; 7:4; 11:14; 12:3, 4, 6; 13:9; 18:13; 19:7, 9–11; 20:4; 21:2; 26:6; 27:15; 28:2, 9; 30:7; 31:2; 33:3; 36:4; 39:4; 44:10; 45:3; 46:3; 47:1; 52:3, 4; 54:2; 63:3; 64:7

pectus, 2:7; 3:4, 8; 12:5; 13:2; 17:3, 4; 31:5; 59:4

peculiaris, 24:1

pecunia, 18:11

peniteo (paeniteo), 3:3; 6:6; 33:2; 39:8; 52:4

penna, 44:9

penso, 36:3

perambulo, 28:8; 40:3

percipio, 19:4

percurro, 13:7

percutio, 2:8; 8:8; 10:1, 5, 6; 23:9; 27:1, 10; 31:7; 32:16; 38:3; 40:1; 43:6; 46:2, 3; 47:1, 2; 54:3; 61:7; 64:6

perditio, 3:10; 10:2; 16:3, 6; 18:8, 10; 43:5; 53:11; 55:3–5

perdo, 6:14; 13:9; 16:3; 18:11; 26:2; 27:7; 28:2, 5; 30:5; 33:3; 34:3; 39:6; 40:3; 44:6; 47:10; 52:2; 55:4; 58:1; 62:5

perduco, 30:5

peremptor, 31:2

pereo, 18:12; 20:4; 27:11; 33:6; 47:6; 51:5; 52:3; 53:10; 54:5, 6; 55:2, 4, 6; 56:4

perficio, 4:11; 12:7; 33:3; 49:6; 51:6

perfundo, 12:1; 50:2

pergo, 31:5; 62:2

periclitor, 62:5

periculum, 9:5

permaneo, 6:9; 9:4; 18:10, 12; 19:9, 13; 21:10; 22:3; 26:4; 28:2; 30:2; 51:5; 52:2, 3

permeo, 40:3

permitto, 23:10; 45:1; 46:4; 58:3; 63:3

perpecco, 28:5

perscrutor, 25:13

persecutio, 31:9; 54:1; 62:5

persequor, 10:2, 4, 6; 31:9; 43:3; 46:2, 3; 47:9; 62:2; 63:5

perseverantia, 37:2

persevero, 3:7; 15:5; 21:10

persona, 20:4

perspicio, 14:3

persuadeo, 18:11; 42:8; 45:2

pertranseo, 10:6

perustus, 6:2

pes, 15:5; 23:10; 24:5; 30:5; 32:4; 54:4; 55:3

pessimus, 3:4; 6:6; 8:2; 9:1; 47:5–7; 52:2; 53:4; 55:2, 9; 60:1

petitio, 36:3; 39:11; 40:3, 4; 51:2; 53:11

peto, 12:3; 18:5, 7; 19:8, 14; 31:5; 35:6, 7; 36:3; 40:3; 51:2; 56:1, 2; 57:3

petra, 6:9; 7:3; 23:4, 5; 35:6, 7; 40:3, 5; 42:9

pictor, 16:5

pictura, 25:11

pietas, 15:7

pinna, 24:6

pinus, 9:12

piscis, 3:11

placeo, 1:16; 3:4; 9:7; 10:2; 18:3; 22:4; 29:1; 44:1; 45:4; 46:4; 48:4; 52:2

plaga, 10:1
planctus, 9:2; 24:6; 28:5; 40:5, 8; 57:4
plango, 9:2; 24:6; 28:10; 33:6; 40:3, 5–8; 64:1
plantago, 18:10
plantatio, 28:4; 30:4; 50:1
planto, 12:8, 9; 23:12; 28:4; 37:2; 39:7
plantor, 28:4
plasma, 53:13
plasmatio, 32:15; 33:3
plasmo, 16:5; 23:8; 44:8; 50:4; 53:6, 13
platea, 45:1
plebs, 14:1, 3–5; 15:4; 16:7; 20:4; 27:2; 30:3–5; 51:7; 52:1; 54:2; 55:2
plectrum, 43:3
plenitudo, 19:15; 21:4; 23:10
plenus, 5:4; 27:12, 14
plico, 11:5
ploro, 14:5; 22:7; 24:2; 28:5; 33:4; 40:3, 5; 46:3; 57:4; 62:10, 11; 64:4
plumbum, 2:9
pluo, 10:7; 19:10; 30:5; 60:2
plurimus, 48:1; 49:7; 51:4
plus, 18:4; 25:12; 26:13; 28:5; 44:4; 50:5; 53:7
pluvia, 3:5; 4:5; 11:9; 13:7, 10; 21:2; 23:12; 44:10
pondero, 29:3
pondus, 36:3; 40:1; 44:3; 49:5; 62:4
pono, 4:11; 5:4, 5, 8; 11:5; 15:6; 16:1; 17:1; 20:4; 22:9; 25:12; 26:1–4, 12, 15; 32:3; 36:4; 39:1, 6; 44:6; 49:2; 55:3, 6, 7; 62:11
populus, 5:2, 3; 6:4, 6, 9, 11, 13; 7:1, 2, 5; 9:1, 2, 4, 7, 10; 10:1, 4, 7; 11:1–4, 6, 14, 15; 12:2–4, 7; 13:10; 15:1, 5, 6; 16:4; 17:1, 4; 18:1, 2, 5, 10, 12, 14; 19:1, 2, 6–8, 10, 11; 20:2–9; 21:1–4, 7; 22:1–3, 5–9; 23:1–4, 7, 10, 12, 14; 24:1–4; 25:1–3, 5; 26:2, 5, 7, 13; 27:1, 4, 5, 7, 12–16; 28:1, 3–5, 10; 29:1, 3, 4; 30:2; 31:2, 5, 7; 32:1, 3, 7, 9, 10, 15, 17, 18; 33:1, 4–6; 34:1, 4, 5; 35:2, 4; 36:3; 37:1, 3–5; 38:1–4; 39:1, 3, 5–8, 10, 11; 40:2, 4; 41:1, 2; 44:8; 45:6; 46:1–4; 47:1, 3, 9, 10; 49:1–6, 8; 51:2, 3, 6, 7; 52:1, 2; 53:8; 54:1, 2, 4; 55:1; 56:5, 7; 57:1, 4; 59:5; 61:2–4, 6; 63:1, 3; 64:3, 8
porrigo, 31:4
porta, 43:3
porto, 11:14; 12:4; 43:2, 3; 65:2
possibilis, 53:7
possido, 12:6; 39:9; 51:4
possum, 3:2, 4; 5:1; 6:11; 9:6, 12; 14:4; 15:1, 2, 5; 16:7; 17:2, 3; 18:4, 11, 13; 19:13, 14; 21:4, 9; 22:3, 8; 24:5; 26:2–4, 7–9, 15; 30:3–5; 31:7; 32:16; 33:2, 3, 5; 34:4; 37:2; 38:4; 39:5; 40:1, 4; 42:8, 9; 43:3; 44:8; 48:3; 49:1, 5, 7, 8; 52:3; 53:13; 54:5; 55:3, 5; 56:4; 62:6; 65:3
posterus, 22:3

postulatio, 40:3
postulo, 49:6; 58:4
potatio, 43:7
potens, 6:7; 15:1; 23:1; 39:2; 47:4
potentia, 43:6; 51:6
potentor, 26:13
potestas, 33:3; 34:3; 47:4; 53:13
poto, 12:7; 31:5, 6
potus, 6:9; 12:9
prasinus, 25:11; 26:10
precedo (praecedo), 6:9; 19:16; 31:5
precessor (praecessor), 29:4; 37:3; 38:2
precinctoria (praecinctorium), 13:1
precingo, (praecingo), 20:2, 3; 27:9; 31:1; 51:6
preciosus, 11:15; 12:9; 13:1; 18:13; 25:10–12; 26:2–5, 8, 13; 40:4
precipio (praecipio), 3:5, 8; 4:3; 5:7; 6:7–9, 12, 14; 9:5; 10:6; 11:3, 5, 9, 15; 12:4; 13:1, 3, 7, 8, 10; 14:3, 4; 15:1, 5; 16:1–3, 6; 19:8, 13; 20:9; 21:7; 23:6, 8; 25:3; 26:3, 4, 7, 8, 15; 27:3, 4, 15; 28:3; 30:5; 31:2; 32:11, 14; 34:2; 35:5, 6; 36:3; 37:2; 38:2; 39:8; 44:5–7; 48:2, 3; 50:3; 51:3; 53:6, 9, 11; 54:2; 57:1; 58:1; 60:2
precium, 25:12
precurro (praecurro), 11:5
predestino (praedestino), 28:6
predico (praedico), 12:9; 21:5; 25:3
prefero (praefero), 39:7
prefoco (praefoco), 60:1
pregnans (praegnans), 55:6
preluceo (praeluceo), 37:3
premitto (praemitto), 6:12; 15:5; 34:5
premo, 39:4
prenumero, 50:8
preoccupo (praeoccupo), 40:3
preparo (praeparo), 27:5, 7; 28:1; 32:7, 17; 40:6
prepondero (praepondero), 40:1
prepono (praepono), 5:1; 9:12; 25:2; 47:6; 50:3; 61:5
presbiterus (Greek), 9:14; 11:8; 22:2; 59:2
prescius (praescius), 22:7
presens (praesens), 6:9; 35:4
presertim (praesertim), 28:3
prespicio (perspicio), 13:6
pressura, 32:14; 35:2; 39:1, 4; 49:1
presto, 37:2; 44:9
presum (praesum), 34:2; 27:10; 38:3
presumo (praesumo), 7:2; 12:3
presumptio (praesumptio), 23:5
preter (praeter), 5:4, 5; 14:4; 26:5; 29:3; 49:5
pretereo (praetereo), 6:12; 39:8
prevaleo (praevaleo), 12:6
prevaricor (praevaricor), 12:4; 24:4

prevideo (praevideo), 12:3

primitivus, 10:1; 12:5; 63:1

primogenitus (primigenius), 18:6; 29:2; 32:16; 39:11; 59:2

primus, 2:3; 6:6; 12:10; 19:9; 20:3; 25:6; 26:10; 27:1; 35:6; 39:10, 11; 44:8; 46:1; 47:6, 9, 11; 53:2; 54:1; 55:3; 61:1

princeps, 5:1, 3; 6:4, 6, 8, 9; 8:9, 10; 9:12; 21:5; 25:2, 3; 30:3; 40:5; 47:11; 49:1, 7; 56:1, 5

principare, 19:2; 20:5; 21:4; 25:2; 29:1; 30:2; 37:4; 39:3; 49:1, 7, 8

principatus, 20:5; 27:16; 37:2, 4, 5

prior, 6:12; 8:8; 12:9, 10; 25:2; 26:13; 27:15; 28:3; 40:1; 48:1; 62:11

priusquam, 19:7; 28:6; 40:3

probo, 11:14; 25:9; 48:1

procedo, 17:2; 28:9

procella, 11:5; 44:6

processior, 21:1

procinctus, 5:4; 39:10

procreatio, 3:4

procreo, 1:11, 21; 15:7; 42:2

prodigium, 9:7; 25:6; 42:5; 53:8

produco, 27:15; 44:7; 45:3

profectio, 11:1

profero, 17:2; 26:13; 32:7, 16; 37:3

proficia, 51:2

proficiscor, 5:7; 6:1, 7, 8, 11, 12; 9:9; 10:2; 18:4, 6–8; 19:6; 20:3; 24:1, 3; 27:8; 29:4; 31:1, 2; 32:2, 15; 33:2; 40:4, 5; 43:7; 44:5; 51:7; 53:12; 55:6–8; 59:2; 61:5, 6

profundus, 10:5; 25:11; 26:4, 8, 11; 39:5

progenies, 3:4; 11:6

prohibeo, 7:2; 12:3; 19:10; 22:9; 42:2, 3

proicio, 9:4, 6, 10, 12, 14; 26:8; 39:5; 64:6

prolongo, 22:3

promitto, 19:16; 40:5; 44:6; 51:2; 53:12; 56:7

promptuarius (promptarius), 32:7, 13

propheta, 23:7; 28:1, 3; 30:5; 35:6; 49:8; 50:8; 51:6, 7; 53:8; 56:4, 6; 57:4; 59:4; 64:1–3

prophetatio, 28:6

prophetia, 18:12; 51:6

prophetizo, 53:11

propheto, 20:5; 28:6; 49:7, 8; 51:1, 6; 53:12, 13; 54:5; 62:2

propicio (propitio), 18:7

propono, 21:4; 26:12

prospeculator, 13:6

prosum, 30:4; 33:5; 49:6; 50:1, 2

protoplastus, 13:8; 26:6; 32:15; 37:3

proveho, 62:6

provoco, 25:5; 52:1

proximus, 2:8; 6:1, 2; 7:3, 5; 11:12, 13; 27:10, 12; 36:1; 39:1; 44:6, 10; 45:5; 47:5; 49:4; 55:4; 62:10, 11; 64:2

prudens, 62:4

prudentia, 21:2

psallo, 21:9; 32:18; 59:4; 60:1, 3

psalmus, 2:7; 21:9; 59:4; 60:1

psalphinga (Greek), 11:4; 13:6; 27:6; 32:18

psalphingo (Greek), 27:6

psalterium, 2:8; 21:8

puella, 31:1; 44:5

puer, 5:4, 5, 7; 7:4; 9:13, 15; 27:3, 5, 6, 12; 31:1, 3; 38:3; 39:7; 42:7; 43:5; 44:5, 9; 45:1; 51:1, 2

pugna, 20:9; 27:2, 5, 14; 31:1; 32:10; 35:5; 36:3; 39:1; 46:2; 47:10; 54:3; 55:1; 57:5; 59:5; 61:1, 3; 62:8; 64:2; 65:1

pugno, 10:3; 20:9; 25:1; 27:6, 9, 14; 32:15; 36:2, 3; 39:1, 6, 10; 46:2, 3; 47:5; 54:1; 57:5; 61:1, 2; 64:2

pulcherrima, 3:1

pulchritudo, 50:2

pulex, 43:2

pullus, 13:3

pulvis, 18:6

punio, 27:4; 31:5; 35:2

punitio, 11:1; 44:10

purgo, 13:3

purpura, 40:6

purus, 25:1

puteus, 10:7; 20:8

puto, 27:7; 35:5; 39:9; 49:6; 64:7

qualis, 34:1; 44:9

quamvis, 52:3; 55:8

quantitas, 19:14

quantus, 14:1, 4; 18:7; 19:14; 25:3; 26:14; 27:14; 28:2, 4; 34:4; 39:9; 62:6

quare, 6:4, 11; 22:2, 5; 38:2; 39:8; 46:2, 4; 49:6; 50:3; 53:3, 9; 59:2; 62:5; 64:5

quartus, 2:3; 4:11; 11:6; 19:7; 26:10; 43:6; 47:11

quasi, 28:8; 33:1; 36:2

quater, 16:6

quero (quaero), 6:6, 9, 14; 19:3; 25:1; 27:11; 38:4; 43:1; 55:8; 56:4; 62:1, 3; 64:3

quiesco, 3:10; 11:14; 33:6; 39:9; 48:4; 55:10

quominus, 6:6; 39:8; 45:3; 60:3

quotidie, 42:1, 2; 43:6; 50:2, 5; 55:4

quoties, 53:3

radix, 12:8, 9; 25:5; 32:8; 49:6

rado, 44:9

ramus, 13:7; 40:7

rana, 10:1

rapio, 8:7; 12:2; 31:1; 39:1; 48:3; 52:1; 59:5; 61:1

recedo, 9:5; 21:10; 22:3; 24:3; 25:3; 28:4; 39:1, 5; 40:5; 42:3; 43:6; 44:6; 60:1

recessus, 9:1; 19:16; 21:1; 33:4

recipio, 11:14; 40:5; 44:10

reclino, 48:1

recludo, 6:12

recogito, 9:5

reconcilio, 18:7; 49:2

recongrego, 26:5

recordor, 19:4

rectus, 9:5; 18:4; 27:15; 47:1

recupero (recipero), 25:12

redarguo, 36:4; 37:4

redditio, 64:7

reddo, 3:10; 6:13; 11:6, 9; 16:6; 18:5; 23:8, 13; 31:3; 32:7, 8; 33:3; 36:1; 39:8, 9; 40:3; 41:1; 46:2; 47:12; 49:7; 62:4; 64:7

redigo, 9:3; 18:11; 34:5

reduco, 55:2, 9

refero, 18:7; 27:14; 28:2; 40:3, 6

refrigero, 12:8

refugio, 47:9, 10

refulgeo, 27:7, 9; 28:3

regius, 6:7; 7:3; 51:3

regno, 37:2, 3; 48:5; 56:2, 3; 58:4; 61:2; 62:2, 4, 11; 63:3; 64:4

regnum, 18:2; 37:2; 56:2; 59:1; 62:2, 9; 64:4

rego, 23:12; 32:10; 63:3

reicio, 54:4

relinquo, 12:4, 9; 13:10; 19:2, 6; 21:6; 33:4; 35:3; 49:3

reliquus, 25:13; 41:1; 63:5

reluceo, 25:11

remaneo, 6:11; 19:14; 20:1

rememoror, 3:9; 16:3; 19:2

remissio, 41:1

remitto, 35:4; 45:3

renuncio (renuntio), 6:18; 20:7; 24:6; 25:7; 27:3, 6; 46:4; 47:1, 2; 50:7, 8; 51:3; 53:12, 13; 54:4; 56:4; 62:3; 63:2

replaco, 30:4

repletus, 19:16; 40:6; 41:1; 53:7

repo, 11:6; 55:4, 9

repono, 23:13; 24:4; 26:13

reporto, 28:4

reposco, 33:3

reptile, 3:8; 55:2

repugno, 15:2; 49:6

requies, 1:20; 19:12; 28:10

requiesco, 3:9, 10; 11:8; 25:1; 31:4; 39:5

requietio, 3:8; 20:5; 49:6

requiro, 19:6; 33:3, 6; 49:1; 59:2

res, 22:3, 6; 29:3

rescribo, 12:10

residuus, 36:2; 39:9; 47:1, 6

resolvo, 27:11; 40:1; 54:6; 64:3

respicio, 7:4; 12:5, 8; 27:11; 31:5; 61:8; 65:3

resplendeo, 26:11

respondeo, 6:4, 6, 10, 11; 9:1, 3; 19:4; 22:6; 23:14; 25:6; 26:5; 27:14; 30:5; 33:5; 38:2; 40:4; 44:3, 9; 45:3; 46:1; 47:3; 49:2, 3; 53:13; 55:7; 57:3, 4; 62:9; 64:3

respuo, 16:3; 39:5

restituo, 3:10; 23:8; 33:3

resto, 16:1

resultatio, 60:3

resumo, 54:6; 56:4, 5

resurgo, 19:3; 32:14

retineo, 18:11; 62:11

retribuo, 39:8; 62:4

retro, 65:3

revelo, 18:5; 19:4; 25:5, 6; 42:2; 51:5; 53:2

reverto, 6:12; 10:3, 6; 15:1; 18:14; 20:6; 24:6; 27:6, 12; 28:10; 30:6; 31:6, 7, 9; 39:4, 5, 10; 40:1, 3, 8; 41:1; 47:10; 58:4; 61:1

revoco, 40:1

rex, 8:10; 9:1, 5, 11, 12; 10:1; 18:1, 2; 20:2, 9; 22:5; 30:3; 39:8–10; 41:1; 48:5; 51:6; 56:1–3, 7; 57:1–4; 58:2–4; 61:2, 4; 63:3, 5; 64:4, 7; 65:4

rogo, 15:5; 18:7; 21:3; 62:6

romphea (rhomphaea or rumpia), 15:4; 27:7, 9, 11, 12; 36:1, 2; 47:1; 54:4; 61:7; 63:2; 65:2, 3

ros, 13:7; 23:12; 26:3, 8

rosa, 31:3

ruber, 10:2; 21:3; 23:10

rubus, 19:9; 37:3, 4

ruina, 55:6; 64:9

rumpo, 46:4

rupes, 27:6; 32:7

sabbatum, 11:8; 25:13; 44:6, 7

sacer, 34:1

sacerdos, 13:1, 3; 21:9; 22:1, 8, 9; 24:4; 25:5; 28:1, 3; 44:2, 3; 46:4; 47:10; 48:2; 50:3, 6–8; 51:6, 7; 53:3, 6, 9; 54:4; 55:3, 4; 61:2; 63:1–3

sacerdotalis, 17:1

sacerdotium, 17:4; 52:2; 53:9

sacrarium, 18:5, 10; 21:7–9; 22:1, 3–9; 26:3, 7; 36:4; 38:1; 42:9

sacrificium, 11:15; 21:8, 9; 22:1, 5; 26:7; 32:2, 3, 18; 40:1, 3, 5; 41:1; 42:8, 9; 44:3; 49:8; 57:4; 59:4

sacrifico, 38:1, 2; 40:5; 50:2; 52:1

sagitta, 18:12; 19:16

salix, 13:7

salus, 18:11; 21:6; 27:4, 7, 12–14

salvatio, 13:10; 32:17

salvo, 6:6, 9, 18; 9:5, 10; 25:3; 27:11

salvus, 8:8

sanctificatio, 11:15; 19:13; 27:14

sanctifico, 11:3, 8; 13:1, 4; 14:4; 26:2, 4; 29:3;
42:3; 44:6; 52:1, 2; 55:9, 59:2

sanctimonia, 15:6

sanctuarium, 19:10

sanctus, 13:1; 18:11; 19:10; 25:9, 10, 12; 27:8,
9; 28:6; 32:14; 33:6; 52:1; 53:9, 13; 59:2; 63:1

sanguis, 3:11; 6:11; 10:1; 16:2; 18:5; 27:11;
35:7; 37:2; 62:5, 6; 64:2

saphirus (sapphirus), 26:10

sapiens, 18:12; 23:7; 40:4; 55:5, 7

sapientia, 20:2, 3; 21:2; 51:4

sardinus, 26:10

sarmentum, 12:8

saturo, 12:9; 23:12; 40:6; 51:4

scandalum, 18:8; 43:5; 44:8; 58:3, 4; 65:4

scapule (scapulae), 43:3

scelus, 3:2

scenophegia, 13:7

sceptrum, 5:4–6; 42:9

scientia, 20:2

scinifes (sciniphes), 10:1

scintilla, 6:17; 28:8, 9

scio, 6:7, 9, 12; 9:2, 6; 10:6; 11:2, 14, 15; 12:1,
4; 13:10; 18:2, 4, 7; 19:5, 9, 12; 20:3, 5, 10;
21:2; 22:3–5, 7; 23:9, 13; 25:1, 3, 4, 7–9, 12,
13; 26:4, 14; 27:5, 7, 8, 11, 14; 28:7; 29:1;
30:4, 7; 31:3, 5, 7; 32:11, 13, 15; 34:1, 4;
35:6; 39:3, 6, 8, 9; 41:1; 42:8, 10; 44:10;
45:2; 49:2, 3, 6, 7; 50:1, 4, 5, 7; 52:1, 2;
53:4, 7; 55:5–8; 56:5; 57:2; 62:2, 9; 64:4

scorpio, 55:2

scribo, 6:2; 12:5; 14:2; 19:7; 21:7; 25:13; 26:1,
3, 10, 11; 35:7; 40:5; 43:4; 56:7; 58:3; 61:5;
63:5

sculpo, 25:11, 12; 26:4, 10, 11; 44:6

sculptilis, 2:9; 11:6; 19:7; 44:7; 47:7

sculptura, 25:11; 26:9–11

scutum, 28:8; 43:3

seculum (saeculum), 3:2, 10; 4:11; 7:1; 9:3;
12:9; 16:3; 18:4; 19:7, 12; 21:4; 23:8, 13;
25:11; 26:4, 13; 28:4, 10; 30:2; 32:3, 7; 34:3;
35:5; 48:1; 50:4, 7; 51:5; 53:4; 59:4; 60:2;
62:9

securus, 32:3, 15; 47:4

sedes, 12:8

sedile, 55:9

sedo, 28:6; 30:5; 31:3; 37:3; 39:2; 40:6; 45:1;
50:3; 51:1; 54:6

seduco, 13:8; 18:14; 21:1; 22:5; 23:5; 30:1;
38:1, 2, 4; 39:9; 43:5; 44:5, 7, 8; 45:6; 46:1,
4; 47:7; 53:3; 62:2; 64:3

seductio, 46:4

semel, 35:2; 36:4; 43:5, 7; 55:4

semen, 3:4, 9, 11; 4:11; 7:4; 8:3; 10:2; 11:9;
12:4; 13:10; 14:2; 15:5, 7; 17:2; 18:5; 19:6;
21:9; 23:5, 7, 12, 13; 43:5; 49:6; 50:2

semino, 4:5

semis, 19:15

semita, 19:10; 20:3

semper, 9:4, 10; 13:10; 21:3; 28:4; 32:4; 39:7;
49:8; 52:4; 63:4

sempiternus, 3:10; 8:3; 9:8; 11:1, 2, 5; 12:6;
13:7, 10; 19:4, 16; 21:5; 23:12; 32:4; 33:4;
44:8; 56:2

senectus, 32:1, 6; 36:4

senesco, 21:1; 52:4; 56:1

senior, 9:2; 11:8; 25:6; 28:3, 5

sensatus, 40:4

sensus, 6:16; 10:6; 12:6, 7; 15:6; 18:10; 19:16;
21:2; 22:5; 28:6, 10; 32:16; 44:7; 50:6

sententia, 6:6; 10:3; 52:4

sentio, 31:7; 47:4

sentis, 37:3

separatio, 62:10

separo, 22:3; 25:1; 62:3, 9

sepelio, 19:12, 16; 24:6; 29:4; 33:6; 36:4; 40:8,
9; 41:1, 2; 43:8; 64:1

sepes (saepes), 33:6

sepulchrum, 19:12; 29:4; 40:8; 43:8

sequestro, 25:12

sequor, 11:15; 15:2; 39:6

sermo, 9:3, 14; 12:10; 14:4; 20:10; 21:1, 5;
23:3; 27:13; 53:2; 61:4

servifico, 32:11

servio, 6:6; 9:1–3, 7; 10:3; 11:2; 12:2; 15:5;
18:12; 19:7; 22:3, 7; 23:14; 24:1; 26:3; 30:1,
6; 34:1, 5; 39:6; 41:3; 61:2

servitus, 9:3; 11:6; 18:11; 34:5

servo, 9:1; 13:3; 39:3

servus, 6:10, 11; 9:1; 15:5; 18:4; 20:2; 22:7;
25:6; 27:7; 38:4; 47:1, 2; 57:4

seta (saeta), 25:12

sicco, 3:8; 5:3; 7:3; 9:10; 10:5; 32:17

siccus, 10:6; 50:1

sicuti, 8:8, 10; 21:7; 26:8; 53:8; 54:2

sidus, 18:5; 33:5

signo, 33:3

signum, 9:7, 10; 13:7; 19:10, 11; 27:7; 31:5, 7;
35:6, 7; 42:5; 51:6; 53:4; 56:7; 59:5

silentium, 60:2

silva, 32:8; 40:7; 47:4–6; 59:5

similis, 12:1, 5; 15:6; 17:3, 4; 20:4; 24:6; 25:8;
26:2, 10; 29:4; 30:6; 32:16; 33:5; 53:2

similitudo, 11:6, 15; 17:3; 25:11; 26:10, 11;
28:8; 33:5; 44:9; 54:2

similo (simulo), 19:11; 26:10, 11

simulacrum, 25:10

singularis, 35:2

singulariter, 25:8

singuli, 6:2–4; 7:3, 5; 17:1; 22:8; 23:5; 25:11; 27:12; 36:3; 39:1; 40:8; 55:4

sinister, 25:3; 31:7; 38:2; 43:3; 53:6; 54:3; 55:7

sinus, 16:7; 40:4

sitio, 4:5; 31:4

sive, 3:9; 35:7; 55:4

smaragdinus, 26:10

socer, 9:5

sol, 11:6; 12:1; 18:10; 19:13; 26:13, 15; 32:9, 10; 34:1, 4; 45:1

solarium, 42:2, 5

solido, 19:8; 23:10; 53:2

solummodo, 44:10

solus, 3:7; 6:11–13, 15; 19:10; 20:5, 6; 23:14; 27:2, 6, 7; 28:10; 31:5; 32:12, 17; 38:1; 49:6; 50:5; 51:2; 53:9; 61:8; 63:2

solvo, 6:10; 8:10; 26:6

somnium, 8:10; 9:10, 15; 18:2; 23:6; 27:12; 28:4, 7

sono, 11:4; 13:7; 21:8

sonus, 18:11; 23:10; 32:7

soporo, 43:6

soror, 8:6, 7, 11, 13; 61:6; 62:7

sors, 20:1, 9, 10; 23:13; 25:1–4, 7; 49:2–7

sortior, 21:1; 49:1, 2, 4

spacium (spatium), 6:6

sparsus, 31:3

species, 31:3; 37:3; 44:5; 50:2; 61:8; 64:4–6

speciosus, 3:1; 13:7; 18:13; 31:1; 51:1

speculator, 20:10; 27:6

speculor, 27:6

spelunca, 7:3

spero, 20:2; 28:6; 31:7, 9; 33:5; 39:6

spica, 12:9

spina, 37:3

spiritus, 3:2; 9:8, 10; 18:3, 10, 11; 20:3; 27:9, 10; 28:6; 31:9; 32:14; 36:2; 39:8; 53:3, 4; 60:1–3; 62:2

splendeo, 12:7; 18:12; 26:15

splendor, 11:4; 12:1; 18:12; 26:13; 27:9; 40:6

spolium, 19:1; 31:1, 9; 47:10

spondeo, 12:4

sponte, 28:2; 43:4

sponsio, 12:4; 13:6; 30:1; 32:12, 13; 35:2, 3

spontaneus, 40:3

spuma, 28:8

sputum, 7:3; 12:4

stabilis, 6:9

stannum, 2:9

statera, 40:1

statim, 9:12; 12:3; 31:2; 32:2

statuo, 9:5; 13:3; 18:13; 21:7, 9; 23:10; 51:2, 3, 7; 55:8; 57:4

stella, 14:2; 21:2; 23:10; 31:2

sterilis, 3:10; 8:1; 23:5; 32:1; 42:1, 3, 4; 49:8; 51:4

sterilizo, 13:10

stigmatus, 25:11; 26:10

stillicidium, 7:3; 12:4

stillo, 51:3

stipendium, 6:7–9

stipula, 7:3, 5

sto, 9:10; 10:5; 11:15; 15:5; 18:6; 22:4; 27:6; 30:3, 5; 32:10; 40:1; 47:3; 51:6

stola, 64:6

stratoria, 40:6

strepo, 11:5

strido, 18:12

stridor, 10:5

stringo, 26:6

stupefacio, 34:4

stupeo, 27:12

suadeo, 13:8; 18:11

suavitas, 12:9; 32:3; 37:2

subdivum, 28:8

subdolus, 39:8

subiaceo, 25:11

subicio, 15:5; 20:4; 30:5; 47:6

subito, 15:5

subsido, 18:9

substerno, 23:10; 28:8

substratum, 28:8, 9

suffero, 25:10; 43:7

sufficio, 29:3; 42:10; 59:2; 60:3

suggero, 29:3

sugo, 55:4

summitas, 42:9

sumo, 9:16; 31:3

superabundo, 22:2; 39:6

superbus, 4:7; 6:10

superduco, 23:5

superexcellentia, 9:8; 12:2; 30:2

superexcelsum, 19:4

superfluo, 18:11; 20:2; 47:11

superior, 28:8, 9; 32:1; 60:2

supero, 15:2; 32:10

superpono, 25:10; 26:7; 27:10; 64:6

supersum, 3:7; 14:4; 18:11, 12; 19:15; 25:10; 29:1; 32:10; 47:10

supervenio, 48:1; 50:2; 55:5

supervolo, 49:5, 6

suppono, 27:11; 43:3

supra, 14:1, 3; 21:8; 26:12; 40:7

surgo, 6:18; 9:1; 12:6; 16:2; 18:7; 19:2; 23:4; 26:9, 14; 27:6, 8, 9, 12; 31:1; 36:1; 39:6, 10; 41:1; 43:2; 44:2; 45:4; 50:3; 53:12; 56:5; 57:2; 58:4; 64:9

suscipio, 6:7; 53:11

suscito, 30:2, 3

suspendo, 23:10; 47:1

suspensorium, 28:7

suspiro, 16:6; 18:12

sustineo, 6:7, 9; 7:2; 15:7; 18:4, 10; 20:2; 21:4; 23:2; 24:1; 27:10; 32:16; 37:2; 42:2; 49:5; 53:2

synagoga, 16:6, 7; 17:4; 22:5; 25:6; 29:3; 57:2

tabefacio, 15:5

tabernaculum, 2:7; 7:3; 11:15; 13:1, 2; 16:7; 17:1; 21:8; 22:8; 24:6; 25:9; 53:9

tabesco, 16:3; 62:9; 63:4

tabula, 12:5, 10; 19:7; 22:5; 26:12, 13, 15

taceo, 6:11; 18:12; 28:3; 30:5; 32:12; 42:2, 4; 45:4; 47:4, 6–8; 51:6; 53:6; 63:3

talentum, 29:3; 36:3

talis, 19:3, 16; 25:11; 26:5, 9, 13; 32:14; 45:5

tam, 45:6; 46:4

tango, 26:6; 42:9

tantummodo, 8:10; 25:13; 49:5; 52:3

tantus, 6:14; 26:6; 27:5, 14; 29:4; 33:2; 47:6; 55:7

taurus, 59:5

tempestas, 23:10

templum, 53:2; 55:3

tempto, 18:4; 34:5; 55:7

tempus (also timpus), 1:16; 2:8; 3:4, 9; 7:3; 8:10; 9:6; 10:2, 3; 12:3, 8; 13:4, 7, 8; 14:2; 16:1; 18:1, 3, 11, 12; 19:1, 3, 6, 8, 9, 12–15; 20:1; 23:12, 13; 24:4; 25:13; 28:4, 9; 29:1, 4; 32:3, 17; 33:2, 3; 34:1, 2; 35:1, 2; 39:3–5, 11; 40:4, 6, 7; 41:2; 43:1; 44:2; 45:1, 3; 47:5, 12; 48:1, 3; 49:1, 6; 51:1, 7; 55:6, 7; 56:1, 2, 4, 5; 58:1, 4; 59:1, 5; 60:1–3; 61:3; 62:2, 9; 63:1, 2; 64:7

tenebre (tenebrae), 3:10; 10:1; 15:5; 16:3; 22:3; 40:7; 51:5; 60:2

teneo, 12:5; 19:12; 43:3; 51:5; 54:3

terebro, 26:11

terminus, 3:2; 9:2; 15:6; 51:3

terra, 1:20; 2:1, 8–10; 3:1, 3–12; 4:3, 5, 9, 10, 16, 17; 5:2; 6:1, 4, 9, 11; 7:1, 2, 4, 5; 8:1–3, 7, 9, 10; 9:3, 4; 10:1, 2, 5; 11:1, 5, 6, 8, 9, 13, 14; 12:4; 13:3, 4, 7, 10; 14:1, 2, 4; 15:1, 4, 5, 7; 16:2, 3, 6; 18:1, 9–11; 19:2, 4, 5, 7, 10–12, 16; 20:1, 4–6, 8, 9; 21:1, 5, 9; 22:2; 23:1, 5, 9, 11, 12; 24:1, 2; 25:1, 6, 9, 11; 26:13, 15; 28:6; 29:2; 30:2, 4; 31:5, 7; 32:7, 9, 13, 15; 33:6; 35:2; 37:3; 38:4; 39:2–9; 40:6; 41:3; 43:5; 44:6, 9; 53:9; 55:10; 57:2; 58:1; 59:4; 60:2; 62:10; 64:1, 6

terremotus (terrae motus), 3:9; 6:17

terreo, 6:18

territorium, 7:4; 20:10

tertius (and tercius), 2:3; 4:3; 9:5; 11:1–4, 6; 18:6; 19:6; 23:2; 26:10; 27:2; 29:2; 32:5; 47:11; 53:5, 7

testamentum, 3:4, 11, 12; 4:5, 11; 7:4; 8:3; 9:3, 4, 7, 8, 13, 15; 10:2; 11:1, 3, 5; 13:10; 19:2, 7, 11; 20:1; 21:8, 10; 22:7, 8; 23:1, 2, 10, 11; 24:3; 26:12, 15; 27:7; 28:2; 30:7; 32:8, 14; 38:4; 46:4; 54:1; 62:1, 3, 11

testificor, 27:15

testimonium, 11:2, 12; 19:11; 22:6; 23:7; 29:4; 32:15, 17, 18; 44:6, 7; 48:5; 51:3; 54:1, 5; 62:10

testis, 11:12; 19:4; 22:6; 32:8, 9, 14, 17; 40:5; 50:5; 57:3; 62:10

testor, 19:4; 21:1; 24:1; 29:4

texo, 40:6

thalamus, 40:6

theca, 27:7

thesaurus, 15:5; 29:3; 58:2, 4

thibin, 9:12, 15

thronus, 12:8; 51:6

thuribulum, 13:1, 2

thus, 44:3

tibia, 55:9

timeo, 6:9; 11:9, 14; 12:3; 18:2; 19:9; 30:3; 40:3; 50:2; 53:3, 13; 55:11; 61:2, 4; 62:5, 11; 64:4, 5

timor, 10:5; 11:14; 12:7; 24:2; 27:16; 64:1

timpanum (tympanum), 55:9

timpus (tempus), 31:7

tinea, 40:6

tollo, 10:5; 16:7; 18:10; 26:15; 65:2, 3

tondeo, 43:6

tonitrus, 11:5; 13:7; 15:2; 23:10

tono, 60:3

tonsor, 43:6

topazion, 26:10

torqueo, 44:9

torrens, 26:1; 27:15

totus, 7:5; 13:6, 7; 19:16; 28:7; 33:2; 42:2; 44:6, 8; 47:6; 56:2; 62:6

tractabilis, 10:1

tracto, 57:3

traditio, 64:7

trado, 8:9; 9:2; 18:2; 19:7; 20:2; 21:3, 9; 27:7–9; 30:7; 31:7, 9; 32:2; 34:5; 35:2, 3; 36:1, 2; 39:4, 6, 7, 10; 40:1; 41:3; 43:2, 5; 44:9; 45:3; 46:1–3; 47:2, 8; 53:13; 54:4, 5; 58:4; 59:4, 5; 61:3; 63:3; 64:8

traicio, 4:16; 25:13

trans, 22:3; 23:4

transadigo, 6:13; 29:3

transduco, 27:15
transeo, 5:4–6; 11:5; 19:13–15; 48:1; 64:4
transfero, 1:16; 21:4
transgredior, 6:4; 13:8; 18:12; 19:4; 23:7; 25:3;
  28:2; 30:1, 2; 34:3; 45:3; 53:10; 58:4
transgressio, 24:4
transmitto, 31:9
transmuto, 27:10
tremo, 2:1; 11:5; 32:7
tremor, 11:14
trenus (threnus), 33:6; 40:5
tribulus (tribolus), 37:3
tribuo, 20:9; 62:4
tribus, 4:17; 6:6; 9:9; 10:3; 11:2; 14:3; 16:3;
  17:1; 19:5; 20:8; 21:5; 22:1, 3; 25:1–4, 8–10,
  13; 26:4, 8, 10, 11; 30:2; 31:5; 42:1; 44:8;
  45:1, 2, 4, 5; 47:2, 11; 48:3; 49:2; 51:2; 53:9;
  60:2; 63:2
triduum, 28:4; 55:1; 56:7
triennis, 23:6
trimus, 23:6
tristicia (tristitia), 40:1, 3; 42:5; 62:9
tristis, 40:3; 50:3; 55:2
tristor, 40:2; 49:2
tubo, 36:2
tunica, 36:3
turbatio, 36:1
turbo, 13:7
turpiter, 45:3
turrificatio, 32:1
turrifico, 32:15
turris, 6:1; 7:1, 2, 5; 12:3; 20:10
turtur, 13:2; 23:6, 7
tympanum, 21:8; 51:7

ubique, 62:8
ullus, 3:10; 9:7, 8; 25:8; 64:3
ultra, 12:8; 16:3; 19:11
ululo, 36:2
umbra, 37:3
umbraculum, 15:5
umquam, 26:3
unanimis, 5:2; 19:16; 25:6; 27:13; 30:4; 39:6
unanimiter, 21:9; 28:5; 32:1, 18; 33:4; 39:7;
  47:9; 51:7
unctio, 13:1; 40:6
ungo, 48:2; 51:7; 59:1–3
unigenitus, 39:11; 40:1, 5, 6
universus, 5:5, 6; 11:8; 13:1; 23:10; 26:5–7;
  27:13
urceus, 12:4
uro, 30:6; 31:4, 6
ursa, 59:5
usque, 6:1, 9, 12; 9:5; 11:6; 12:6, 8; 14:1; 15:6,
  7; 19:2, 9, 10; 22:8, 9; 25:6; 26:5, 15; 28:5;

29:3; 30:4, 7; 32:9; 34:3; 36:1; 38:4; 39:6;
  45:3; 47:7, 10; 53:4; 54:3; 56:6
uterus, 9:5, 12; 55:4, 10
uti, 40:6; 45:3
utinam, 62:4
utraque, 26:4; 35:7
utrum, 25:13; 40:1; 42:2
uxor, 2:8; 3:1; 4:10; 8:3, 8; 9:1, 9; 31:3; 42:6;
  43:5; 44:5, 6, 10; 49:8

vacca, 55:6–8
vaco, 52:3
vacuus, 50:4
vado, 9:10; 10:4; 18:8, 9; 27:5, 11; 31:5, 7;
  32:13; 35:5; 40:3; 42:8; 48:1; 50:6; 53:3;
  55:1; 58:1; 59:1; 64:1, 9; 65:5
valeo, 27:12
validus, 55:7
valles, 6:9
vanus, 6:9; 9:4; 11:7; 12:6, 9; 15:5; 18:11; 20:2;
  23:13; 28:5; 35:3; 39:2; 40:3, 5, 6; 42:4; 44:6,
  7; 45:6; 47:6; 49:3; 50:2; 52:2; 55:1, 4; 62:2,
  5, 11
varietas, 25:11
varius, 17:3
vas, 13:1; 22:8; 31:1; 62:10; 65:2
vectis, 15:1
vehementer, 30:3
velamen, 12:1
velut, 25:11; 26:11, 15; 31:5; 39:5; 43:4; 50:6;
  53:3
vena, 23:10; 28:7–9
venio, 5:1, 2; 6:1; 7:3; 9:1; 10:3; 11:1, 14; 12:2,
  8; 15:6; 17:3; 18:2, 4, 7, 9–13; 19:5, 12; 21:6;
  22:1; 25:1; 26:8; 27:6, 12; 28:4; 30:2–5; 31:2,
  8, 9; 32:3, 8; 33:2; 34:1, 3; 35:1–4; 36:1, 3;
  37:2, 3; 38:4; 39:1, 3, 4, 6, 9; 40:1, 4, 5, 7;
  41:1; 42:4, 6, 7, 10; 43:3; 44:3, 5; 45:1, 3, 4;
  46:2, 3; 47:8, 9; 49:5, 7; 50:3, 8; 51:3, 7;
  52:1; 53:6, 10; 54:3, 4; 55:1, 3, 6; 56:3, 4, 6,
  7; 58:4; 59:2, 4; 61:1–3, 6; 62:3, 9; 63:2–4;
  64:2, 7; 65:2, 4
venter, 9:2, 5, 6, 14; 22:3; 32:2, 4; 39:11;
  44:10; 47:4, 7; 50:2; 55:4
ventus, 11:5; 13:7; 23:10; 32:7
verbum, 6:12; 7:1; 9:7, 11; 11:1, 2, 6; 12:3;
  14:2; 15:4–6; 16:4; 18:12; 19:1, 2; 20:4, 6, 7;
  21:3, 4, 7, 9; 22:2, 3, 5, 7; 23:7, 13; 24:3;
  25:3; 26:1; 27:6, 9, 10, 13, 15; 28:3, 10;
  32:18; 33:1, 4, 6; 35:6; 36:2; 38:4; 40:4, 5;
  42:3, 4, 6, 7; 46:1; 47:3; 51:3, 4, 6; 52:2;
  53:10, 11, 13; 56:1, 2, 6; 57:3; 58:1; 61:3, 4,
  6; 62:4, 8; 63:5; 64:4, 9; 65:4
vere, 11:14; 21:9; 49:6; 55:7

veritas, 22:8, 9; 25:5–8; 28:3; 37:3; 39:9; 46:1; 47:2; 51:4; 62:4, 7, 11

vermis, 40:6; 44:9; 63:4

vero, 1:6; 3:4; 4:7; 5:4–6; 8:2, 11, 14; 11:1; 12:7; 18:10; 22:9; 23:7; 26:4, 10; 29:3; 37:3; 38:4; 42:10; 44:5; 50:1

versutia, 47:7

versutus, 26:5; 45:6

vertex, 26:3, 4, 7, 9; 54:5

verumtamen, 3:11

vesper, 6:7; 28:5; 31:3; 32:10

vestimentum, 13:1; 20:2, 3; 27:12; 46:4; 54:4; 64:4

vestio, 20:3; 40:6; 64:6

vestis, 9:10

veterasco, 55:1

via, 6:4; 9:7; 11:6, 7; 12:4; 13:8–10; 15:7; 16:5; 18:3, 7, 8; 19:4; 20:3, 4; 21:9; 22:2, 3, 7; 24:4; 27:12; 28:4; 30:1, 2; 32:12; 33:2, 3; 35:5; 36:4; 39:6; 49:3; 52:1, 2, 4; 53:12; 55:7, 8; 56:1, 5; 61:6; 63:1

vicio, 44:8

vicis, 31:3; 47:6

victoria, 9:3; 12:6; 49:6; 59:5

video, 3:1, 3; 4:5; 7:2; 8:3, 10; 9:1, 8, 10, 15; 10:6; 11:11, 14, 15; 12:1, 5; 14:4; 15:2; 18:3, 8–13; 19:7, 9; 20:1; 22:2, 3; 23:2, 3; 24:4; 26:5, 6, 10, 13; 27:6, 9–15; 28:2, 4, 6–8, 10; 29:4; 31:1, 3–5, 8; 32:8, 15; 34:1; 35:7; 36:1; 38:2, 3; 39:1; 40:1, 2, 4; 42:5, 7, 10; 43:2, 5; 45:2, 6; 47:3, 4, 6–8; 49:1, 4, 6; 50:2, 3, 6; 53:2, 4, 8; 55:1, 2, 4; 56:2, 4; 58:3; 59:2; 61:3, 8, 9; 62:1, 4, 8; 64:3–5; 65:1, 3

viduo, 22:5

vilis, 12:9

vinco, 7:1; 12:1; 15:2; 39:4

vinculum, 43:4

vindico, 2:10; 11:2; 22:6; 36:4; 39:9; 43:5; 45:4; 47:6, 8; 53:8; 55:2; 61:6; 64:2

vindicta, 35:4, 5; 39:9

vinea, 12:8, 9; 18:10, 11; 23:11, 12; 28:4; 30:4; 37:2, 3; 39:7; 42:3

vinum, 31:6; 50:6

vir, 1:3, 10, 12, 14, 19; 2:10; 4:13, 14; 5:5; 6:3, 4, 7–10, 12–14, 18; 8:2; 9:2, 10; 10:5; 11:2; 12:3; 15:1, 2; 16:1, 4, 7; 18:4, 7; 20:1, 2, 6; 21:4; 23:4; 25:4, 8–11; 26:1, 2; 27:1–6, 10, 11, 14, 15; 29:2, 3; 30:4; 31:1, 2; 35:1; 36:1, 2; 38:1, 3, 4; 39:2, 7; 41:1; 42:1, 2, 4, 6, 7; 43:3, 8; 45:3, 5; 46:2, 3; 47:1, 10; 49:4, 5; 50:1–3; 52:3; 54:6; 55:10; 61:1, 2; 63:3; 64:4; 65:3

virga, 9:5; 10:5; 17:1–4; 19:11; 52:2; 53:9

virginitas, 40:7

virgo, 40:4, 7, 8

viriliter, 20:5

virtus, 5:5, 7; 6:7; 12:5; 20:4; 23:1; 24:6; 26:6; 27:7, 10, 11; 30:3; 31:1, 2; 32:11; 34:1; 39:2; 43:5, 6; 61:5

virtutifico, 5:4; 12:3; 24:4; 31:7; 36:2; 49:3

vis, 6:11; 39:4, 9; 45:3; 53:6

viscera, 9:2; 54:6; 64:8

visio, 59:2

visito, 1:20; 13:8; 19:12, 13; 26:13

visus, 12:7; 18:5; 23:5; 27:13; 43:7

vita, 10:3; 11:15; 13:8; 16:3; 18:11; 19:8; 22:6; 23:12, 13; 26:14; 29:1; 30:7; 32:3; 33:2, 3; 36:4; 40:7; 59:4; 62:5; 65:1

vitis, 37:2

vitulus, 12:3, 5, 7; 13:2; 23:6, 7; 25:9; 44:5; 45:6

vivifico, 3:4, 10; 9:1; 25:7; 38:4; 51:5; 58:2–4

vivo, 1:2, 5, 7, 9, 11, 13, 15, 18, 20–22; 2:4; 3:9, 11; 4:12–15; 5:2, 8; 6:6, 11; 11:14; 16:3; 18:12; 19:9, 13; 20:2, 6, 10; 21:4; 23:8, 10; 27:11, 14; 30:6; 33:2, 5; 39:6; 44:4; 51:7; 53:12; 55:1; 57:4; 62:9; 64:6, 7

vivus, 11:6; 13:3; 21:4; 38:4; 44:9

voco, 1:20; 4:11; 6:7, 9; 7:5; 8:3, 10; 9:16; 11:2; 18:6; 19:4, 9; 23:1, 8; 24:4; 25:10; 28:1; 31:1; 40:1; 42:3; 43:1, 6, 7; 51:1; 53:3, 5; 54:6; 56:4; 60:2; 63:2

volatilis, 3:4, 8; 6:14; 15:2

volo, 6:6, 11; 10:3; 15:6; 18:3, 7, 10, 11; 22:6; 24:1; 25:8, 9, 13; 26:6; 27:11, 12; 29:3; 34:1, 3, 5; 35:7; 37:1, 4; 44:3, 5, 10; 45:1, 4; 46:3, 4; 47:1; 50:4; 51:5; 53:2, 8, 13; 56:2; 61:1; 63:3

voluntas, 6:4, 11; 12:7; 25:5; 49:6; 50:5; 58:4

volvo, 11:5

votum, 40:1

vox, 2:10; 11:4, 14; 15:4; 18:11; 20:4; 21:9; 24:2; 28:5, 8; 32:1, 4; 33:3, 4; 39:10; 42:3, 6; 44:2; 47:1; 50:5; 51:3; 53:2, 3, 5

vulnero, 27:9; 63:3

vulpes, 43:4

zaticon (possibly Greek; diatheke), 9:15

zelo, 9:6; 11:6; 18:11; 20:5; 32:1, 2; 39:2; 44:10; 45:6; 47:1, 7; 50:5; 59:4; 62:1, 11; 64:8

zelus, 44:7; 47:1; 58:1; 62:11

zona, 20:2, 3

Index of Modern Authors

General Index